To Ride the Tiger

By Robert L. Parker

ISBN 0-7414-1903-3

Published by:

PUBLISHING.COM

1094 New DeHaven Street, Suite 100
West Conshohocken, PA 19428-2713
Info@buybooksontheweb.com
www.buybooksontheweb.com
Toll-free (877) BUY BOOK
Local Phone (610) 941-9999
Fax (610) 941-9959

Printed in the United States of America

Printed on Recycled Paper

Published February 2008

To ride the back of the raging tiger is ultimately terrifying, but you must desperately hold on. To fall off would be signing your death warrant, for the grisly beast would surely eat you.

Another Day

So tall the trees and so green the grass,
I wondered to myself, how long will it last?
Up in these mountains, with Heaven-To-Touch,
I cherished the outside I love so much.

The alluring sky was spacious and blue,
The crisp, cool air made my senses run true.
The birds sang to me a sunrise song,
Mother Nature's theme — not a note was wrong.

The animals jumped as I roamed in and out,
Chattering and screaming as I walked about.
They hated humans, and I knew why;
No use fooling myself, or trying to lie.

Then I heard a sound, a man-made machine,
And sadly enough, I knew the routine.
The chopper flew low to find where I am;
I survived another day in South Vietnam.

Song/Ballad
Female Recording Artist

Sergeant Parker

Sergeant Parker, when will you come home?
Sergeant Parker, you left me all alone.
Now you're fighting, way across the sea,
In a war God knows shouldn't be.

Now you're back a hero, medals upon your chest,
But in your heart, there seems to be unrest.
You say you have to fight in still another war.
Then I kissed you softly, and you had to speak no more.

I listen to the radio almost every day;
You're wanted by the law — "a criminal," they say.
The FBI wants you, and the CIA does, too.
They say a lot of people died. Is this true?

You say that this war is one that must be,
Though it's to be a war of the Lost Victory.
And so, Sergeant Parker, to me you'll never be wrong;
With all my love, I give to you this song.

Introduction

True courage is a contradiction in terms. It takes the form of a determined willingness to live and die. This book is about such courage. Sergeant Parker was not the methodical killer that his friends and superiors thought him to be. He was just good at his given job, which took him into Laos, Cambodia, and North Vietnam. As an Army- and CIA-trained communications and intelligence expert, he had access to top intelligence information gathered in Indochina. Much of this information still remains highly classified. After two years in Vietnam, he came home to become a quiet and fearful force. His name would be associated directly and indirectly with drug traffickers, hit-men, thieves, Army Antiterrorist Teams, the CIA, Military Intelligence, an Italian-American Mafia Organization, a Syrian Multimillionaire, a Sicilian Mafia Organization, and more.

After years and years of incarceration in county jails, psychiatric institutions, and prisons like Sing-Sing, his true story can now be told. As you read about his experiences and the tragedies that have befallen him, decide for yourself if he is as dangerous and vicious as the law claims. No matter what he has to say, some readers will never like him; others, though, will understand and recognize him as being just a man, no more and no less. Either way, he will not be an easy man to forget.

The names of most people have been changed in this book. This was done to preserve the privacy and reputation of these people, both living and dead, and their relatives. Some locations in Southeast Asia have been changed in this book due to MACV-SOG still keeping many of its operations top secret.

Chapter One

Late 1969 / Vietnam

The chopper flew high, soaring boldly through the afternoon sky. It was a combat chopper equipped with a grenade launcher, rocket launcher, and two M-60 machine guns. My eyes were closed, and I sat with my CAR-15 assault rifle between my legs. My name is Robert Parker, and I was a U.S. Army Special Forces Sergeant. Besides the chopper crew, there were seven of us. The other six were Montagnard men from the Rhade tribe; they had Special Forces training, too.

The Montagnards, nicknamed "Yards," were the proud, brown-skinned mountain people of Vietnam. They disliked the lowland Vietnamese people, who considered them primitive savages. I liked working with them much more than with the ARVNs (or South Vietnamese Army Troops) I've dealt with. I'm a black man myself, but I was taller, more physically built than my loyal Yards. They carried the standard American M-16 rifle with their own personal choice of sidearm.

We were headed for a small hamlet called Kham Luc, which was near the Cambodian border. The hamlet was a main-force Viet Cong sanctuary, marked for destruction by Intelligence. The Kham Luc assignment had been handed down through the channels to my team.

As usual, when I feel I'm in a temporarily secured area, my mind started wandering. And as usual, against my better judgment, I started thinking about Carol Wilson, the girl I'd left in Buffalo, New York. I'd written that woman countless letters, and she hadn't replied to any of them. And the only time she ever wrote was when she needed more money. I never could understand Carol and her wild ways. My friends constantly told me I was too passive with her. They said I always let her do what she wanted, whenever she wanted, but I loved Carol in my own way. How the hell was I supposed to know she'd take my kindness for weakness? It hurt me to know that she realized this, but didn't care.

1

I snapped back to the present reality of war as the chopper suddenly went into a steep dive. It circled a jungle clearing at treetop level, attempting to draw fire. When none came, we dropped swiftly into the clearing, hovering about four feet from the ground. My team and I jumped, zigzagging for the cover of the jungle. As the last Yard jumped, the chopper rose rapidly back into the sky.

In the cover of the jungle, we checked our equipment again: ammo, web-belts, canteens, knives, frag grenades, white phosphorous grenades, smoke canisters, blocks of C-4 plastic explosives with time detonators, machetes, an M-60 machine gun, M-79 grenade launchers, first-aid kits, salt pills, malaria pills, iodine pills for water purification, compasses, and C-rations for three days. The hamlet was a few miles away, so we started our forced jungle march. I took the point-man position ahead of the team, as I'd done many times before. My Yard companions were always amazed when I did this. They'd never seen an American walk the dangerous point-man position so much. I knew there were times when they'd wanted to ask me why, but they never quite got it out. In a way, I'm glad they never asked; I really wasn't sure why myself. Maybe, just maybe, it was my own personal kind of death wish.

I moved steadily through the bamboo clusters, vines, high elephant grass, and poisonous plants that would kill if eaten, irritate if touched. At times I would stop, look, listen, smell, and check my compass bearings. I looked for enemy ambushes, snipers, booby traps, snakes, scorpions, and insects that could all be threats to our well-being. We came closer to Kham Luc, each of us knowing the hamlet and its people were doomed.

Hours later, the hamlet was in sight under a double canopy of trees. For fifteen minutes, we observed the activities in Kham Luc, which had a population of well over two hundred people. A few of the men, women, and teenage children were boldly armed to the teeth with rifles, pistols, grenades, explosives, and knives. At a few areas in the hamlet, elderly adults made sharp punji sticks and spears from pieces of bamboo and wood. These items were used for certain types of severe and fatal booby traps. In the marketplace, where many of them were gathered, they briskly argued about buying and swapping things from fish, chicken, cows, rugs, and clothes to freshly cut meats, sugarcane, fruits, vegetables, rice, and shiny, decorative trinkets.

My men kept looking from the hamlet to me during this time, waiting for my thumbs-down doomsday hand signal. Staring with remorse at the children in the village, I finally gave the signal, knowing my orders clearly. We moved out, silently crawling and crouching low to surround the hamlet. No words were spoken between us. None had to be. We'd been through a hell of a lot together already. As a covert operations team leader, I'd lost team members: Americans, ARVNs, Chinese Nungs, and Yards. The Yard team I was with now, though, was the best I'd ever had, and we hadn't lost a man yet. We'd been shot up, bombed, ambushed, sniped at, and surrounded by the enemy, but somehow, we managed to survive our wounds and live. In short, we were just plain lucky with the percentages growing grossly against us.

We avoided dozens of crippling and deadly booby traps while closing in on the hamlet. We planted plastic explosives behind many of the hooches, and we also booby-trapped pathways leading out of the hamlet with frag grenades. The M-60 machine gun was set up for the main dirt trail through the center of the hamlet. We also put explosives as close to the marketplace as possible and readied the grenade launchers. Frag grenade pins were straightened for fast pulls and throwing. In less than an hour, we were all set up, just waiting. The time detonators on the explosives had fifteen more minutes left.

The last few minutes seemed to go by like seconds. Contact! Contact! Tremendous explosions shook the earth violently, taking an undetermined number of lives instantly. Insane screams and dying moans mixed with low, sobbing cries rang through the air. Some of the survivors ran out onto the main dirt trail, as expected. The M-60 opened up on them along with the M-79s. We all threw several frag grenades apiece into the hamlet, contributing to the number of maimed, crippled, and dead. We opened fire with our rifles, aiming at anyone shooting back, running, or crawling. The surprise attack kept the enemy fire short and to a minimum.

After firing a few magazines of rounds, we advanced carefully into the hamlet. We kept shooting, but more selectively, now, making sure everyone within sight was dead. Three young adults, two men and a woman, ran out of a burning hooch for the safety of the jungle. Instinctively, I opened up on them with my rifle, shooting all three. One of the men died instantly, but the other man and the woman were still alive, though gravely wounded.

I stood directly over them, briefly looking into their eyes. Slowly, I pulled the four-inch .357 Magnum pistol out of my side holster. Hesitating for a second, I shot both of them in the forehead. Bloody tissue, bone slivers, and brain matter splattered my jungle pants, shirt, arms, and face. Quickly, I wiped the warm blood and mucous-mixed flesh from my face and bare arms, not wanting it there. Only hearing sporadic fire, now, I cautiously walked toward the center of the hamlet. I tried my best not to step on body parts, mangled dead bodies, or into the puddles of blood that seemed to be everywhere. I wasn't doing very well, though, and the soles of my jungle boots were caked with blood and dirt.

My team met up with me in the center of the hamlet. Two of them had been superficially wounded. With all enemy resistance having ceased, I gave the go-ahead for Phase II. Methodically, we shot and killed all the remaining animals in the hamlet that survived the assault. We collected all the enemy weapons, ammo, and radios we could find, dumping them in the center of the hamlet. We found important maps and documents pertaining to potential targets and movements of some VC and NVA (North Vietnamese Army) units. We torched all the hooches that were still standing and put explosives in the caches of food and medical supplies we found. Then we poisoned the hamlet water well and laid counter booby traps of our own. We put explosives into the weapons pile and poured all the remaining kerosene and oil we found on the pile, too. We headed out of the hamlet fast, keeping alert for any unknown enemy forces nearby. Gasping and coughing from the thick smoke all around us, we were only too glad to be leaving.

A half hour later, we heard all the explosives in the hamlet go off in sequence. We'd already called for our extraction at a prearranged area close by. Altogether, we spent about an hour and a half inside the hamlet, and in less than an hour after leaving, we were on our way back to Ban Me Thout. Ban Me Thout was the name of our home-base compound. It was also designated by military intelligence as CCS (Command and Control South), which was part of our joint Special Forces and CIA operations. Officially, we were known as a Studies and Observation Group, but that was just a cover name to conceal our operations. Secretly, we were MACV-SOG (Military Assistance Command Vietnam-Special Operations Group). SOG was classified top-secret and created solely for high-intensity, black-bag, dirty tricks warfare and for highly technological military intelligence gathering. For instance, SOG would lay and maintain small listening devices on known and suspected enemy trails, do long-range recon patrols into Laos, Cambodia, and North Vietnam, perform search and seizure and search and destroy missions, assassinate or kidnap NVA and VC officers, torture, kill, or imprison infrastructure personnel, and harass enemy communications and supply routes. SOG operated its own radio stations, too, with powerful transmitters like the one in Hue, which was called the Voice of Freedom. This type of radio station in psych-ops (psychological operations) was called a Gray Station because its location was never revealed. Black Stations never revealed their positions, but they were located in North Vietnam and run mostly by North Vietnamese dissidents under SOG control. Lastly, SOG had to oversee the tribesmen mercenaries in Laos who worked for the CIA The tribesmen launched paramilitary attacks against the NVA and VC in Laos. In return for their badly needed help, we aided them in their opium trafficking.

It was dark by the time the chopper made it back to Ban Me Thout. Reporting in to my section leader, Captain Brian Miller, I briefed him on the completed mission. I knew the CIA and military intelligence would be pleased that the hamlet was finally destroyed. As I left the captain's office, I checked to make sure my team didn't have night ambush patrol. We didn't.

After reaching my tent, I stripped down to my pants and boots and stretched out on my bunk. I was mentally and physically exhausted again. By force of habit, I still kept my holster and pistol on. I pulled out a half-bottle of bourbon from under the bunk and took a couple of deep, long swallows before putting it back down. With my eyes closed, I tried relaxing every muscle in my fatigued body. While dozing off to sleep, I romantically envisioned Carol with me in bed. We were making tantalizing love together, locked in a wet, passionate embrace. As I fell into serene sleep, I felt Carol wrapping her brown, silky legs around my back, forcing me deeper inside her.

My sleep was interrupted at about 3 o'clock in the morning when a hardcore Viet Cong unit hit us. As usual, they started by dropping mortars on the compound. Some landed in the motor pool, destroying several trucks. Others landed throughout the triangular compound, with one landing near the tent I was in. The roaring explosion set the tent on fire, throwing the bunk and me into the air. The tent was filling with smoke as I pushed the bunk off me. Getting up, I ran out of the tent like a madman, heading for the motor pool. The enemy had opened up with small-arms fire, now, and I heard Russian, Chinese, and Czech rifles on automatic.

Their mortars were still dropping sporadically, each one sounding like sharp, cracking thunder. I wasn't running because I was fearful; I was running because I was pissed off. In Special Forces, we're taught that fear is an emotional reaction that can be controlled. When a person allows himself to be controlled by fear, the next thing that person does is panic. When this happens, that person is no longer useful to himself or anyone else. Therefore, we're taught to push fear to the most remote spots of our minds, rendering it ineffective. And in the place of fear, we are taught to project anger mingled with a methodical yet impulsive retaliation.

I had to run about a hundred fifty yards through enemy fire, shattering explosions, and flying shrapnel. Flares were high in the moonless night sky, lighting up the area outside the compound. Tracer rounds, orange, yellow, green, and red, could be seen flying high, low, and ricocheting off objects.

I felt hot, stinging sensations in several places on my sweat-drenched back while I ran. I finally entered the motor pool and spotted what I wanted. Leaping up on an APC (Armored Personnel Carrier), I slid into the driver's seat. I started up the engine and took off at full speed toward the perimeter of our compound. I was heading toward the area where the heaviest enemy fire was coming from. The steel treads of the APC strained and clanged loudly, throwing up dirt for several yards in all directions. Our perimeter consisted of several strands of constantine and razor wire, a cyclone fence, trip flares, punji sticks, broken glass, and electronically controlled claymore mines.

Our compound was returning fire at a stupendous rate with 81-mm mortars, 106 recoilless rifles, .50 and .30 caliber and M-60 machine guns, M-79 grenade launchers, and small-arms fire. A reactionary force consisting of several APCs, each filled with eight combat men, Americans, Yards, and ARVNs, was going out of the gate to closely engage the enemy. As I neared the perimeter, an enemy mortar exploded near my APC, shaking the ground and throwing tiny pieces of metal debris that stung my face and neck. The explosive blast rocked the APC slightly off-course. Deliberately, I crashed through and past the perimeter, dragging fence and wire with me for several yards.

I set several trip flares off, but luckily, none of the mines went off. About fifty yards outside the compound, I stopped, jumped behind the .50 caliber mounted on top of the vehicle, and started shooting. I showered rounds at enemy rifle and mortar flashes and at the area in general. I could hear enemy rounds zinging past my head within inches, and others ricocheted off the steel hull. Another mortar exploded close to the APC, rocking it roughly and throwing me off. As soon as my body slammed awkwardly to the ground, I had my .357 Magnum out. From my prone position, I rapid-fired with both hands on the pistol. Only after feeling the trigger-hammer on empty cylinder chambers several times did I realize I'd fired every round. Dropping the pistol, I leaped back up behind the .50 caliber and continued firing until my ammo ran out. I quickly loaded another heavy box of ammo to the machine gun and started my constant firing again.

Just as unexpectedly as the enemy assault had started, it stopped. They weren't firing anymore, but I kept shooting for a few more minutes, as did everyone else in the compound. Automatic weapons fire from our reactionary force outside the perimeter could be heard now. The enemy knew their assault had to be swift and deadly. They realized from past experience the mass firepower they attracted by attacking our compound. Shortly, the night sky would be full of army combat choppers and air force fighter planes. Right now, I knew the enemy was gathering up their wounded and dead as fast as they could. They took their dead whenever they could due to their religious beliefs. Unrealistically, they felt it profoundly confused our intelligence reports, too.

It took several hours to get the compound back up to maximum operational level again. Seven ARVNs and five Yards were killed, and several were wounded. Two Americans were killed and three seriously wounded. Medivac choppers came to take the dead and seriously wounded away. I had about fifteen tiny pieces of shrapnel and debris taken out of my back, neck, arms, and face by a medic. A soothing salve was applied, and I was given more to rub on for the next few days. I was a little sore and stiff but otherwise in good health.

I was told to report to my section leader at eleven a.m. With an hour to wait, I took a few aspirins for my headache and lay down until almost eleven. As I walked toward Captain Miller's office, I wondered what he wanted now. I was hoping he'd surprise me with another ten-day R&R trip to Bangkok, Thailand, but maybe that was hoping for a bit too much.

Nearing the captain's office bunker, I saw a familiar jeep with the MACV initials on the bumper. I knew then that whatever the assignment was, the CIA was involved again. I didn't like the CIA station chief for our sector or any of the other CIA operatives I've met. They seemed to exhibit a know-all attitude and smugness about themselves. I was plainly told that I had to give them respect out of courtesy to the military and their federal GS rating, so I respected them, but I'd be damned if I had to personally like the bastards, too.

Stepping into the captain's office, I came to attention, saluted, and waited. As expected, Frank Connally, the station chief, was sitting with the captain. They were looking through two classified files on the desk. Captain Miller was a damn good man and leader, in my estimation. He was in his early thirties, was about 6'2" tall, and had coarse tan skin, a muscular build, and dark brown hair sprinkled with gray. He was from Georgia, and the first thing I noticed about him was his poker face and piercing brown eyes. The captain and I liked each other a lot. We'd never said it openly to one another, but we knew. Connally was in his mid-thirties. He was 5'9" tall, had crew-cut blond hair, small shifty eyes, and was about thirty pounds overweight. His stout, round face was always flushed and nervous looking.

"Relax, Parker. Have a seat," said Captain Miller in a firm Southern drawl. Connally never said anything to me as far as cordial courtesies went. He'd perceived some time ago that I didn't particularly like him. As such, he kept his distance from me when roaming the compound. It was also rumored that Connally kept his distance because he felt I was one of the most dangerous men he'd ever met. Coming from an experienced CIA station chief and caseworker, I wasn't sure if he meant that remark as a professional compliment or a gross slur. Either way, he had some damn nerve calling me dangerous. I was just an expendable item being manipulated by the CIA and military intelligence to carry out the dirty little schemes they conceived but had no stomach for themselves. It was people like Connally, with their warped ideologies and power, who were the truly dangerous ones in the world.

Captain Miller handed me the two files they'd been looking at, saying, "Lom Hai and Ong Tinh. Both Vietnamese, and both are traitors. Lom Hai is forty years old, and Ong Tinh is twenty-two. They were reliable agents, obviously, when the Agency started payrolling them a few years back. Well, a few months ago, they got together and turned over, and they're working for the commies' NLF (National Liberation Front) in the south here. Neither of them has ever had any political ideologies of any kind, but they responded well to money. We believe the commies lured them over by paying them a lot more money than we were, or else the commies are blackmailing them through relatives in the north. Exactly why they turned is really academic at this stage. When they deserted, they stole some portable cryptography deciphering equipment and some classified documents. Just recently, Connally got hard intelligence on where they are. The Agency wants us to retire both of them permanently."

I glanced at the pictures of Hai and Tinh before skimming through some of the data on both. I still heard every word the captain said while I sized up Hai and Tinh as unmarried, intelligent, and dangerously ambitious ex-ARVN soldiers. They loved women, and their main motivation was money. It was hard to rationalize how the Agency ever trusted these guys around sensitive paperwork and equipment.

"I have to point out again," Connally stressed worriedly, "that Hai and Tinh must be eliminated as soon as possible. With them in possession of the portable crypto equipment, they've already cost the lives of a Special Forces Intelligence expert and two Vietnamese agents. They must have been in a hurry because the classified papers they took were low-priority and really unimportant. The main concern is the crypto-equipment because they have a partial key to deciphering messages. We've kept this whole thing contained; only a handful of people know what they've done. If it were disclosed or rumored to other Asian agents how easily Hai and Tinh turned, we could have a mass defection or have our whole Southeast Asian intelligence network filled with double agents."

Captain Miller stood up, stepping over to a large geographical map of Southeast Asia on the wall. Pointing to a spot on the map, he stated, "They're here, about sixty miles north of us at a deserted village called Phu Lom. All the cryptography gear they took is set up there, too. You're trained in this type of equipment, so you know how they're eavesdropping and deciphering some of the classified messages from American and South Vietnamese intelligence sections. If they continue like this, the consequences would be disastrous in terms of money and manpower. You have to hit them at Phu Lom and destroy that equipment before they change locations again."

I understood the concern involved. If Hai and Tinh kept deciphering most of what they picked up, it would cost thousands in American and Vietnamese lives. It would also cost Uncle Sam a lot of bucks, too, in the millions it would take to replace some of the present crypto ciphering and deciphering equipment.

Connally spoke again, blurting out the importance of terminating these two guys. "You've got an hour to get yourself ready, Parker," the captain continued, interrupting Connally. "This is solo, so just tell your team you're going to Qhin Nhon or Pleiku as my courier again. By the time you're ready, there'll be a chopper on standby. Your insertion point is four miles west of Phu Lom. Primary extraction is one mile south of Phu Lom if everything goes smoothly. Any problems and secondary extraction will be three miles southeast of the primary. Forty-eight hours is the max we're giving you before going to a contingency plan to zap these bastards. Your personal codename remains the same, Nighthawk-One. Now, are there any questions for Connally or myself? If so, let's hear them now, while things are still fresh in your mind."

There really wasn't anything more I needed to know. The briefing was informative and precise, as usual. Personally, I wished they had picked someone else for this assignment. Though destroying hamlets and villages wasn't anything new to me, taking out Kham Luc yesterday just wasn't settled in my mind yet. Maybe I was getting soft, moralistic, or something; I don't know.

I've always been a damn good soldier, gung-ho and super-patriotic, but for the last couple of months I'd sensed something extremely wrong about this war. All wars are wrong as far as I'm concerned. At the same time, though, I considered myself and Special Forces a necessary evil in protecting the free world and oppressed people.

There's no getting around the fact that I was an intelligently trained assassin. As such, I held a strong belief that any man who deliberately went around trying to cultivate a killer reputation had to be some kind of demented psychopath. This goes for soldiers in war and people on the streets. I simply followed my orders to the letter, no matter how questionable I felt those orders were. If necessary, I'd forfeit my life to follow my orders, too. But within the last couple of months, I'd sensed something enormously wrong about this war.

I stood up, telling Captain Miller and Connally I was fully satisfied with the briefing. Laying the two files on the desk, I came to attention, saluted, and went for the door. As I opened it, Captain Miller spoke sharply in a raised voice, "Sergeant Parker!" I turned abruptly, looking with raised eyebrows at my poker-faced section leader. Relaxing his voice to a soft, steady tone, he said, "Take it easy, Sergeant, and good hunting."

"Thanks, Captain," I replied with a rare smile. Glancing at Connally, I was tempted like hell to give him the finger, but I left.

The captain knew something was troubling me, but he didn't know what and he didn't ask. Even if he had asked as a friend, I would have lied to him. Though he was a friend, he was still a Special Forces officer and part of the Special Operations Group. Had he known what was troubling me, he would have relieved me of my duties immediately. He wasn't a hard-ass, but as a professional soldier, he would have seen me as a liability to future solo and team missions. I would have done exactly the same thing had I been him and known.

I talked to my team briefly before getting my gear ready for the trip. Taking my time, I had several sips of bourbon before finding the chopper. Except for a short conversation with the chopper crew, I said nothing to them in the air.

For the first time, I contemplated how many more assignments and missions I'd have before I was captured or killed. Percentage-wise, I was overdue for one or the other, or both. There were times when I felt so lonely and tired. I felt like I could be in the middle of a massive riot and still feel pathetically lonely. I sat quietly, watching the deep green and brown countryside with its many rice paddies sweeping by below. I observed how beautiful and alluring it always was. It gave me a strong sense of peaceful tranquility from the air. Though I'm a realist, I had a love affair with Vietnam from the sky. It was a heart-throbbing, splendid sight, and the more I saw its beauty, the more I wanted to submit to its noble deception. For a second, my entire body shook in an involuntary spasm that ended with goose bumps.

It took some roundabout flying with security precautions to reach my insertion point. The chopper crew gave me their good-lucks as I hopped a few feet to the ground. I watched the chopper as it soared noisily away. Then, checking my compass, I headed for Phu Lom. By the time I reached the village, it was already dark.

There was a small fire in the center of the village, and I noticed four noisy people around it. I carefully inched forward, wary of booby traps, until I had a better view. I recognized Hai and Tinh; they both seemed drunk and high. They were drinking from a large bottle and smoking what appeared to be a Thai-stick reefer joint. Their movements were clumsy as they talked, laughed, and fondled the women. I assumed the two young women with them were girlfriends or paid prostitutes. There were two whole chickens roasting on a metal rod over the fire that smelled damn good, too.

Climbing a tree, I tied myself to a large branch and got comfortable. Then I loosely tied my rifle to me so it wouldn't accidentally fall. I intended to sleep, catnap style, until early morning. I'd decided to let Hai and Tinh enjoy themselves and party that night. I'd let them drink all the booze they wanted, smoke all the reefer they could, and even get all the sex they could handle. And then, early the next morning, I'd waste them both and end their brief liaison with the commies. It was too dangerous to take them now, in the dark. I was too unfamiliar with the village and its immediate surroundings, and I couldn't confirm if there were others around, so I waited.

I smacked, swatted, brushed, and cursed mosquitoes, ants, wood ticks, and other insects away from my face and arms. The monkeys and rock apes weren't exactly thrilled with me commandeering the tree, either. They showed their moody disapproval by shaking branches, making fast chattering and screeching sounds, and occasionally throwing an object at me. I ignored the testy bastards, though, because hell, they didn't own the damn trees! I was determined to show mankind's superiority over beasts by keeping my ass parked in this tree. I gave the finger to the few glaring monkeys and rock apes I could see.

At the first light of dawn, I was out of the tree. I circled Phu Lom, checking the immediate outskirts first. I avoided a dozen fatal booby traps, knowing full well that there were others in the area, too, and went in. I ended up behind a medium-sized thatched hooch. I listened for movement, voices, a cough, anything signifying human life in the hooch. I listened for ten minutes before taking my double-edged commando knife out. I made a small hole through the hooch wall. Then I peeked in to visually confirm the hooch was empty and unused. Then I widened the hole until it was large enough for me to squeeze my gear and six-foot frame through. I remained stationary on the dirt floor in the prone position, making sure I was still safe. After a few minutes, I crawled to the doorway and carefully peeked out at the village. I saw nothing but hooches on both sides of a large dirt pathway. Hai, Tinh, and their cuties were in one or more of these hooches, and I had to find out which ones they were. I preferred doing it without warning them in advance.

I wasn't enthused about checking out each and every hooch in the village. I'd be exposing myself too much and lowering my surprise advantage that way. I decided to wait for a couple of hours to see what developed. If there was no movement in that time, I'd have no choice but to search the hooches.

Every few minutes, I would cautiously look out of the entryway for my targets. I did this for over an hour before my patience finally paid off. Bingo! I saw Ong Tinh come out of one of the large hooches over a hundred yards down on the other side of the village. He was armed with a Chinese SKS rifle with the bayonet extended out of the barrel. Tinh walked sluggishly to the side of the hooch and relieved himself in some bushes. Yawning and stretching his slim body, he crossed the pathway to my side of the village. He started walking slowly in my direction. He carried his rifle carelessly, and he walked with too much recklessness to suspect that anyone else was in the village. He was probably pulling his regular guard duty time, becoming relaxed and bored with the routine.

Laying my rifle down, I stood up next to the left side of the entryway. The commando knife was in my right hand, razor sharp and lethal. I was going to take full advantage of this by taking Tinh out right now. I was drenched in sweat from the hot, humid air and my outright exhaustion. I knew that if I screwed this up, Tinh would kill me for certain.

Adrenaline burst through my fatigued body, making me light-headed while the seconds ticked away. Thoughts quickly flashed through my mind about how I should kill Tinh. Should I go between the ribcage and up, to collapse the heart? Should I go midway down his back on the spine or at the base of his neck? Maybe go for a kidney, or through the side of the neck to sever one or both carotid arteries, or through one of the eye sockets to pierce the brain.

I heard Tinh approaching the hooch in his sandals, and I tightened the grip on my knife. Midway past the entryway was as far as he got before I lunged for him. In one swift motion, I quietly covered his nose and mouth with my left hand. Bending him halfway into the entryway, I twisted and bent his head back, exposing his throat. He was so stunned that he dropped his rifle, which wasn't very smart. Had he been trained in good instinctive reaction in combat, he would have reflexively fired a round into the air or the ground. This wouldn't have saved his life, but it would have alerted his partner, Hai.

Brutally, I plunged the knife into his throat, aiming at the base of the brain, viciously twisting it. Still holding the knife in his throat, I bent his head down on it, muffling the gurgling sounds from the fatal wound. Blood flowed freely all over Tinh and me. At this point, I'd pulled him all the way into the hooch. From the smell, I knew that Tinh had defecated on himself. He was dead, but I didn't release him until his body settled some from the twitching and jerking nerves. About a minute flew by before I dragged his limp body into the far corner, leaving a bloody trail in the process. Leaving him there, I got into the other far corner with my rifle ready. Squatting low, I was listening and preparing to shoot anyone who walked into or near the hooch. I didn't care who it was, Korean, Australian, Vietnamese, Montagnard, Chinese-Nung, whoever. If they didn't look right, they were getting wasted. I stayed in the corner for about ten minutes, watching the ceiling, the walls, the entryway, even the dirt floor for hidden trapdoors. Finally, I went back to the entryway, peeking out again. I focused on the hooch that Tinh came out of, wondering if Hai and the two women were inside the hooch or if Tinh's woman was the only one there. I had to find out.

Crawling back out of the hole I'd made in the hooch, I circled the village by going back into the jungle. Slowly but surely, I closed in on Tinh's hooch. Several feet from the rear of the hooch, I heard garbled American and Vietnamese voices on radio frequencies. Getting closer, I heard the crackling, humming, and static of more radios. I listened for a few minutes to Hai and the two women talking.

They were speaking in their native tongue. I understood almost every word, having learned Vietnamese while at Fort Bragg. Hai, who did the most talking, spoke about relatives in Saigon. Then Hai mentioned that Tinh should have been back by now, and I immediately became concerned. Hai had mentioned him in a calm, passive tone, but still, I had to move fast. Hai was no fool, and he would probably bring the subject of Tinh back up within the next few minutes. Then he'd go looking for him, fully armed, alert, and suspicious. *That* I didn't want if I could avoid it, especially since I had the chance to surprise all three of them in a closed area.

I checked my stubby CAR-15 assault rifle, which was set for automatic fire. I slowly eased my way around to the front of the hooch. There was only an army blanket hanging over the entryway, covering it. I stood silently to the right of the entryway, looking up and down the village. Listening to them still talking inside, I took a deep, settling breath and made my assault. Quickly, I stepped through the blanket with both hands tightly on my weapon. Once inside, I stopped, shouting, "*Dung Lai! Dung cu don!* Halt! Halt now!" Judging by the shocked looks on their faces, to say I surprised them would be an understatement. It didn't stop Hai and one of the women from reaching for the pistols in their side holsters, though. I fired a burst of several rounds at Hai first because he was farthest from me. The rounds hit him in the face and upper chest, slamming him backward and through the rear wall of the hooch. The burst of 5.56 mm rounds I fired at the woman hit her in the midsection, almost ripping her in half. Blood splattered all over the hooch, the radios, the crypto equipment, and me.

I leveled my weapon on the remaining woman, but she hadn't moved an inch. She was pretty, in her early twenties, with long, raven-black hair. Her big brown eyes were unblinking. Her small mouth hung wide open, and she just stood there, traumatized. She kept staring, unbelieving, at the dead woman, then at the hole in the rear wall. Her distressed mind was having difficulty registering what had just happened. I yelled for her to unbuckle her holster and let it drop to the ground. Three times I yelled this before she came out of her self-induced trance. She stared at me like I was her worst nightmare come true. With tears welling in her eyes, she nervously unbuckled the holster. It fell to the dirt floor; our eyes were still fixed on each other. *"Cho toi xem gian cau cuoc!* Show me some identification!" I shouted. Shaking, she pulled her plastic I.D. card out, and I snatched it from her. Stuffing the card in my pocket, I searched her hastily with one hand from head to toe. Then I ordered her to face the wall and kneel with her hands on top of her head. I glanced at Hai's body through the hole in the wall to make sure he was dead. I did this more out of habit than anything else, and with no recognizable face, he was surely dead.

I turned my attention to the noisy equipment. There were some tools in the hooch, so I took the vital parts out of all the radios and crypto equipment. I threw the parts in the middle of the dirt floor. There were two medium-sized cardboard boxes full of classified papers, code booklets, electrical manuals, and various CIA manuals. I dumped both boxes on the dirt floor. I took the woman's I.D. card out, knowing it could easily be a fake. It stated that she was Mai Chinh, age twenty-two, residing in Quang Tri. After reading this, I told her to turn around. I knew that a reasonable percentage of hardcore Viet Cong women were made into squad and platoon leaders, and although they were small and looked fragile, some Viet Cong and NVA women could easily kill a two-hundred-pound man with their bare hands and feet. *"Ong lam gi o day? Ongo dau den?* What are you doing here? Where are you from?" I asked roughly, watching her eyes. I interrogated her for fifteen minutes, trying to sound as harsh and intimidating as I could. I was using my sixth sense, perceptiveness, and experience to determine if she was Viet Cong, plain-clothed NVA, or an outright civilian enemy spy. I felt she had lied to me about some minor things, but those things were unrelated to my assignment. My final opinion was that she was not the enemy, and she was therefore not a direct threat to me.

Hai and Tinh had paid both women for their company and sexual favors for a few weeks. The women had been friends for years, but they were new to the prostitution game. Tearfully, she said that Hai and Tinh made them wear the pistols for self-protection. And she said that both of them bragged about working for the Americans and getting paid lots of money for it. She kept repeating in between statements that she and her girlfriend were never enemies to the Americans. I believed her. Her girlfriend, I felt, just overreacted to my sudden presence, causing her own death.

I returned her I.D. card and told her to stand up and go outside. She slowly stood up, trembling nervously, but she didn't budge from her spot. She was horrified, with tears spilling down her face. I told her again to walk outside, and again she wouldn't budge. In sheer panic, she started begging me not to kill her. She pleaded frantically, saying we could make love if I spared her life. She said there were special sexual things she knew that all American GIs liked. I didn't say a word while watching her wild-eyed, terrified face. For the third time, I told her to go outside. She didn't move.

With one hand, I grabbed her by the arm, pushing and dragging her outside. She fought me like a wildcat every inch of the way, biting, kicking, scratching, cursing, and screaming. My whole damn body was battered and bruised before I let her go. She lay breathless on the ground, chest heaving, with one breast exposed, nipple rigid. Her stare was fiery now, mixed with rage and fear.

"*O day khong duoc yan. Didi mau, biet?* It's not safe here. Go now fast, understand?" I said to her. She just lay there, glaring at me in defiance. I was getting irritated because I wanted to get out of the village fast. Pulling her up, I gave her a push to get started. Her eyes filled with tears again, and she momentarily covered them with her hands. Then she glared oddly at me, showing more hate than fear this time. Turning away almost gracefully, she slowly started walking away. Her steps were feeble, timid, and very shaky. I watched her walk farther and farther away until she finally disappeared into the jungle. I kept thinking how foolish she was to be convinced that I'd kill her. There was enough killing in this land already; there was no reason in hell that she had to die, too.

I pulled Hai's body back into the hooch, then threw four white-phosphorous grenades, nicknamed "willy-peters," in there. White-phosphorous grenades, like napalm, burn with a white-hot intensity, even underwater. They could melt some metals and burn damn near anything else, too. The vital parts of the equipment, the equipment itself, and the papers would be totally destroyed. I threw two frag grenades into the hooch Tinh's body was in. Not one of the three dead bodies could ever be identified by anyone, for any purpose. I left the village thinking about the woman I'd released. The desire to take her up on her sexual offer was almost overwhelming. I needed a passionate sexual climax to temporarily soothe my frustrated mind and body, but the village of Phu Lom was clearly the wrong place at the wrong time, and I'd be doing it for the wrong reasons.

A few hours later at my primary extraction point, I called for pickup on my PRC-25 radio, nicknamed Prick-25. A combat chopper had been designated to be in the area at certain times to serve as my backup and pickup. It was coming to get me. A few minutes later, I heard the chopper, but I couldn't spot it yet. I released a smoke canister, which filled my immediate area with thick, red smoke. The chopper zeroed in on me for a swift pickup. It was late afternoon by the time I made it back to Ban Me Thout.

For the rest of the day, I was moody and got drunk as all hell. Even my Yard team members avoided me like the black plague. I ended up in one of the ammo bunkers that night, working on my second bottle of bourbon. So much was going on in my mind about so many different things. The bunker was totally dark, and I sat there in intoxicated solitude. I felt jittery, tense, panicky, and my hands shook nervously. The weird part was that I didn't know what was wrong with me. I'd had this type of spell dozens of times within the last few months. Maybe I was on the verge of a nervous breakdown, or maybe I was ready to go insane or something.

I thought about Carol in Buffalo and wondered what she was doing — and what guy she was doing it with. Regrettably, she wasn't exactly a one-man woman by any means. I had to accept that fact once and for all, no matter how much it hurt. Unexpected tears began filling my eyes. My God, I was falling apart with no place to escape to. How the hell could I escape my own mind, my own thoughts? The killing was starting to bother me.

Then it happened. Suddenly, I started having flurried flashbacks of fierce firefights, violent killings, and brutal interrogations of enemy prisoners. I saw myself helplessly surrounded by hundreds of Viet Cong and NVA troops. None of them had eyes, only blood-dripping sockets. Every one of them was armed, shooting relentlessly into my body. I didn't die, but I felt every agonizing bullet. And I saw the petrified look on my face as I watched blood spew out of my body. I begged and pleaded for mercy, but their only response was shrill laughter.

The very earth stood still as I perspired heavily, reliving the war in my imaginary hell. My heart was pounding like crazy, my teeth rattled, and my whole body went into a wild, trembling seizure. Then the loud, piercing explosions started, huge, blinding explosions going off in my head. Excruciating and powerful, they numbed my brain, leaving me lifeless and drained. *Oh my God, I'm going to die in this strange land! I know it! I just know it!* I yelled! I screamed! I yelled and screamed in such a bone-chilling, tormented, beastly way that several rodents scurried out of the bunker. Over fifty armed men responded to my inhuman screeching. I was so horrified that I somehow screamed myself back to my normal sense of reasoning. I vaguely overheard a few of the men at the entrance to the bunker. They were grumbling and cursing because they couldn't shoot or throw grenades in without blowing the bunker sky-high. In my groggy, drained state, I was certainly relieved to hear that. I felt mentally and physically paralyzed, and I needed a few minutes to settle my nerves.

I was drunk, shaking, weak, had a piercing headache, and I vomited until my stomach muscles ached. Minutes later, I called out to the guys in a weary voice, identifying myself and staggering out. Embarrassed, I stretched the truth, saying I fell asleep in the bunker, had a nightmare, and started yelling. A few skeptics cautiously went inside the bunker, intent on finding some kind of wounded beast. They couldn't believe a human being was capable of that kind of noise until they found the bunker empty. After that, everyone calmed down and started teasing me about the whole thing. Needless to say, I wasn't in the mood for kidding around, and I told them all to kiss my ass. They joked as they watched me stagger off on rubbery legs, and I cursed them and their family trees.

Later, stretched out on my bunk, I realized that I had experienced the most intense spell I'd ever had. I also sensed that these spells were going to get worse before they got better. What the hell was wrong with me? What was grinding me up into a nervous wreck? Maybe it was Carol and the crummy way she always treated me. Or maybe it had to do with me not wanting to hurt anyone again. If that were the case, I might as well stick my head between my legs and kiss my butt goodbye, because that was no way to feel in the middle of a jungle war, thousands of miles from home. Maybe it was a combination of Carol, the war, and my emotions that were getting to me.

I knew that the best thing I could do for myself and for Special Forces was to get transferred. I was a liability because I wasn't functioning at my maximum. Just the thought of someone being hurt or killed because of this worried me a lot. I had to contain my pride and do what I felt was right for myself. Hell, I only had a couple more months to do before my DEROS (Date Expected to Return from Overseas). I'd be leaving this war for good then. But there was no way I could finish my time here in this unit without cracking up.

I'd had it. I had to change units. And why shouldn't I? I'd done more than my share with the Fifth Special Forces Group. All my solo and team missions, my assignments, my confirmed kills, they all gave me an outstanding performance rating. If anyone had the right to request a unit change, I did. Damn right! I decided I'd go to the captain's office the next day and put in for a unit transfer.

Chapter Two

Two weeks after putting my transfer request in, I was ordered to the Fifth Special Forces Headquarters in Nha Trang. I kept wondering what the Major wanted with me. Major Small was a West Pointer in his late thirties. He was 5'8" tall, of average weight, and had a square chin, deep blue eyes, and closely cut light-brown hair. He was noted for his aggressiveness, quick temper, and loud, deep voice that even made some colonels quake in their boots. Whenever I saw him on compounds and firebases, I never saw the bastard smile.

There were several detachments in the Special Operations Group, and Major Small was in charge of the one I worked for. SOG had its permanent headquarters in Saigon, just north of the Cholon district on Pasteur Street. It was located in a white five-story former French villa. I'd been there a few times on the top floor, where the intelligence section was located. The place was always packed with CIA, DIA (Defense Intelligence Agency), ARVN and American military personnel.

For the major to personally order a mere subordinate like me to his office wasn't good. I started getting a little angry at myself for being so concerned about the whole matter. Whatever he wanted, he wasn't going to stand me up blindfolded against a wall and have me shot or anything. He was probably putting together some ultra-secret team again, and some bigmouth had volunteered my name.

At Nha Trang, I hitchhiked over to Fifth Group Headquarters. The major's clerk, a burly black corporal armed with a .45, showed me into the major's office. Major Small was sitting behind his big oak desk, which had official papers, letters, and files all over the top of it. He was reading one file with particular interest as I entered, presented myself, and waited for his response. The bastard left me standing at attention while he continued reading through several more pages. His office was air-conditioned, and all four walls were filled with maps, citations, plaques, certificates, medals, and pictures. "At ease, Sergeant Parker. Take a seat," he finally said in his deep voice, gesturing to the chair in front of the desk.

He went through several more pages before looking at me. Sighing heavily, he took his glasses off and placed them gently on the desk. Calmly rubbing one side of his head, he said, "Parker, let's forget formalities and talk straight turkey, okay? This meeting is strictly confidential, and what's said here remains here. Is this clear?"

"Yes, sir," I promptly replied.

He opened one of his desk drawers and pulled out a bottle of good bourbon and two plastic cups. Pouring some bourbon in both cups, he handed me one, saying, "I hate to drink alone, and I don't trust any soldier that don't drink and curse." I thanked him for the drink and took a sip. After tasting his, he put his cup down. He pulled a few sheets of paper from the desk drawer and placed them down directly in front of me. Thumping the papers hard with his finger a few times, he suddenly roared, "What the hell is this?" I looked carefully at the papers and saw that it was my unit transfer request. Before I could answer, he continued loudly. "If I read this accurately, you want out of the Fifth Group and SOG, to any available unit. Is that correct?"

"Yes, sir," I responded. In my mind, I tried to reason out why he was so belligerent about it. I was the one requesting the transfer. It was my name on the form, not his, so what was the big deal? All I needed was his signature on the form for it to go through the channels. But I'd be damned if I was going to sit here meekly and get chewed out for no reason. He was probably concerned that my request would make him look bad among his peers. He wouldn't want them speculating on why a good soldier wanted out of his SOG detachment.

"All right, Parker," said the major in a lower voice. "What's the problem at Ban Me Thout? Is it your team? Captain Miller? Someone else there? What? Why the hell do you want out of the Fifth Group and SOG?"

No way in hell was I going to explain my true reasons for wanting the transfer. If I did, he'd put it all down in my files as my operations commander. Doing that would ruin my army career, my personal performance ratings, my promotions, and on and on. I didn't need those kinds of problems. The army would use the truth against me instead of using it to understand me better as a person. They'd take a dim view of an unconventionally trained soldier with a sudden case of morality and conscience. I joined the army to make a career out of it, and I wasn't about to sabotage myself. I enlisted for three years the day after my seventeenth birthday. In the early part of my third year, I reenlisted for six more years while here in Vietnam. When I leave Vietnam, I'll have about three and a half years left in active service. After six to seven active years, I'd seriously think about going to OCS (Officer Candidate School). I didn't have any fancy West Point, ROTC, or military academy schooling before the army. That is why I tried so hard in Vietnam to be an above-average soldier and leader. I needed a good combat record because it would help me later in my career.

Still looking at the major, I finally answered his question, stating, "Sir, I'm not having a problem with anyone at Ban Me Thout. I'm requesting the transfer due to sensitive personal reasons of my own. And with all due respect, I cannot and will not discuss those personal reasons. I'm sorry."

Major Small seemed disturbed and irritated at the determination in my voice. Narrowing his eyes menacingly, he said harshly, "What if I gave you a direct order, Sergeant, to tell me what those personal reasons are?"

I was starting to get angry as this meeting went from informal to formal. The bastard was going to pull rank on me. I didn't want to tell him a lie because he'd try to reason out whatever the lie was. What was the big damn deal with him, anyway? Hell, I only had a month and a half to go before my DEROS! The egotistical bastard should be glad to be rid of me because I was a short-timer. A lie wouldn't work and neither would the truth. He knew that if I refused a direct order, he could have me arrested, court-martialed, and sent to LBJ (Long Binh Jail). Just the thought of him doing that enraged me even more. He'd be ruining my entire career, and there wasn't a damn thing I could do about it.

He was still glaring at me, waiting for a response. So I gave him one. "Sir, if you order me to give my reasons, I would still respectfully decline to answer. My reasons are purely personal and in no way threaten the Operations Group."

Major Small leaped angrily out of his chair, slamming both his fists down on the desk. "Don't piss me off, Parker," he growled, "because I can make life fucking miserable for you! This isn't the bush, soldier, and your reputation means diddly shit to me! Understand?"

It took all the willpower I could conjure up to keep my mouth shut. I didn't want to egg him on. At the same time, though, I meant everything I told him. He regained some of his composure and clasped both hands together behind his back. With a slight smirk, he shook his head from side to side, staring at me. My mind propelled itself into full alert when I saw that sly smirk.

Walking over to the small bulletproof Plexiglas window, he quietly stared out at the busy compound. In a placid tone, he said, "I've been reading over your classified file. I'm reading it more out of curiosity than anything else, I'll admit. I knew you only by reputation, hearsay, and by your written reports. When I received your transfer request, I took the liberty of getting your complete classified file. I've seen you before, I think, at a few briefings, debriefings, and prisoner interrogations. You have to appreciate, Sergeant Parker, that I'm a covert operations commander, and it's impossible to know all my men personally. Correct me if I'm mistaken, but your primary schooling was in field radio repair at Fort Gordon, Georgia. Then you were sent to Fort Benning, Georgia for airborne ranger training. From there you were stationed in Germany, assigned to a communications unit called STRATCOM. An impressive unit, too — a brains outfit. You were taught cryptology and cryptography there along with electronic surveillance. From STRATCOM you were sent back to the States, to Fort Bragg, North Carolina for Special Forces training. While there, you were also sent to an NCO Academy and language school to learn Vietnamese as part of your training. After that, you were sent back to STRATCOM in Germany. A few times, you spent TDY (Temporary Duty) with the Tenth Special Forces in Bad Tolz as a communications expert on field training exercises. Am I correct so far, Sergeant?"

"Yes, sir," I replied with hidden agitation, wondering what kind of psych game he was up to. The mention of Germany and STRATCOM (Strategic Command) brought back some forgotten memories. STRATCOM was a sophisticated, high-tech communications unit specializing in microwave, tropo-wave, and teletype

24

equipment. Everyone had to have NATO and CRYPTO security clearance to work in that unit. To make a civilian comparison, STRATCOM would be almost equal to the highly secret NSA (National Security Agency). The NSA and STRATCOM were far more effective than the CIA in high-tech intelligence gathering and surveillance.

Major Small turned away from the window and faced me. "From Germany, you were sent to Nam, here," he continued, "and assigned to the First Logistical Command, a direct-support unit. Your job as an all-around commo expert was fixing field radios, radar, crypto, and electronic surveillance equipment. After a month or so, though, you seemed to lose interest in fixing equipment. You became a permanent perimeter guard, part of a reactionary force that you helped create to protect the company from enemy attacks. You ultimately submitted a transfer request to the Fifth Special Forces. At Nha Trang, here, you were put through an advanced CIA course in the field of intelligence and communications. Your motivation, leadership ability, and plain guts got you assigned to SOG and my detachment. Now, out of the clear blue sky, you want to transfer out. For what? What's the problem? Let's get it out in the open! Work it out between us! I'll do all I can within the bounds of my power to help, but I have to know the situation first! You know that!"

I sat there, wondering for a split second if maybe I should tell him, but my sixth sense warned me against trusting him with such personal information. No, I couldn't tell him my innermost thoughts or my deep self-conflicts. Not ever.

He saw that I wasn't going to say anything, so he added more bourbon to our cups. After we both had another taste of the warm booze, he started fingering through my file. "See this?" he said, trying to control his temper. "This letter is from the CIA station chief in your sector. It's a commendation letter signed by him and the deputy director of Special Operations. This letter alone grants you a secure job with the Agency when and if you ever leave the army." He flipped to more letters of commendation about me, stopping to name the sources: letters from Colonel Chung, a Korean; from Major Ngoc, an ARVN; from Chief Bao, a Montagnard; and from Captain Miller and a few others in Special Forces. I was honestly bewildered that Connally had written a commendation letter on me. He never mentioned it like the others had.

Slamming the file closed, he said, "What the hell am I going to tell my conventional superiors? They're all paranoid types as it is on covert operations. An experienced covert-ops man wanting completely out of the intelligence field might raise a few eyebrows. And this is how ugly rumors, myths, and half-truths start about clandestine and covert operations in general. How am I going to explain to competing detachment peers that one of my best men left for personal reasons?"

I sat there looking at him as calmly as I could. My anger started growing again; I knew that all he cared about was his image. And yet, I strongly sensed that one day, Major Small, the bastard, would become famous. He was a good detachment leader, and somehow, somewhere in his military career, he was going to write his name in American history, but it would only be done through the blood, sweat, and tears of men like me.

I was determined to keep my mouth shut before I worked myself up into a violent rage. My silence should be enough for him to tell how I still felt. Bastard. About a minute went by in silence as we stared at one another. Finally, in angry, precise whispers, he said, "You report to me in this office at exactly oh-nine hundred hours tomorrow, Sergeant! You be one minute late, and I'll have you court-martialed so fast it'll make your head spin! Now get the fuck out of my office! Move it, soldier!"

I stood up, saluted, and left. In a quiet rage, I walked over to the transient barracks with my gear and got a bunk. My next stop was the NCO club, where I got good and drunk. Lying on my bunk in my underwear, I still had Major Small, the bastard, on my mind. Why the hell was he keeping me in Nha Trang? I could be back in Ban Me Thout by now, away from the son of a bitch. He wanted to put me through the grinder again, I knew, but still, it wouldn't work. Not in a hundred years, not even if my life depended on it. I dozed off to sleep, cursing the major, this war, Carol, and the whole damn world.

The next morning, I stepped into the major's office at nine o'clock sharp. The irony was that the major wasn't in yet. His clerk told me to wait in the office, saying the major would be along shortly. The waiting was one of the challenges I was to be put through. I knew this and adjusted to it without much anger. A half-hour later, Major Small casually walked in with a handful of papers. He offered no excuses and no apologies, and I didn't expect any, either. Rank had its privileges in the military, and right now, the major was exercising his. As soon as he sat down, his clerk hurried in with a hot cup of coffee for him. Only after the clerk left did the major put the papers down and look at me.

In a normal but stern voice, he said, "For the record, I'm going to ask you once again, and once again only. Do you still want to transfer out of Special Forces and SOG? If so, are you still refusing to grant me a reason?"

The major was getting ready to have me arrested and court-martialed. With my heart pounding, I braced myself, waiting to hear the words that would destroy my career and ruin my life. Raging anger surged through my veins, burning my flesh and stomping my brain. In a fierce but weak voice, I answered, "I haven't changed my mind about anything, Major."

"I expected as much, so let's get down to business," he snapped impatiently. "And don't interrupt me until I'm finished, goddamn it. I can't stop this transfer request from going through the channels. As your operations commander, though, if I put my disapproval on it, headquarters will do the same. I'd be willing to approve your transfer on one condition. I want one last mission out of your ass first: a search and destroy. Finish it, and I'll have you out of this unit within twenty-four hours of your return. Understand one thing right now: I can disapprove this transfer and still order you on this mission if I so choose. But with your DEROS a couple of months away, I'd be losing you as a team leader anyway. The mission itself would take from one day to two weeks maximum. I want your answer now, though, before I continue. I refuse to waste my time and breath if you're not interested."

I was totally baffled and surprised beyond belief. The last thing I expected from the bastard was something like this. I started relaxing some, but I was still agitated at the thought of being utilized one last time. Then it dawned on me. The bastard or someone else in SOG Headquarters or Fifth Group Headquarters wanted me on this search and destroy. I wondered how long this mission had been on the planning board. My sixth sense told me that I was designated for this long before my transfer request went in. One last mission with a two-week max left me about a month to do. There was no way I wanted to do that final month in this unit. In a month alone, I could be sent on several different missions or advisory consignments. And with my anxiety spells and intense flashbacks, I didn't see myself lasting even a month. Probability, the X factor, and Murphy's Law were all running against me. Hell, I could be killed on this mission, but if I were, I wouldn't have to be concerned about a transfer. In the long run, I was better off taking the major's offer. If I didn't, he was going to screw me. He'd said so himself in so many words, and he'd do it with twice the determination and vigor he had used the day before. I'd go on the damn mission, and if I survived, I'd be out of the unit like I wanted. If I got killed, I'd still be out of the unit; I'd just get out of it the hard way.

I started to realize that at my young age of twenty, I'd made many life-and-death decisions pertaining to myself, my teams, civilians, and the enemy. It was enough to give any young man multiple heart attacks, gray hairs, and a permanent case of diarrhea. I didn't regret any of the decisions I'd made in this war, though, whether they spared lives or took them. I've always felt that I did the best I could with what I had. If it wasn't for that self-assured attitude, I would have gone stark raving mad.

"What's it going to be?" Major Small growled with slight anticipation.

"You don't leave me much choice, Major," I answered solemnly. "If I refuse, you'll probably have me court-martialed. Or, as you said, you'd disapprove my transfer and order me on the mission anyway. My answer's yes, so I can leave the unit after the mission's over. You already know how strongly I feel about leaving, and I'd prefer to leave with a good performance rating and no problems."

The major gave me another sinister smirk, remarking, "You hit it right on the nose, Sergeant. Your file may rate you with above-average intelligence, but you're a stubborn man and pain in the ass. Still, I never felt for a second that you'd let your stubbornness override your common sense."

As far as having common sense went, I'd often wondered if I had lost or misplaced it somewhere. I also wondered what else I might have lost or misplaced of myself in this war.

The major went on to explain the mission to me. An elite company from a Viet Cong main force battalion was raising hell in the Second Corp area of South Vietnam. They were constantly hitting American and ARVN compounds, firebases, and LZs (Landing Zones). They were also destroying and terrorizing Vietnamese and Yard villages loyal to Americans. Some of the army's conventional combat troops were spending too much time searching for them, too. The main enemy company would strike, withdraw, break up into small groups, and disappear. When they were ready to strike again, they'd get together as a company and attack their target. Seven days ago, they totally destroyed a small Yard village near the Cambodian border. Through our Asian intelligence network, we finally got some hard information on them. When the enemy company split up this time, the directions of several of the small groups were noted.

"What we're going to do," the major went on, "is send in small search and destroy teams to track, locate, and destroy each of the known groups. Each team will be led by Special Forces personnel, meaning you'll be leading one of them. Headquarters feels it would be nice to give the enemy a psychological and physical blow by taking out one of their best companies. Each of the known groups has been codenamed, and the one you're after is called Bluebeard. Intelligence doesn't know the exact strength of each known group, but they estimate the strength to vary from ten to twenty-five troops per group."

Unrolling one of the many maps in his office, the major showed me the location of the last destroyed village. It was only five miles from the Cambodian border. Intelligence knew that some of the unknown groups had crossed into Cambodia.

Next, the major gave me coordinates of where Bluebeard had been as they left the area near Cambodia. Bluebeard could have changed directions, anything, but the coordinates were good as a starting point. The last intelligence report still had them inside Nam. "Now," said the major, "if Bluebeard changes course drastically and crosses into Laos or Cambodia, you're still to pursue with all due intent and purpose. You know the game here concerning crossovers. You've been on penetration crossovers before in these countries. Officially, American soldiers don't have the legal right to cross over into either neutral country, so on the official records, it'll state that you were transferred today to a transportation company in Pleiku. In fact, once the mission's finished, that's the company you'll be transferring to, and you'll finish up your time in Nam there.

"If you're captured in Laos or Cambodia, we can't officially acknowledge your capture, and you know as well as I do that it's better to be dead than captured with the mental and physical torture you'll be subjected to. And that isn't even counting the bullshit propaganda and other enemy politics you'll go through as a POW. You'll be totally on your own, as usual, if your team crosses over. Any screw-ups at all and the Department of Defense will use your open official records as plausible deniability. Your classified records will never be brought into play under the National Security Act. If you're killed in a crossover, we couldn't even officially accept your body back, and you'd be openly listed as Missing in Action within the confines of South Vietnam. Whatever you do, Sergeant, don't get captured. If you do, you'll be a pawn for the enemy, and they'll make you wish you were dead. I know you're aware of these procedures, but I have to go through them. It's regulations."

We talked for over an hour about the mission, charting my team's insertion point, checking weather conditions, terrain, the closest known enemy position, etc. Toward the end of the briefing, Major Small unexpectedly added, "The team you'll be leading will consist of five men other than you. They will not be ARVN Special Forces or Rangers, either. In fact, the five men will not even be Yards or Chinese Nungs."

"Okay," I acknowledged, "the men will be other American Special Forces or Ranger personnel, then. No problems."

"I'm afraid not, Sergeant," the Major smirked, still seated. "Your five men will be from the First Infantry Division from around Lai Rhe."

"What?" I shot back, dumbfounded. "The First Division? You want me to take First Division grunts on a mission? This is the team you're talking about? You're crazy! You're trying to get me killed!"

Major Small catapulted out of his chair, bellowing, "Now hold it a goddamn minute! I don't know who the fuck you think you're talking to, but you shut your face and shut it now, soldier!

That's an order! This shit wasn't my idea! It came from SOG and the Fifth Group's planning board! These men are conventional grunts, but you're stuck with them! Those are my orders, and I intend to follow them — and so will you, soldier! All my other six-man teams will only have two or three men from the First assigned to them. The remainder of their teams will consist of ARVNs and Yards. It was random chance that you ended up with five. Cut the crying and bitching! I'm pissed off enough about this setup without hearing your shit, too!"

This was just great. Just wonderful. Just what I needed! I was supposed to go running around Southeast Asia with five regular grunts. Most of the guys in those conventional units weren't even Ranger-qualified. Why me? Why the hell me? Bastard!

Still angry, Major Small roared on. "Your five men are wait-ing for you in front of the transient barracks. You leave tomorrow at oh-seven hundred hours on a chopper. It'll stop in Quam Ky for refueling. You're to call in then for any last-minute changes, so make sure the call's scrambled. Everything I've told you has been thoroughly explained to each man from the First assigned to us. Their official records have been manipulated, too, until they've returned. As far as anyone knows without privileged information, these guys never left their companies. Your team is designated Indigo-8. Now, unless you have any questions, I want your ass out of my office."

I left the major's office angry, but at the same time, I felt relieved. I had one last mission to do, but at least I wasn't being court-martialed. I walked over to the barracks, not enthused at all about meeting my team. As soon as I saw the three white and two black men, I felt sick. I just wanted to dig a hole and cover myself up in it. The next thing I noticed was that one of the men wore second lieutenant bars. It wasn't unusual in covert operations for a sergeant to be placed in charge over an officer. The most experienced man was normally put in charge, regardless of his rank. The lieutenant spotted me and called the other four men to attention. Why he did that, I'll never know.

"Sergeant Parker, I'm Lieutenant Steven Collins," he cheer-fully said. "We're assigned to you as your team."

I never wore a nametag on my tiger-striped fatigues or on my jungle hat. I also wasn't wearing any rank, so I was a little startled

31

that this Lieutenant Collins identified me so easily. He was 5'10" tall, slim, and had high cheekbones, light blue eyes, red hair, and freckles. He looked about twenty years old and didn't seem very experienced to me. No one with even basic guerrilla experience would have such a wholesome, innocent smile on his face like he did. I was pissed off about this whole thing. I paused for several seconds before curiously asking, "How did you know I was Sergeant Parker, Lieutenant?"

With that wholesome smile, Collins answered shyly, "Well, uh, Major Small told us to just wait here for a very pissed-off-looking black guy." Hearing that crap pissed me off even more. The major wasn't only an egotistical bastard; he was a goddamn wise-ass, too.

Sourly, I inquired, "How long have you been in this country, Lieutenant?"

"Almost a month now, down around Lai Khe, mostly," Collins answered with that irritating smile still plastered on his face.

"Have you had any enemy contact yet?" I asked, dreading the answer.

"Well, a couple of firebases I've been on were mortared a few times. That's about it, I think," replied Collins, still smiling.

I didn't need this shit. Not on my last mission. I shook my head slowly from side to side, sighing heavily.

"Are you okay?" Collins asked, finally wiping that damn smile off his face.

"Hangover," I snapped tiredly. "Just a hangover, that's all."

I walked over to the four men, who were still at attention. I asked them their names, and then I asked each one a few questions. Specialist Fourth Class Frank Vitani was the only one out of all five who had good training and experience. He was a LRRP (pronounced *Lurp*), which was a Long Range Recon Patrol expert, trained at the Recondo School here at Nha Trang. The Recondo (Reconnaissance and Commando) School was run by Special Forces instructors who taught jungle survival, guerrilla tactics, ambush, counter-ambush, unarmed combat, map and compass reading, small arms, explosive ordinance, psychological warfare, and airborne training. Many of the conventional combat units would send some of their men through this school so they could be the eyes and ears for their companies in the bush.

Vitani was in his early twenties. He was short, stocky, and tanned, with fairly long black hair and dark eyes. He was from Oakland, California with eight months "in-country" so far, and he'd killed NVA and VC personnel in numerous ambushes and firefights. I'd use him as the team's rear guard in the bush because I'd be walking point. Rear guard was just as dangerous as point; they were the two most hazardous positions to walk on a team.

Standing next to Specialist Fourth Class Vitani was Private First Class Robert Ordowski. He was nineteen years old, from Madison, Wisconsin. Ordowski was well over six feet tall, and he was a powerhouse with wide shoulders, a thick, hairy chest, huge arms, and beefy hands. He was a curly blond human dynamo, and he looked more like a pro defensive lineman than an army PFC. Ordowski had been in-country for two months, and he had seen very little action. Well, I wasn't looking for miracles at this stage, and I didn't expect any, either.

Next to Private First Class Ordowski stood nineteen-year-old Private First Class Dwight Austin, from Tampa, Florida. Austin was dark brown, about 5'9" tall, of average weight, and had beady brown eyes, a thick black mustache, and a medium-sized afro hairstyle. He'd been in-country for about a month, and he'd been in only one firefight.

Last was Sp4 Edward Jones, who was from the Bronx in New York City. Jones stood about six feet tall, was skinny, and had a deep black complexion. He'd only been in two firefights, and he'd been in-country for two months. He tried to look confident and ready, just like the others were doing.

I felt terrible. I felt depressed beyond words. I wanted to suddenly wake up and find that this mission and these men were only a dream, a figment of my imagination that I could just laugh about and totally discard. A minute or so passed by while I silently waited to wake up. It also took that amount of time to fully accept the fact that this was all too real and that my ass was up shit's creek without a paddle if I couldn't pull these guys together as a fighting team. I wondered if they fully understood that if we didn't work together, we'd be killed together. There wasn't time to train them in small team search and destroy tactics, thanks to Headquarters.

Why the hell did they send me mostly inexperienced men? Mostly friendly guys like these? They shouldn't be this friendly with me! I hadn't earned their respect, and they hadn't earned mine yet, either. I suddenly became angry at myself. The friendly part of me, which I'd kept deeply buried, was yearning to thrust forward. That terrified me to no end. In war, you learn from experience or plain cold logic not to become too friendly with another soldier. One second, that soldier's a walking, talking, breathing friend, a human being. And the next second, that same soldier could be a bloody, lifeless mass, unresponsive and inhuman in shape and form. I knew this all too well; I was stupid, and I learned the hard way. But never again. Never. Not for all the money in the world. Because money has no significance to a man gone insane.

So no, I couldn't be friends with them individually or as a group. But yet, at the same time, I felt a deep desperation to have friends. To just be accepted for the person I was, not because of my rank and training. I seemed to be in more and more emotional conflict with myself. I saw myself as an intelligent and reasonable person, but I was filled with mixed emotions that seemed overwhelming.

I suddenly realized that I was being stared at by five pairs of eyes. I couldn't honestly blame them for their expressions, either. There I was, standing in front of them all, daydreaming my ass off. Looking intently at them, I knew what I had to do. I had to intimidate and scare the hell out of them all. I wanted them to fear me now so they'd fear me in the bush. I needed them totally aware of my presence from this moment on. My orders had to be obeyed reflexively in the bush; they couldn't hesitate. Their awareness had to be heightened so acutely that they feared me more than they feared the enemy. Team survival had to be the priority, the only priority. Only then would we have a chance of surviving without ever having worked together before. Without this, we were just walking dead men looking for a piece of real estate to die on.

I didn't like role-playing the hardcore sergeant, but I had no alternative. Taking a deep breath, I started my verbal assault, shouting, "You assholes from the First think you're hot shit, don't you? You think your shit don't stink because of bullshit run-ins with the enemy! Well, I'm not part of the First, ladies! You bastards want to fight? Well, I'll show you all the slant-eyed gooks in the world to fight! I'll overdose you bastards on gooks! If you want to cut their ears off for trophies, that's your goddamn business. Just understand that with me, you'll damn well fight, and you'll damn well kill gooks! If your number comes up, you'll die like a fucking man with me, too! If just one of you bastards freezes up on me or fucks up, I'll kill you my goddamn self. I'm your team leader, with total authority, and I can and will legally blow your brains out if I'm forced to! You got a loving mommy, daddy or wife back home? Fuck them! You mess up on me in the bush, and your ass is history! I've been ordered to take you guys on this mission, but no one, I repeat, no one has ordered me to bring you back alive! If you want to live, you have to survive me first — *then* the enemy! And if you think I'm a mean black son of a bitch with a fucking attitude problem, you're right!"

Not one of them dared to speak. They just stood there, startled and shocked. I was giving them the most demented facial expression I could conjure up, too. My dark-brown, bloodshot eyes were fanatical and dangerous looking. My nostrils flared, my bottom lip trembled nervously, and my left eyebrow twitched wildly. It took a long time staring into mirrors to perfect this maniac look.

Their expressions changed in a flash. They went from being startled to being worried as they glanced at one another. This was what usually happened, though, whenever I whipped the maniac look on someone. Right after the initial shock wears off, the questions about my sanity naturally pop up. I wanted them worried and skeptical about me having all my marbles. I knew they were briefed on me being an experienced covert operations sergeant, and since I was appointed team leader, they knew I had to be a tough survivor and a tough leader. I needed them to obey me instantly in the bush. Right now, a good percentage of their hostility would be focused on me. I had challenged their male egos, their courage, worthiness, and psychological strength as individuals and as a team. But once they were in the bush, they'd turn that hostility toward the enemy with stronger determination. And that's what I wanted, an above-average determination from them, a survivor's fierceness in the bush. Of course, they'd still speculate about me being an escapee from some psycho ward, but they'd know as soldiers that I was a formidable ally with the expertise to bring them back alive. With this in their minds, I told them to be here at 0630 hours tomorrow.

By 0700 hours, we were in the air, heading for Quam Ky. I had an irritating hangover. I briefed them on how to leave the chopper as a small team if the insertion point was enemy-free. Then I explained how to do it if we came under fire at or near the insertion point. I ended my conversation with a wild, threatening glare. During the rest of the flight to Quam Ky, they talked among themselves but not to me.

At Quam Ky, I radioed the Operations section at Fifth Group Headquarters for the final go-ahead. Everything was still green for go with no changes. The chopper finished refueling, and we lifted off again for the final lap. I noticed that there was little talk now on the chopper. I'd been ignoring them anyway, and I closed my eyes again. I had so much on my mind; I didn't know if I was coming or going. I avoided staring at the countryside rushing by below. Vietnam, with its artistic beauty, kept creating a false sense of serenity deep within my heart. It ate my guts up when I tried to understand how a small, beautiful country like this could contain so much violence. So much killing, maiming, crippling, blood-shed, and slaughter. So much crying, suffering, misery, and grief. And so many emotionally numb and misguided children, with fear, hate, hunger, larceny, and murder in their eyes. And that didn't even include the infants. I've seen them all: men, women, children, babies, wounded, dying, and dead. The horror of this was that all these people could not possibly have been the enemy. I reversed my thinking abruptly, wondering who the hell I was to think such thoughts, anyway. I was just one of the insignificant minor actors being used in an all-star cast of geopolitics. My life and my thoughts were totally irrelevant to the overall scheme of things here. I couldn't keep tormenting myself about things beyond my immediate control.

Still, my emotional conflicts were twofold because I was both a civilized man and a savage man. The civilized man within me was my true being, my natural, passive self, moral and emotion-ally logical. He was a friendly, loving, peaceful entity who had a strong sense of integrity and fair play. And he abhorred violence of any kind, in any way, form, or fashion.

The savage man within me was a brutal predator who dealt with total logic and pure reasoning. Rage, hostility, revenge, and barbaric violence were the things essential to his functioning. In short, survival was everything and all things to the savage man. Survival equaled hate, and hate equaled violence with no remorse. Survival made every man and woman a subject of distrust and suspicion. Compassion, love, and friendship were emotional threats to the savage man's existence. And last, the savage man was manufactured within me; Nighthawk-One was created by some of the most diabolical and immoral minds known to mankind. Robert Parker and Nighthawk-One shared the same physical body and mind, but they were extreme opposites, as different as two entities could possibly be.

I forced myself to stop thinking about my dual self. It was a thought I didn't like dwelling on. My mind fluttered, and reflections of Carol suddenly appeared. Beautiful, lovely, enchanting Carol. I'd put so much faith and love in our relationship only to be victimized. And I was the last person to know. She cheated on me and manipulated my feelings to no end. Carol was a few years older than I was, but my maturity surpassed hers in many ways. She enjoyed fast money and the fast street life, never tiring of parties, drinking, smoking reefer, and loud crowds.

How blind, innocent, and foolish I was then. I was addicted to the graceful movement of her sensuous form when she walked, and I was spellbound by the bewitching passions trapped within her alluring body when she danced. All our lovemaking was satisfying. At times, we were romantic in bed, boldly experimenting, softly probing and tenderly petting. At other times, we were breathlessly erotic, almost animalistic, in our cravings, desires, and boundless imaginations.

Carol and I were perfect sexual mates, but outside of sex, we were strangers, opposites in almost every way. My true being, Robert Parker, will always be hopelessly in love with her. I refuse to forget the pleasurable memories of the time we spent together. There weren't many, but still, they're cherished within the civilized part of me. And it was for that reason only that I sent money to Carol whenever she asked.

My created self, Nighthawk-One, thought I was a weak, stupid fool who was being led by passion instead of pure logic.

Nighthawk-One never failed to remind me that because of Carol's immense selfishness, she could easily pose a threat to my physical and mental survival. Passion equaled weakness, and weakness equaled death, screamed Nighthawk-One.

I stopped playing mental chess with my thoughts and feelings. It was becoming more tiresome and frustrating all the time. I found myself becoming instantly angry, but I didn't know what I was angry about. Everything! I just had to be angry about every damn thing! I was oblivious to the constant noise of the chopper's engine and the whooshing rotors, and I hardly noticed my hands trembling, my abnormal sweating, and my shortness of breath. These and other physical symptoms weren't unusual when I was in deep, concentrated thought. I did notice, however, that my team members were giving me inquisitive stares.

Even the chopper's two machine gunners were staring curiously at me. When I stared back menacingly, all eyes shifted frantically. Inside, I was laughing at the humorous way they tried to avoid my glare.

As the chopper flew onward, I tried settling my mind for just a little while. I wanted my mind in a complete state of limbo with no past, present, or future thoughts interfering, but as hard as I tried, I couldn't even relax myself temporarily anymore. My mind fluttered involuntarily again, and from the depths of my subconscious, another thought was thrust forward.

This unyielding thought centered on the mass firepower and high-tech intelligence equipment the United States Military had compared to North Vietnam. Even with all this, we still couldn't wear the enemy down or even kill enough of the elusive bastards. The U.S. Military had dropped endless amounts of bombs in North and South Vietnam, bombs weighing 250, 500, 1,000 and even 15,000 pounds. A B-52 bomber group could literally saturate an area with each one dropping over twenty-seven tons of bombs.

I remembered one big village near Laos that was in the middle of a heavily infested enemy area. I was one of three American advisors who surrounded and entered the village with an ARVN Ranger battalion. Six interrogation teams questioned each villager, looking for suspected Viet Cong. Over one hundred fifty people came under heavy suspicion of being VC or enemy collaborators. The rest of the villagers were flown away in big Chinook choppers to a resettlement area for their own safety and protection. This had been our main assignment, to remove the villagers and destroy the village, thus denying the enemy the chance to control the place.

After the villagers were gone, American combat engineers came in with their heavy equipment. They dug a huge hole in the center of the village. Several thousand pounds of explosives were put in the hole with a chemical time detonator. Then the hole was covered up by bulldozers. The gigantic earthshaking blast flattened all the thatched, wood, and stone structures in the village.

My mind drifted to the modified C-47 cargo planes that were equipped with electronic Gatling guns, nicknamed Spooky or Puff the Magic Dragon. They had an awesome firing capability, from 5,000 to 25,000 rounds per minute. Some specially equipped planes could fly over an area and snap thousands of high-speed still photographs in a couple of minutes. Still others could examine the air for sweat or urine molecules to locate enemy troops. There were others that could drop small acoustic and seismic detectors in the jungle. This was done to detect human movement. And there were sensitive listening devices dropped, too, that could pick up normal tone conversations between enemy troops.

The U.S. Military had other technological gimmicks, as well, like particle detectors that could detect carbon trails through the sky to locate the cooking fires of enemy troops. There were planes with special film, too, that could detect camouflage covering in the jungle and even detect warm truck engines through a double or triple canopy of trees.

There was the "cluster bomb" that could toss out eight hundred little explosive bomblets. And there was the "smart bomb" that could be guided to its target with laser beams. There were the huge blankets of special herbicides that could be dropped and ignited from the air to suffocate anything living beneath them. I thought about Agent Orange, too, which was used by the military to kill trees and mangrove forests. Agent White was used to kill the underbrush and bushes, while Agent Blue was used for killing rice plants.

All this was only a small portion of the technology being used in this war, but we still couldn't seek out the elusive enemy and destroy them all. If all this firepower and high-tech surveillance gear was so goddamn good, then what the hell was I doing on this chopper? It seems that no matter how technologically advanced mankind gets, there will always be room for plain old manpower and ingenuity. As the intelligence reports had shown since 1968, American fatalities were been rising. Sometimes, there were as many as 400 to 500 deaths per month, excluding American wounded. And knowing American intelligence and warfare as I did, one of the major contingencies had to involve the use of small, tactical, low-radiation nuclear weapons if American deaths kept rising. The only other way to avoid a continuously high body count would be the mass invasion of North Vietnam by sea, air, and land, but this type of large, logistical invasion would have involved too many units of the Army, Air Force, Navy and Marines.

Chapter Three

For some time, I was deep in thought about all the mass fire-power and high-tech equipment. Then I heard someone yelling at me over the noise of the chopper. The crew chief was yelling and signaling with his hand that there were five minutes left to insertion. I nodded several times, letting him know I'd heard him so he would quit shouting. I checked my small rucksack, weapons, and other gear, making sure everything was secure. I had four bandoliers of ammo crisscrossed around my shoulders and chest, and I was carrying an M-l6 this time.

My team members began checking their gear, too, and I saw their nervousness suddenly intensify. The insertion point was a single canopy jungle clearing. Once I saw it, I had doubts about a chopper even squeezing into it. Intelligence had reported no NVA or VC activity within a thirty-mile radius, but intelligence also said that the area was infested with Cambodian, Laotian, and Chinese-Nung paramilitary gangs. These types of warlord gangs would ambush American soldiers, Viet Cong, NVA, and each other. They were cold-blooded killers and scavengers who would waste you for your weapon, a pack of American cigarettes, or the gold in your mouth.

The chopper flew over the insertion point area three times to draw fire. Nothing. Hovering over the small clearing, it descended steadily, straight down. Startled birds flew off and I could see small animals scurrying away. Tall elephant grass, shrubbery, and tree branches swayed recklessly. Leaves shook wildly, too, and the spinning rotors flung debris and dirt in all directions.

The two M-60 machine gunners on each side of the chopper scanned the jungle foliage sharply. They were ready to open fire on anything moving, man or animal. Between the noise of the engine, the small clearing, and the debris blowing all around and through the chopper, the situation was nerve-wracking and almost unbearable. The chopper hovered a few feet from the ground, and I leaned out, putting a foot on one of the skids. Cautiously, I studied the whole area in front of me, the trees, bushes, elephant grass, and ground. I was only inches away from one of the chopper's helmeted machine gunners as I leaned out. He was

41

pimple-faced, wide-eyed and chubby, with dirty blond hair sticking out of his helmet. Sweating profusely, he swung the barrel of the M-60 from side to side, looking for something to kill.

I quickly gave the thumbs-up sign for my team members to see. Then I jumped. My weight was barely on the ground before I started zigzagging for the cover of the jungle a few yards away. Once inside the dense jungle, I squatted behind a big tree with some of its roots protruding from the ground. I was surrounded by five- to six-foot-high elephant grass. Glancing around, I expected to be encircled by my whole team in a tight group. I saw no one. I'd explained in flight about leaving the chopper on the double and on the heels of the guy in front, so where the hell were they, damn it? Only seconds had passed, and I still heard the chopper clearly. I took a peek around the tree, expecting to see my team stampeding toward me. I saw the chopper still hovering near the ground like a giant green insect with wings. My team had not even jumped out yet! A split second later, I saw Lieutenant Collins leap to the ground.

Then it happened. Without warning, all hell broke loose. *Phu Kich! Ambush!* Just as Lieutenant Collins hit the ground, he was shot twice in the stomach. The machine gunners on the chopper opened up spontaneously, firing into the jungle. Before Collins' body even hit the ground, three RPG-7 mortars landed in the clearing. The shattering, deafening explosions rocked the chopper violently, ripping half the rotor blade off and flinging it wildly into the trees. Hundreds of pieces of hot shard and shrapnel slammed into the chopper. There was no firing from the chopper, so the machine gunners had to be dazed, unconscious, wounded, or dead. Thick black smoke appeared from the damaged, sputtering engine as the chopper flopped heavily to the ground, breaking its right skid.

Lieutenant Collins was still alive on the ground with his helmet blown off. Dozens of shrapnel wounds littered his back, buttocks, and legs. Weaponless and with a dire desperation for life, he tried crawling on his elbows. My God, his distorted face showed the agony he was in. Collins got about three feet before a flurry of rounds made his head explode. His head was gone! His face! Nothing was left on his shoulders but a bloody, moist, fist-sized skull fragment. Everything else was gone, splattered into chunks, bits, and pieces all over the place. Blood flowed and sprayed from the headless torso to the ground, forming puddles. There was a brief silence for several seconds when nothing was heard except the expiring chopper engine.

Then Private First Class Austin charged out of the tilted chopper like a madman, tripping at the door. He fell hard to the ground just as automatic fire swarmed at him from the jungle. Like countless angry bees, the horde of deadly rounds dug up chunks of earth all around him. Forty to fifty rounds must have struck him from head to toe before the firing stopped. Numerous rounds had hit the side of his head, and his left arm hung awkwardly from a shredded muscle tendon. His right foot was shot completely off with the boot still on it. Austin was dead. Gone.

Austin should have been firing his weapon when he left the chopper. Would that have stopped him from being killed, though? No. I wanted to yell for the rest of them to stay in the chopper instead of running out, but to yell now would give my exact position away and doom my ass for sure. I wouldn't be able to run ten yards before they dropped mortars and heavy small arms fire on this area. I wasn't even sure if telling them to stay in the chopper was really the lesser of the two evils. Before this thought could fully streak through my mind, my doubts were answered.

Mortars struck the clearing again like hail. The ground-shaking concussions stunned me, and I briefly lost my hearing. One of the mortars struck the chopper squarely. Another blew the tail off, and still another one landed squarely, as well. Four more mortars were dropped in the area, which was filled with twisted steel debris and bodies. The main portion of the chopper was demolished and on fire; automatic weapons from the jungle sprayed the clearing with hundreds of rounds.

I smelled human flesh, burning and scorched. I hated the smell, despised it, and could never compare it to anything else I've ever smelled. It was distinct and unusual, a heavily scented, almost sweet, nectar-type aroma that assaulted my nostrils and bloated my lungs. I felt like I was suffocating, like the very smell itself destroyed all the oxygen in the air. I couldn't see the smoldering chopper or the charred, mangled bodies anymore. Black smoke filled the whole clearing and blew through the trees, and they were still firing heavily into the clearing.

I leaned back behind the tree, my legs drawn up tightly to my chest. My whole body was drenched in a nervous sweat, and I suddenly became severely dizzy and disoriented. My heart was thumping like a jackhammer, piercing pain stabbed the right side of my head, and my lungs screamed for sufficient air. My rifle was on the ground, my right hand barely touching it. The thick smoke, the roaring blasts and weapons fire, watching my team and chopper crew dying, the smell of burning flesh, the need for oxygen, and the sunlight filtering through the trees to taunt my very existence were overwhelming.

In just seconds, all this! All of them dead! Gone! I was hyperventilating, and my eyes bulged out of their sockets. In a nervous frenzy, I rocked my legs from side to side while saliva drooled from the corners of my mouth. I could hear my heart clearly, as if it were right in my head. It pounded away like mad, drumming and drumming relentlessly on the sharp, piercing pain in my head. It was unbearable torture. I tried yelling, but only gurgling, incoherent stammering sounds came out. I was slipping into a shock-induced catatonic state.

This is it! This is what I've always dreaded! My mind was being impelled beyond panic and terror. It was daylight, my eyes were wide open, and the temperature was over ninety degrees, but all I saw was pitch darkness, all I heard was total silence, and a freezing chill rattled my body to the bone. I was no longer walking the thin red line between sanity and insanity, normality and abnormality. I was being nudged into a twilight dimension of complete and absolute madness, a demonic, diseased, and fanatical dimension that seared my very soul at just a glimpse. *Hell was not fire and brimstone! Hell was this! All this!* I was mentally falling apart. I was on my way to becoming a raving lunatic with no sense or reasoning. *Jesus Christ! I don't want this! Please! I don't want this!*

The civilized part of my being was breaking into pieces and disintegrating. I felt myself tumbling deeper and deeper into a dark abyss. The civilized part within me was no match for the supernatural specter that heaved madness among mankind. The civilized part inside me would be totally destroyed, and as a result, the savage part inside me would also be destroyed. Although they were complete opposites, they were still helplessly and bitterly part of each other's being. The savage part in me had always ventured for total dominance over the natural, civilized part, but it never, ever did that at the risk of a mental breakdown and outright insanity. That would be self-defeating and self-destructive. What it wanted to do was survive.

The savage part within me was ferociously determined to survive, not as a mentally insane entity but as a purely reasoning entity shrouded in logical thoughts. Survival equaled violence! Violence equaled savage man! And savage man was Nighthawk-One! From the deepest depths of my essence, from the very core of my celestial soul, there surged forth a strange, extraordinary force that was vital to my mental and physical wellbeing. It was an unnatural force so tremendous and overpowering that I was no longer falling into the dark, bottomless pit but ascending from it, faster and faster. I no longer saw darkness but light, and I no longer felt cold but blazing hot. This holy or unholy force penetrated every ounce of flesh and every drop of blood in my body, every cell and molecule. It fused itself into my being, bringing me back, back to the reality of this world, my life, and the moment. I could breathe again, and I hungrily inhaled and exhaled deeply. Bitter hate was the first emotion I felt, hate so vicious and brutal that it was staggering. Seething rage and beastlike hostility were thrust forward next with impulsive and explosive fury. Nighthawk-One was back!

I grabbed my rifle and did a swift forward somersault that took me deeper into the elephant grass. My mind started clicking like a living apparatus, like the lethal machine I was created to be. There was still loud automatic fire, though not as much as before. I analyzed my status and options as a lone survivor. What was the time factor since I left the chopper? A minute? Two minutes? Maybe three? I was many miles away from the nearest friendly outfit, a Special Forces A-Team camp. I had to move and vary my position as much as possible. Then I'd find a secure place and evaluate my choices. Escape and evasion thoughts flashed through my mind like red-alert signals.

On a grassy knoll to my right, about 150 yards away, stood a tanned, uniformed, pith-helmeted NVA soldier. Holding his AK-47 assault rifle in one hand, he triumphantly pointed in my direction with his other hand. He yelled excitedly to others I couldn't see, who were in the tall elephant grass like I was. Then he quickly fired a burst of several rounds at me.

45

I took quick aim and squeezed off a burst of automatic fire at the him. I missed the bastard! As soon as I had finished firing, I took off in the opposite direction, running away from the grassy knoll. I ran in a zigzagging fashion for about fifty yards. Holding my weapon tightly while running, I thumbed the selector switch from automatic to semi-automatic. I knew there were others closing in on me fast in the elephant grass. They were probably flanking me first on both sides. Then they'd surround me and tighten the circle for the kill. Still, the biggest and most immediate threat to me was the NVA soldier on the knoll because he would keep on pointing out my changing position.

He fired another volley of rounds in my direction. I heard two or three of the bullets zip through the elephant grass just inches from me. That was it! I'd had enough of this! Turning quickly, I held my rasping, panting breath and took a few seconds longer to aim. Then I squeezed off several steady, well-directed semi-automatic shots. I got the snitching bastard! His body jerked as he gave out a short scream and bent over, both hands clutching his midsection. Another round hit him and he fell backward off the grassy knoll. I heard angry Vietnamese voices to my left, and I bent low in the grass. I changed the near-empty magazine in my rifle for a full one. There had to be about a dozen of those bastards, less than fifty yards away and closing in. From their loud curses, it sounded like they were in close proximity to each other, too. I had to take advantage of that so I could temporarily disorganize their search and escape.

Pulling the small Montagnard rucksack off my back, I grabbed three of the five frag grenades in there. I put the rucksack back on, staying low, and pulled the pin of one grenade, throwing it in the direction of the voices. I quickly did the same with the other two, landing each grenade about ten to fifteen yards apart.

The roaring, ground-shaking explosions were staggering. Then I heard the screams of pain, the panicked yelling of others, and the firing of weapons. The survivors were spraying the area randomly, hoping to kill me. Stumbling to my feet, I took off running. I ran like I'd never run before. My legs were pumping and straining. I held my rifle up near my face to protect my eyes as I crashed blindly through the elephant grass. Humidity was high and the sun was hot, my mouth pasty dry. My heart was pounding like crazy as I ran. Winged and crawling insects battered my face, going up my nose, my gaping mouth, and into my eyes.

Thorny shrubbery and needled plants scratched and cut my face, hands and arms, but I fumbled onward. I tripped and fell four times from tangled vines, thick bushes, and small ground holes. My jungle hat was ripped off my head, but I didn't stop. Minutes later, I broke free of the elephant grass, grunting and gasping like a wild man. I didn't break my stride and plunged into the dense, wooded area directly in front of me. Images of the bloody ambush fluttered through my mind as I tore through the jungle. I tried to force them away because I couldn't deal with them. The ambush and massacre were too traumatic, too emotional and personal to think about them adequately.

I broke through the wooded area smack into bamboo clusters and more trees. I still heard distant firing, which was now mixed with explosions. The bastards were dumping mortars into the elephant grass, hoping to blow me to shreds. *Just let them believe I am still in the elephant grass, for just a little longer*, I thought. I sprinted across a narrow dirt trail in the jungle, which was something I normally wouldn't do. I crashed back into the jungle, not daring to use the trail. I came to a small, foul-smelling creek with red, sandy banks. It was filled with stagnant pools of grayish-green and grayish-red fungus.

Without hesitating, I splashed into the water, which came up over my waist. The stench was terrible. The cool, slimy water gave slight relief to my aching legs and sore feet. I felt drowsy and nauseated and had painful stomach cramps, too. I struggled with each step in the creek because my boots were being sucked into the soft, muddy bottom. On the other side, the wet, muddy portion of the bank kept collapsing under my body weight. I kept sliding helplessly back into the creek. I finally had to throw my weapon to the dry portion of the creek bank and crawl out slowly, inch by inch, on my hands and knees. I was bone-tired and out of breath. I stayed on all fours for a few minutes, breathing hoarsely. All the muscles in my body ached like never before, but still, I picked up my weapon, got to my feet, and took off at a suffering trot.

It hadn't dawned on me yet that I had every right to be afraid. I was too filled with rage and hate to even understand what fear was. Fear did not compute; survival did. It was rage that made my cramped, inflamed leg muscles move. And it was hate that drove my heart and lungs to the limit of physical endurance. As Nighthawk-One, I could never pinpoint who or what it was I hated so much. I only knew that I hated with every beat of my heart and with every breath that I took. To Nighthawk-One, raging hate was far more enduring and much more powerful than love or fear could ever be. It was hate, not love or fear, that numbed my brain, canceling some of the excruciating pain ripping through my body. Love and fear, or both, would have been Nighthawk-One's downfall, not his salvation. To hate, to cripple, to kill again, Nighthawk-One knew he had to survive.

I forged onward, stumbling, ducking and dodging low branches and vines. I fell repeatedly; my pants and left boot were torn. Exhausted, I trotted weakly through a tick-infested area, across several more trails, over small ridges, around boulders, trees, and more bamboo clusters. I startled birds, monkeys, and other jungle animals. I saw a pit viper, a krait and a cobra, large spiders, scorpions, and tarantulas. I saw the trails of rabbits and other small animals, and I ran smack into a wild pig with three piglets. The full-grown, black, bristle-haired pig was about one hundred pounds and had sharp tusks. We saw each other at the same time, a few feet apart. The pigs were so surprised that they just froze in place. I heard high-pitched squeals, but by the time the whole incident fully dawned on me, I was already past them. Ordinarily, the grown pig would have attacked me instantly, thinking I would harm her babies. Maybe the sight of a cut and scratched-up human being with a strange, wild gaze was enough to make the pig consider a more cautious option. Besides that, the quickness with which I appeared and disappeared and the fact that my human scent had no trace of fear in it may have added to the pig's caution or confusion.

This most certainly would not have worked with a tiger or a bear, I knew. I would have to shoot them on sight. There was a small but reasonable chance I could survive such a fight, I was taught. My present physical state was a big liability, but still, I would fight like a crazed wild animal — with bullets, my knife, a rock, anything — until I was dead. Tigers and bears didn't back off in the jungle. A sighting of one of them would have left no choice for either of us except to fight. It was that type of law in the jungle, with predators like tigers, bears, and Nighthawk-One.

48

I was not afraid of death. I knew it was inevitable, that every human being, rich or poor, white, black, or yellow, would face it someday. I also felt it was something that should be accepted and openly discussed as simple reality, not under or overly discussed, just openly understood without fear, leeriness, or inhibitions. I'd always been more concerned about how I would die than about death itself. So no, I didn't shun death like many others did. Death was not the enemy. Death was a sneaky and mysterious companion that had spared me so far, but it would one day turn on me, I knew, without hesitation or regret. In my own strange way, I'd come to respect that, respect in the sense that I didn't feel special, but I was secure in the fact that it would happen to all others, too.

All this and more flashed through my weakening mind as I trotted. My mind was intact, but I felt hazy and distant. The aching in my head was no longer piercing, but a dull, constant, throbbing pain that hurt just as much. As brain-numb as I was, every muscle, ligament, and tendon in my body still twitched in agony. My knees and shins were swollen, bruised, and bloody. I felt more faint and nauseated, and I'd gone from a slow, exhausted trot to an even slower, limping, staggering one. How far had I run? A mile? Over two miles? I didn't know. I was oblivious to time and distance. I had cramps and severe tightness in my thighs, my sides, and my stomach. The aching tightness in my left thigh flourished, reached its peak, and made my leg buckle. I collapsed on my stomach, face down on the ground. I squeezed my eyes shut, and my face contorted in agony as the many pains suddenly hit me full force.

I felt a yearning deep inside me to cry from the frustration, unbearable pain, and sheer desperation of it all, but there was another part inside me that was against it, wouldn't allow it, and considered crying a flaw and a weakness. So although my eyes were strained and filled with tears, I refused to cry, but my God, I wanted to.

I lay flat on the ground, dizzy and unmoving. I was completely exhausted, my breathing still noisy and uneven. There was no way I could move another inch, not even if my life depended on it. With so much physical pain and fatigue, the thought of death quickly became secondary to rest. I needed sleep, just for a few minutes. That's all, a few minutes. In a matter of seconds, I'd fallen into a deep unconscious state where there was no pain, no memories, and no war.

Hours later, my head jerked up a few inches from the ground. I was barely conscious when I began to retch and finally vomited. My breakfast splattered from my mouth to the ground. It brought me back to full consciousness as my stomach muscles contracted painfully. My spew was mixed with blood, and my stomach heaved, but nothing more came up. Had I been lying on my back unconscious and vomiting, I could have choked to death.

My legs and arms felt like deadweight as I gingerly took my rucksack off. Then I rolled over on my back, away from the smell of my vomit. Different piercing, throbbing, and quivering pains kept shooting through my body, but they weren't as intense as before. With swollen red eyes, I stared up at the shrubbery, brightly colored flowers, and twisting vines. I saw endless slivers of sunlight streaking through the greenish-brown, single-canopied trees, and insects buzzed all around me. Large, pretty butterflies and dragonflies flew by, monkeys chattered and shrieked, and parrots and other birds filled the air, chirping, hooting, and cawing. It flashed briefly through my mind how beautiful and peaceful it all seemed. The jungle's elegance was shocking, yet danger and death could appear at any time.

Judging by the sharply angled rays and the increasing darkness of the jungle, the sun seemed to be getting low. I had to keep moving, find shelter, a cave, a deserted hooch, anything. There was no way I could climb a tree and sleep in my present physical state.

After several minutes, I raised myself up on my elbows, checking myself out. My feet were sore, and I could feel the bleeding blisters on both of them. My left jungle boot was ripped at the toe and caked with dirt and dried blood. Both my shins were bruised and bloody, and my pants were ripped and bloody, too. My plastic water canteen was gone, snatched out of its pouch by a branch, bush or vine. My shirt was torn and bloody in several places, and I had scratches and cuts on my stomach, chest and sides. Both my arms and armpits were scratched and cut up, too, and caked with dry blood and pus. My face and neck were in the same condition, and my fingers and knuckles were scraped and bloody.

Flies, red ants, gnats, mosquitoes, and other small insects and bugs, some I'd never seen before in my life, were crawling all over my body. They were invading the many scratches and cuts I had. In sheer panic, I weakly brushed most of them off my body, killing some. Vaguely remembering the slimy creek I waded through, I pulled both my pant legs up. Several reddish-black bull leeches bloated with my blood fell off. A few more were still attached to my legs, sucking themselves full of my blood. I didn't smoke, so I had no cigarettes in my rucksack. I had matches in a waterproof container, but I didn't want to waste them on leeches. I always carried a handful of small salt packets with me, in the waterproof container, just for leeches. I sprinkled salt on them, and they quickly shriveled and detached themselves. Leeches were nasty; the saliva they left in their tiny bites made it take longer than normal for the blood to coagulate.

I slowly stood up, first getting on all fours, placing one foot down, then the other, then rising. I was still dizzy, and my legs remained shaky and weak. Taking off my utility belt, I unbuckled my pants belt and unbuttoned my fly, letting my pants drop down. I pulled my green cotton undershorts down and looked for more leeches. I also checked my stomach, sides, and armpits, but I didn't find any. I wanted to take my boots off and check my feet, but I didn't dare. My feet were so swollen that I'd never get my boots back on again.

Dressing slowly, I realized I had to move. In slow motion, I grabbed my rucksack by its shoulder straps. I picked my weapon up with my other hand, thumb near the safety release. I started walking, forcing myself to ignore my weary and painful body as much as possible. I walked about half a mile before stopping on a small, rocky ridge. I saw Chu Pong Mountain clearly, now, which I had noticed earlier. I recalled its name from briefing maps I'd seen. It had to be about five to six miles away. It looked invincible and magnificent in its green, brown, and purple hues.

Carefully, I walked down the other side of the ridge, leery of the sharp, jagged rocks that protruded dangerously from the ground. I headed directly for the mountain, desperately wanting to get to high ground. I felt that there would be less risk if a rescue chopper picked me up from high ground than from the jungle floor. Even under double- or triple-canopied trees, a chopper with a cable and loop could pluck me up while hovering in the sky, but if it couldn't, I'd have to find a small clearing large enough for a chopper. I had two pen-sized flares in my rucksack to signal with.

By now, Headquarters knew something had to be drastically wrong because none of the prearranged radio checks had happened. The chopper's radio and my team's radio were destroyed in the ambush, adding insult to injury.

I walked about a mile, passing a burnt-down hooch and several more trails. Then I trudged down and back up a shallow ravine and through thick foliage.

A half mile farther through dense thickets and tall elephant grass, I glimpsed the straw roof of a large hooch. Getting closer, I saw it was built several feet off the ground because of monsoon rains. I smelled cooking as I inched closer, and I saw smoke coming out of the hooch. In the small clearing, I saw about ten chickens, two pigs, three goats and a young water buffalo. Except for the buffalo, all the animals were contained in small bamboo pens. For about fifteen minutes, I just waited and watched. Then I saw Poppa-san walk out of the hooch, wearing only a soiled loincloth on his skinny frame. Barefoot, he carried a large clay pot. He was in his early- to mid-sixties and had leathery brown skin. His short black hair was mostly gray, and his teeth showed reddish-black stains from chewing betel nuts all the time. His face was worn and weary, riddled with wrinkles that spoke of hardship.

At each bamboo pen, he put the pot down on the ground. He dipped both hands into the pot and threw handfuls of dried corn into the pens; the animals scrambled noisily for the corn. I'd finally found a secure resting place, hopefully. I wanted to take Poppa-san before he went back inside the hooch. It was getting darker and darker in the jungle, and I hurt too much to go any farther. I needed refuge, rest, and time to eat.

I snuck up behind him until I was only a few yards away. With my rifle pointed at him, I yelled hoarsely for him to halt. Surprised, he spun around, almost falling, with his eyes wide and back pressed against the pen. He quickly raised both hands high above his head. In Vietnamese, at the top of his lungs, he yelled, "Don't shoot! Don't shoot! I live here! I swear by Buddha, I'm not Viet Cong! Don't shoot!"

His yelling made my head hurt worse, so I told him to shut up. Then I asked if anyone was in the hooch and told him not to lie. Poppa-san paused before answering, his eyes shifting to the ground, then back to mine. I told him that if he didn't tell me who was in the hooch, I'd go and shoot everyone in there. With moist, sad eyes and both his trembling hands extended out to me, he sobbed, "I beg of you, American. Do not kill me or my daughter. Take what you will, but do not harm us. We live alone and only farm rice and vegetables for ourselves. We are not Viet Cong."

I motioned with the barrel of my rifle for him to go inside the hooch. With his head sagging between his bony, frail shoulders, he started walking. I was right behind him with the barrel of my rifle poking him in the lower back. I was hurt, bleeding and exhausted, but had he tried anything hostile, I'd have shot him without hesitation. My mind was mostly on his daughter, who wasn't secured yet and was therefore still a threat.

Poppa-san climbed up the makeshift ladder to the entryway. I was right behind him as he entered. My eyes scanned the room like radar. Inside the round hooch squatted his daughter. In her hands, she held a cocked crossbow with the arrow pointed in my direction. I ordered Poppa-San to stop, keeping his body between the frightened woman and myself. I heard whimpering sighs from Poppa-san, and no one spoke for several seconds.

I preferred having their cooperation to intimidating them. Way out here in the bush by themselves, it was hard for me to believe they were Viet Cong. They could be VC collaborators, but I wasn't sure about that yet. It was worth a try to gain their cooperation.

I told the woman to put the crossbow down, that I wasn't there to harm them. I told her I'd only fight if I was attacked. I pointed my rifle barrel up toward the roof to support my words. Turning to look at me for a few seconds, Poppa-san then told his daughter to put the crossbow away, because I was hurt and sounded sincere. Again, he told me that he and his daughter were not VC, only farmers. Nervously, she took the arrow out of the crossbow and put them both down. Relieved but still cautious, I set my rifle and rucksack down. I sat down on the floor with my legs extended, back against the wall. Exhausted and tense, my body ached all over. With a flick of my hand, I unsnapped the holster strap over my pistol and unbuttoned my knife strap. I was hoping they didn't notice the casual move. I didn't want them getting uptight again. I tried to look as relaxed and trusting as I could while staying prepared for any physical threat from them.

Poppa-san squatted on the floor across from me; his daughter stayed where she was. She wore baggy black pants and a loose black top, which were the standard for civilians — and also the Viet Cong. She looked to be in her early- to mid-twenties, and I suddenly realized how beautiful she was. Her long, shiny black hair flowed down her back. She kept staring at me with distrust, her arms wrapped firmly around her knees. Poppa-san lit his long-stemmed opium pipe, and they both just stared at me for a few minutes. Their facial expressions in that time seemed to go from suspicion to curiosity.

I took that time to check out the hooch more closely. There were mats of woven palm covering most of the bamboo floor. There was an altar with photographs, a small brass statue of Buddha, and joss sticks on it. I saw a large, expensive-looking black trunk with gold trimming all around it. There were a few rattan shelves built along the wall with over a dozen cans of American C-rations on them. Near some of the C-rations were a few balls; they resembled small potatoes, but they were actually opium balls. On one shelf were a few serving bowls and spoons made out of wood. I saw two small kerosene lamps made from perfume bottles, and I saw two oil lamps. There was also an open stone fireplace in the hooch with a big hole in the wall behind it to ventilate most of the smoke.

The smell of cooking was nauseating and filled the entire hooch. I spotted a fishing net and a sheathed machete nearby. The place was sturdy, solidly built, and furnished too well. Besides that, there were connections with many of the items I noticed. I had to question them about some of their possessions. They could very well be enemy collaborators, being paid off in items and food. Or else they had a damn good black market connection to work with.

"How long will you stay, American?" Poppa-san asked curiously.

"Two or three days at the most, with your permission," I replied.

He looked blankly at his daughter, then back to me, saying, "Two or three days is good, American. I will honor that. But then I must ask you to leave. I want no trouble with the VC. My daughter and I are only farmers, not fighters."

With my eyes half-closed from fatigue, I said, "Thank you. You and your daughter are very honorable for your kindness and understanding." I was hoping like hell that Poppa-san and his daughter weren't VC or enemy sympathizers. I was hurting badly, and I silently prayed that he meant what he said.

"I mean no disrespect, but how did you get the C-rations?" I inquired carefully. Poppa-san frowned bitterly at me, then glanced at his daughter. Then his old red eyes fell back on mine as he continued puffing on his pipe. Poppa-san's glare told me he wasn't answering my question. I glanced toward his daughter for a possible answer just as she stood up. She lit the kerosene and oil lamps because it was dark outside. Then she went over to the fireplace and picked up a steel rod that was about three feet long. Sticking it into the pot hanging over the fire, she vigorously stirred whatever was in it.

I started having stronger doubts about this hooch being a safe place. My sore body muscles tensed up automatically, leery of anything and everything. I put my hand on the butt of my pistol, finger on the trigger guard. If they forced me to fight, my pistol and knife were best for close quarters. I watched them carefully, keeping my peripheral vision on the hooch door. Poppa-san, the old bastard, had turned sour on me, so I tried his daughter. I wanted to find out where they got the C-rations and who the extra bedroll was for.

I saw two bowls of rice and two sets of chopsticks near the fireplace. "What is it you're stirring? It smells good," I said to her, lying.

She stopped, staring at me as if wanting to smile, but hesitating. "There are chunks of monkey, pigs' blood and peppers in the pot, GI," she answered. She started stirring again but kept peering oddly at me. A few minutes later, she asked shyly, "Are you hungry, GI? I'm told American GIs are always hungry."

My stomach felt like it was being squeezed in a vise. Even though I didn't feel like eating, I knew I had to force something in my stomach. I had brown plastic packets of freeze-dried spaghetti and beef stew in my rucksack. These packets were lighter and more preferred on long-range missions than regular canned C-rations. I wanted hot, freshly cooked food in my stomach. It had taken a while for me to start tolerating Vietnamese food, but it would be a cold day in hell before I ever really got used to it. I'd eaten monkey hips and rice, snakes, dog, rat, worms, wild pig, raw fish heads, various birds, and more. I'd also had water buffalo blood brewed with strange Montagnard mixtures that made me want to weep and puke my guts up.

Answering Poppa-san's daughter, I told her I'd be honored to eat with them. She looked at Poppa-san, needing his final permission. He just nodded approvingly without missing a puff. She seemed relaxed now, almost relieved for some reason while she fixed the meal. Taking a long-stemmed dipper made out of wood, she dipped it twice into the hot pot. She poured the strong-smelling mixture over a bowl of rice, then gave it and a pair of chopsticks to Poppa-san. I hadn't noticed the big pot of rice that was almost hidden from my view near the fireplace. Taking two more bowls from the shelf, she filled them with rice and mixed in the hot concoction.

Surprising me, she came right over and squatted down next to me to eat. She was about 5'7" tall with a firm shape. Her deep brown eyes radiated a stunning brilliance, and she had a dainty, petite nose and well-composed lips that seemed flawless.

I ate slowly, taking small morsels and chewing well. My face grimaced in pain as I swallowed. "Your body bad, much blood, GI. Same inside you too, yes?" she said in English. That shocked the hell out of me. Now I was wondering where the hell she learned English! Not wanting to question her about it right then, though, I tiredly replied, "I'm afraid so. I have great pains inside and outside my body."

She suddenly frowned, saying in English, "VC do this to you, I know. They crazy! They hurt many people. Father, me, pray all American GIs come South Vietnam. Kill all VC."

My head started spinning terribly again, and twice I almost vomited. I felt severely faint, but I couldn't pass out now, not yet. I still had doubts, especially now, about this place being safe. Could it be I was destined to die here in this hooch? My eyes suddenly rolled weirdly in their sockets and closed as my head slumped down. I was passing out when someone grabbed me abruptly by the arm and started shaking me. Pleading loudly, she said, "No die! No die, dark one! I help you! No die!" She kept shaking and yelling at me until I regained consciousness. Focusing on my surroundings, I slowly reoriented myself. With her hands, she gently wiped dirt, sweat, dried blood, and pus from my swollen face.

"What's your name?" I gasped weakly, wanting to talk and be talked to.

"My name is My Ling. What your name, GI?" she asked.

"Parker, call me Parker," I slowly answered.

"Par-ker," she said over and over again, breaking my last name up into two distinct parts.

"Where did you learn to speak English, and where did you get the C-rations?" I questioned.

Without hesitating, she responded. "My brother, Nguyen, he be sergeant, South Vietnamese army. He teach me good English. He fight VC, like American GI. Sometimes he come home, maybe day, maybe week, bring much home. He good brother, help sister, help father. That good, yes, Par-ker?"

Being relieved to hear that, I said, "Yes, he's a good brother, My Ling. You and your father must be very proud of him." She kept talking in English, probably because she didn't have many people to do it with. I kept thinking that she could be lying, but I really wanted to believe her. Given my condition, I wasn't sure if it mattered anymore. I was probably going to pass out shortly again, anyway.

"Before, I have brother name Pham, and husband name Truong, Par-ker," she continued. "VC kill Pham, Truong, three year ago. Father no like talk that. Father, me, hate VC, wish they all die."

"I have to rest now, My Ling. Just let me close me eyes and rest a little while," I moaned in a low voice.

"No!" My Ling cried. "First medicine, later rest. Think maybe you have good heart, Par-ker. I help you." She went over to the large trunk and opened it. What she took out was an American military morphine syrette.

I never carried morphine syrettes with me because of my leeriness of drugs. I preferred drinking to opium, coke, hash, reefer, or anything of that nature. Drinking helped me cope.

Thinking about drugs brought back what a friend of mine had said while I was stationed in Germany. He was an officer with the Tenth Special Forces there, and he was a Vietnam veteran. He told me that there was little control over the use of amphetamines in Special Forces within the past few years; commanders were having the stuff passed out like it was bubblegum. They wouldn't order speed to be used, but they let everyone know it was in their best interest to use it. This was being done with Special Forces in Panama, Okinawa, Germany, and especially Southeast Asia. The speed was never intended for recreational use in Special Forces, my friend had said. It was intended to help soldiers maintain a high level of alertness while engaged in covert and extremely dangerous combat duties. Most of these types of duties called for soldiers to stay awake for two to three days at a time. "If you didn't stay awake and highly alert, you were killed," my friend said.

I tried the amphetamines on two long-range recon missions. I didn't like them at all. The speed gave me a false sense of invincibility along with a slight moodiness. Besides that, I was so hyped-up that I actually thought I heard a rat pissing on cotton fifty yards away. Using speed twice was enough for me, and I stayed with the booze. Many other guys I knew didn't stop and stayed on the stuff. It got to the point where they had to smoke a lot of reefer just to come down from their speed high.

I felt My Ling tugging at my left arm before I actually focused in on her. She had my shirt halfway off and my left arm exposed. No way did I want her shooting me up with that crap! I'd be nodding like a dope-fiend and then pass out cold. I made a feeble attempt at snatching my arm away while shaking my head from side to side, but with an unexpected strength that left me dumbfounded, she forced my arm back. Not being able to defend myself against a 125-pound woman made me cease all resistance. I was in too much pain to care anymore.

I just watched her passively. Her army brother, I assumed, must have taught her first aid. She jabbed the syrette into my shoulder. Military morphine syrettes were used for intramuscular injections and not for veins. That's why the point of the needle was always wide and dull instead of sharp and pointed.

I got an immediate head rush that was awesome. With my eyes closed, I thought for sure she'd put a grenade on top of my head and pulled the pin. Opening my eyes, I watched in slow motion as she took my rifle, pistol, and knife. I couldn't stop her! I could barely move! *Who gives a shit, anyway?* My head suddenly stopped pounding and I felt no pain. My muscles felt totally relaxed. Too relaxed. Damn! I couldn't feel my body anymore! With an extremely numbed brain, I started searching for my body. Hell, it had to be here somewhere. I felt light as a feather, floating through the air. I was floating! Droopy-eyed, I stared through a foggy mist at two oblong forms sitting side by side. I giggled at them while tears streamed down my face. The giggles suddenly turned to loud laughter. My emotions were out of control and played games with me. I felt peaceful and not peaceful; fearless and fearful; defeated and undefeated. I laughed loudly and cried noisily, all at the same time, until I slumped over and passed out.

Chapter Four

The next day, in the early afternoon, I started coming around. I still would have been out if it weren't for My Ling putting cold cloths on my face. I was in the middle of one of my nightmarish flashbacks, and I didn't know where I was. Half awake and terrified, I jerked straight up like a bolt of lightning. My survival instinct brought my hands swiftly to both sides of My Ling's head, with my thumbs on the inside corners of her eyes. I applied pressure, trying to pluck both eyes from their sockets. In my semiconscious state, I mistook My Ling for an enemy soldier trying to kill me. She quickly grabbed both my arms, screaming and trying to push away. "Par-ker?" she yelled hysterically. "Par-ker? I no VC! Par-ker!"

Her high-pitched shrieking brought me to full consciousness and I quickly let her go. She fell on her back, still frightened, gasping heavily and crying with both hands over her eyes. "I no VC!" she kept sobbing.

Still sitting up, I took in my surroundings. My chest was heaving, I was sweating heavily, and my body was shaking. I was on a bedroll, naked, with a pretty hand-woven spread partially covering me. My Ling had washed all the grime, blood, and pus off my body and rubbed a sticky black salve over the bruises and cuts. Then I remembered. Major Small, the mission, my team, the ambush, the jungle, Poppa-san, My Ling. My Ling! Oh my God! She was crying, trembling, and moaning on the floor.

On all fours, I rushed over and started tugging at her hands so I could see her eyes. I prayed to God that they were still in their sockets with no permanent damage. "Let me see, My Ling," I said softly but nervously. "Let me see your eyes so I can help you. I'm sorry!" She started calming down some and I examined her eyes closely. They were still in place, but her right eyeball had a deep red mark on it. I saw a wooden bucket half-filled with the cold water she had been using. Picking up one of the cloths, I dipped it into the bucket. I did this several times, squeezing the soaked cloth directly over both of her eyes. She tried rubbing her eyes a number of times, but I kept telling her no. About ten minutes went by before she started regaining her normal sight. I told her there was only a red mark on her right eye and that it would go away in about a week.

The loose, dark-blue two-piece pants outfit she had on made her smooth skin vibrant and enticing. Our arms were wrapped tightly around each other as we sat there on the floor. She felt so delicate and warm in my arms, so flawless, with her head pressed firmly against my bare chest. I swear, it was as if she were meant to be in my arms. I felt her heart beating softly as it settled to a normal, contented rhythm. Long-forgotten emotions consumed my heart and mind. Oddly enough, I became very compassionate toward this strange woman.

Running my fingers gently through her soft black hair, I mumbled that everything was going to be all right. I was still sore with pains and stiffness, but I felt a little better and stronger. About fifteen minutes later, I asked her where my clothes and weapons were. "I wash clothes," she said, looking at me. "I take you river, wash medicine off." I wanted a towel, and she got me a large red one out of the trunk. I wrapped it around my waist and got out the bar of medicinal soap I always kept in my rucksack. "Why you put towel on, Par-ker?" she asked, snickering. "I see many man, no clothes. I no little girl, Par-ker."

She'd said a mouthful there. Hell, I guess if a woman has seen one naked man, the big male mystery was gone forever. She kept staring at me with that devilish smile on her face. I didn't mind going native, but I wasn't a damn exhibitionist. *If she thinks I'm ripping this towel off so we can go frolicking through the jungle like Tarzan and Jane, she's crazy!* Not really knowing what to say, I simply smiled and replied, "My Ling, shut up."

I retrieved my weapons from the trunk and put on my utility belt with my ammo pouches, knife, and custom-made holster attached to it. I slung my four bandoliers of extra ammo on and grabbed my rifle. My Ling said she took my weapons last night so I wouldn't accidentally hurt myself.

With both of us barefoot, we walked along a narrow trail, laughing and playing like two kids. I enjoyed myself for the first time in a long while. Instinctively, I still watched the trail for trip-wire, the shrubbery for ambushes, and the trees for snipers. She kept trying to snatch my towel off, so being a gentleman, I kept trying to pull her pants down.

We reached the river, which was a half mile away. We stopped in the middle of a small, scenic clearing. There were no trees, just low grass and blue, white, purple and red flowers covering the clearing like a tiny paradise. Before I could get my gear and towel off, My Ling had undressed and jumped nude into the water. I followed. The cool water felt good; it refreshed and stimulated my body. We splashed and swam around for a while, hugging, kissing, and touching each other. As each minute passed, I became more fascinated by the honesty and affection within this woman. Only my true self, my natural being, could feel such warmth and tender-heartedness. Nighthawk-One could never feel such wondrous emotions, not in a million years. I felt alive! For the half hour that we swam, played, and bathed, I recklessly disregarded security and my survival instincts. This was something I had never done before.

With little effort, I picked My Ling up in my arms, carried her out of the water, and carefully set her down on the towel. With my tongue, I gently stroked her glossy lips and sleek neck before lingering on her well-formed breasts. Bringing my lips back up to hers, I kissed her softly, then passionately harder. We made love with a profound desperation and urgency. My Ling was just what the doctor ordered for me emotionally, mentally, and spiritually. Her intoxicating kisses, fiery warmth, and organic wetness plunged me into a blissful void that went beyond this jungle, this war, and this very earth. We became intricately absorbed into one form with one function and one ultimate goal.

Later, while walking back to the hooch, My Ling begged to carry my rifle. I let her have it without a second thought. Pointing the rifle repeatedly and clumsily into the bushes and high trees, she made loud shooting sounds. "You kill many VC, Par-ker?" she asked breathlessly with childlike excitement. I thought about the confirmed kills I'd accumulated and realized it was something I'd never tell anyone. The average combat soldier would give his right arm to have the kills I'm credited with. For a time, I was proud and praised for such a high body count. As I walked with My Ling close to me, though, just the thought of killing brought shame and guilt to my mind. Her genuine innocence and forthright sincerity were devouring me. She reminded me of a teenage tomboy playing cowboys and Indians on some street corner back in the States.

She looked at me with a puzzled expression, saying, "You no want talk VC? Okay, Par-ker, no sweat! I talk VC, okay? I hate VC. They kill brother, husband! One day, I kill maybe two, three VC."

With sad eyes, I stared at My Ling, and the depth of her innocence hit me squarely. It was soul-stirring and made my heart throb with a tingling sensitivity. How could I explain to her that violence wasn't the answer? Violence breeds violence; it never ends. She shouldn't be caught in the middle of this war. It wasn't right! She was a noncombatant! *She shouldn't be here!*

I must have been staring rather hard at her, because with a childlike pout, she stopped playing with my rifle and said, "I do bad, Par-ker? You no like me?"

"You didn't do anything bad," I answered, kissing her lightly on the lips. "It's something you and I will never have any control over." I put my arm around her small shoulders, holding her close to me while we walked.

"I no understand, Par-ker," she replied with a puzzled look.

Smiling soberly, I said, "I don't understand it, either."

We walked in silence all the way back to the hooch. There was a deep, nurturing closeness between us when we looked at one another. My clothes and boots were dry, so I put them back on. The feel of my jungle fatigues and boots brought me back to a security-conscious state again. My Ling told me that Poppa-san had gone to the village and wouldn't be back until late tomorrow. While she was busy in the small rice and vegetable field near the hooch, I checked the immediate jungle area for a few hours.

It was late afternoon when I returned. My Ling fixed two packets of freeze-dried spaghetti for us to eat. For hours, she questioned me with wide-eyed fascination about the United States. It was dark outside when she and I made slow, erotic love again. She revitalized my whole being and taught me the meaning of harmonious ecstasy.

Afterward, she teased me, saying she had a big surprise. Reaching deep inside the big trunk, she brought out a full bottle of

American whiskey. My heart skipped a beat and my taste buds bulged when I saw the booze. "You like, Par-ker?" she asked with a broad smile. "Brother Nguyen say all American GI like drink. I souvenir you, okay, Par-ker?"

Opening the bottle, I took two big swigs. The warm whiskey was soothing as it flowed down my throat. Several more swigs later, I was feeling nice and mellow. My Ling was having a ball watching the tipsy grin I had stuck to my face. I offered her some of the whiskey, but she didn't drink. She said that when her brother visited, he brought whiskey and opium for their father. For over an hour, she laughed uncontrollably at the funny faces I made at her while she wove a basket. She talked about children and how much she loved them, even though she had none. She explained that her husband didn't like kids and never wanted any. She asked if I had any children, and I said no. With a shy, deeply dimpled smile, she reminded me about our lovemaking and the possibility of her becoming pregnant. That, she said, would make her a mother and me a father, with the baby being half American and half Vietnamese. I couldn't help but laugh at her practical deduction.

I was lying bare-chested on a bedroll with just my pants and boots on. I've always adored children, and hearing her talk about possibly being pregnant with my child made my muscular body quiver warmly. Quietly, she came over and lay down with her head on my chest. Both her arms were wrapped snugly around my waist as I ran my fingers through her silky black hair.

In my relaxed, intoxicated, half-awake state, I relived a year of extreme combat duty. Then I thought about yesterday's bloody ambush. Massacre was a better word for it, an outright fucking massacre. Lieutenant Collins, Ordowski, Vitani, Jones, Austin, and I didn't even know the names of the chopper crew. My God, I've never lost an entire team before, and the guilt I felt was staggering. I was the most experienced man on the chopper, and I should have spotted something wrong. Altogether, nine men were dead, yet I survived. Why? Why did I live while they all died? It didn't balance out. It didn't seem right. I should have died with my team. *I should be dead, damn it! I should be dead!* I wanted to die! I had to die! Frantically, I pulled my pistol out with trembling hands and stuck the barrel in my mouth. I cocked the trigger hammer as tears streamed down my face. The tears were blinding, and I didn't see My Ling grabbing my hands. She yanked the pistol out of my mouth, twisting the barrel away from my face. I'll never know if I pulled the trigger or if my finger jerked when My Ling redirected the barrel, but the pistol went off. The shot sounded like a small cannon blast. "No, Par-ker! No!" she cried, terror-stricken. "No! No!"

My heart was beating chaotically, and beads of sweat dripped off my face. I couldn't believe what I just tried to do! Not me! I wouldn't kill myself! But my God, I almost did! My Ling grabbed the pistol from me and ran to the other side of the hooch where she squatted down, shaking like a leaf. With both hands, she held the pistol tightly to her chest. Breathless and sobbing, she stared wide-eyed at me. Her head swayed from side to side while she nervously chanted, "No! You no die, Par-ker! You no die, Par-ker!"

I looked from her to my hands, wondering how the hell I could attempt suicide. "Oh, shit! What the fuck?" I kept repeating to myself. My Ling was still staring at me from across the hooch. Damn, she saved my life! I took another swig from the bottle, saying, "I'm all right, My Ling, I'm okay." I just couldn't get over the fact that I had tried to kill myself. Talking out loud, more to myself than to My Ling, I said, "I'm exhausted. I wish I could just stop the world and get the hell off. I had a lousy ghetto childhood. I have a so-called girlfriend who doesn't give a shit about me. I'm in a war I now hate. And no one's ever given a damn about my feelings. No one cares!"

Still crying, My Ling said softly, "I care, Par-ker! I care! You no do crazy thing. You no die! I take care you! I love you, Par-ker."

Damn! What did she have to say that for? Was it possible to fall in love in just twenty-four hours? I knew that emotional love wasn't logical, rational, or timely, and the wonderful feelings I was having for My Ling all spelled love in a hundred different ways. Maybe my loneliness and depression were finally playing the ultimate game with my emotions.

My friends in Buffalo said I fell in love too easily, usually with the wrong type of woman. Maybe now I'd finally found someone who would love me like I loved her. I sensed that My Ling's love was honest and sincere, just like mine. There was only one kind of true love in the world, and that was honest love, which didn't come along every day.

I got up and walked toward My Ling, wanting to hold her close and feel her warm body. Apparently, she thought I was still intent on blowing my brains out. She slid the pistol behind her back in one fluid motion, crying, "No, Par-ker! No! No!"

"I'm okay now, really, My Ling," I said calmly. "I won't do anything like that again."

I stood her up on her feet, kissing the tears on her face. Dropping the pistol to the floor, she got on her tiptoes, threw her arms around my neck, and said, "I love you, Par-ker. I take care you. No die!"

"Okay, okay," I replied. "Take it easy. Relax, everything's okay."

We undressed and lay quietly on the bedroll, caressing each other. We stayed like that for a little while, cherishing the quiet time. I had a few more swigs of whiskey while I lay there, deep in thought. *I swear, if I had the balls, I'd become a deserter. I'd quit this man's army right now, take My Ling to Sweden, find a job, and settle down.* I had the urge to desert, but the more I thought about it, the less appealing it became.

I thought about my army career and briefly questioned it. Could I really do twenty years without the United States getting into another dirty little war somewhere? I wasn't sure if the U.S. Army was the best thing for me anymore. I'd already reenlisted, though, so I had about six years to think about it. I thought about my three uncles and how the oldest one did twenty years in the Marine Corps; he spent three of those years in Vietnam. My second-oldest uncle was an Army Airborne Ranger for several years. Then he got out of the army in the early 1960s and tried to become a New York State Trooper. He found out soon enough that troopers at that time didn't want blacks in their ranks. He was subjected to so much harassment that he finally gave up and joined the Navy for twenty years. My third uncle was never in the military. He was a paralegal in Cleveland, Ohio, but he had a third-degree black belt in karate. All three of them would have given me a lecture, then kicked my ass if they knew the things I thought about sometimes.

Carol popped into my mind next. I still had feelings for her, in my own way. But I decided not to send her another penny. I had to put my feelings for Carol in the proper perspective. She was my past, now, not my present or my future. *Her manipulation of me stops here*, I decided.

I thought about My Ling next. She was God-sent, a sincere sign of hope for better things in my troubled life. I couldn't deny or question my feelings for her any longer. I cared for her, and I loved her. I'd been hesitant to admit that outright. Once I did, I felt a strange, comforting relief. I stroked the side of her face gently, knowing she was still awake. I felt so close to her emotionally, but I wanted even more closeness. If I could have, I swear, I would have crawled all the way up inside her and lived the rest of my life within her being. I believed that My Ling loved me in the same way, and I adored that. She even saved my life, and I was going to do the right thing and save hers. My mind was made up. I was going to ask My Ling to marry me so I could take her back to the States. I truly believed she was God-sent. Through her sincerity, I'd wipe out the hopelessness and futility in my life. I needed her honesty and loyalty. They were rare in this world, but with them, I could be my moral, civilized self. Without her honest caring, I would never have the willpower to put Carol in my past. So yes, I'd give My Ling all the love I had, and I had lots of love to give.

My mind focused back on the ambush. The memory accelerated my heartbeat and left me breathless. I thought about my team's primary objective: to track and destroy Bluebeard. The major would enjoy seeing me come back with my tail between my legs. He would relish writing up my only failure with his bullshit comments about what I did wrong. He'd be protecting his West Point ass while labeling me a screw-up. These were just things off the top of my head I knew he would do. With his rank, position, and clout, he'd probably have even more ways to screw me. Despite all the missions I'd completed, the major was capable of ruining me over one failure. It was almost unbelievable, but it was true. I was on the bastard's shit-list because of my transfer request. And the more I thought about it, the more I thought that he might a little envious of the respect I got from other Special Forces and indigenous troops in the field. There was really no telling why the bastard disliked me so much. I couldn't care less about him disliking me, but he was using his rank and position to screw me.

Mixed images of Major Small and the bloody ambush filled my thoughts. Suddenly, I made up my mind. I was going to finish the mission myself, or at least try like hell. I was determined not to give the major satisfaction from my failure. I'd question My Ling about whether she had seen or heard about any VC in the area within the past few days. If she didn't know anything, maybe I'd send her into the village for rumors about recent VC activity.

With her still in my arms, I questioned her. Snapping her head up from my chest, her bewildered eyes burned deeply into mine. Astonished, she blurted, "How you know VC here before?"

My body went rigid when I heard those words. Unnerved, I grabbed her by both shoulders, saying sternly, "My Ling, my God, are you crazy or what? Why didn't you tell me this before? Don't you care about my life, about yours?"

She started crying again, and that melted away all the annoyance I had. It hit me then how much I hated seeing her cry. Just watching her tore away at my strength and left me weak and vulnerable. Throwing her arms around me, she said, "I sorry, Par-ker. I no want you go VC! They maybe kill you. You stay, Par-ker, you no go! I take care you! I love you!"

I told her to stop crying because I wasn't upset anymore. Wiping the tears from her face, I smiled, kissing her on the lips. "Tell me everything you know about the VC, okay?" I asked. "Then I'll tell you something I think you'll like."

"VC come maybe seven day ago, Par-ker," she said. "They take rice, five chicken, one pig. They no pay, Par-ker. I fight VC. They laugh, beat father, beat me. They no good, Par-ker. VC scare me. I be afraid."

Her body was trembling again as she relived the incident in her mind. I had a feeling this might be the VC group I was after. "How many VC were there?" I questioned.

"Five VC, one North Vietnamese soldier, Par-ker. One VC hurt, much blood, maybe die soon," she answered.

"Which direction did they go when they left?" I asked.

She pointed confidently with her finger, saying, "They go mountain, Par-ker, I see."

It took several minutes of bittersweet arguing for My Ling to understand why I had to go after them. I told her about Major Small and the attitude problem he had with me. To survive the major, I had to pursue the enemy so I could put it into my official report to the Fifth Group and SOG. I knew he'd probably suggest a lie-detector test to see if I actually pursued the enemy. My team being neutralized was not a viable reason for me to abort the mission. I couldn't abort the mission unless I was so physically and mentally incapacitated I could no longer function. In plain English, a soldier of theirs had better be dead, one tiny step from death, or so mentally unstable that he was literally eating shit and barking at the moon to abort a mission.

I really didn't want to explain all this to My Ling, but I needed her to know. I doubt if she understood everything I told her anyway. I also let her know that after the mission, I was coming back to marry her — if she wanted me — and take her back to the States. Stunned, she stared at me in disbelief, her eyes wide and her mouth gaping open. It looked as if she were getting ready to cry again. "No crying," I told her.

"You be for real, Par-ker?" she gasped excitedly. "You no play? You take me America?" It took her several seconds to realize I was serious. When she did, she jumped up so fast that she startled the hell out of me. Rushing over to the altar where the Buddha statue was, she bowed down from the waist in front of it. Then, dropping to her knees, she bowed her head low to the ground. Praying to Buddha, she rattled off a flurry of Vietnamese words so fast, I gave up trying to understand her. I just sat there admiring my future wife, the human savior of my worthless soul and very life.

Jumping quickly to her feet, she came at me at a dead run. She threw her whole body on top of mine, wrapping her arms around my neck. She knocked me flat on my back, saying joyously, "I be happy, Par-ker, thank Buddha! I no shame you! You be proud!"

After calming her down some, I reminded her I was still going after that enemy group in the morning. I told her I really had no choice in the matter, that I had to try. Her immediate response was that she was going with me. I was unprepared for this particular response, and I didn't like it.

"No way. Forget it, you hear me? I'm not taking you. Understand that right now," I growled, pushing her off me. I took a couple more swigs of whiskey, glaring at her like she was crazy.

Pouting now, she muttered, "You no take me, I follow you! You go VC, they kill you. You die, I die too. Be together, Par-ker!" I wasn't too thrilled with her rationalization, to say the least.

Suddenly, her big brown eyes gleamed as she smiled, saying, "I help you, Par-ker. I know fast way, go mountain, I show you, okay?"

Standing up, I put my index finger in her face and screamed, "No!"

Most people would have been alarmed at a sudden scream like that, but My Ling didn't flinch or even blink an eye. She just stood there, blank-faced, her head held high. This led me to believe the subject was finally closed. I was wrong. With a defiant act that shocked the hell out of me, she stuck her finger right under my nose, stating slowly, "I no go, you no go. You go, I go!" Then she squatted down right in front of me with her arms wrapped around her legs. Her head was angled sharply as she stared at me with a hard, challenging look.

I couldn't believe this! Vietnamese women were supposed to be humble to their fathers and husbands. Where the hell did she get this defiant crap from? After another taste of booze, I went over and kicked the hooch wall, putting my boot through it. To further discourage her, I whipped my famous maniac look on her, shouting, "No!" A few of my military peers once told me I could curdle milk with that pissed-off, crazy look.

It didn't faze her! Not one damn bit! She simply pouted sweetly again as she looked around the hooch. Then she got up and walked over to some shelves. She flung all the wooden bowls and C-ration cans down to the floor, screaming, "Yes! Yes!" Then she squatted right down again with that challenging look on her face.

The argument was going nowhere, so I did what any rational man would do when arguing with his woman. I surrendered. Unconditionally. I took a swig of whiskey and sat back down on the bedroll. My Ling kept looking at me, and I saw a smile gradually appear on her face. Throwing my hands up in the air, I laughed, shaking my head. "You and I, little lady, are going to have a long talk after this mission's over with," I stated firmly. "Understand?"

Letting out a short, victorious scream, she ran over and dove on top of me. I didn't consider a hundred pounds of free-falling weight soaring down on my body to be much fun, but she was enjoying herself, so I took my lumps in stride as I tickled and kissed her. I'd take my surprisingly ill-tempered future wife with me, but I was determined to keep her out of harm's way at all costs.

I told her to rest because we'd be leaving at first light. With our arms and legs entwined, thoughts about the past two days swept through my mind again. I cursed Major Small by force of habit. At the same time, I had to reluctantly thank the bastard, too. If it weren't for him, I wouldn't have met My Ling. Just the thought of being grateful to him left me sick to my stomach. I thought about the weird luck I'd had in this war. I'd been told that there was something unnatural about my survival luck. I'd been ambushed, under heavy crossfire, and in hand-to-hand combat, but I continued to survive. I couldn't even blow my own damn brains out.

It made me wonder if every human being had a preordained destiny. With My Ling at my side, I was determined to seek out and find my true destiny. I couldn't imagine anything worse than what I'd already been through. In less than two days, My Ling had somehow wound herself around my heart and mind. She turned me from a walking zombie into a caring human being again. I could tell by her breathing that she was asleep. I stroked her hair, pushing it out of her eyes, and watched her closely for a while. Then I fell into a comforting sleep with no thoughts of the major or nightmares of any kind.

Chapter Five

At dawn, My Ling and I started off toward the mountain. We carried food that would last about three days. She walked a few yards in front of me because she knew where the enemy booby-traps were in the area.

It was common for the enemy to put some type of identifying sign near each booby trap so the traps could be spotted and avoided by their peers and nearby villagers. The signs could be anything — small marks on a tree, rocks placed on the ground in a certain way, dirt, weeds, or flowers moved slightly away from their normal positions — and the signs were hard for many American troops to spot.

We moved slowly and cautiously; My Ling examined every-thing in front of us. A dozen times, she whispered for me to stop, showed me a deadly booby trap, and pointed in another direction for us to walk.

It took several hours to walk a few miles through the rough terrain. It was early afternoon, and the base of Chu Pong Mountain was only a half mile away. We sat, resting against a huge boulder, our clothes soaked in sweat. I gave My Ling another salt tablet and some water. I let about fifteen minutes go by before telling her she wasn't going any farther. I told her if I wasn't back in a few hours, she should go home. As expected, she objected to this, but I didn't compromise this time. No way would I take her up on that mountain with me. Getting this far without spotting or engaging the enemy was a miracle in itself. I expected no such miracles on the mountain.

I wanted to leave her with a weapon, but I wasn't sure what it should be. She'd never used an assault rifle before, so it wouldn't suit her. My magnum pistol was too big and powerful for her. I decided to leave her my commando knife, one frag grenade, and two flares. I told her to shoot a flare in the air if she needed help, and if I saw it, I'd start back. I wasn't satisfied with the meager items I'd given her. They weren't adequate, but I didn't know what else to do under the circumstances.

My Ling's tearful, worried face hurt me deeply, but I had to go alone. I kissed her, tasting her wet, salty tears. Damn it, I didn't want to leave! My passionate instincts told me to grab her and run, never looking back. But I couldn't do that. I'd never be able to live with myself or look her in the face if I did that.

Ever since I joined the Army, my highest priority was to be a good soldier with a soldier's values. But not now, not this time. I'd committed myself to finishing this mission because I was a man long before I became a soldier. The VC had beaten My Ling, slaughtered my men, and drove me to the brink of insanity. I'd be a coward if I didn't see this through.

I turned to walk away, not wanting to wait another second. Hesitating even for a moment would have had my stomach churning and my eyes filling with tears. Trembling, My Ling grabbed my arm with both hands, digging her fingernails into my skin. With the most frightened expression I'd ever seen on her face, she whispered, "Par-ker, you no go mountain. I beg you, no go mountain. I see death, Par-ker. Old people live village say bad spirits in mountain. Many people go mountain, no come back. They die, Par-ker. You go, you no come back. I know, Par-ker."

I'd almost forgotten how superstitious the Vietnamese and Yard people were. I reassured her that I was going to be all right, though I didn't know what was in store for me ahead. With her viselike grip on my arm, her nails pierced my skin, drawing blood. She wouldn't let go of my arm. "Par-ker," she tearfully begged, "you go, I go! Together we die, Par-ker." As calmly as I could, I explained again that I'd be okay. Using my other hand, I pried My Ling's fingers from my arm. Clutching her stomach, she screamed hysterically, "You want die, Par-ker? I no want you die. I love you! You no go mountain! I see death, Par-ker!"

The best thing for me to do was walk away without another word. She was convinced I'd die today on Chu Pong Mountain, and she could be right. If my destiny was to die on that mountain, so be it. *But I'll be damned if I'll be the only man to die today.*

The very last thing I felt like doing was smiling, but I smiled, wanting her to see that I was confident about the mountain. Inwardly, I wasn't so confident, but I was still going. Maybe I was stupid, stubborn, crazy, I don't know, but I was going all the same. I kissed her again, then walked away like the fool or man I was.

She started crying loudly, "Par-ker! Par-ker! Par-ker!" I disappeared into the jungle foliage, walking faster. She kept screaming my name, and each time she did, it was like someone stabbing me in the heart. Her hoarse voice kept echoing through the jungle, haunting me. I continued on, and after awhile, I could no longer hear her heartbreaking screams. I felt relieved about that, but at the same time, I was deeply depressed. Seeing her cry and hearing her screams had left me emotionally devastated. In leaving her, I'd left a part of myself behind, too.

My God, this is crazy! How could I love her so much? I'd only just met her a couple days ago. Was it possible? And how could she speak of love to me? I had enough common sense to know that there was more to us humans than just the physical self. There had to be something supernatural, something mystical, a fleshless, soulful essence, an inorganic spirit, something that contributed to making us what we are as human beings. As unexplainable as these things are, and as unexplainable as they may forever be, I firmly believed in their unequaled and unparalleled powers. So with the right spiritual bonding, it was possible for me to love My Ling, and it was possible to believe that she loved me, too.

Being born is a risk in this world; life is risky, and love is risky, too. Any person, man or woman, who doesn't want to gamble on something, who doesn't want to dare the odds at least once, is a meaningless person to me with no courage and no true individuality. So I'd risk loving My Ling. If I lost her to someone else, I'd be heartbroken, but I'd have no regrets. I would rather love her for a short time and enjoy our love together than never love her at all. This was love in all its infamous and unexplainable ways, love in a world that was complex, moody, and dangerous.

I was so lost in thought that I almost missed the thin wire in front of me. I froze. Slowly and meticulously, I checked the immediate area around me for secondary booby traps. Finding none, I turned my full attention back to the wire. It was about a foot away from me, and it was about seven feet high off the ground. I followed the wire, most of it having been expertly camouflaged, to the nearest tree. It was connected to an American frag grenade with the pin straightened. It amazed me how the enemy could steal, capture, and buy so many American weapons and turn them on us. This type of booby trap was made for the radio-man in a team, platoon, or company. The radio-man, being the only source of communication, was usually near an officer positioned in the middle to protect him and the radio. While the guys in front of him could walk safely under the wire, the radio-man's antenna would hit the wire and pull the grenade pin out. Because the grenade would be several feet off the ground, its explosion would have the maximum killing and wounding range. This particular type of wire wasn't usually hard for experienced GIs to spot. When the enemy used monofilament fishing line, though, the clear stuff, there were usually fatalities and injuries. I had to put My Ling completely out of my mind and concentrate on my surroundings, but to put her fully out of my mind was something I just couldn't do.

I came closer and closer to the base of Chu Pong Mountain. I started being more cautious as I slowly approached it. Through the thick jungle, a circular clearing appeared out of nowhere. It was small, a little over fifty yards in radius, right at the base of the mountain. The clearing looked naturally made, but it could also be a man-made kill zone. An unsuspecting person or persons would walk into the kill zone, and the enemy would open fire from camouflaged ground holes, or from the trees, or, in this case, possibly from the side of the mountain. I wasn't taking any chances, so I decided to bypass the clearing. I skirted the left side of the clearing, getting about halfway around before a mortar shell exploded a few yards from me. The thunderous impact propelled my body into the air, sending me crashing into a tree.

I was unconscious for a few minutes. When I came to, I was severely dazed. A painful lump the size of a half dollar was swelling on the right side of my head above my ear. Blood oozed out of the lump in several places. My head felt like someone had bashed it in with a baseball bat. My right eye was bruised and swollen. My right side ached, and it felt like I'd fractured or broke a rib or two. I was bleeding from stinging hot shrapnel in multiple places on my right leg and shoulder. I was momentarily oblivious to the many rounds zinging through the foliage around me. They were splintering branches, the bark on trees, and chewing up chunks of dirt close to me. Though dazed and in pain, I had to change my present position or die. My rifle was a few yards away, and I crawled achingly through the hail of bullets to retrieve it. Every movement was agonizing and brought tears to my eyes.

My rifle looked functional, so I continued crawling out of the area. The piercing pain in my head was terrible, and my bruised right eye only gave me partial vision. My right leg felt numb, and my right side hurt with every breath. With labored exertion, I continued crawling until the enemy rounds were no longer in my immediate area. I finally stopped to rest in some tall shrubbery and elephant grass after crawling about fifteen or twenty yards. My heart raced as I coughed up blood and tried to settle my nerves. This had to be the enemy group My Ling told me about. They spotted me near the kill zone and waited for me to walk into the trap. When I didn't, they unloaded with mortars and small-arms fire.

I could still hear shooting and the occasional mortar blast as I lay wounded on my back. I stared straight up through some single-canopied trees at the deep blue sky. Throbbing pains thrashed my body while I fought back my sudden fear. Fear was a rare emotion for me, and the feeling was startling. Then it dawned on me why I felt like that. It was because of love, damn it! I was in love!

Because I loved My Ling so much, I wasn't my old self any-more. This was something I hadn't truly appreciated or fully comprehended until now. By myself, I'd been bold as a lion, gutsy, and fearless, with no regrets or second thoughts about putting myself in danger. Countless times, I'd violently flirted with death with an audacious callousness. But no more. I couldn't. The arrogance and recklessness were gone.

I felt afraid as I stared up at the deep blue peacefulness, so high and far away. Damn! I wanted to live! My Ling loved and needed me. I was no good to her if I were crippled or dead. Something deep within me suddenly snapped. *Fuck Major Small and his lie-detector test! Fuck them all! I'm disengaging my pursuit here and now, and that's the way my report's going to read, too! If SOG kicks me out because of it, then so be it. I'll serve out my six-year reenlistment, and then My Ling and I will decide if I should stay in or get out. With her by my side, I'll deal with anything the army, Major Small, or the world throws at me. I'm going back to get her, and we're getting the hell away from this mountain.*

I desperately yearned for My Ling, to touch her and have her nurse my wounds. She needed me close to her, and I was prepared to crawl, hop, or limp to get back to her.

The enemy had stopped firing and dropping mortars, probably thinking I was dead or gravely wounded. Most likely, they'd wait for a while, then search for my body to confirm the kill. I still didn't know exactly where they were, but I didn't care. By the time they came searching, I'd be long gone. I stared at the sky for almost ten minutes. That was too long to stay in one position. Clumsily, I put a gauze pad on my head wound. My head was spinning as I stood up and tested my right leg. It supported my weight, but I knew the leg wouldn't hold up for long.

I heard sudden screams, high-pitched screams. Instinctively, I ducked down, expecting enemy fire in my direction. The screams became clearer, more distinct. It was My Ling! She was screaming my name. "Par-ker! Par-ker!" She kept screaming as I looked around frantically in all directions. I couldn't spot her. My panic grew and my heart pounded wildly.

There. I saw her. She'd just broken free of the dense jungle at a full run. *No!* She was in the clearing. The kill zone! *No!*

"Par-ker! Par-ker!" she cried, running farther into the clearing.

My God, no! "My Ling! Go back! Get out of there! Go back!" I shouted. "Go back, please!"

The enemy fired. The rounds hit her first in the chest and stomach, twisting her body around. More rounds splattered her back, then both legs, as she crumpled to the ground. Blood-soaked holes were scattered all over her body, and still, the enemy kept firing. The rounds literally disintegrated her head and kept her headless torso rolling on the ground until she was just a distorted mass of pulverized bones and flesh. Still, the enemy fired on and on. She looked like a headless rag doll that someone had ripped apart, dipped into red paint, and thrown brutally into a corner. I stood there, paralyzed, not wanting to believe what I'd just seen.

"Motherfuckers!" I cried out. "Motherfuckers! Motherfuckers!" Through my tears, I saw the general direction of the enemy fire. I fired off a whole magazine of rounds in their direction on full automatic. Because of the tears and my bad right eye, I could barely see, but still I fired. I hollered out a bellowing scream that reverberated harshly through the jungle. Between my wounds, dizziness, frustration, and exhaustion, I felt faint and fell helplessly to the ground. Enemy rounds flew over my body, narrowly missing me. They concentrated their fire in my direction in a wide arc. Crying loudly, I stared blurry-eyed at the sky again, mindless of the enemy rounds flying chaotically around me.

I didn't understand. Why did she have to die? Why, God? Why? Why not me? Why her? She was a noncombatant, guilty of nothing but loving me! Hear that, God? She loved me!

The enemy had stopped firing, but I was too traumatized to realize it. I wouldn't have cared anyway. My physical wounds were secondary to my grief and mental anguish. I lay there with tears streaming down my face. The deep blue sky was no longer serene and peaceful; it was ugly to me. Contemptuously, I yelled at the sky, "Why, God? Damn it, do you hear me? You never hear me! Well, fuck you! Did you hear that, God? Up your royal fucking ass! You've never listened to me! Never! Where's the understanding? The compassion? Why hurt me like this?"

Rolling over, I pounded both fists savagely into the ground until they were numb. I kept crying uncontrollably. "My Ling, can you hear me, sweetheart? What am I to do? Help me, please!"

All my willpower was gone, drained. I felt abandoned and terribly lonely again. Why was God destroying my life and damning my soul like this? For a half hour, I lay weeping and cursing out loud. I cursed the war and everyone I knew and everyone I'd ever heard of. Happiness and joy were nothing but a fool's paradise.

For a few minutes, I slipped into a deranged mental state, thinking that all this had to be a dream. This war — Major Small, the Fifth Group, SOG, the ambush, My Ling — all had to be a bizarre dream. I was really at home, sound asleep in bed, and all this was just in my head. My Ling never died because she never existed. Some say that dreams are windows to the subconscious created by the imagination running wild. If I'd been dreaming, I'd concocted My Ling in my mind. But why, then, did I feel such a deep loss within me and such emotional pain?

I don't like this dream. It grieves me. I want to wake up! Now! With a sudden outburst, I yelled, "NOW!" Surprised, I glanced around as if I were seeing my surroundings for the first time. The last few minutes had been blank to me, a blackout or something. The only things I could feel were my aching injuries and a deep, morbid feeling from losing My Ling. I had cried so much that I had no more tears to shed. What was left for me now? What could I do? Should I get angry? There was nothing but anger left to fill my emptiness and loneliness. Desire for ruthless revenge began pulsating through my mind with a quivering rage. I wanted my pound of flesh. I demanded it. Revenge and my death wish would both be granted today on Chu Pong Mountain. The acute pain in my head was intolerable, more than flesh and blood could bear, but I would bear it. My other wounds were starting to ache more, but I would endure them, too.

God, the Supreme Creator, whatever name he preferred, took My Ling and he didn't have to. There wasn't any need for him, with such infinite power and wisdom, to take her like that. But he did. He used the VC group as his earthly instrument of death to destroy her. Maybe this was his way of punishing me for the enemy lives I'd ruined and taken in this war. Watching My Ling die was an unforgettable punishment and a haunting tragedy combined. I wanted revenge. I would try to kill every one of them before I died. I just couldn't live with My Ling's death on my conscience. I would die on this mountain like she had superstitiously predicted. What she hadn't foreseen was that her own death was hopelessly entwined with mine.

The more I thought about the VC group, the more savage and enraged I became. Hate pumped extreme amounts of adrenaline through my blood, making my body quake uncontrollably. My mind began regimenting itself, becoming alert and disciplined. My survival instincts were reaching their peak again, making me feel stronger and able to think more clearly. Once again, I became the predator I was trained to be. Revenge equaled violence. And violence was Nighthawk-One.

I looked around, seeing everything with a different perspective. I gazed up at the sky, and it was neither peaceful nor ugly. To Nighthawk-One, the sky was just layers of meaningless clouds with no immediate significance. Fearlessly, I analyzed my present situation with sterile and unemotional thoughts. I had to do something to permanently neutralize the VC group. There'd be no strategic withdrawal this time, no retreating, and above all, no surrendering. I had to find out exactly where they were, and there was only one way to do that. Getting to my feet in a low crouch, I held my rifle tightly. Then I stood straight up and took off running. The enemy would have to be blind and dumb to refuse such a tempting target.

They opened up on me with a heavy machine gun and AK-47s. I ducked low, changing directions, running about twenty-five yards before dropping behind a tree. The enemy continued spraying the area while I lay there, catching my breath. I'd seen exactly where the rounds were coming from. The bastards were in a camouflaged cave or dugout at the base of the mountain. I saw the rounds shredding vines and other foliage around the hideout while they fired.

Once I knew where the bastards were, a basic plan began forming in my cold mind. From my rucksack, I took the last pen-sized flare and frag grenade I had. Though my rucksack still contained personal items, I angrily threw it away. My head wound still ached, I still had blurred and partial vision, my fractured or broken ribs still hurt, and the shrapnel wounds in my right leg and shoulder still bled. But I didn't care, wouldn't care, and I wasn't going to let the pain force me to care. Not yet. Not now.

The enemy was still firing into the area as I started crawling low toward their hideout. I didn't stop until I was within throwing distance. After I rested for several minutes, I threw the ignited flare followed by the frag grenade. When the grenade exploded, I fired a full magazine of automatic rounds at the hideout. Then I took off running — not toward the enemy hideout, but away from it. Despite the pain, I ran in a wide semicircle up the side of the mountain. With the flare, grenade, and burst of rounds, they'd be expecting a frontal assault from me. It was a suicide attempt to charge them directly, and I'm sure they knew it. I wanted them speculating that I was crazy enough to make such a move. What I was really doing was going up the side of the mountain, looking for a back door entrance to their hideout. I hadn't heard about or seen any underground enemy complexes that didn't have a few emergency exits. Some of the complexes were small; some were huge, with connecting tunnels running for miles. They contained large training classrooms, shooting ranges, sleeping quarters, mess halls, hospitals, weapons, ammo, and countless booby traps. We had a nickname for these enemy tunnels: Hell's Back Door.

The thick jungle foliage and my injuries slowed my pace. I still heard sporadic fire below while I moved on. I was exhausted, with sweat dripping heavily out of every pore. I had new scratches and cuts, and some of the old ones were bleeding again. About an hour later, I found what I was looking for. About thirty yards away, sitting against a tree, was an NVA soldier. A few yards from him, I saw part of a bamboo ladder that stretched down into a hole in the ground. I'd found one of their rear-door exits, but this was the first time I'd seen one being physically guarded. Usually, the enemy just set booby traps in and around the exit as a warning system. The young, black-haired NVA was muscular, probably in his early twenties. He had an AK-47, a water canteen, and a small radio with him. He didn't seem concerned or excited about the sporadic shooting below.

I had to waste this guy quietly with no shooting. I didn't have my knife, so I had to use my hands. Inch by inch, I started toward him, moving silently. It took over an hour of crawling to cautiously cover the distance between us. I was being careful not to startle any animals or birds or snap any twigs. I was only a few feet from the tree he sat against as I inched closer. I anticipated snapping his neck, crushing his throat, or strangling him in a quick-kill maneuver. Quietly, I eased myself into a squatting position behind him with the tree between us. The NVA soldier had only seconds to live as I eased my left hand around the tree to grab him.

It was at that instant that the fickle finger of fate decided to screw me. I accidentally snapped an unnoticed piece of dry twig under my jungle boot. The noise was loud and crisp, dooming my plan. I was in trouble.

The NVA soldier, after hearing the noise, quickly jerked away from the tree. Instinctively, I followed his fluid movement. On his feet, a few yards from the tree, he started turning with his rifle. He was surprised when he saw me right there with him. Grabbing the barrel and butt of the rifle, I twisted it counterclockwise and kicked him in the groin. His face warped in pain, and he gave out a piercing scream as I snatched the rifle away. Falling to the ground, he rolled out of my immediate grasp. I flung the rifle as far as I could into the jungle. The NVA soldier got back on his feet, legs spread wide. He was gently rubbing his groin with his left hand. In his right hand, he held a pocketknife with a four-inch steel blade. His black eyes and pimpled face showed an angry fury that would only be satisfied with my death.

His left arm was in front of him, his knife hand close to his side. This stance told me he was an expert knife-fighter. Spreading both my hands out in front of me, I angled my palms downward. I bent my knees, shifting my weight to the balls of my feet for mobility. I hoped that seeing me in a defensive fighting stance would make him leery of trying quick-kill strikes. With the wounds I had and being so tired, I couldn't fight off several quick-kill strikes back to back.

Still, I was in serious trouble. He'd attack with slashing and thrusting strikes to wear me down, immobilize me, and finally kill me. Slashing and thrusting by an experienced knife-fighter was nothing less than a slow, torturous killing procedure. With about a yard or so between us, he made a deceptive slash at my midsection, then swiftly brought the knife upward, lunging for the side of my neck. My knife instructor had taught me to always expect to be cut in a knife fight. In a situation where I was knifeless and on the defensive, I was taught to sacrifice non-artery areas and the least important muscle areas. There was no choice sometimes but to take a cut in order to get in on an enemy to immobilize or kill him. Although I was on the defensive, it would be my fast, aggressive attacks that would decide my fate.

As the NVA soldier lunged for the left side of my neck, I stepped back and to my right. Because of my wounds, my movement wasn't quite fast enough, so I brought my left hand close to my neck. I did this so I would block his knife-arm safely or take a slash on the back of my hand. Either way, it was better than being slashed in a critical area like my neck. With blurring wrist action, the NVA soldier slashed me twice on the back of my left hand. Before he could retreat out of my striking range, though, I gave a sharp blow to his nose with the rigid palm of my right hand. His nose splattered and broke. Blood flowed freely into his mouth and down his chin. Breathing heavily, he wiped some of the blood away while gurgling sounds rose from his throat. In a rage, he gave a crazy shriek and charged me. More than likely, he'd attack with slashing, thrusting, and killing strikes combined, making him unpredictable and more dangerous. While backing up, I quickly dipped, dodged and blocked his many deadly and injury-causing knife strikes. I had to do something fast or die. I did a low roundhouse kick using my right foot, hitting him hard on the side of his right kneecap. Excruciating pain and numbness shot through my wounded right leg as I broke his knee.

The NVA soldier screeched as his knee cracked and muscles ripped. Limping back a few steps, he glared viciously at me. The broken knee had slowed him down considerably, and a cautious confidence filled my mind. Though we were both limping now, I'd try crowding him, hoping he'd make a mistake. With a loud yell, he lunged wildly at me, the knife barely missing my throat. The momentum of the lunge twisted his body awkwardly around, forcing him off balance. Most of his back confronted me now as he started falling into me and down. This could have been a desperate trick on his part to get closer to me, but I had to take the risk. With both arms, I grabbed him around the neck in a stranglehold. This particular type of deadly stranglehold was called the "rear takedown and strangle technique," with the snapping of the neck as a failsafe precaution. This technique was normally used for silent kills, taking out sentries and guards from behind.

We fell hard to the ground, and I took the full force of the fall on my back. With all the strength my wounded body could conjure up, I tightened the hold more. Because my strength wasn't at its maximum, I wrapped my legs around his body to keep him from twisting and kicking so much. The NVA soldier desperately stabbed the inside of my left thigh and slashed me twice on my right arm, directly above the elbow. Suddenly, his movements slowed, and blood spewed out of his mouth. It was then that I broke his neck with a sharp, twisting jerk of his head. My arms felt like lead weights as I slowly removed them from his neck. I was too weak and hurt to even push his body off me right then. Only after several minutes was I able to wearily shove the dead weight off.

The two knife slashes on my right arm bled profusely but weren't deep. The stab wound inside my left thigh wasn't as deep as I'd thought. Taking the dead man's knife, I cut strips from his bloody shirt. I wrapped and tied a couple of strips around my slashes and stab wound. It wasn't sanitary, but I had to stop the bleeding fast, or at least slow it down. After retrieving my rifle from the jungle, I fell to the ground for a short rest.

My head ached. I was dizzy, nauseated, and blood seeped from all parts of my body. I was weak with severe shakes, and my bruised right eye had swollen shut. I just wanted to lie there, go to sleep, and die peacefully, but the rage in the pit of my stomach wouldn't allow me to lie there, let alone die there. Not right now. I had to survive long enough to get My Ling's killers.

With the help of a tree and my own stubborn determination, I dragged myself to my feet. After a few minutes, I was able to support my weight on my unsteady legs. I put a full magazine of twenty rounds in my weapon and made sure it was on automatic. Then I hobbled over to the bamboo ladder leading down into the dark tunnel. I descended about twenty feet, slipping twice before I hit the bottom. I was in pitch darkness, not knowing which way to go. I saw a flickering light far to my left. The walls of the cave were damp and cool as I carefully made my way toward the light. The light turned out to be a candle in a large glass jar on top of a flat rock. The cave made a sharp right turn at the candle, and farther down, another light flickered. Taking a few painfully deep breaths, I continued on along the wall. As I approached the second light, I heard the enemy fire more and more clearly. I heard Vietnamese voices near the sharp right turn of the cave at the next candle. Peeking around the corner, I saw that the cave walls ran for several yards, opening into a large, well lit, circular area. I saw bright kerosene lamps and candles, and four Viet Cong soldiers stood inside the room, shooting out of four portholes. They were evidently shooting into and around their manmade kill zone, which was directly in front of them.

I recalled My Ling saying that there were five VC and one NVA that stopped at their place, and that one of the Viet Cong men was gravely wounded. The NVA soldier was no longer a threat, and the wounded VC was probably dead, which left these four. I moved carefully toward the open area. This was it. A chill sliced through my body just as I began the assault. I shot the heavy machine gunner first, killing him with four rounds in the back. I sprayed rounds from left to right in a quick burst. I changed positions, moving a few yards to my left. I heard surprised cries while dust, dirt, ricocheting rocks, pebbles, and bullets filled the area. In my changed position, I quickly fired another burst of rounds, emptying my magazine. I knew I'd wounded the remaining three, but wasn't sure how badly. Throwing my empty rifle into the dusty fog, I drew my pistol out, dropping flat to the ground. Several enemy rounds had already been fired in my direction, and another burst was fired in the area where my rifle bounced off the cave wall. To my right, I faintly saw bright sunshine when a bamboo door was pulled open. A staggering form was trying to escape, so I fired one round from my pistol. I rolled over a few times to my left, changing positions again.

The magnum round hit the VC in the upper back. It lifted him a few feet off the ground, propelling him awkwardly out the door. I heard another VC, who sounded seriously wounded, yelling hoarsely for his comrades. His voice sounded low to the ground, so I fired two low rounds and heard a fatal scream. I stayed put this time, swinging my pistol continuously from left to right and back, anticipating return fire. I got none. I lay still for about five minutes while the debris and smoke settled some. A few kerosene and oil lamps had been shot up, and a couple of small fires were burning. Even after I'd spotted the bodies of the three VC, I still didn't budge. I didn't want to move too fast and find out the hard way that one of them was still alive. I fired one round into each of their bodies as a precaution before painfully getting to my feet. I could barely stand up with my dizziness and my wounded right leg. I fell hard against the cave wall for support. I was standing, but I had to bend over slightly due to the pain in my ribs. After a few minutes, I found that the double vision in my left eye wouldn't go away. I forced myself to move with merciless willpower; I didn't want to die in an enemy cave. I'd crawl over broken glass to get out of there if I had to. Out in the open jungle, with the sun shining on my face, was where I wanted to die.

I hobbled over to my rifle and put a fresh magazine of rounds in it. I replaced the six spent rounds in my pistol with live ones. Dragging my rifle with me by the sling strap, I stumbled out the open bamboo door. Right outside the camouflaged door was the fourth VC. He had a few small bullet holes in his lower back and a much larger one in his upper back.

Staggering into the kill zone, I saw My Ling's body. The inhuman sight was too nerve-wracking for me to bear. Almost fainting, I fell hard to the ground on my hands and knees. I was too weak to cry, run, or even walk. My stomach cramped painfully as I vomited. For a few minutes, I became delirious again, no longer remembering who I was. I finally made it to my feet after three tries. The jungle kept swirling while I stumbled and swayed out of the kill zone. I had walked only a short distance when a small trail appeared out of nowhere. I followed the trail, not knowing why other than the fact that it was there.

Somewhere along the trail, unaware, I dropped my dragging rifle. Where was I? What place? Who was I, and what the hell was I doing in the jungle? I was bleeding, in pain, and dying, but why? My inner and outer strength finally crumbled, and I fell hard to the ground. Then I saw her! My Ling! I saw her! She was floating hazily in the air a few yards from me. Her serene eyes showed no hint of happiness or sadness as she stared mysteriously at me. With my trembling, bleeding hand, I reached into the air, wanting her to take it. *Please, My Ling, take my hand! Take me with you! Don't leave me again!* In slow motion, she moved her head from side to side, saying no. I started crying hopelessly, opening and closing my hand. I yelled hoarsely, "My Ling, please, don't leave me here! I'll believe in God, I swear! Take me with you!"

Through my tearful, blurred double vision, I thought I saw movement close by. Several moving forms seemed to have suddenly appeared. I blinked my eyes several times, trying to focus on whatever angels or demons confronted me. I surmised that my death was very near as these blurred images came closer in slow motion. I laughed. Blood sprayed out of my mouth, gagging me while my mad laughter agitated my pain. It was true! It was true!

In the regular army units, there was an old saying that the Marines guarded the Gates of Heaven, but the Green Berets guarded the Gates of Hell. *It was true.* I laughed and laughed while painful, spasmodic cramps tore through my body. My laughter quickly ceased as my mind sank into a deep coma.

Chapter Six

The big Vietnamese town of Qhin Nhon was located right on the South China Sea. There was a large U.S. Army and Air Force compound there with a medical hospital in it. Waking up in a two-man room, I saw the white walls first, then the I.V. needle in my left arm. There was a wooden chair and a metal cabinet in the room. The bathroom door was open, and I assumed the other smaller door was the closet. Looking past the blue curtains and out the window, I saw part of an airstrip, a few buildings, and passing military vehicles. I was bare-chested, wearing blue hospital pants. My chest and back were tightly wrapped with white gauze strips. My right side ached slightly. My head, right eye, left hand, left thigh, and right arm above my elbow had all been bandaged. All over my body, I had scratches, cuts, and small shrapnel wounds that were healing. The other bed was empty with fresh sheets and a spread on it. The antiseptic smell of rubbing alcohol filled my nostrils.

It became evident to me that I was still alive, which suited me just fine. I couldn't remember how I got there or how I got my injuries. I started getting frustrated as I tried to recall what had happened. I finally gave up after I gave myself a headache and my vision blurred.

About a half hour after I woke up, an army nurse peeked into my room. Seeing me awake, she smiled and walked in. The first thing I noticed was the first lieutenant bar on her collar. I wasn't crazy about officers, but looking at her made me forget about my headache. She wore a starched, tightly tailored set of fatigues. She had a nice tan, was about 5'5" tall, had short, blonde hair, large, firm breasts, a small waist, impressive hips, and a healthy rear end. Coming over to the bed, she put a hand on my forehead. "Fever's gone, Sergeant Parker. That's good," she said, smiling. "I'm Lieutenant Anderson. You've been unconscious for three days. How long have you been awake?"

"I don't know," I answered. "For a little while, I guess." She took my pulse. Her fingers were velvety soft, and her perfume was titillating. She was an eyeful, making my heart beat faster and stronger. Patting me gently on the wrist a few times, she smiled teasingly, saying, "It seems like you're going to be just fine, Sergeant."

When she turned to stroll away, I asked, "What happened to me? How did I get here?"

Concerned, she responded, "You don't remember anything that happened to you, Sergeant?"

Impatiently, I said, "No, Lieutenant."

"Oh," she said. "Well, even if I did know what happened, I wouldn't be at liberty to discuss it with you. I'll notify Captain Acker, who's your doctor, and tell him you're conscious, okay?" She didn't wait for a reply; she just smiled and scurried out into the hallway

She probably didn't know anything about me, but somebody knew. Damn it, I wanted to know. A few hours later, it was dark outside, and this Captain Acker still hadn't shown up. I made a big commotion about this until I was given a shot of sedative that knocked me out. As I slept, I started to remember everything that had happened. I relived the events from my last trip to Nha Trang all the way up to falling unconscious on the trail. The memories were terrifying, and I thrashed about in bed, getting cold chills. All the emotions and feelings I'd experienced out there swept through my mind. I laughed, cried, and screamed in mental anguish as I relived it all.

Later that night, my anxiety finally broke through the sedative. I became fully conscious. My eyes opened wearily as I stared into the gloomy darkness. My muscles kept twitching while I lay there, drenched in sweat. My God, I had to think this through before I went insane. Tears filled my eyes when I thought about My Ling. I really loved her, and she was dead. I didn't want her to be dead, but she was dead. I had to pound it into my head that there was nothing I could do about My Ling. I had to accept her death and my survival. I didn't have to like it; in fact, I hated it. But, my God, I had to accept it. I didn't feel complete as a person, and I wondered if I ever would. I still had memories, precious, sweet memories, that would forever be priceless and dear to me. My Ling would want me to go on with my life, to seek out my destiny. Though she was dead, I still loved her and always would. I had to go on. My sanity demanded it.

I thought about the nine guys lost in the ambush. Nine guys! Trying to rationalize their loss brought on an intense headache. With a fixed determination, I tried to accept their deaths and my survival. I saw that my guilt complex would never be totally settled in my mind. Merely accepting their deaths wasn't enough, but it was the best I could do. Staying awake the rest of the night, I desperately tried to avoid more thoughts about the ambush and My Ling.

The next morning, at about nine o'clock, I saw Captain Acker. We talked for about fifteen minutes about my wounds. He told me how lucky I was that my wounds weren't any worse, especially the concussion. He said that rest was the best thing for me. I remembered everything except how I got there, and questioned him about it. He didn't know much; he only knew that I was choppered in, but he told me that I'd be having visitors later on in the day from my unit.

Around one o'clock in the afternoon, my section leader, Captain Miller, and two sergeant friends came to visit. They greeted me rather vigorously with pokes and jabs to my body. Though they meant well, the pokes and jabs hurt like hell. I said nothing, and I didn't complain when I heard the same corny jokes I'd heard before. After several minutes of discussing the current events at Ban Me Thout, we settled in for some serious talking. "Captain Acker thinks you have a mild mental block," Captain Miller said with concern.

"When I first woke up, I couldn't remember anything," I answered, "but last night, everything came back to me, except for how I got here. Did I make it back on my own? Did peasants find me What happened?"

Captain Miller responded, "You were found by another SOG team sent in a day after you left."

Hearing about another team surprised me. "What other SOG team?" I asked. "I wasn't briefed on another team in my AO (Area of Operation)."

Taking a deep breath, Captain Miller said, "Calm down. I have lots to tell you — good and bad. Working yourself into a frenzy isn't the answer, that I do know."

"Let's hear it," I groaned in a tired, restrained voice.

"I was surprised, too, when I learned about the other team," Captain Miller said. "They had the exact same mission your team had."

"Wait a minute, slow down here," I interrupted. "Let me get this straight. My team was assigned to take out an enemy group codenamed Bluebeard. Major Small briefed me, and my team was the only one assigned to do this. Now you're telling me, a day after I left, another SOG team was dispatched to take out Bluebeard too?"

"That's right. Now, don't get bent out of shape," Captain Miller said. "Major Small had no knowledge of this when he briefed you. I'll get back to that son of a bitch in a minute. Right now, I want you to clearly understand, if it weren't for the second team, you'd be dead. A few hours after your team was dispatched, a colonel on the planning board was in the Officers Club. He overheard two lieutenants talking about the inexperienced team you had on your mission. One of the lieutenants said that it wasn't likely for you and your team to make it back. The two officers were Special Forces men, but they weren't cleared for privileged info about SOG. The colonel, after overhearing this security breach, wrote their names down. He called the other Board members, telling them what happened. The Board convened immediately and sent for Major Small to confirm or deny the inexperienced team story and to find out if he personally breached security in any way. He told the Board he never uttered a word about the mission to anyone, and that you blatantly disregarded his orders by taking a team of five First Infantry men with you. He emphasized that direct orders were given to all team leaders; each team would have only one or two First Infantry grunts at the most. He gave the Board the overall impression that you were insubordinate, incorrigible, and caused dissension among the troops."

In a fury, I pulled the I.V. needle from my arm and leapt out of bed, heading for the door. I never made it. Strong arms tackled me to the floor and wrestled me back to bed. At the top of my lungs, I yelled, "I'll kill that bastard! He's dead meat! He's fucking lying, damn it! He's lying! That bastard's lying!"

A few staff members tried to enter the room, but one of my sergeant buddies kept them out. Captain Miller and the other sergeant had me pinned down on the bed. "Get your shit together before it's too late! You hear me? This is Captain Miller, your section leader talking! Get it together now, soldier! That's an order!"

No one spoke for a minute while I calmed myself down. I knew Major Small was a bastard, but I never realized he was a lying snake, too. I was still angry, but I felt calmer and told them to let me go. I had to hear the rest, no matter how much bullshit was involved. "I'm okay, thanks," I grumbled. "But I couldn't help it. He's lying, Captain, he's lying!"

"I know that because I know you," Captain Miller said. "You're a fanatic about teamwork and experience. I know he's lying through his teeth, Parker. But right now, I want you to contain yourself. You hear me? You've been through an extremely traumatic experience, and if you keep these outbursts up, they'll transfer you straight to the psycho ward. Keep a low profile, understand? I'm telling you again, get it through your thick skull that you're alive. You survived against the odds while nine men were scraped into body bags. I didn't see them die, and I don't know how I would have dealt with it myself. But you have to deal with it, understand? You don't have a choice. You made it this far. Don't let yourself become your own worst enemy. Don't give up. I will not allow one of my soldiers to give up!"

Deep in my mind, I knew he was right. But he'd never know how traumatic it really was with My Ling dying, too. I had to start pacing myself, taking things in stride with some degree of patience. I couldn't change what had already happened, no matter how hurt or enraged I got. I knew the captain had more to say and passively prepared myself to hear it.

Captain Miller said he was ordered to Nha Trang to meet with a Special Inquiry Board several hours after I left. They had my classified file, which was above-par, but they wanted an on-the-spot oral report from him concerning me. He said he gave me an excellent evaluation on character, leadership, motivation, the whole works. According to Captain Miller, Small was squirming in his seat, giving him the evil eye. Captain Miller was under oath and he said he simply told the truth.

Captain Miller continued. "The two lieutenants were there, and you've worked with one of them before. He stated he overheard two Special Forces sergeants talking about you and your team while drinking in a bar-hooch the previous night in the town of Nha Trang. He made it clear that he didn't know these two sergeants, and he was too drunk at the time to ever recognize them again. He explained that he related the story to the other lieutenant while in the Officers Club in the compound the next day. It's well known among the officers that Small has a loose mouth when he's drinking.

"There's a good probability here that he breached security either consciously or unconsciously. But then again, our counter-intelligence community hasn't exactly been at its maximum since we entered this war. Honestly speaking, this lapse in security could have come about in several ways. The Inquiry Board is full of shit. There's five officers on it, and three of them are Small's friends. They did agree after some arguing that your team was insufficient for your assigned mission. That's when they ordered another team out. The enemy had already salvaged what they could from the ambush site, and your handiwork was found around the mountain: one NVA and five VC dead."

My mouth flew open as I started to correct him about My Ling. Suddenly, I stopped, not wanting to share my experience with him or anyone else. When she died, she was armed with my knife, flare, and grenade, so they'd taken her for the enemy. They could call her VC if they wanted, but I'd always know otherwise.

Captain Miller was still talking. "The Inquiry Board had planned on talking to your team members to shed some light on this. Obviously, that can't be done. Their deaths brought even more serious concerns to the Inquiry Board. The person or persons responsible for forming the team could be court-martialed and charged with major negligence and incompetence. Don't lose your temper again, Parker. You know as well as I do about military politics in this man's army. Like I told you, I believe Small is guilty of giving you the team outright. But the Inquiry Board's protecting him and screwing you in the process. Within the last twenty-four hours, interest has shifted drastically from Small and nine dead men to you. Incredible and highly questionable, isn't it? To cover their devious asses, the Board busted you down to private and kicked you out of Special Forces and SOG. They've given you a thirty-day leave, then reassignment to Fort Lewis, Washington."

Captain Miller explained that trying to court-martial Small would have been difficult. The Board's official conclusion was that even with an inexperienced team, I, as the most experienced man and leader, should have noticed some minor or major irregularity at the insertion point and aborted the landing. The sons of bitches used my classified file against me by stating my expertise, accomplishments, and confirmed kills in the field. Captain Miller said they made reference to the fact that I did all this at a minimum loss of life and injuries to my men. In a nutshell, they said I was a short-timer and that my mind wasn't on the mission as it normally should have been.

Captain Miller said he knew it was bullshit, but they had to rationalize their actions on paper. I had every right to be pissed off. He said he was pissed, too, but that I needed to maintain myself. Small wanted me court-martialed for negligence, incompetence, and insubordination. The Board ruled against it. Captain Miller said that they didn't do it as any type of restitution to me, though. With the good combat record I had, it simply would have been tough to prove such serious charges.

They were also concerned about certain conventional military officers and civilian news reporters who disliked Special Forces and Covert-Ops finding out about the incident and exploiting the situation. Captain Miller said a court-martial would have simply brought too many undesirables into the picture. Also, they doubted that I'd take a court-martial sitting down. To fight back, they said I probably would have exposed SOG, with all its illegal activities in the war, to the media. With the anti-war sentiment back home, there would have been pro-war politicians and military hawks pissed at every member of the Inquiry Board if all that came to light. Their careers wouldn't be worth a crock of shit; it would be like opening Pandora's Box in the Intelligence community.

Captain Miller told me the Board thought about putting me in for a couple of medals, but Small was arguing venomously against it. He felt that the sensitive nature in which the mission ended and my insubordinate attitude didn't warrant me any more medals.

"I'm still your immediate superior until your new orders are cut," Captain Miller said. "I'm submitting my own written report, stating my dissatisfaction with the conclusions of the Board. It's not much, I know, but the Board has to file it. Who knows, maybe one day after this war's over with, this incident will be brought to light by some honest politician or curious news reporter hearing rumors about it.

"Because of my report, my name's officially on file in dis-agreement. I'm telling you now that if I'm ever subpoenaed to a special military hearing or a Washington subcommittee hearing on this mess, I'm telling them all I know. I'll probably be retired by then, so I won't give a damn about military bureaucracy."

Captain Miller explained that he was not telling me what to do, but legally, I had a right to appeal the Board's decision. He said that since I hadn't even submitted my own mission report yet, the Board couldn't be too interested in what I had to say. They hadn't even come close to adhering to the regulations of investigative procedures.

"You being out cold in this hospital for three days proved very convenient for them," he said. "Personally, I'd advise you to submit a detailed report as soon as possible. There's a good chance your report will be purposely lost or destroyed. Then again, some clerk may unwittingly file it. Now, as for the appeal, I can give you a few reasons why you should do it and a few reasons why you shouldn't do it. The choice is yours."

I was so angry that I shook all over, but I controlled myself. I couldn't believe this crap. Major Small deliberately gave me those men. He forced them on me when he didn't have to. Why the hell did he hate me so much? What was with him? *That bastard got nine good men killed and damn near killed me, and he's going to get away with it!*

He and that Board did me in, but they could have done worse. Fuck the stripes! They could keep them, damn it. I wanted out of Special Forces and SOG, but I didn't want to be kicked out. *But fuck that too! The only thing important to me now is that I'm out.*

As far as the Board giving me a thirty-day leave, it wasn't a gift. Most of the guys leaving Nam were automatically given a thirty-day leave. I had to admit, though, that I was overjoyed with having leave time. Any medals they might have wanted to give me they could shove up their brass asses. I didn't ask for them. All I cared about was my leave time. Screw everything else. I'd had it with clandestine and covert-ops games and the Intelligence community. I didn't want to be a leader of anything anymore, not ever again. All I wanted was to be an average soldier with average responsibilities. As for appealing the Board's decision, I was against it. All I'd do was stir up a lot of crap, and I'd still end up being the scapegoat. I could just see Major Small strutting around like a peacock. How many other people had he killed through negligence?

Captain Miller touched my shoulder, asking, "Are you okay? I'm sorry to be the bearer of bad news, but I'm your section leader and friend, Parker. I felt an obligation to give it to you straight. We have to go now. I don't know how long you'll be here, but I got your personal belongings locked up. We'll see each other before you go home. No more temper tantrums. I want you out of here and on your leave as soon as possible. You're one of the best soldiers I've ever had the pleasure to work with. And that's a fact, not a compliment. The rest of the guys send their respects and say to hang in there."

Captain Miller was a man I'd follow to hell and back, and I was proud to have served under him. I learned a lot by observing and listening to him. It wasn't easy being an elite soldier and a caring human being, but he balanced both wisely and I respected him for that. After another round of pokes and jabs, they left. Their visit had somehow revitalized some inner strength in me. I slept that night feeling relaxed, and I had fewer nightmares.

The next morning, a clerk came from Fifth Group Headquarters, wanting my mission report. I dictated everything in precise detail while he scribbled on a pad in shorthand. I mentioned nothing about my personal experience with My Ling. They thought she was the fifth VC, and I said nothing to make them think otherwise. Besides, my report might never make it into the files if Major Small or one of the Board members read it, and I highly suspected that Major Small was anxiously awaiting my report. Fuck him, I just didn't care anymore. They wanted my report, and I was giving it — with my added opinions. What they did with it was their damn business. All I cared about was my leave time.

Later on in the afternoon, a captain who was a psychiatrist came to see me. He told me that the interview was a standard procedure for combat patients in the hospital. The interview lasted for about an hour, with him occasionally jotting down notes. His conclusive opinion was that I wasn't a nutcase.

I was awake for most of the night, thinking about that psychiatric interview. I didn't consider myself crazy, but I did acknowledge that I had some self-destructive habits. My relationship with Carol was destructive, and deep inside, I'd known that from the beginning. I'd always wanted her physically more than mentally because she wasn't very bright. I always ended up being attracted to needy people, and I always overcommitted myself to their problems and injustices. I tended to get myself so deeply involved that I didn't have anything left for myself, emotionally or mentally. Carol seemed incapable of love, yet I chased after her like a dog in heat. And I put up with a lot of emotional pain along the way, too.

I thought about Sergeant Becker all of a sudden. He was an acquaintance of mine who was involved in the NCO Club scandal here in Nam. Some officers and sergeants had conspired together to rig the slot machines in the NCO and EM Clubs throughout South Vietnam. Becker was a boozer with only a few months left before his retirement, and he'd been about to lose everything in his upcoming court-martial for being part of the scandal. He was given an option: by repaying some of the money, he'd be allowed to retire honorably with full benefits instead of getting a dishonorable discharge. He was given a week to come up with exactly four thousand dollars.

Around this time, I'd just gotten paid about five thousand dollars for my six-year reenlistment. Most guys reenlisting sent their money home to be saved, but not me. When I reenlisted, I held the belief that I'd probably be killed in Nam and never make it home, so I carried a brown paper bag with me and had the finance clerk pay me in cash. I planned on spending half the money in Nam, drinking and screwing. The other half I'd spend on another R & R to Bangkok, where I'd try drinking and screwing myself into the Guinness Book of World Records. I wanted to live the high life before I was stuffed into a body bag.

My plans abruptly changed when Becker came to me. He was literally on his knees, begging me for the four thousand dollars. He rambled on and on about his wife, his kids, and that he'd kill himself if he got court-martialed. He swore on his mother's grave that he'd pay me a few hundred dollars a month out of his checks until the debt was paid. A needy person had found me again, and I hadn't even had to go looking for one. Sure enough, I overcommitted myself. I took him at his word and gave him the money with no written, notarized agreement of any kind.

Shortly after that, we got separated, and I've never received a penny from him. Looking back, him swearing on his mother's grave was bullshit. He'd told me once that she was alive and well, living in Arizona, but I'd forgotten that until it was too late. Why did people have to be like this, so devious? Had our roles been reversed, I'd have made sure he got money every month until my debt was paid.

I really pissed myself off at times. I was endowed with good intelligence and common sense. I was even too logical at times. And yet, I fell for one of the oldest street-corner con games in the book. Carol and Becker were just two of the many situations in which I'd foolishly gotten involved.

I was raised in a one-parent household smack in the middle of the ghetto. My mother was a hard worker, but she was also an alcoholic who beat me a lot. I busted my ass as a kid trying to be the perfect person she wanted me to be, but I never seemed to satisfy her because she always expected more. Maybe there was a rational connection to all this, but I'd be damned if I could reason it out. What I could reason out, very simply, was that I had to stop this crap.

Drifting in and out of sleep, I thought about My Ling, missing her. She could have helped in motivating me to stop my self-destructive habits. I realized, of course, that ultimately, I had to help myself. But My Ling would have been such an inspiration had she lived. As it was, I had neither the motivation nor the inspiration to do anything. I cared about myself, and yet, I didn't care about myself. That was my present attitude and frame of mind. It didn't make much sense, but it was the way I felt.

The next day, I was x-rayed and fully examined. Captain Acker said I'd have mild headaches for a couple of months from the concussions and that I'd have slight pain for a time from my fractured ribs. He said not to worry because it was all part of the healing process. He added that things could have been worse, had I not kept my body in good physical condition. I asked when I'd be discharged to start my leave, and he said next week.

After leaving the hospital, I flew back to Ban Me Thout, packed my gear, and went to the transportation company I was assigned to in Plieku. After a short stay there, I was flown to Camranh Bay. The army flew me in-country to a place called Long Binh, but was sending me home from Camranh Bay. Fort Lewis, Washington was one of the receiving bases we went to after leaving Vietnam. It would also be my duty station with the 75th Airborne Rangers after my leave time was over. I had my .357 Magnum pistol packed after I got a permit to bring it into the States. Along with copies of my transfer orders, I had paperwork with orders to attend the Debriefing and Reorientation Program at Fort Lewis. This program was standard procedure for many combat soldiers, and it was designed to reorient soldiers to society for leave or discharge.

Chapter Seven

My stomach churned while most of the guys clapped and cheered as the plane lifted from Camranh Bay. I felt a great relief, knowing I was putting more and more distance between myself and Vietnam. At the same time, I felt depressed, realizing how deeply I'd miss my combat buddies. And I felt an odd sensation, too, knowing I'd miss the strange art of combat, of man-hunting, man-trapping, and living on the very edge. I tried limiting my thoughts some, because I was becoming upset and nervous on the flight. In forty-eight hours, I'd been processed out of Vietnam and flown halfway around the world to Fort Lewis. The base was overcrowded and chaotic with soldiers everywhere. You couldn't stop and turn around without bumping into another soldier.

It was early morning and still dark. We were led to a large mess hall and served a ceremonial steak dinner. After eating, a master sergeant told us that buses were outside to take us to the airport. I talked to the master sergeant later, while guys got their gear and boarded the buses. I showed him my Debriefing and Reorientation Orders, wanting to know where the place was located. He shook his head tiredly as he read the orders. He said the D & R Section was in the process of being moved from one building into a larger one to accommodate the backlog they had. He said it would be three or four weeks before D & R started back up again and they caught up with the backlog.

Three to four weeks took up my whole leave, I explained to him. Wearily, the master sergeant glanced around the area at the many soldiers rushing around. Then he simply shrugged, saying I wasn't the only soldier who was pissed off at D & R, and most of them just left. After stating this, he walked a few steps, then turned, saying, "If you want to leave, then leave." Then he walked away into a crowd of soldiers. Without a second thought, I grabbed my duffle bag and boarded the nearest bus.

At the airport, I bought a ticket to Buffalo with a changeover in Chicago. When the plane descended at the Buffalo International Airport, tears filled my eyes. I just couldn't express how good it felt to be back for a while. I had honestly thought I'd never see home again. I was still wearing my green class-A winter uniform, and I still had my Fifth Special Forces Group Flash on my beret. Sergeants and officers were mostly in the Fifth Special Forces Group. The other Special Forces Groups consisted of officers, sergeants, corporals, specialists, and privates. While I still wore my Fifth Group shoulder patch, I only had private stripes on my sleeve from being demoted. I didn't care, though, because this was the last time I'd wear the beret, flash and shoulder patch.

Walking through the airport terminal, I was excited and stopped at the first vacant phone I saw. I called home, and George, the stepfather I'd never met, answered. My real father divorced my mother when I was about five years old. While I was in Nam, my mother had sent me a letter, telling me she'd married again. She said George worked at the large Bethlehem Steel Plant. Talking to my deeply-voiced stepfather, I wondered if I'd like him or not. He sounded like a nice person, and I rattled off a flurry of questions. My mother was a registered nurse, but she wasn't home; she had gone to the store. I had no brothers, and my sister, Deborah, was a nurse, too. She still lived at home, but she hadn't gotten in from work yet. I was surprised when George said he and my mother had adopted a four-year-old boy named Maurice. Having an adopted brother tickled the hell out of me. George said he wanted to come and get me, so I hung up. I was smiling from ear to ear as I walked into the cocktail lounge for a few drinks.

The exact location of my home was in the small city of Lackawanna, nicknamed "The Steel City" due to the huge Bethlehem Steel Plant there. Lackawanna was only a few miles outside of Buffalo. I was born in Buffalo, raised mostly in Lackawanna, and spent a lot of time between both cities.

About two hours later, I headed for the main entrance of the terminal. Snow covered the ground everywhere, but it wasn't deep. Fifteen minutes passed, and then I saw a small, green, two-door compact car pull up with a man and a little boy in it. The man honked the horn and waved at me as he opened the passenger door. I dashed to the car, throwing my duffle bag in the back seat, and hopped into the front. About twenty cars honked their horns behind us as we took off. After several minutes of talking to George, I sensed he was a fairly quiet person. He was about 5'9" tall, dark-complexioned, slightly overweight, and wore glasses. I had Maurice sitting on my lap, and he quietly stared at and touched the ribbons and badges I wore. He was shy and hesitant, which was understandable. Maurice was a good-looking child, and he kindled a deep warmth within me. He made me realize how much I wanted a child of my own. Cautiously, I thought about My Ling, wondering what our son or daughter would have looked like.

At home, my mother and sister smothered me in hugs and kisses. When I'd left home, my mother had been living in a poor projects complex. Now, she had a nice two-story house with a garage. The difference in living status was like night and day. I was given the spare bedroom on the bottom floor. After a few hours at home, Maurice and I were the best of friends and inseparable.

Over drinks, George asked me endless questions about Nam, and I became apprehensive. I didn't want to talk about Nam. I didn't even want to think about that place. At the same time, I didn't want to offend George by not answering. Though my answers were tactful, my internal memories became full-blown, making me feel panicky.

I was the last one to go to bed that night. Before I did, I checked the bottom floor's doors and windows, making sure they were locked. I placed my loaded pistol under my pillow. A few hours later, I was still wide awake, peering into the darkness. No matter how hard I tried, I couldn't fall asleep. I felt leery, nervous, and tense. I became acutely aware of mixed smells in the house: tobacco, food, perk-coffee, perfume, and household disinfectant. I could pick out distinct, subtle sounds, too: the kitchen faucet dripping water, the sounds of the refrigerator, the ticking of the dining room wall clock, the furnace clattering, screeching car tires on the streets, a police siren in the distance, the barking of dogs, the crisp, clear beating of my heart, and the wailing wind blowing coldly against the windowpane.

In my mind, these sounds began to intensify until the noises were violently resonant and ear-shattering. My heart started pounding faster and faster. The bedroom started spinning as I erupted into an icy sweat. Mixed smells of the jungle slowly penetrated my nose. I started gasping. Deep, scarred memories took me back, plunging me smack in the middle of the hot, steaming jungle. I trembled. I was being hunted. The ticks of the dining room clock became the sounds of enemy bullets chasing me. The barking of dogs became the sounds of loud, crashing enemy mortars. The screeching car tires became the sounds of high-pitched screams. The wind blowing against the windowpanes became the chilling voice of death itself, beckoning to me, demanding my soul.

A tree branch, a pebble, or something slammed against my bedroom window. In a split second, I had my pistol out and cocked, aiming point blank at the window. About a minute passed before I started coming out of the frightening flashback. How and why the flashback even started, I didn't know. I didn't know how or why the flashback ended like it did, either. Maybe my survival instincts sensed that there weren't any hostile forces close by. Lowering my arm, I uncocked the pistol, but I still held on to it tightly. I was home, not back in the war, and I slowly realized that more and more. I felt depressed; I'd just had my first flashback, anxiety attack, or whatever it was right at home. I wondered what the neighbors and police would have thought had I blasted a magnum-round through my bedroom window. That was close!

This was the United States, not Vietnam, I kept reminding myself. I had no enemy here! I wouldn't be shot, knifed, or bombed here. I wouldn't be ambushed here. Right? I kept trying to convince myself that hostile forces were halfway around the world, not here. There was nothing menacing in Lackawanna or Buffalo, right? I'd almost convinced myself of all this when a terrifying voice from the depths of my being suddenly screamed, "WRONG!" Total logic and pure reasoning began rapidly assessing my present situation and environment. In seconds, my mental computations concluded that I was indeed wrong. The savage man that was created as a functioning, living machine within me showed that survival meant everything and all things. Survival equaled violence! Violence equaled savage man! And savage man was Nighthawk-One!

Nighthawk-One knew that the whole world was hostile and threatening. Lackawanna and Buffalo were urban jungles filled with drug-traffickers, drug addicts, pimps, armed robbers, murderers, and other dangerous elements. Nighthawk-One knew that violent death was just as certain here as it was in Nam. Violence was part of mankind's essence and a major part of its history. Nighthawk-One also realized that he would destroy any man or animal that threatened his survival.

Sliding silently out of bed, my senses once again became keenly tuned to minute sounds. I put on my pants, shoes, and undershirt. With my pistol held in combat readiness, I quietly checked under my bed. Then I checked the bedroom closet and peeked cautiously out the window. I considered the upstairs area of the house secure, but anyone on the bottom floor was the enemy, a direct threat to my survival. Coming out of the bedroom in a soundless crouch, I looked, listened, and smelled. In the darkness, I checked the bathroom, the den, the hallway, kitchen, dining room, and living room. I went down into the basement, checking every square foot before I came back up. I went outside in the freezing cold; snowflakes fell heavily to the ground. Walking around the fenced-in yard, I checked for fresh boot-prints, sandal-prints, and bare footprints. I checked the garage thoroughly, too, before coming back inside the house. My whole body was shivering uncontrollably as I walked back to my bedroom. Taking my clothes off, I dried myself with a towel.

While my tension slowly seeped away, I thought about my friends and relatives here. Could I still give them adequate friendship and love? Would I still freely accept their friendship and love? Was I still capable of giving and receiving affection after seeing and doing so much? I'd changed and I knew it, but was the change a positive or negative thing for me? I felt so mature and so knowledgeable, but at the same time, I felt used, like I'd been emotionally and mentally raped, like part of my true identity had been violently stolen against my will.

Vietnam was like living in a dream world, a no-man's land. A serious price was paid for trusting other people in Nam. And when you tried acting like a normal, emotional human being, you got ridiculed. I still remember the voices of some combat buddies after enemy kills, saying, "Cut off their ears or cut off their heads." This was a peer pressure chant that challenged one's male ego and savageness as a combat soldier. Guerrilla and counter-guerrilla training encouraged these types of acts as well as the unleashing of violent rage.

Civilian-reality and jungle war-reality were as different as night and day. To survive in Nam, I became almost completely emotionally and ethically numb. Many times, I only found inner peace by devising a dead space within my psyche where memories lived on, cut off from their emotional impact.

Combat GIs referred to themselves as Grunts, which symbolized someone who was no longer capable of thought. Instead of using the word "kill," words like zapped, wasted, terminated, bumped-off, and blown away were used. Many words were regularly used in the dehumanization of the Vietnamese people by describing them as gooks, dinks, slopes, or Charlie. Even Green Berets were labeled by other GIs as gangsters, rat-eaters, snake-eaters, crazies, hit-men, or assassins. It was weird, but there were slang names for damn near everything in Nam.

I thought about all this and more. I hoped I could still learn to love as much as I'd learned to hate. I was still having trouble getting to sleep. I got up and went into the den, where there was a large drinking bar. Behind it was about twenty bottles of assorted liquor. I took a full bottle of bourbon back to my bedroom. Sitting on the side of the bed, I opened the bottle and took a few sips. I had nothing in particular on my mind while I sat there, drinking in the dark. About an hour later, I got up from my bed, my pistol in hand, and carefully checked the doors and windows again. After this, I placed my pillow and quilt blanket on the floor beside the bed. I actually felt more comfortable on the hardwood floor than on the mattress. Putting my pistol under the pillow, I took a few more sips of bourbon, then went to sleep. I dreamed about My Ling. We talked, laughed, and embraced, even as the tears rolled down our faces. I kissed her sensitive lips and warm, salty tears, staring romantically into her eyes. Wherever I was with My Ling, I felt happy. *Do I have to wake up from this, My Ling? Oh, please, I don't want to wake up! Please! Let me stay!*

Chapter Eight

Christmas was only a week and a half away when I'd come home on leave. During my first week home, I stayed in the house. I didn't even walk to the corner store. I stayed awake for most of the nights, sitting at the kitchen table. I'd clean my pistol every night, read newspapers, magazines, and books, and drink heavily at the table. My flashbacks increased until I had several every day and constant nightmares when I slept.

During my second week home, I started spending several hours a day in the closet with my pistol. When I slept, I still had my pistol with me, along with my stepfather's hunting knife and my adopted brother's toy M-16 rifle. My family had gotten me new clothes for Christmas, but I didn't wear them. I refused to eat meals with my family, preferring to eat by myself in the dark closet or bedroom. At times, I would just stare out my bedroom window for hours while drinking. In the kitchen at night, I would sometimes glare intensely at my pistol, contemplating suicide. I started sleeping in my clothes and taking fewer baths. I was depressed, and I just didn't care about anything. The only thing important to me was making sure I had enough booze. The war was constantly on my mind, day and night, awake or asleep. The memories kept taunting me and tearing me apart inside.

My family became concerned about my behavior and often spoke to me about it. Sometimes they spoke in normal tones, and at other times, they screamed. I'd just listen until they were finished, then go back to drinking. The only one I felt relaxed around was my adopted brother, Maurice. He'd crawl up on my lap to play, or lie down beside me on the floor, or come into the dark closet with me to sit. My judgment started getting worse, and at times, I considered Maurice the child My Ling and I would have had.

During my third week home, I started venturing out of the house to nearby bars, stores, or just for walks. I never left the house without my pistol and knife. I avoided large crowds, public restrooms, and buses. In bars, I sat with my back to the wall so I could see everything that was going on. At night, I walked in the shadows, stepping wide around corners, and peering cautiously into bushes and trees.

During my fourth week home, I got into two fights. Both incidents were in bars in Lackawanna. The first fight was with a black guy about my age. He'd been in the Marine Corps for a few months but was dishonorably discharged for assaulting an officer.

In this particular bar incident, I was drinking by myself, as usual, at a table. The bar was half full, and James Baker sat on a barstool near me. For reasons of his own, Baker started yelling at me over the jukebox music. Cursing, he called me names like army-shit, scumbag, and asshole. He said an army man wasn't shit compared to a Marine. My survival instincts came to full alert, and I labeled him an instant threat. The barmaid and two patrons tried to calm him down, but he only got angrier. He yelled that Marines were on Vietnam soil first, not army punks like me.

Baker had touched a sensitive nerve. I could recall quite a few times when the Marines have needed the army's help. As for the Marines being first in Nam, he was wrong. Army advisers were in Southeast Asia as far back as the mid 1940s. In the late 1950s, the CIA and army advisers were in Laos, fighting the Communist Pathet-Lao guerrillas. The fighting eventually centered on Vietnam. Baker had evidently been misinformed, and by his yelling, I'd say he'd been misinformed about a lot of things.

Not being able to contain myself any longer, I started cursing back at him. The dispute was quickly settled outside. In seconds, I'd broken his right arm. About twenty people had been watching the fight, some from the bar. I went back inside and sat down to finish my drink. I kept my eyes on the front door, which was the only way in or out. I wasn't trying to kill Baker; I just wanted to hurt him. I wouldn't run away if he came back armed and with friends. I'd use whatever force was needed to protect my physical wellbeing. He could be calling the cops, demanding my arrest. I didn't care. Whatever might happen would happen.

Instead of coming back to the bar, Baker went to the hospital. He told the doctor he'd been drinking and fell down a flight of stairs. Two nights later, I saw him in a bar with a cast on his arm. I prepared myself for anything, always expecting the unexpected, but even I didn't expect him to do what he did. He apologized! He took full responsibility for starting the fight, and he added that he wanted no more problems between us.

Of course I didn't believe him. He seemed sincere, but so could any smart, streetwise person. Emotionally, I wanted to believe him, but strict logic dictated that time would tell, not words. He bought me a few drinks, and outwardly, I projected a relaxed state. Inwardly, I maintained full mental alert, still expecting the unexpected. Baker never bothered me again.

My second fight was in a bar closer to home. It was about nine o'clock at night, and there were only a few people in the place. I sat on a barstool at the far left of the bar, a place where I could see everything. Janet Smith came through the door and sat down beside me. Janet was twenty-one, about 5'6" tall, and had a short afro and brown complexion. She was slightly overweight with average looks. This was the first time I'd seen her since our high school days. I bought her a few drinks while we talked about school days and friends we both knew. She'd been married, had two children, then gotten divorced.

About an hour later, her ex-husband came into the bar. His name was Steve Bishop. He was about six feet tall with dark skin, and he had a big afro hairstyle, a big nose, and a heavyset body. What Janet failed to tell me was that her ex-husband was insanely jealous and beat her a lot. Even after their recent divorce, he still harassed her whenever he could. She'd finally gone to the police and got a restraining order. The order specified that he was to stay away from her and the kids or be arrested. That didn't stop him, though, because he continued harassing and beating her.

Bishop walked right up to her and started calling her a whore, slut, and bitch. My mind instantly went to full alert. Still yelling, he suddenly slapped her, knocking her to the floor. She was afraid and trembling, screaming at him to leave her alone. The old black bartender told Bishop repeatedly to leave her alone.

Janet was a nice person, and she didn't deserve to be slapped like that. At the same time, though, this was a domestic battle and none of my business. Even if she had asked for my help, I'd have reluctantly refused. Bishop wasn't being verbally or physically threatening to me, so I said nothing and did nothing. While she was still crying on the floor, he slapped her again. Hysterical now, she made a desperate lunge for my coat, pleading for help. I ignored her. It wasn't my business. Then, Bishop suddenly made it my business.

Seeing Janet tugging on my coat, Bishop got even angrier. Reaching into his back pants pocket, he pulled out a large knife. I heard a click and saw the shiny blade quickly snap out, a switchblade. Standing only a few feet away, he yelled at me to let go of his woman. I will never understand why he even said that! I wasn't holding Janet! She was holding me!

Bishop had threatened me, and there was no way I could ignore that. I was still sitting on the barstool with him off to my immediate right. I saw him out of the corner of my right eye and through the mirror behind the bar. He was working himself up to do some kind of physical act against me. He yelled that I was a dead man as he stepped toward me and raised the knife over his head. He was in aggressive motion, and I deliberately paused for a split second until the blade was just about to thrust down on my vulnerable neck. Still sitting on the stool, I angled my head, neck, and right shoulder sharply backward. With my drink in my left hand, I tossed it into his face. My right hand was already in motion, jamming his knife hand on top of the bar for a second. He was too close for me to deliver an effective punch or kick to his body. With my left hand in a fist, but keeping my thumb rigidly extended, I gouged him in the left eye. Bishop backed up reflexively, and I jumped off the stool, punching him between the eyes. His knees buckled and he fell to the floor. I didn't stick my thumb in his eye as far as I could have because the results would have been irreparable. His eye would be all right in a few weeks with daily eye medication. There was a bleeding gash on his forehead where I'd hit him. He was on his back when I stepped on his arm that held the knife. My pistol was already out and cocked. With my arm extended, I held it point blank in his face.

Janet was suddenly at my side, putting her hand on my shoulder. Weeping, she begged me not to shoot him. The bartender begged me not to shoot, too. Pointing the pistol toward the ceiling, I uncocked it and put it away. I glared angrily at Bishop for a few seconds, then glanced softly at Janet. I wondered briefly how the hell she ever got mixed up with such an asshole. I walked out of the bar and went up the street to another one to continue my drinking.

Both of the bars that I'd had these confrontations in were in the black community. The average black bar in the ghetto shied away from calling the cops to their establishments unless it was absolutely necessary. I was lucky in both these incidents that the police weren't called in.

I went into my fifth week of being home. It didn't fully register with me that my leave time was over and I was AWOL (Absent Without Leave). Between my drinking, flashbacks, nightmares, and lack of proper sleep, my normal judgment was becoming more impaired. I cared about nothing and valued nothing except my drinking. And I reverted back to staying in the house again.

At the beginning of my sixth week home, my grandmother sent for me. She sat me down in her house for a lecture on my behavior. I had to admit that my grandmother was an important person in my life. I loved her very much. I literally called my grandmother "Momma." As far back as I could remember, my grandmother was always good to me. She was fair, always talking to me and making me feel wanted and loved. She gave me the proper love, warmth, and discipline I should have been getting from my own mother. Needless to say, this brought about endless arguments between the two because they could never agree on how to care for me properly.

My grandmother's house was within walking distance of my mother's. I had only visited her a few times since I got home. I wasn't sure why. Maybe, deep inside, I knew that my grandmother still held influence over me. A good example was when I had visited the last time. I was drunk, dirty, armed, and angry at the world. I was still planning to go back out and do some more drinking. My grandmother was strongly against that. She asked only once that I spend the night there and not go back out. I did as she asked without question and without argument. Had anyone else asked me this, I never would have listened.

We sat at the kitchen table, playing one of her favorite games: Dominoes. I had a slight problem with the game because I was so drunk; I kept seeing twice as many dots as she did, and I almost fell out of my chair from nearly falling asleep twice.

I felt emotionally secure and loved around my grandmother. She could tame the savage man inside me with just an affectionate glance or a simple touch. Calmly, she lectured me about drinking and fighting so much. She suggested I find something constructive to occupy my time. After a few games of Dominoes and then checkers, I took a bath. I ate a full meal that she'd prepared for me. I was wearing one of my uncle's old robes while she washed, dried, and ironed my clothes, and I lay on the living room couch, watching TV. By the time she had finished, I was sound asleep.

Within the next few days, my grandmother loaned me some money, so I tried taking her advice. With the money, I went and leased myself a used brown Fleetwood Cadillac. Then I bought a small wardrobe of clothes. With my military license, it didn't take long to get my civilian license. I cut down on my drinking a bit; instead of being stumbling drunk, I was just plain drunk.

I started driving around Lackawanna and Buffalo, just sight-seeing at first. In Buffalo, I drove around the east side, which was predominantly black. I drove around the "Fruit Belt" and "Cold Springs" sections that I knew so well. I couldn't believe how the "Fruit Belt" and "Cold Springs" sections had changed, some for the better and some for the worse. Jefferson Avenue, Broadway, East Ferry, and William Street were basically the same. The young black women were gorgeous to look at as I drove around. More than once, I almost wrecked my car as I stared at their pretty smiling faces and shapely bodies. The next week, which was the first week of February, I started doing some serious bar-hopping. I was even going across the Peace Bridge into Canada, visiting some of the Toronto bars there.

One night, during the second week of February, I came home depressed and drunk, as usual. Once I was in the house, my mother and sister started lecturing me loudly about my behavior. My mother and sister were experienced experts at teaming up on me. As far back as I could remember, my mother had always favored my sister over me. My sister could do no wrong, whereas I'd been constantly told I did everything wrong.

The TV was on in the living room while I stood there, listening to them bark at me. My sister, Deborah, kept commenting on how embarrassed Mother was in the community due to the rumors circulating about me. My mother shouted that I was a drug addict, like all Vietnam veterans were. She said she was ashamed to look her friends in the face because of me.

I wasn't a drug addict, but assuming I was made it easier for my mother to rationalize my strange behavior. My mother was highly respected in the area; she was involved in several community organizations and functions. She was also a former policewoman and a former hairdresser. Once, she even ran for a seat on the city's Board of Education. Her true concern wasn't for me. She cared more about what her friends and neighbors were gossiping about. Deep inside, I always knew this. No matter where we lived, my mother always put neighbors, friends, and gossip in high regard.

When people were introduced to my mother, they'd feel that she was one of the most gracious and kindest human beings they'd ever meet. My mother was literally a genius who could dazzle most people with etiquette and intellect in just minutes. But I knew the other side of my mother, the dark side. She was not the easiest person to live with or be friends with, by any means. Her dark side consisted of raging anger, frustration, materialistic greed, and never wanting to be wrong about anything. She drank booze like it was water, and she was overly competitive in community affairs. Most people who knew her realized it was better to be a phony friend or acquaintance than it was to be an outright adversary. She was known to be cold and cunning when it came to discrediting someone in the neighborhood. I'm convinced that if the late FBI Director, J. Edgar Hoover, had known my mother, she would have had him peering cautiously over his shoulder, too.

My sister was a heavy drinker as well, and she was into abusing legal drugs. They would always team up to ridicule me, but they fought each other like crazy. Still, no matter how much they fought, they couldn't do without each other. They seemed to be dependent upon each other, emotionally and mentally.

I continued standing there in the living room, listening to my sister call me names in a loud voice. I listened to my mother calling me an ungrateful drug addict, saying I should have died in Vietnam. My whole body trembled, I gasped, and my knees wobbled when I heard that last statement. It hurt me. My mother's keen observation didn't miss my reaction to that last statement, either. Instead of backing off, she continued shouting obscenities like a vicious predator going in for the kill after wounding its prey. She told me I was an unexpected baby, that she had tried to give me away to another family.

Tears were welling in my eyes while I stumbled backward. I felt like someone had just punched me full force in the stomach. I just stood there, needing to disbelieve, but reluctantly believing. This answered so many questions about her abusive treatment toward me as a child when I was growing up.

During the few minutes that I stood there, I hadn't spoken a word. What could I say in my defense? And if I could say something, if I could suddenly comprehend my strange behavior, she wouldn't have listened. She'd never listened to me. Everything always had to be her way with no compromises. Damn it, I was pissed! I was powerless against her. She always knew the right buttons to push. I wouldn't argue back, and she knew it. I'd lost too many arguments to her and gave up trying long ago. I was seething with so much rage from just listening to her that it seemed to rattle my body and scorch the marrow in my bones.

She continued her screaming, stating that I was just like my real father: stupid, lazy, and no good. I couldn't take it anymore, and I staggered again, shouting, "NO!" Just as loudly, my mother responded, "YES! You bastard! You two motherfuckers are just alike! Just alike!"

The room started spinning faster and faster until my mother, sister, and the room were just blurry images. Bright yellow, orange, and red spots appeared before my eyes, then suddenly changed into flaming clusters. Then I heard rifle shots, machine gun fire, loud explosions and chopper engines. I saw dripping blood that turned into puddles of blood, streams of blood, and then an ocean full of thick red blood appeared. Human blood. I stumbled, falling hard to the floor on my hands and knees. I was breathing rapidly, chest heaving and sweating profusely, and I started crying. I was in a frustrated, helpless rage, and a firefight was swarming in my head. I was fed up. Fed up with being baffled and confused about the war, frustrated with the turmoil in my head, and tired of being defeated by my mother and this damn world. I had no right to be on this earth! I couldn't fit in! I wanted out!

At that moment, it seemed to me that only my physical destruction would stop the hurt in my heart. Peace was being with My Ling. Happiness was in her world. While on my hands and knees, time and space abruptly ceased. Mentally, I was in a dark void; I was neither here nor there. My pistol appeared in my hand, though I had no recollection of pulling it out. All I felt was the need to die. Dying meant relief. Dying meant escaping this reality by taking refuge in another. It meant the ultimate strategic withdrawal, with no hope of ever returning. Most of all, it meant being with My Ling, and I needed that desperately.

I started laughing uncontrollably while tears continued down my face. I had the pistol cocked with the barrel pressed under my chin. My hand trembled as I squeezed the trigger. *Click!* In my emotionally agitated state, I pulled the trigger several times, not realizing the pistol was empty. After suddenly comprehending that using the pistol was futile, I dropped the pistol to the floor. I hadn't known it, but before I went out drinking, my mother and sister had taken the bullets out of my pistol.

I was up on my feet in an instant. I staggered recklessly out of the living room, through the dining room, and into the kitchen. I wanted to die. The explosions in my head got louder, and the blood was thicker. The whole right side of my head was in piercing pain. I saw no knife on the table or in the sink to stab myself with. All I saw was a blurry quart container of Clorox with the cap off. I grabbed the plastic container with both hands. Tilting it to my mouth, I started gulping down the Clorox. Then, falling to my knees, I began rocking back and forth. Swaying and nauseated, I fell to the floor. I kept sobbing, no longer capable of feeling anger. There was excruciating pain in my head, and I felt totally lonely and absolutely hopeless.

I had no idea how much time elapsed while I lay there in the fetal position. I vaguely recalled pairs of strong hands lifting me up and putting me on a stretcher. Securely strapped in the stretcher, I was carried outdoors into a waiting ambulance. My family had called the police and ambulance to our residence. I was rambling incoherently in English, though at times I'd lapse into Vietnamese. I chattered on and on, giving radio frequencies, coded messages, code names, and map coordinates. I cursed Major Small with a vengeance in English and Vietnamese, and I became quietly complacent when I thought about My Ling. I was rushed to Our Lady of Victory Medical Hospital on Ridge Road, where my stomach was pumped. Then I was taken by ambulance to Meyer Memorial Medical Hospital in Buffalo. I was strapped to a bed on their psychiatric floor. My mother and sister came along, giving the doctors my basic history: age 20; birth 7/25/49; single; Negro; Methodist; male; unemployed; admitted 2/10/70; overdose Clorox; service army; and recently home from Vietnam.

They said that ever since I got home, I stayed unclean and liked sitting in the dark, mumbling to myself. They went on, saying I avoided social contact with guests, ate by myself, and only enjoyed the company of my adopted brother. And they said I came home drunk, argued about buying a car, and then attempted suicide.

My mother was good at covering herself, which is why she told them I was arguing about buying a car. The truth of the matter was that I already had a car, a leased one. I wasn't interested in owning a car. But my mother had to give them a reason about why I tried killing myself. She mentioned nothing about her screaming and verbal insults that really set me off. She wouldn't dare mention that because it would be detrimental to her sacred image.

The next morning, I was untied from my bed after talking to a psychiatrist. I was alert, coherent, and the doctor found no evidence of any acute psychotic ideation. In plain terminology, it meant that I wasn't a loony case. His final diagnosis was "pathological intoxication." I stayed in the hospital for one week before being released. At home, my mother told me the police had confiscated my pistol. For some reason, I've never believed that. I avoided thinking about my attempted suicide. Twice I've had the warped nerve to kill myself, and twice I've screwed up royally.

A few days after getting out of the hospital, I stopped at a bar called Maxims on Ridge Road in Lackawanna. It was after midnight and I was dressed neatly, wearing a black cashmere coat and a dark-brown, three-piece suit. The bar was large, crowded, noisy, and smoky, with the jukebox blaring loudly. The tables were full, so I sat at the bar for a while. About a half-hour later, I quickly claimed a vacated table near the wall. I watched the people closely while they drank, danced, and laughed.

You can tell a lot about a person simply by observing their body language. I sat there picking out the pimps, drug pushers, drug addicts, prostitutes, hustlers, and the ones with honest jobs. I observed numerous guys who were carrying concealed weapons.

After sitting for about fifteen minutes, I started noticing a woman staring at me. She was unwavering and steady with her stare, which was why I finally focused in on her. She was sitting a few tables over with a guy around my age. The guy sat with his legs crossed and arm around her shoulders. Looking at him, I knew he was a pimp. He was dressed in an expensive purple suit, black silk shirt, wide-brim black hat, thick gold neck-chain, gold watch, and several expensive rings. He looked to be over six feet tall, was solidly built, had a medium brown complexion with wavy black hair, and a morbid expression on his face.

Staring harder at the woman, I realized she was someone I knew. It was Carol Wilson. I barely recognized her with the fake eyelashes and mole, orange lipstick, blonde wig, and heavy makeup on. I'd thought about Carol many times since I got home, but that was the extent of my concern. Looking at her now, though, her face appeared pale and weary instead of vibrant and refined. Her eyes didn't sparkle with excitement like before. Instead, they looked hollow and spiritless. She seemed burnt out and sickly, not at all like the woman I'd known. When she saw I had recognized her, for a few scant seconds her eyes did sparkle. She wore a tight, red, low-cut sleeveless top that showed off her voluptuous braless breasts. Pleasurable times flashed through my mind as I stared at her protruding nipples. We stared emotionally at each other, our concentration and thoughts focused. The guy with her must have sensed a mood change in her because he turned unexpectedly toward her. Looking aggravated, he followed her stare until his eyes locked menacingly on mine. If dirty looks could kill, I would be dead in my seat. I ignored the bastard and continued staring at Carol.

It took a moment longer for her to realize she'd been caught staring at me. Seeming unnerved, she lowered her eyes to the table, picked up her drink, and sipped it. Then she took her lit cigarette from the ashtray in front of her and puffed on it. Her hand was shaking as the guy whispered something to her. Frightened, she looked at him and quickly shook her head from side to side. Then she gave him a phony smile, puffing nervously on her cigarette again. A few minutes passed before she slowly raised her eyes. She looked around the bar, sipping her drink and smoking another cigarette. Her hollow eyes gradually roamed back to me, and she began staring again. This time, she seemed prepared for the bastard next to her. Whenever he glanced at her, she'd swiftly divert her eyes away from me.

This cat-and-mouse game went on for several minutes until she got up and went to the ladies' room. She was wearing black leather knee-high boots, a black miniskirt, and red fishnet stockings. Her body was still stunning. She made heads turn as she wiggled gracefully through the crowd. About ten minutes passed before she reappeared again. Instead of walking back to her table, she passed it and continued toward me. Stopping on the other side of my table, she just stood there, staring. Her face looked so gloomy. There were healed knife scars and needle track marks all over her arms.

"Hi, Bobby," she said, awkwardly. Her voice was sensitive but hoarse.

Warmly, I replied, "Hi, Carol, it's been a long time." Her nearness made my mind go further down Memory Lane.

She looked nervously over her shoulder, then wearily back at me. "Your sister said you were back. I missed you, Bobby, I really did," she expressed sincerely.

"Is it me you really missed, Carol, or was it my money?" I snapped, instantly regretting my remark.

Tears suddenly filled her eyes and her hands quivered even more. Sighing, she said, "I'm sorry for hurting you, Bobby. Please don't hate me. We had our good times. You were always sweet to me, but I kept hurting you. I'm sorry! You want to kick my ass, go ahead, but don't hate me, Bobby!" She glanced nervously over her shoulder again, wiping tears from her face. "I didn't come to beg for money or anything," she said solemnly. "I just wanted to say hi, that's all." Again, she glanced uneasily over her shoulder. With some apprehension, she stated, "I'd better go. You take care, Bobby. I'm sorry I bothered you."

She turned to walk away, but I quickly called her name. "Who's your friend?" I asked. Leaning to the side a bit, I looked casually at the guy. He was really pissed off because Carol was talking to me. I simply stared back at him with a blank expression on my face.

"He's not my friend; he's an asshole!" she snarled back. Her eyes were fiery, and I'd obviously hit a sensitive nerve. "I may as well tell you before the gossip catches up," she said. "I'm strung out on dope — heroin." Glancing over her shoulder again, she nervously continued. "He got me hooked on the shit over a year ago. Kept getting me drunk, giving me pills, coke, then started shooting that junk in my arms. There's five other girls working for him, too, all junkies like me. He's a drug-dealer, pimp, thief, and all-around scumbag! A real fucking animal, Bobby!"

She worked herself up into a jittery frenzy talking about this guy. Still curious, I inquired, "Why stay with him if he treats you like shit?"

"Because I'm weak and scared, goddamn it, that's why!" she cried. "I've got a two-hundred-dollar-a-day habit to support! I can't do without a fix, Bobby! I just can't! He knows how to get the good, high-grade stuff. And besides that, he's a monster, and you don't fuck with monsters. He's got me selling my ass in filthy motels, pissy alleyways, and the backseat of anybody's car for a few bucks. I can't tell you how many times I've been tied up, beat senseless and cut by tricks. Three goddamned times I've been stabbed. I tried leaving him once. Know what happened? He beat me so bad, I was in critical condition for a week in the hospital!"

Tears kept flowing down her face. My intellect dictated non-involvement; but my emotions screamed with outrage. With a calculated coldness to my voice, I grumbled, "Sit down, Carol."

"I can't!" she snapped, flinching in fear. "He's going to kick my ass just for talking to you!"

In a louder voice, I repeated, "Sit down, Carol."

"No!" she blurted in panic. "No! Don't mess with him, Bobby! He'll kill you! He's crazy, I'm telling you! I've got to go! Goodbye!"

By the time she'd turned and taken a few steps, I was out of my chair and beside her. Grabbing her arm, I forced her back to the table. I pulled a chair out and pushed her down in it. Then I sat back down in my chair and stared across the table at her. She was scared to death. Breathlessly, she pleaded, "Let me go, Bobby! I'm in deep shit already! Don't make it worse, please! I knew I shouldn't have come over here. He's going to kill me for sure. I'm dead!" She lowered her head and started crying like a baby.

Looking over at her table, I calmly waited for this guy to make his move. Still glaring, he finally leaped up, knocking his chair over. He started walking in our direction. His twisted expression and eyes showed violent, psychotic rage. There was a bulge in his right suit-coat pocket that looked like a pistol. My muscles became taut, and my mind peaked in animalistic awareness again. *If this guy walks within arm's reach of me, I'm attacking him.*

With my martial arts training, there was a time when I could kill a man with just one blow. With my excessive drinking habit, though, I knew it would probably take me a few blows. I had no intention of trying to kill this guy, but if I had to use deadly force, I knew I would. On the other hand, this guy could easily stand out of my reach and pump me full of bullet holes. *Well, whatever happens, happens.*

Instead of coming around the table to confront me, he stopped directly behind Carol's chair. Bringing his left hand down on the side of her neck, he squeezed her neck muscle roughly. Carol shrieked in horror, her body jerking off the chair, then back down again. Her wet eyes were tightly closed, and her face was distorted in pain. "Yo, bitch!" he yelled in an angry, deep voice. "You one hardheaded ho! Get yo narrow black ass out that chair fore I stomp yo guts out!" Carol opened her eyes. There was a depressingly submissive look in them.

"Yo, the sister's chillin, man," I said. "Dig yourself and step off, brother." I spoke in black street lingo because I knew that was the only language he'd fully understand. In plain English, I told him that Carol was staying with me, and he should think about what he was getting into and just leave us alone.

He got angrier, surprised I had even opened my mouth. "Yo, what up, nigger?" he yelled. "You don't bum-rush me, tryin to strong-arm my bitch! Step off fore I murder you, boy! That's right! Me, Tyrone Jackson, the Ice-man, will blow yo black ass away! Step the fuck off or die!"

The jukebox was still churning on, playing a slow, soulful song. Most people had stopped talking to watch, while some eased away from the confrontation. The veins in his neck were straining and pulsating. With his left hand, he snatched the wig off Carol's head and threw it to the floor. Then, with his other hand, he grabbed a handful of her real hair. "Bitch, you bought and paid fo!" he boomed, yanking her out of the chair. He started dragging her across the floor by her hair. Carol was too terrified to scream from the pain or even plead for help.

I was already out of my chair and moving around the table by the time he had her on the floor. Seeing me, he quickly let Carol go and stuffed his right hand into his coat pocket. He was going for his pistol. Had he been a street-smart survivor, he'd have kept the pistol in his pocket and just fired. He would have nailed my butt easily like that. The split second needed to pull the pistol out of his pocket was the only thing that saved my life.

As he pulled his hand out of his coat pocket, I grabbed his wrist with both hands. He was gripping the pistol tightly, so I twisted his wrist down first, then backward behind him. His finger was on the trigger, and I could have easily made him shoot himself in the back. Twisting his wrist even more, I made the barrel point up toward the ceiling. His wrist snapped, and the pistol fired once from an uncontrolled muscle reflex. The bullet ripped harmlessly into the ceiling. He screamed, attempting to twist and punch me in the face with his other hand. I was still behind him, though, keeping him off balance, moving with the flow of his body.

I forced Tyrone Jackson, the Ice-man, to his knees. Holding his broken wrist, I came crashing down on the arm with my right elbow, breaking that, too. His short scream was guttural this time. Then I punched him, hard, right behind the left ear, which I knew caused severe dizziness. Moaning, he slumped to the floor. Taking the .22 revolver, I took the bullets out and scattered them on the floor. Then, dropping the pistol, I gave it a kick. It skidded across the floor, into the crowd, and disappeared. Pistols were valuable on the street, so I knew someone would pick it up quickly.

I was in a rage. I glanced around the bar, looking for Carol. I spotted her curled up under a table near the wall. Walking toward her, I kicked two chairs out of my way and pushed over the table she was hiding under. Snatching her up, I slammed her hard against the wall. Her eyes flew wide open. She looked confused and she tried to speak, but only low, rasping sobs came out of her twitching lips. "Listen to me, Carol," I growled. "I almost killed this punk for you. Get your shit together, you hear me? There's drug rehab centers all over the damn place! Kick the fucking habit, stupid, because it's killing you! What happened to the woman I used to care about? Look at yourself, you make me want to puke! Don't you ever fear that piece of shit on the floor again, you hear me? Next to God, it's me you better fear from now on! If I hear about you selling your body or buying dope again, I'll put my foot up your ass so far you'll choke to death! And if this punk fucks with you again, just let me know! I'll deal with him again."

I took a handful of bills from my pocket, about five hundred dollars. Stuffing the money down between her breasts, I said, "Use the money to get yourself started! If you need more, let me know! If you buy dope, do yourself a favor and buy enough to overdose and die on, okay?"

She looked so sad as she stared, ashamed, into my eyes. My heart poured out to her. I wanted to take her in my arms and comfort her, but logically, I didn't dare do that. To show her outright affection now would be defeating for her and me. Ultimately, she would mistake my affection for weakness and try to manipulate me. If I was going to help at all, I had to keep her thinking that I'd become hardcore. She'd never seen me angry or seen me fight before, and I knew it was startling to her. Hopefully, it'd help her raise serious questions about her present lifestyle. As for myself, I'd be wise to stay away from her. I had my own problems to deal with without committing myself to hers.

I turned to walk away just as two policemen came bursting through the crowd. One of them had his .38 pistol leveled at me. The other cop had a pump shotgun aimed at me. He yelled, "Freeze or die! Your choice!" Sighing, I put both hands on top of my head. I was arrested and jailed, charged with assault. My bail was twenty-five hundred dollars. My mother and sister said they had no money to get me out, which was a lie. My stepfather said he didn't want to get involved. My grandmother finally got me out after three days.

My family was angry and highly opinionated about my be-havior. As for myself, I was surprised that the tough guy, Tyrone Jackson, the Ice-man, who had a violent criminal record, would press criminal charges on me. I could have gotten away with self-defense if the cops had found the pistol, but I kicked it away. For the next week, I continued barhopping between Lackawanna, Buffalo, and Toronto. I couldn't care less about the assault case pending against me. *Whatever happens, just happens, that's all.* Tyrone Jackson might try to kill me, or he might be smart enough to pay someone else to kill me. I swear, if he messed with me directly or indirectly and I survived, his ass would be history.

Chapter Nine

It was Sunday afternoon when I returned to Buffalo from an overnight trip to Canada. I was hungry and stopped on Main Street at the Swiss Chalet Restaurant. I stuffed myself with chicken, knowing I wouldn't be hungry for some time. Several inches of snow covered the metropolitan area, but the roads and sidewalks had been cleared. Walking out of the restaurant into the cold air, I thought briefly about seeing a movie. I noticed a woman in an old, silver, dilapidated compact car trying to park in front of my Fleetwood. She started backing in nicely when her car suddenly bucked, sputtered, and zoomed backward. Her car slammed into the front of mine with a loud *ba-bammm*. I stood there several feet away with my mouth wide open. I couldn't believe it! She rammed my car! With that piece of shit she was driving, she rammed my car! I saw the dented, rusty door of her car begin to open. I prepared myself for an argument I damn well intended to win. *She'd better have every type of car insurance known to mankind on that piece of junk, too!*

Before the woman could fully exit her car, she became more than I'd bargained for. She was superbly shaped and breathtakingly beautiful, and that left me tongue-tied and dazzled. Standing about 5'7" tall, she seemed to be in her early twenties, weighing about 125 pounds. Her hair was black and shoulder-length with rippling curls, and she had dark Mediterranean features. Her deep brown eyes held a rare brilliance that increased the symmetrical beauty of her face. She wore a light-brown winter coat and black shoes with a black two-piece pants outfit and a frilled pink blouse. Jumping out of the car, she flung both hands to her face. She looked worried, and it seemed as if she were about to burst into tears. She kept staring at the dent on the front fender. "Oh, no! Oh my God! Not again," she moaned nervously. "I'll lose my insurance this time!" She was talking out loud to herself while I just stood there, looking at her. Then, turning abruptly, she noticed me standing there. She was fidgety and seemed afraid to speak, but she cautiously asked, "Excuse me, but do you know the owner of this vehicle?"

Though her voice was tension-filled, it was still nice and sweet to me. With a grim look, I glared at her, saying, "I happen to know the owner quite well. *I'm* the owner." I would never have been so blunt or looked so stern had I known her reaction would be one of sheer panic. Her mouth flew open, her eyeballs bulged, and she seemed terrified. Her trembling hands fell from her face momentarily while her body swayed. For a few seconds, I thought she'd either faint or start screaming hysterically. I quickly replaced my stern look with a gentler expression.

Glancing at the dented fender again, she seemed to relax a little and lowered her hands again. Sagging her shoulders in defeat, she muttered, "There's no need for a scene, please. I'm entirely at fault and I apologize. You'll want to see my license and insurance card, of course. I'll get them."

She looked really distressed as she turned away. Unknowingly, she was making me feel guilty, like I was a real heel. "Wait!" I heard myself saying. "I'm sure this can be settled without involving our insurance companies. It's not a big dent, anyway. Tell you what, let's get out of the cold, have a drink, and discuss this maturely, okay? There's a nice, warm nightclub right up the street. It'll help take the tension out of the air, and I could use a drink anyway. And with all due respect, I'd really appreciate the company."

At first she appeared doubtful. Then, as she tilted her head slightly, I glimpsed an encouraging gleam in her eyes. "Oh, well, okay. I guess it's okay," she said. "I'll just get my purse and lock the car." I stood there in shock, watching her lock the doors. The most desperate car thief in the state wouldn't be caught dead within fifty yards of that wreck!

At a table in the nightclub, we talked over drinks for about an hour. She was Italian and her name was Antoinette Tartaro, but she liked being called Toni. She worked as a secretary for a life insurance firm in downtown Buffalo. She was single, living on the west side in a modest apartment. She had no sisters and only one brother, and her parents had gotten divorced when she was fifteen years old. Her father and brother still lived in Buffalo, but her mother had chosen years ago to live with a sister in Italy.

Besides being beautiful, Toni was witty, intelligent, and refreshingly warm. I enjoyed watching her smile, seeing her deep dimples, glossy lips, and sparkling eyes. She was simply fascinating, and I relished every minute with her. She was dating a guy, but she said there wasn't anything serious between them. She let me know I was the first black guy she'd ever decided to have a drink with. After I asked, she wrote her phone number down for me. When she had to go, we walked back to her car. Watching her drive away into traffic, I knew I had to see her again and soon. I never would get around to getting the small dent fixed on my car.

I'd planned on waiting a few days before calling Toni, but I ended up calling her the very next day. During the following week, I took her out to supper three times. The week after, we spent four days together in Canada. During the third week, I moved most of my personal belongings into her apartment. She knew that I was a heavy drinker, but that didn't seem to bother her even though she only drank moderately. We went to the movies, musicals, museums, art galleries, and nightclubs together.

Back during our first week together, we'd become sexually active. We were constantly making love in bed, on the living room rug, the couch, in the kitchen, against the walls, and in other unique places. We showered together and enjoyed rubbing lotion all over each other. Then there were simple times, too, when we just played and laughed like two kids around the apartment.

By the last week of March, I was starting to feel miserable again. The little bit of money I had in the bank was almost gone. Without telling Toni, I'd even gone out a few times, looking for a job. I'd found none. I cared for Toni too much to be a financial burden to her. Finally sitting her down, I told her how I felt and why it was best I moved out. Her sudden fury surprised me as she tearfully cursed me. She was so infuriated that she hauled back awkwardly with her little fist, ready to punch me. I'd heard that Italian women were generally temperamental, but damn, I was speechless. I couldn't figure out what I'd done wrong. In between curse words, she said she didn't care if I ever found a job. She explained that it didn't matter if I ran out of money because she'd take care of us both. With her secretary job, and being able to borrow from her father, she said we'd be able to make it. She added that if she needed to, she'd get a second job to help support us. She said she loved me and that I'd hurt her when I started talking about leaving. I apologized, then kissed her after making sure it was safe to approach her.

124

I may have been wrong in talking about leaving, but I wasn't wrong about money. My belief was that without money, a person had no status in this world. Money bought necessary things as well as the extra comforts of life. To me, a person or family without adequate money was considered insignificant in this overly competitive world. Some people say that having lots of money destroys good homes, crumbles sincere love relationships, creates violence, and turns honest men into devious ones. This is probably true in some respects. Some people say that money isn't everything, and I also believed that to a certain extent. But I also believed that money was something that couldn't be ignored. I didn't want to set any unrealistic goals for myself by wanting to be a millionaire. I just wanted enough money to take care of Toni and myself. She was my good friend, my warm lover, and my charming woman. I wanted the best for her because she deserved it. She didn't understand all this, but I did. And somehow, I had to make her understand the importance of money, too.

For the next few days, I was drinking so much I could barely stand up or remember my name. I was depressed and worried about our financial status. To some men, this was the perfect setup — to lie back and be supported by a woman. I wasn't that kind of man and never would be. Toni got angry at me a few more times, but I couldn't help the way I was feeling. I felt worthless, too ashamed to even look her in the eyes. Here was a woman I cared for so much, and I couldn't even take proper care of her!

One night, during the first week of April, I'd just come in from a drinking spree. It was around eleven o'clock. I was tired, and all I wanted to do was sleep. In the living room, Toni sat talking to two men I'd never seen before. Both men had dark hair and mustaches, and they were in their mid-to-late forties. The shorter-haired one with the crooked nose wore a black two-piece suit and a white shirt. His heavier buddy with the double chin wore powder blue pants, a royal blue sports coat, and a black turtleneck sweater. I had no idea who they were or why they were there. All I cared about was going upstairs to bed. Toni and I didn't smoke, but we kept ashtrays handy for guests who did. Both men were seated on the couch, smoking, while Toni sat in the cushioned lounge chair.

She jumped up, smiling, and came over to kiss me, saying, "Hi, honey. This is Sal and Tony. They're close friends of my family." Both men stood up and came over with their hands extended. I shook their hands, and the one in the black suit said, "How are you, Mr. Parker? I'm Salvatore Amato, and this is Tony Greco. Like Toni said, we're old friends of the Tartaro family. I can still remember bouncing Toni off my knees and buying toys for her to play with. I can't get over how she's grown. Looking at her makes me feel ancient, I tell you."

Toni blushed and giggled as she put both arms around my waist. I was tired and only half listening to them. My stomach ached, my head hurt, and all I wanted was some sleep. "Mr. Parker," Amato said, smiling, "we didn't just come to see Toni, but you, too. We were sent on behalf of a friend. He'd like to meet and talk with you at your earliest convenience. This Friday night at about ten o'clock would be a good time. Toni's invited, too, of course."

I was drunk, exhausted, and moody. I'd heard what Amato had said, but I wasn't the least bit interested. I didn't want to meet Toni's family friends, now or ever. All I wanted to do was sleep, and these two guys were holding me up. With an annoyed and tired look, I replied hastily, "No, thanks."

Toni responded quickly. She looked at me with a surprised expression, saying, "Robert!" Amato and Greco both seemed to take offense at my reply, giving me slightly irritated looks. I didn't care. I undid Toni's arms from around me and went upstairs to bed.

About fifteen minutes later, Toni walked quietly into the bedroom and turned the light on. I was in bed, lying on my back with my eyes closed. Sitting on the side of the bed, she started massaging my shoulders. Then she kissed me wetly all over my chest. As tired as I was, I started getting aroused and opened my eyes. Looking into her eyes, I began unbuttoning her blouse. When the blouse was off, I undid her bra. Her breasts were exceptional and well proportioned for a woman her size. Her dark, rigid nipples could excite a dead man. I kissed and nibbled both. At the same time, I gently massaged her warm thighs while gliding my hand up her leg.

"Honey?" I heard her saying breathlessly. "Let's talk for a minute first, please? Then I'll undress and come to bed, okay?" I stopped gliding my hand up her legs, but I didn't stop kissing her breasts. "You got them angry, sweetheart," she moaned

"Who?" I mumbled.

"You know who. Sal and Tony," she responded, pouting a bit.

"Fuck them!" I mumbled back.

"Honey, please, stop. I can't think clearly," she gasped. "I have to tell you something. It's a secret I kept from you. I'm sorry, baby, but it's about my father and brother. They're into organized crime."

I choked. I gagged. My poor heart skipped a few beats. I became hysterical. "Organized crime?" I yelled. "Organized crime? Your father and brother? The mob? You mean the Mafia?" Toni slowly nodded her head yes. My eyes glazed over and I started hyperventilating. My mouth kept opening and closing like a fish out of water. "What about Sal and Tony? They're in it, too?" I asked nervously. Toni reluctantly nodded.

"Oh, shit! Are you nuts, woman? Crazy? I'm dead meat! I'm fucking history!" I yelled at the top of my lungs. I startled Toni by leaping out of bed so fast that she slipped and fell to the floor. I put my clothes on at record speed, yelling frantically, "Oh, fuck! They're going to kill me! They're sizing up Lake Erie for me right now! I just know it! Just my fucking luck! Of all the Italian women in Buffalo, I have to find one whose family and friends are mobsters! I bet they're really thrilled about a black guy living with you, right? They just want to talk, wish me good luck, that's all, right? They're going to kill me, woman, don't you understand that? Well, I got news for you! They want me, they'll have to find me! I'm leaving you, this state, the whole fucking country if I have to!"

I dressed so fast that my shirt was inside out, the right leg of my pants was stuck inside my sock, and my shoes were on the wrong feet. Toni was sitting back on the bed now, crying. She'd been trying to talk ever since I started my raving speech. "I'm sorry, Robert," she sobbed. "I should have told you before you moved in. Everything's okay, it'll work out. I talked to Sal and Tony after you came up here. I fixed it, honey. I told them I'd change your mind, so we can still go Friday night."

I was still upset. Sitting down next to her on the bed and putting my arms around her, I said, "Baby, understand what's happening here. If I go to this meeting, they're going to kill me. Understand that, will you?"

"Honey," Toni replied, "if they really wanted to kill you, they would have done it by now. I've never liked any of them or what they stood for. My mother left my father when she found out he was in the mob. They fought for custody of my brother and me in court, and my mother lost. When I graduated from high school, the first thing I did was get a job and move out of the house. My father and brother knew exactly how I felt. I love them, but I hate them for being with the mob. You don't know what it's like growing up overhearing phone conversations and arguments. It was terrible, some of the things I heard. I'm smart enough to know we should go Friday night. I don't want to go either, Robert. I hate those people. But if we don't go, they'll never leave us alone."

"Where do they want us to go? Who the hell is this friend they talked about?" I asked, feeling skittish.

"Let me try to explain it this way, honey," Toni said. "The whole Buffalo area is controlled by the Stefano Maggadino mob Family. He's controlled the area for a long time, even before I was born. I've seen him with my father a few times when I was small. On Friday, we're going over to Mr. Angelo Alfano's house. He's one of the Capos (Captains) in the Maggadino Family. My father's a lieutenant working under and for Mr. Alfano. He must be in his sixties by now, and I met him once when I was a teenager. It's more complicated than I can explain, but that's the way I've always understood it."

Her arms around my neck, she kissed me, saying, "Don't worry, honey, I'll be there. I won't let anything happen to you. They just want to talk, I'm sure of it. They're just being nosey. After we talk to them, they'll leave us alone."

Toni was confident about what was going to happen, but I damn sure wasn't. They wouldn't dare hurt her. It was my butt on the line. I was still upset as I sat there with her, figuring out what to do. It took about ten minutes for me to decide to go. Of course, Toni was thrilled about my decision. As for me, I wasn't thrilled at all.

Toni helped me undress because I was still a little trauma-tized. In bed, lying on my back, I watched her undress. In spite of my anxiety, I felt myself bursting with passion as she mounted me. The intensity of our sexual climax propelled us into a tranquil space between the very earth and stars themselves. A short time later, Toni was fast asleep, but I was still wide awake. Since I met her, my flashbacks and nightmares had decreased drastically. Only once in a while would I wake up in the middle of the night screaming. While we lay in the spoon position, I softly kissed the back of her neck a few times. With our bodies pressed so firmly together, I was hoping not to disturb her sleep. I adored having her so close to me like this, and I could smell faint traces of her perfume. I was surprised when I felt Toni rotating her sensuous body into mine. We made love slower and longer this time, until once again we'd attained the ultimate physical ecstasy.

Friday night came around and I was a nervous wreck. It was only eight o'clock, and I was already dressed in a black three-piece suit. I tried to slow down on my drinking so I'd be tipsy instead of drunk. Toni kept giving me pep talks all evening so I wouldn't change my mind. With her dressed in a pink blouse and a pretty, white, pleated skirt, we left the apartment around nine o'clock. All the way to the suburban town of West Seneca, she kept pep-talking me while driving. In a calm, patient tone, I finally had to tell her to shut up.

Minutes after entering the town limits, I spotted a late-model Oldsmobile following us. There were two men in the car, but I couldn't see their faces clearly. Most of the houses and apartment buildings we passed were middle class to upper middle class. We turned down another residential street, and Toni told me we were there. She turned into the driveway of a large, green ranch house with a big picture window and a double-door garage. The house had a big front lawn surrounded by hedges.

The garage door was closed, and through the small windows I observed the outline of two cars. Getting out of the car, I saw that the Oldsmobile had stopped in front of the house, its engine idling. Large brown drapes were drawn across the picture window of the house. A dark-haired, middle-aged man with average features stepped through the side door into the cold night air. Wearing gray pants, a white shirt, and a black sweater, he embraced Toni and kissed her on the cheek. Then, glancing at me with a blank expression, he suggested we get out of the cold. With him leading the way, we went up a few stairs and turned left into a large, modern, eat-in kitchen. Going through the kitchen, we entered the spacious dining room. From the dining room, we entered the large living room. Glancing behind me, I saw that the other end of the dining room led to a hallway with three doors and a back patio. Several men were in the smoke-filled room. They'd been talking in Italian but became silent when we entered. There was a man sitting in a black leather lounge chair to my immediate right, and I assumed he was Alfano.

He was short and slim with mostly gray, wavy hair. His skin was pale, wrinkled, and hung loosely around his face and neck. He wore black pants, a long-sleeved blue shirt, and a pair of gold-framed glasses on his face. He was smoking a terrible-smelling cigar, and I noticed that his feet barely touched the shaggy, dark-brown carpet. Amato and Greco stood on either side of Alfano, and another man stood directly behind the chair. One man stood near the front door. Off to my left, almost opposite Alfano, sat two men on a black leather couch. Both were casually dressed, and they were the only ones in the room who were giving me dirty looks. The older man on the couch — he seemed to be in his late forties — glared like he wanted to kill me. The man sitting next to him was in his mid-twenties, and he stared menacingly at me, too. I had a strong feeling that I'd just met Toni's father and brother.

The man who had escorted us into the living room sat down in the dining room. For a moment, Toni stood with me near the elegant glass coffee table. Then she rushed over, kissing and hugging both men on the couch. Looking a little nervous, she sat down between them while giving me a weak smile. My insides started churning as I stood there, not knowing what was expected of me. I was very leery and started to get a little angry because these guys were silently glaring at me like I was from outer space. By force of habit, my mind started calculating defensive options in case of a physical confrontation. I assumed that all of them were armed and dangerous. For a minute, I glared back at them, and my knees got weaker out of nervousness. All the defensive options I'd come up with seemed futile and suicidal. I'd only seen the men in the Oldsmobile outside, but I knew there had to be unseen men in the area, too. I didn't know anything about Alfano personally, but as a capo, he couldn't be stupid. He had to maintain a reasonable security level at all times. A responsible leader would never let an unknown person get this close without having unseen security forces close by, too.

In a scratchy, authoritative voice, Alfano broke the silence. "My name's Angelo Alfano, as I'm sure you're aware." Then he called to the guy in the dining room. "Bring Mr. Parker a chair. He's going to be here awhile." I sat down facing Alfano, my back to Toni and her family. I made sure my hands remained clearly in sight and open. Alfano crossed his legs, still puffing on the cigar, and bluntly asked, "Are you armed, Mr. Parker?"

"No, sir, I'm not," I answered in a nervous tone.

"You don't mind if one of the boys gives you a quick pat, do you?" he asked flatly. He pointed at Greco, and I stood up with my hands on top of my head and my feet spread. Greco gave me a quick but thoroughly professional patting, and then I sat back down. There was no way in hell I'd come here armed, and I believe that Alfano knew this, too. If they were really concerned about me having a weapon, they'd have patted me down outside or in the kitchen. Having me sit down, stand up, then sit back down again was a form of subtle harassment by Alfano. It was his way of telling me this was his show, and he did whatever he wanted.

Somewhat tiredly, Alfano said, "There's a serious problem at hand, and it will be resolved before anyone leaves this house tonight. You, Mr. Parker, stand as the object of this problem, along with Antoinette here. You see, we know about you two living together. It was brought to my attention by her father, Joe, and her brother, Dave. They're quite upset about this mixed relationship, of course. Joe's not just a made member; he's also one of my lieutenants. Dave's also a made member, so it's impossible to ignore their complaint. I felt the best way to handle this was to get everyone together in the same room."

Toni's father and brother were having tantrums because I was black, and therefore I wasn't good enough for her. They wanted the relationship stopped. I realized, though, that Joe and Dave couldn't rightfully touch me without permission from Alfano. Hurting or killing me without going through the chain of command would have been disrespectful to Alfano, especially if something went wrong that brought unnecessary attention to him or the crime-family.

"Do you love Antoinette?" Alfano asked, staring at me now.

"Yes, I do," I answered. "I love her very much, and no matter what the outcome of this meeting is, I'll still love her." I saw a slight, irritated twitch in Alfano's left eyelid when I said that.

"Speaking hypothetically, Mr. Parker," Alfano continued, "if Antoinette were in a life-threatening situation, would you forfeit your life to save hers?"

"That goes without question," I answered. I heard a low sigh from Toni. I wanted to look around and see her face, but I didn't dare do that yet. I was looking into Alfano's eyes, trying to figure out what was on his mind. He was an experienced pro, though; his face gave no hint of what he was thinking.

"Joe," Alfano said, "the floor is yours. You've chewed my ear about this long enough. The concerned party is here, so tell him what you've told me. It'll make you feel better."

Joe stood up, placing himself between Alfano and me. He fumed with anger, pointing an accusing finger at me, saying loudly, "I want this nigger motherfucker to stay away from my daughter! He's touched her! This fucking nigger bastard has touched my daughter! I demand the right to cut his goddamn balls off. Niggers are animals, the scum of the earth, and he's disgraced my daughter. I want this son of a bitch's balls to feed to the sewer rats! It's my right!"

Toni jumped up angrily and started screaming at her father in Italian. Her father yelled back in Italian, still pointing and jabbing his finger furiously at me. Toni rattled back a flurry of Italian words. Then her brother jumped up, also yelling angrily in Italian. Toni rushed over to me, throwing her arms around my waist, weeping loudly. In between sobs, she yelled something in Italian to her father and brother that transformed their anger into outright rage. I don't know what she said, but all hell broke loose. I saw it coming, but I did nothing as Toni's father punched me squarely in the jaw. Still holding me, Toni screamed as she and I went sprawling to the floor. Her father tried to kick me twice, but Toni covered my body with hers. They continued to yell at each other. Toni's brother dashed over and tried to pull her off me. He started screaming at her again. Whatever leeriness I had before somehow disappeared. I was angry as all hell. I wanted to get up and fight these two boneheads, but instead of getting up, I just lay there with the inside of my mouth bleeding. If I'd gotten up fighting, the other men would have surely jumped on me, too. And in the confusion, I could very well be stabbed or shot, leaving Toni's father and brother quite happy.

Alfano was allowing this whole scene for two reasons, I felt. Because they were made members, he was letting Joe and Dave release some of their frustration. At the same time, he was once again letting me know, rather crudely this time, that this was his show. I saw Alfano mumble something to Amato, Greco, and the man behind him. All three went into action: Amato restrained Joe, Greco restrained Dave, and the third guy pulled Toni off me. Joe and Dave kept screaming and cursing at me while they were being led back to the couch. Toni was still yelling at them both, and she sat on the opposite end of the couch, away from her family.

All three kept up the loud noise, pointing at me as I lay on the floor. Then, in a slightly raised voice, Alfano said something in Italian and the whole room became silent. "It was wise to remain on the floor, Mr. Parker," Alfano said with a sly grin. "Is your jaw broken?"

"No," I replied, taking out my handkerchief and wiping blood from my mouth.

"Get up off the floor and sit down," Alfano ordered. Toni and I had knocked the chair over when we fell. Tilting it back up, I sat down quietly. Alfano knew I was more angry than afraid, now. It showed in my face as I stared back at him.

"Do you still love Antoinette?" Alfano asked, his face blank.

"Do what you want; I don't care. We chose to be together!"

Alfano stared hard at me, then glanced over at the couch. Taking a deep breath, he closed his eyes for a few seconds. He said, "I was talking to a close friend recently, straightening out some business, and during idle talk afterward, I briefly brought up the subject of mixed relationships. He and I go back a long way, long before you two kids were even born. We're both aware that most things are constantly changing all around us, and if our structure is to survive and remain a serious force, we have to adjust with those changes in our society. Years ago, had I been confronted with this situation, you would have been shot down

133

like a dog. For the record, though, I've decided to let this mixed relationship continue."

Toni's father and brother catapulted from the couch, screeching their objections in Italian. Angrily, Alfano slammed his small fist down on the armrest of the chair. Amato and Greco stepped forward menacingly, facing Joe and Dave, who got quiet fast and slowly sat back down. They seemed to be enraged beyond words. Pointing at them both, Alfano said, "I've warned you both before. Never do that over a final decision, you hear me? Personal or business-wise, don't ever do that to me again or you'll both regret it. Understand?" Cautiously, they both nodded. "Hear me well," Alfano continued. "You both stay away from this guy, understand? Stay far away — no accidents, no disappearances, no contract hits, nothing! You sons of bitches kill him, and you both better kiss your asses goodbye. You want to go against me, then go ahead and kill him!"

I thought my hearing was malfunctioning. He was actually telling them to back off and leave me alone! My mind started to race as it tried to figure out Alfano's angle. What was he up to? Was he tricking me, playing head games?

"Do I make myself clear," Alfano raved on, "or do I need you two replaced?" Joe stuttered an apology. Toni seemed perplexed, and she told me later that she was worried not only for me, but for her father and brother, too. "This is why I made sure you two carried no weapons here tonight," Alfano continued. "Like father, like son. You're both hotheads, crazies. I want you two cowboys to shake hands with this man, then leave my home. This problem's resolved as far as you two go."

Joe stood up first and walked over to me. I stood up quickly, not wanting to be sitting in case he clobbered me again. If he did, I wouldn't strike back, but I'd be damn sure to block his blow this time. He extended his hand with a grim, disgusted look on his face. Squeezing the hell out of my hand, he said hoarsely, "By God, you take care of my little girl. You hurt my baby, there won't be a hole big enough for you to hide in." Joe's eyes were red, tearfully moist, and fiercely intense. I knew he meant, with a fanatical vengeance, what he'd just said. He walked out the living room, and I heard the back door slam a few seconds later.

I was in the process of shaking Dave's hand as he eyeballed me with distaste. "She's my little sister, my only sister," he grumbled. "I'm warning you now. You hurt her in any way, and you'll answer for it!" Then he left, slamming the back door. I sensed very strongly that this wasn't settled. They were probably going to find a way to get back at me, and it'd probably be something indirect so they wouldn't expose their involvement. I had to be more careful on the streets with those two maniacs on my case.

Alfano motioned with his hand for me to sit down. He said something in Italian, and Amato rushed out of the living room. Greco went over to a marble table, opened the drawer, and took out a manila folder. Giving it to Alfano, Greco resumed his position alongside the chair.

"Mr. Parker," Alfano said, "I hope I've been of some help. I'd like to know, though, if you have plans of marrying Antoinette in the near future?"

Toni and I had never discussed marriage before, but we did love each other. While some men didn't think marriage was a good thing, I actually preferred to be married. Marriage doesn't ruin people; people ruin marriages. Toni would make me a good wife, so I told Alfano, yes, I planned on marriage in the near future.

"I think that would be the respectable thing to do," he said. "Especially with her carrying your child."

Child! What child? Jumping out of my chair, I just stood there, gaping at her. "Child?" I mumbled in a squeaky voice.

Toni stared at me with sympathetic eyes, wrapping her arms around her stomach. "I'm sorry, honey," she moaned softly. "I was going to tell you. I wanted to surprise you, that's all." She's surprised me, all right! Now I understood why her family flipped out on me. *Hell, I'm going to be a father. Me! I'm I going to have a baby!*

She kept staring sadly at me, probably thinking I was angry. She was wrong. I started toward her and she met me halfway. Our arms around each other, she sobbed, "Forgive me, honey. I'm sorry, I'm sorry!" Holding her warm body firmly, I told her I wasn't the least bit angry.

"Excuse me, Antoinette," Alfano said. "I'd like to talk with your future husband privately, if I may. Would you be kind enough to wait in your car? I won't keep him long."

Toni glanced at Alfano, the folder in his lap, then back at me. "Don't be long, honey," she said, giving me a quick kiss. Then she kissed Alfano on the cheek, thanking him for his understanding. With a smile, Alfano nodded and gently patted her shoulder. Toni left. The guy in the dining room went out with her.

I sat back down, happy that Toni was pregnant. I also felt good that Alfano had ruled in our favor. I was personally indebted to him, and I'm sure he realized this. Amato came back, pushing a small silver-and-glass bar on wheels. He fixed Alfano a glass of red wine first, then poured me some bourbon. When he gave me the bourbon without asking what I preferred, I realized how closely they'd been watching Toni and me. After Alfano took a sip of wine, he placed the glass down on a wooden stand next to him. He put the cigar back in his mouth for a second, took a deep puff, then opened the folder, saying, "What I told Joe and Dave wasn't exactly the whole truth. I never mentioned the subject of mixed relationships to any of my friends. As a capo, I can handle this situation in any way I choose. I feel I've done that appropriately and objectively. I must tell you again, though; had this situation arisen years ago, you'd have died without question. Joe and Dave were well within their rights as made members to be upset about Antoinette. I'd hoped that in this day and age, with so many things changing so rapidly, and with Antoinette choosing you and with child, they'd have considered a milder approach. It seems I was hoping for a bit too much again, because they were their typical hotheaded selves."

He asked again how my jaw was feeling. I told him it was a little sore and had a small cut, but that was all. "When I first heard about you and Antoinette," Alfano continued, "I had a background check done on you. The results are right here. Being an Army Green Beret is interesting, you know. It lends credibility to you being intelligent, for a black man. Don't misunderstand that remark. Everyone is entitled to his or her own opinion, regardless of the subject. For myself, I firmly believe in intelligence in all races. My general opinion of black Americans is that they could be a much more powerful political force if they'd stop the in-fighting and petty politics among themselves. Personally, I don't expect

136

you to agree or disagree with my opinion. This is my home, so you're stuck with my views."

Turning a few pages in the folder, Alfano said, "You're trained in high-tech communications, small-arms weapons, and anti-terrorist tactics, and you're cross-trained in demolition, intelligence, psychological operations, political assassination, prisoner interrogation, et cetera, et cetera. You also hold a black belt in karate. It says here you worked closely with the CIA in Vietnam. All this is interesting, which is why I wanted to talk without Antoinette or her family present. To be blunt, I want to use some of your military talents. You'll be paid for your services, of course, and you'll answer directly to me. Naturally, I'll expect a code of silence concerning our joint venture."

So that was it. He wanted me working for him without his boss or anyone else knowing about it. Alfano was shrewd, and this had been in the back of his mind all along. I knew Toni and I could use the money, and like it or not, I was indebted to him. "I'll do whatever you want," I told him. "I'm indebted to you for your help tonight."

"I hope you prove to be worth it, young man," he said. Giving the folder to Greco, he sipped some more wine while I tasted more of my bourbon. He seemed to be contemplating something. "I do have a job for you," Alfano said suddenly. "I had two of my boys working on it, but I want you to handle it. There's a black businessman on the east side named Brian Walker. He's got a wall safe in his bedroom we want to get into. I don't want any valuables in it touched except for the stack of bearer bonds. These bonds, you'll find out, are worth three hundred thousand dollars."

Alfano explained that Walker was a business associate of the Colombo Family in New York City. He'd brought the bonds into the Maggadino Family's territory without consulting them. "The cheap punks didn't want to pay a percentage or be indebted to our Family, so they sneaked the bonds in. They probably got a buyer in the area." The Maggadinos had been tipped off by a Colombo soldier on their payroll.

"We know the kind of bonds they stole, so we're going to get them ourselves," Alfano said. "I've had worthless duplicate copies made up. It's simple: snatch the real bonds and leave them the fake ones. Walker's going to have to do some fast talking when they try to sell those worthless bonds. They'll probably kill him unless someone figures out they've been screwed by the Maggadino Family. Even if they do figure it out, we'll just deny it. They'll never be able to prove otherwise.

"Walker and his wife left today for a two-week vacation in Florida. They have no children, and he has no burglar alarms we know of. I hear he's got some type of electronic gadget in his bedroom, though. The more I think about it, the more I want a listening bug in his bedroom. What kind would you suggest? I'll have it ready for you in twenty-four hours."

If Walker didn't have any intrusion alarms, I figured that he didn't sweep his house for bugs, either. Off the top of my head, I came up with the picture-hook bug. It was highly concealable, supersensitive, and could easily be made from scratch. The average picture-hook bug was an inch long, a quarter inch in diameter, and had a picture-hook on the flat end. I explained all this to Alfano, and he gave me a sly grin for my choice.

"I haven't heard of that one," he chuckled, "but I'm sure my boys have. By the way, how about locks? Can you pick one with the right tools? And what about small dial safes — can you open one with an electric stethoscope?"

After I said I could handle both areas, he gave me three days to get the job done. He gave me Walker's address on Brunswick Avenue, and I memorized it along with Alfano's telephone number. He said he'd have Amato deliver the phony bonds, bug, and lockpick set to the apartment the next night. Before I left, he warned me about double-crossing or betraying him. He said my family in Lackawanna would die brutal deaths if I did. I told him he had nothing to worry about. Finishing my drink, I thanked him for his help, shook his hand, and left.

I drove back to Buffalo, and Toni kept apologizing for not telling me about the baby. She was happy with the way Alfano had dealt with her family, though. She explained again that she loved them, but she wasn't going to be pushed around like a little girl. Smiling and giggling, she smothered me in hugs and kisses while trying to tickle me so I'd laugh. She succeeded, too; I started booming with laughter and tickling her back. All the while, the car was swerving and rocking down the road.

Back in Buffalo, I stopped at a liquor store to buy a bottle of champagne and a bottle of bourbon. After a few drinks at home, Toni challenged me to another wrestling match on the living room rug. I gave up only minutes after we'd started; I wanted her to be careful with the baby. Besides, she had bitten my little finger, which I protested as unfair play.

After making love on the rug, Toni unexpectedly asked what Alfano had wanted. Damn! I was hoping she'd forgotten about that! I didn't want to lie, but I had to. She wouldn't understand why I was dealing with Alfano. We needed the money, and with the baby coming, we needed money even more. She wouldn't understand, but when the money started to roll in, she'd thank me.

"Oh!" I answered. "He just wanted to talk about our relationship some more, that's all. Everything's okay, baby. Everything's going to be just fine. You'll see."

"I know," Toni responded. "I just had a weird feeling he might be trying to get you to work for him. We don't need people like him, Robert. They're nothing but trouble, and they're degrading to good Italians. Now kiss me, my black knight, before I bite you again!"

The next night, it was snowing lightly. Toni was asleep upstairs while I looked out the window, waiting for Amato. I didn't want him banging on the door and possibly waking Toni. I saw a late-model Ford stop in front of the house with two men inside. Amato jumped out from the passenger side, carrying an attache case. Meeting him quietly at the door, I told him that Toni was in bed. With a friendly pat on my shoulder, he gave me the case and wished me good luck. Then he got back in the car, and it sped off into the night.

I checked out the stack of fake bonds, the electric stethoscope, the small lock-pick set, and the bug. I also added a writing pad, pencil, hammer, small pen-size flashlight, and a quarter-inch nail to the attache case. After having a few more drinks, I went to bed. Alfano didn't tell me how much I'd be paid if I pulled this off, and he didn't tell me about any legal representation if I got busted, either. He was letting me pull this job off alone, but I knew he didn't entirely trust me. With three hundred thousand dollars at stake, I knew I'd be under surveillance until he had the bonds.

During the afternoon the next day, I did some recon on Walker's home. Brunswick Avenue was a quiet area with well-built homes. I drove by the two-story white house he lived in twice and walked by it once. The temperature was in the low forties, the sun was out, and most of the snow had turned to slush.

That night, I told Toni I'd be going out at about three in the morning for a couple hours. When she asked why, I simply told her I had some business to take care of. She gave me an odd look, and I thought she'd push the issue, but she didn't. She spoke very little to me the rest of the night, and I didn't get my usual goodnight kiss.

It was three-thirty when I parked my car on Jefferson Avenue, a block away from Brunswick. I wore my black paratrooper boots, black pants, black turtleneck sweater, black ski cap, and a dark, navy-blue coat. Wearing a pair of tight leather gloves, I walked quickly but casually, carrying the attache case in my left hand. I didn't pass many people, and only a few cars went by on the street.

As I neared Walker's home, I checked his neighbors' houses for lights and any activity. I saw none. My biggest concern was being stopped by the police. Explaining the contents of my case would be impossible, and I'd be arrested on the spot. I'd be charged with possessing burglary tools, and the arrest would buy them time to find that the bonds in the case were fake and the real ones had been stolen. I'd be charged with forgery and possibly attempted fraud. Weirdly enough, I felt a sense of excitement, of gambling with the odds. I was living on that dangerous edge again, like I was in Nam, putting my talents and my life on the line to complete an assignment.

Without stopping, I walked up Walker's driveway to the backyard. Staying close to the house in the darkness, I waited for a few minutes to spot any activity around me. Seeing none, I walked up the four wooden steps to the screen door. It wasn't latched. The type of lock on the back door was a wafer lock. This type of lock was easy to pick, and in less than a minute, I had the door open. I stepped quickly through the door into a small den with a carpeted floor. Closing the door, I turned on my pen-sized flashlight. All four walls were covered in wood paneling, and a few cheap oil paintings hung from them. To my left was a floor-to-ceiling bookcase filled with various sizes of soft and hardcover books and stacks of magazines. In front of the bookcase against the side wall was a leather couch. In front of the couch was a wooden coffee table with scattered magazines on it, a half-filled ashtray, and a glass vase with plastic flowers. To my right was a small bar with two high stools behind it. On impulse, I checked out the bar. Finding an open bottle of whiskey, I took a few swallows.

From the den, I stepped into a large bedroom with beige walls and gold, floor-length drapes across the window. A gold quilt covered the king-size bed, which had two dust-covered gold pillowcases on it. Large dressers stood against two walls, and a floor stereo sat against another wall. The dressers had assorted items on top of them, and the medium-sized framed paintings on the wall looked expensive. I walked silently around the bedroom on the thick, dark shag carpet, observing the paintings closely. I found the one the safe had to be behind, but the painting wouldn't budge.

Remembering that Alfano said Walker had some type of electronic gadget, I noticed the black oblong box on the nightstand near the phone. On the front side of the box were five buttons. For several seconds, I looked at the picture, then walked over to the box. As I stared at the buttons from left to right, I decided to skip the first three. I didn't know Walker personally, so I had no idea about his thought patterns or behaviors, but I did know about human behavior in general, which is why I skipped the first few buttons. I guessed that the first few dealt with personal pleasures, like opening and closing the drapes, turning the stereo on and off, et cetera. If one of those buttons could move that wall painting, it had to be the last or second to last one. Luck was with me. When I pressed the fourth one, I saw the framed painting separate from the wall on three sides. Stepping over to the painting, I opened it all the way and saw the steel safe.

There was no dial. There wasn't a combination lock on the safe. After a few seconds of feeling surprised, I realized that this was all for the best. A dial safe would have taken me an hour or so to open with the stethoscope; I would have had to draw a square block graph on paper for each combination number. This type of safe made things a lot easier and faster for me. Going back to the box, I pressed the last button, feeling sure that it opened the safe, but nothing happened. I pressed the button again. Nothing happened. I stared at the last button, wondering what was wrong. Then I saw a toggle switch on the back of the box. I flipped the switch, then pressed the last button again. Bingo! I heard the safe as it popped open a few inches. Checking the safe out, I found several diamond bracelets and rings, gold chains, signed business contracts, a .45 automatic pistol, the bonds, a safe deposit key, and about fifty thousand dollars in cash. Walker's stash was seriously tempting, but I only took the bonds, replacing them with the fake ones as instructed.

After I closed the safe and put the wall painting back in place, I walked over to another painting and took it down. With the claw of my hammer, I pulled the nail out. Taking a nail that was a quarter inch in diameter from my case, I carefully hammered it into the hole to widen and deepen it. I pulled the nail back out and found that the picture-hook bug fit firmly. I hung the painting back up, closed my case, and went back to the den for another swig of whiskey. Then I left the house, making sure the back door was locked.

Getting into my car, I drove off, wondering how big the surveillance team Alfano had on me was. There were countless surveillance techniques that could easily be applied on me. I felt relieved and good inside for completing the assignment. At the apartment, I put the attache case in the living room closet, then went to bed.

I called Alfano in the morning, and he wanted to meet me at two-thirty that afternoon in the Peace Bridge Park. This park was small and close to the Peace Bridge, which connected the United States and Canada. The turbulent Niagara River flowed scenically by the park and under the Peace Bridge. At exactly two-thirty, I was slowly driving through the park. After passing several parked cars, I spotted the one Alfano was in. I parked behind him, got out, and slid into the passenger side of his car. I handed him the attache case, and he fingered through the bonds with a grin on his face. "Nice job, Parker. Good work," he said. "Those punks will think twice before coming into the area unannounced again. The bug's in place, right?"

"Whatever's said in the bedroom or adjoining rooms will be on the air, loud and clear," I answered.

"I knew you'd turn out to be a good investment," he remarked. "You're going to do just fine, Parker, just fine."

"Thanks, Mr. Alfano," I said. "Any time I can be of service, just let me know."

"I'm glad to hear that," Alfano responded, "because there's another matter I want taken care of on the east side."

Reaching under the seat, he pulled out a bulky manila folder and gave it to me. I looked inside and saw nothing but hundred-dollar bills. "There's twenty grand in there. It's yours," he said. "You satisfied with that, or do you want more?"

Alfano was testing me again. He wanted to see if I was greedy. I wasn't like that and didn't want him thinking it. "I'm more than satisfied with this," I answered. "It's very generous."

"I agree with you," Alfano said, laughing as he lit a cigar. "I've got plans that'll bring in more money for the organization and us, too."

He took a half bottle of whiskey out of the glove compartment and gave it to me. I took a few swallows and offered the bottle back. "Keep it," Alfano said, handing me a piece of paper. On the paper, I saw two names with addresses, and next to each name was the amount of money they owed. "I loaned these two punks money four months ago," Alfano grumbled. "I did it with no collateral up front, just a handshake agreement. Whatever happened to honor? It's getting to mean nothing these days. I must be getting soft for giving a few loans up front. So what happens? I get screwed! This is mostly Family money I'm messing with here, not mine. I want that money back — with the interest included. My boys want to hit these two punks, make an example out of them. I prefer a little diplomacy first to see what happens. They're both black, so I'm sending you to talk to them. Make them understand that not paying will result in serious health complications.

"The first guy, Thorton, is a criminal lawyer, married with kids. His home and business address are both on the paper. He's a good lawyer, but he likes the whores and horses a lot. I gave him twenty grand for forty back in three months. He's overdue and never tried reaching me, nothing. I don't like that. The other one, Robinson, alias Boots Robinson, is a drug pusher and hustler. The address on the paper is a bar he owns on the east side. He got fifty grand for a flat seventy-five back in two months. He's two months overdue. Try reasoning with them first. If they don't listen, I'll have them both hit and chalk up the loss. Try getting this done within a week if you can. If you need more time, just let me know. I'm flexible. By the way, how're things with you and Antoinette? Any problems with Joe and Dave?"

"Toni's okay," I answered. "No problems with her family yet, and hopefully never."

"Well, keep your eyes open and watch yourself," Alfano remarked. "Joe and Dave are going to try something as soon as they figure out a way to do it and cover their asses at the same time. I've got to go, but keep me posted."

We said our goodbyes and I got out, taking the bottle and folder with me. The next day, I drove downtown, still feeling happy with the money. The first thing I did was extend the lease on my car. I bought Toni two watches, an expensive one and one for daily wear. I also bought her an expensive gold chain and bracelet. We could pay the rent several months in advance now, and pay her credit card bills off. I'd give her a few grand for new clothes and some pocket change, too. Stopping by a supermarket, I bought four shopping bags full of groceries. My last stop was the liquor store, where I bought several bottles of bourbon and vodka.

Toni was in the kitchen cooking by the time I got home. I set the shopping bags on the kitchen table, and she peeked excitedly into each one. Surprised, she asked, "Ours, honey? Ours? Where did you…?"

Stopping her in mid-sentence, I gave her the gift-wrapped packages. Each gift brought a deeper and brighter smile to her face. In a joyful frenzy, she kept hugging and kissing me. The happiness on her face made my body tingle. Then I dumped all the money from the manila folder onto the kitchen table.

A dazed look crossed her face and she gasped. "Oh my God! Robert!" she panted. "Where did all this money come from, honey? What did you do?"

Suddenly, she backed away from the money like it was contaminated. Her eyes burning deeply into mine, she asked sharply, "Robert, you didn't, did you? You wouldn't." Still holding the dress watch in her hand, she angrily flung it at me, screaming, "Damn you!" Then she ran into the living room and threw herself across the couch, crying.

I rushed in after her and sat on the couch, gently stroking her hair. "Baby, let's talk," I said, feeling ashamed.

"I don't want to talk," she screamed. "You're just like my father and brother! Alfano's going to ruin us, Robert! How could you?"

"I'm sorry," I responded, trying to soothe her, "but we needed the money. With the baby coming, we have to be money conscious. Alfano asked me to do one small favor for him, and I got paid, that's all. Nothing violent, I swear."

"I don't care! I won't live like this!" Turning over, she looked at me, hissing, "No more favors or I'll leave. I mean it, Robert! I'll do it! I won't have our baby growing up like I did! I don't care about their money. We don't need it. No more favors or I'm gone! You won't see me or the baby ever again! I love you so much it hurts sometimes, Robert! You don't know how many nights I lay in bed worrying about you, waiting for that phone call that you've been found dead in some alleyway. That was how I felt before we even saw Alfano! Can you possibly understand how I feel now? Don't you love me, Robert?"

Toni's eyes were filled with sadness as she stared at me in frustration. Why was she making me feel so guilty? Couldn't she understand I did it for us? We needed the money, and once she saw the money, I thought she'd understand that. I couldn't let her know I was still working for Alfano. Right then and there, I decided that when I'd made enough money, Alfano and I were through. Toni and I would get married and put a down payment on a good house. By then, I'd have a decent job, even if it was digging ditches for a paycheck. "I won't go near Alfano or his men again, okay?" I told her. I was lying through my teeth. Telling the truth would have kept us arguing. "But don't ever talk to me about leaving again," I added, getting angry. "You didn't have to give me an ultimatum like that. Don't compare me to your family. What I did, I did for us. Hopefully, you'll understand that one day. Now, like it or not, that money on the table is ours. I worked for it, and I'm not flushing it down the toilet. You say I'm wrong, so I won't do it again. But give me a little consideration at least for caring."

Not waiting for a response, I stomped angrily upstairs with a bottle of booze. For the rest of the day, Toni and I didn't speak. By choice, I slept on the couch that night. The next morning, before she went to work, we both apologized for arguing.

Two days later, in the afternoon, I paid a visit downtown to Thorton's office in the Ellicott Square Building. I carried my attache case with me. After finding his name on the main floor directory, I took the elevator up to his office floor. Passing a few rooms and rounding a corner, I found his office. When I stepped inside, I was confronted with his secretary, who was busy typing. She was in her mid-to-late fifties, nicely shaped, with thick black glasses, platinum blonde hair, dark lipstick, and too much make-up on. She was trying to look younger, but the wrinkles around her eyes and mouth told a truer story. Her glossy red fingernails moved fluidly across the keys of the typewriter. Stopping, she peered sourly at me as if my presence were a rude invasion. "May I help you?" she asked in a sarcastic tone.

"Yes," I answered, faking a smile. "My name is Parker. I'd like to speak to Mr. Thorton, if he's in, please."

Fingering through an appointment book, she said, "He's in. Do you have an appointment?"

"No, but I'm expected," I responded, still smiling. "If you'd let Mr. Thorton know that a Mr. Alfano sent me, I'm sure he'll see me."

"I'd be disregarding my duty if I did that," she blurted. "Mr. Thorton frowns on being disturbed unnecessarily."

Wiping the smile off my face, I said, "Look, just buzz him and tell him Mr. Alfano sent me, okay? If not, I'll just barge into his office unannounced."

She snorted. "We have an efficient security force in this building that is very capable of handling rowdy people."

"Well, they'd better be damn efficient and capable if you expect them to get between me and that door in the next few seconds." I sat on the side of her desk, smiling and winking at her. By the expression on her face, she must have thought I was nuts.

She pressed the intercom on her desk and said, "Excuse me, sir. I'm sorry to disturb you, but there's a rather rude man here demanding to see you. He says his name is Parker, and he has no appointment. He insists he's expected, sent by a Mr. Alfano. Would you like me to call security, sir?"

There was no immediate response, but then a deep voice slowly replied, "Security's not necessary, Miss Burns. I'll see the gentleman."

She seemed surprised that Thorton didn't want security. "Thank you," I smirked, standing up. "Oh, by the way, have a nice day, Miss Burns." She gave me such an evil, venomous look that I actually felt a bit intimidated. I walked promptly into Thorton's office after giving Miss Burns another wary glance.

I closed the door and faced Thorton. His office was small. He was sitting behind his metal desk, wearing a gray three-piece suit and tie. Thorton was in his late forties. He was slim with a dark complexion, had short hair, and a thin mustache with long sideburns. He was wearing gold, wire-framed glasses, and he seemed fidgety, giving me a baffled look. "You're Parker?" he questioned. "You're black!"

"No shit!" I snapped in mock surprise. "You're black, too!" I pulled a chair up to the desk and sat down. "Let's get down to business, Mr. Thorton," I said in a slightly angry voice. "I'm a busy man with a tight schedule. You're into Alfano for forty grand, and you're a month overdue. I don't know the go-between you normally contact to get in touch with Alfano, but whoever he is, I'm sure he's been in contact with you. You had to be aware that Alfano would be sending someone again sooner or later. Well, I'm that someone, and he wants his money now."

"I, ah, I don't have the money," he said nervously, lighting a cigarette. "I need more time. I was going to ask for more time, but I never got around to it. You know how it is. Things get pretty busy around the office."

I gave him a level stare. "No, I *don't* know how it is. I'm here for the money, not elaborate excuses. Understand this right now: I can have you wasted with a simple phone call. Or I can have you crippled, and you can be a wheelchair lawyer for the rest of your life. I can be compassionate, too, and just have a family member kidnapped until the money is paid in full. If I have to leave this office unsatisfied, Mr. Thorton, you're going to be in shit up to your ears. So quit insulting me and let's get to the money, okay?"

Thorton looked desperately out his window, then back at me. "Please, I'm begging you. Just another month, that's all. Just another month!"

"No!" I answered angrily. "I want the money now or your ass is history! If you're thinking about going to the cops, I'll give you a ride there myself. Just remember that those Italian boys have a reputation for long memories. No matter what, you're not getting around this. What it simply boils down to is how you want to do it, the easy way or the hard way. I want the money now — borrow it, steal it, I don't care — but I want the money now!"

. His face flushed with anger. He took a noisy pull on his cigarette and glared out the window again. About a minute went by, and his eyes got watery and red. Crushing his cigarette out in an ashtray, he snapped, "I've got twenty-five thousand in the bank right now. It's all I've got to my name. I'll pay the remainder off in thirty days. Give me a fucking break, goddamn it. I've got a family and problems, you know."

"You've had your thirty days," I answered. "And voluntarily telling me you have twenty-five grand tucked away makes me believe you really have a little more. You and I are going to your bank — now. You'll withdraw thirty grand in cash for me, and I'll give you two weeks to pay the ten grand. After you get the rest, contact your go-between to Alfano, and he'll send someone to pick the money up. My offer isn't open for discussion. It's that or nothing."

I stood up and stuck my hands in my pockets, waiting. He stood up, too, and grabbed his overcoat and hat. Passing his secretary on the way out, he growled, "I'll be back in about an hour."

His bank was within walking distance of the building. I gave him the attache case in front of the bank and waited outside. It took about forty-five minutes before he came back out. He looked angrier than when he first went in. Unexpectedly, he flung the attache case down in front of me. It bounced off my left foot and onto the sidewalk. My toes ached; I wanted to bust every bone in his body. My insides shook in raging tremors, but I refused to flinch.

"There's your fucking money, you blood-sucking black bastard. You want it, pick it up!" he yelled. "You could have given me more time! You'll get the rest of your fucking money, but remember one thing. You're just a nigger flunky for that wop son of a bitch, and one day, he's going to drop you back in the fucking gutter where you came from, or else he'll kill you! I know his kind. I hope he kills you slowly, but if he lets you live, your young smart ass will be all mine. I'll get you for this! No matter what, I'll get you for this!"

People were slowing up and staring as they passed. A few even stood a safe distance away, listening. Thorton spun on his heel and stormed away. I wanted to chase him and smash his face on the sidewalk a few times, but I didn't move an inch. I was so enraged that I couldn't even trust myself to blink until Thorton was out of sight. *Who the fuck does he think he is, talking to me like that? Bastard!* Snatching the attache case up, I forced myself to walk away calmly. I stopped at a nearby bar and had several drinks to settle my nerves. At home, I called Alfano and made another appointment for the next day at the Peace Bridge Park.

The next afternoon, I didn't see Alfano's car when I drove through the park. I pulled over to wait, but I kept the motor running and cracked the window a few inches. For several minutes, I watched the water of the Niagara River rush by. I was still a little keyed up from the Thorton incident, so I closed my eyes and tried to relax. When I closed my eyes, my mind forcefully recalled past haunting memories, and the smell of death penetrated my nostrils. My mind fluttered recklessly through a series of war experiences in the jungle, and I could hear the shattering explosions, loud chopper engines, and chattering machine guns of Nam.

The place was Bong Song, where the 173rd Airborne Division was located before it moved to the Charang Valley. The special operations team I was part of then had just come down from a three-day intelligence-gathering mission in the nearby mountains. After briefing the 173rd on enemy NVA activity in the area, we decided to stay in Bong Song for a couple of days. It was here that Eddie Cole found me and died.

Eddie was black, nineteen years old, and from New York City. We met on the plane that brought us to Vietnam. We wrote several letters to each other while we were in Nam, and we became friends. Eddie had joined the Marines after turning seventeen. After that plane flight, we didn't see each other again until he landed at the Bong Song airstrip on a chopper.

Eddie was in an elite Marine recon unit and had spent a few days looking for me. For the first few hours, we drank and laughed and talked about old girlfriends and friends. A Japanese porno movie was about to be shown in a nearby shed, so we went to watch it.

The open shed was big. It had a flat, aluminum roof and eight thick, wooden utility poles evenly spaced around the roofing. There were fifty to sixty guys sitting inside the shed on metal folding chairs. Eddie and I sat toward the front, and each of us had a six-pack of beer. I was bent over in my chair, elbows on my knees, with a can of warm beer in each hand. Eddie was sitting straight up in his chair to my immediate left, holding a cigarette in one hand and a beer in the other. There was a lot of loud talking, laughing, yelling, and howling going on, and Eddie and I cheerfully added to the noise.

One solitary bullet came through the top of the shed, piercing the aluminum roof. No one heard it over all the noise. We never found out if the bullet was fired by the enemy or someone in the compound playing games. The bullet came spiraling in at a sharp angle, passing only inches behind my head. Had I been sitting straight up in my chair, the bullet would have struck the right side of my head, killing me instantly. The bullet hurled past me and struck Eddie in the neck. I heard him gasp, and at first, I mistook the warm fluid splashing the side of my face for spilled beer. When he grabbed my jungle shirt, I looked over at him. There was blood spurting out of a hole in his neck.

Men all around us started jumping up and panicking, shouting that we were being hit. I heard rifles clanking and bullets being injected into chambers. There was shoving and pushing as everyone headed for nearby bunkers. Grabbing Eddie, I threw him over my shoulder. Leaving my M-16 lying on the ground, I hurried out of the shed, my pistol in hand. Forcing my way through the confusion of running men, I was pushed off my feet to the ground. I got back up quickly, put Eddie's limp body over my shoulder again, and continued onward. Once inside the nearest bunker, I lay him gently on the ground. I put his head on my lap; his eyes were open, but he was already dead. I just sat there, rocking back and forth. I was drenched in blood. I blamed myself for Eddie's death. If he hadn't found me at Bong Song, he would still be alive.

The Marine Corps sent Eddie's mother a letter explaining his death, and I'd written her, too. Eddie was from a one-parent home like I was, and his mother didn't take his death very well. She had a nervous breakdown and was under psychiatric care for a few months. She wrote me harsh letters, blaming me for Eddie's death. It would take many years for me to accept Eddie's death as just plain fate.

My mind shifted drastically, and Major Small suddenly filled my thoughts. I wondered where the murdering bastard was and what he was doing. Wherever he was, I wished him dead with every fiber of my being. My body trembled as my mind shifted in rapid detail to my last ambush. I couldn't breathe. I was choking. Beads of sweat poured down my face. My heart pounded faster and faster, and I thought for sure it would burst. Suddenly, My Ling's mangled body vividly appeared in my mind. I cried out to her. I reached for her and yelled. My whole body was twitching, and I jumped so high that I bumped my head on the ceiling of the car. I'd accidentally honked the horn of the car, too, as I struggled against an imaginary force. Looking all around me, I quickly remembered where I was. I lowered my window some more and inhaled deep breaths of cold, crisp air to settle my nerves.

A few minutes later, Alfano parked directly behind me. When he got into the passenger side of my car, he was coughing and complaining about a cold he'd caught. I explained what had happened between Thorton and myself in detail. Alfano laughed loudly, patting me on the shoulder, and then blew his nose. "I haven't had a good laugh like that in a long time," he roared. "Thorton's got balls. Instead of threatening me, he ends up threatening you. He knew the setup when he came begging for money. We didn't go to him."

I gave Alfano the attache case. He counted the money and gave me five grand to keep. "Forget about Thorton and the rest of the money. I'll send one of the boys around for the balance," he said. "You're all right, Parker. I like you. We're going to do good together. Watch out for Thorton. Don't forget, he's a criminal lawyer, so he knows a lot of street punks."

We made small talk for several more minutes about the Buffalo Bills and the Sabres hockey team. Then Alfano left, but only after reminding me about Robinson. I took the five grand home, but I said nothing about the money to Toni. I put the money in a shoebox and slid it in the bottom drawer of my bedroom dresser. For the rest of the day, I stayed in the house, drinking and watching TV.

The following Friday night, I decided to pay Boots Robinson a visit at the bar he owned on East Ferry Street. If I couldn't find him there, I'd call Alfano the next day for another address. It was about midnight when I parked my car on a side street off East Ferry. The name of the bar was Touch of Love. I walked a half block to it. There were a few men standing out in front of the bar. Even on the street, I could hear music blasting from the jukebox inside. The men in front of the bar were talking loud, drinking beer, and smoking reefer. As I got closer, I heard two of the guys conversing about a woman named Marlene. They kept saying how Marlene could give dynamite head with her sexy mouth and tongue. They said they couldn't wait to see her again. As I walked into the crowded bar, I wondered who and where Marlene was.

The bar was big with a red carpet, brightly colored walls, and a long, L-shaped bar with a huge mirror behind it. All the barstools were filled, as were all the tables. Couples danced wildly while other people just roamed the floor. Thick cigarette smoke filled the air like smog, irritating my eyes and nose, and people had to yell to be heard over the blasting jukebox.

As I bumped my way to the bar, I got some inviting stares from a few women. Three pretty barmaids were working diligently behind the bar. The one closest to me was light brown. She had shoulder-length black hair with a streak of red running through it. She was in her mid-twenties and shapely, with an innocent, shy smile. I wondered just how innocent she really was.

I had no idea what Robinson looked like, so I hoped to get this barmaid to tell me if he was here or not. Waving and yelling her down, I ordered a double shot of bourbon straight. When she brought my change, I said loudly, "Yo baby, what's up? Where's Boots Robinson tonight? I owe him some money, and it's burning a hole in my pocket."

She stared at me for a few seconds, and I assumed she was trying to decide if I was a cop. Evidently deciding that I wasn't, she picked up a phone from under the bar. Ignoring a few people who were calling her, she asked, "What's your name?"

Pretending to be offended, I answered, "Yo, what's up, Momma? I ain't hittin' on you for your name, so don't stick me up for mine. I owe Boots some money, so if you want to screw your boss out of three grand, then cool, don't call him. I'll just keep my money."

She glared at me as more people yelled at her for drinks. Then, putting the phone to her ear, she pressed a button and whispered into it. I took a sip from my drink and looked around the bar while she talked. People were still calling her when she slammed the phone down and pointed at a door marked "Private." "Go to that door. I'll buzz you through, Mr. No-name," she said in a sassy tone. "First door on the right. Just knock."

Giving her a fake smile, I yelled, "Thank you, Sister." Just as cordially, she yelled back, "Fuck you!"

When I got to the metal door, I heard a buzzing sound as it clicked open. I stepped through into a narrow hallway and shut the door. The hallway was dimly lit by a light bulb hanging from the ceiling. I walked a few steps to a solid oak door on my right and knocked hard on it. No one answered.

Knocking harder on the door, I began to wonder if I'd been set up for an ambush. I purposely wasn't carrying any weapon because all I wanted to do was talk. Putting my ear to the thick door, I vaguely heard music. I still had the option to turn around and leave this joint, but I couldn't do that. I had to see this all the way through.

Still, no one answered the door. I started pounding my fist on the door, and suddenly it flung open. Damn! Oh, shit! Confronting me in a two-piece black suit was the biggest man I'd ever seen in my life! This guy filled the whole doorway and more, and was as tall as the door frame was high! He was huge! He had to be over four hundred pounds! His hands were enormous and oddly deformed, and heavy perspiration drenched his face and soaked his yellow shirt.

Hostility radiated from his eyes as he stared down at me. Cigarette smoke mixed with the distinct smell of reefer rushed out into the hallway. The instrumental jazz music was louder, and I gazed unbelievingly at this bulky, powerful force. Holding a lit cigarette in his beefy hand, he slowly brought it to his mouth. Inhaling deeply, he quickly exhaled, purposely blowing smoke in my face. *Why the hell didn't Alfano tell me that Robinson had King Kong for a fucking bodyguard?* The smoke had me blinking my eyes and coughing, which really pissed me off. As I focused back in on Kong, though, logic strictly dictated that this guy could be extremely hazardous to my health. I chose to resolve my anger through a more liberal form of compromise. Simply stated, I wasn't about to get this son of a bitch pissed off.

"What you want, motherfucker?" he boomed angrily.

"My name's Parker. I want to see Robinson," I answered.

"Yo, Boss," Kong yelled out. "The dude's here they called about. Gotta shake you down, man." I put my hands on top of my head, and he patted me down unprofessionally. Then he shuffled aside, allowing me to walk in.

The room was large with dark brown walls and a thick, black shag carpet on the floor. There was a couch, two lounge chairs, and two fancy wooden end tables with marble lamps on each one. In front of the couch was a wooden coffee table with a glass top. There was a stereo set in the far right corner with an 8-track tape playing in it. To my left, I saw two men sitting at a card table, smoking and playing poker. There was money, a pair of dice, ashtrays, a bottle of booze, and two glasses on the card table. Near the coffee table was a floor console color TV set. The room was well lit, had no pictures on the walls, and the only window was covered by curtains.

Stopping at the coffee table, I stared at the man and woman on the couch. They were into some heavy caressing and petting. I assumed that the busy man on the couch was Robinson. He was dark, solidly built, and in his early- to mid-forties with a medium afro. He wore a blue, short-sleeve knit shirt and black silk pants. A large gold chain hung around his neck, and he wore an expensive diamond watch on his left wrist, a gold bracelet on his right wrist, and a few rings on his fingers. He had to be about six feet tall or so when he stood up. The woman was in her early twenties. She was light brown, very pretty and shapely, with curly black hair just passing her shoulders. She was wearing a black miniskirt and a long-sleeve pink blouse, but no stockings.

They both seemed to be good and high, probably from alcohol, reefer, and coke. Over the sound of the music and the noisy poker game, I could hear them moaning and breathing heavily. Robinson's shirt was unbuttoned, and in a passionate frenzy, the woman was licking and kissing him all over his bare chest. Her blouse was unbuttoned, and she was not wearing a bra. He had her miniskirt pulled all the way up to her waist. She wasn't wearing panties, and he had his left hand working between her thighs in a slow gyration.

The wetness between her legs was evidence of the enjoyment she felt. I was spellbound by her sensuous body, glistening wet essence, heavily scented perfume, and the way she moaned and rotated her graceful hips. With no qualms, my body betrayed me, and I became aroused just by watching her. I began to fantasize about tasting her sultry wetness and feeling myself deep inside her.

My sexual fantasy ended abruptly when I sensed someone close behind me. It was King Kong. Glancing over my shoulder at him, I smiled, saying, "It's no fun unless I get some." I had to get someone's attention, and that seemed like a quick way to do it. I was hoping Kong wouldn't suddenly rip my head off. I was gambling that with his low mental ability, he wouldn't anything rash without checking with Robinson first.

"Boss? Boss?" Kong bellowed angrily. "Hear this motherfucker? Want me to break his face, Boss? Huh, Boss?" The two guys at the card table stopped their game. They stared at me, prepared to commit any act of violence ordered by their boss.

Robinson gave me a disgusted look while sighing heavily and withdrawing his hand from between the woman's thighs. He smiled and wetly kissed the woman. Then he picked up one of the reefer joints from the coffee table. Lighting it up, he took a few deep hits before looking at me again. He gave the joint to the woman, rubbing her soft thighs as he said, "You hawking my lady kind of tight, man. She's super fine, a cold-blooded freak, ain't she?" In plain English, he told me that I was staring at his woman. Then he bragged about how beautiful she was, wanting me to agree. Then he slid her blouse back, exposing her firm breasts. Touching them both, he smiled. "You want some head, man, a good fuck? She'll do whatever I tell her, man."

The woman smiled and flicked her wet tongue out at me. It pissed me off that Robinson knew I wanted his woman sexually. "You want her, man?" he smirked. "I'll let you two have the couch. Me and the boys, we just want to watch, that's all."

Robinson obviously got his rocks off by watching other men screw his woman.

I lied, stating, "I'm not interested in your woman, man. She's not my style."

Anger showed in his eyes and he wiped the smirk off his face. "You must be a faggot then, man. I don't like faggots."

The woman and the other guys laughed at this. Ignoring the remark, I said boldly, "Let's cut the bullshit and get down to business, okay?"

Robinson glared at me, then looked at Kong behind me. There were two whiskey bottles on the coffee table, one empty and the other half full. Picking up the bottle, he poured some whiskey into a glass. He gulped down the whiskey and sat back, crossing his legs. After asking what my name was, he said coldly, "Okay, Parker, my man, you wanted to see me, so you're seeing me. State your business or I'll have Cyclops bust your head open and throw your ass out."

So the huge bastard behind me was called Cyclops. It was a fitting nickname. "Alfano sent me," I explained. "You know the deal. It's seventy-five grand we want. If you're going to start lying to me, make it a good lie, okay? I don't need my intelligence insulted with petty bullshit."

Robinson uncrossed his legs and gave me a weird look. The woman next to him got nervous all of a sudden. I don't think she cared to be around him when he was angry. Cyclops was breathing harder down my neck, and the guys at the table stared relentlessly. What I really felt like doing was excusing myself and getting the hell out of there. But I had to play this all the way through, whether I liked it or not.

Glaring bitterly at me, Robinson snarled, "You got a smart mouth, young blood. I got the old dago's money, man. I got word he'd be sending somebody around. But I don't like your shitty attitude, and I'm seriously thinking about reneging."

"That wouldn't be a good idea," I countered. "Your crew wouldn't be nothing but light exercise for those west side Italian boys."

Jumping up, he yelled, "Why? Because we're black and they're white? You're an oreo nigger, black on the outside and lily white on the inside!"

Trying to contain my anger, I responded in a slightly raised voice. "Call me anything you want. I'm not insecure about my identity. What I said about your crew and the west side crew had nothing to do with being black or white. The whole idea of any war is not just knowing yourself, but knowing your enemy well, too. You're a good drug dealer, and you're probably a good pimp and hustler, too. But I don't believe you know shit about real organized crime wars, and dirty wars in general. I'm talking about having to check your car for a bomb every time you want to drive it. And not just under the hood, but the gas tank, under the seats, behind the dashboard, and unscrewing the door panels to check inside there. Or wondering if the car parked next to yours is rigged to explode when you walk near it. And every time you use your toilet at home, you'll have to wonder when you flush it if you'll be blown to bits. You won't be able to sit in your living room without constantly checking your couch, chairs, and lamps for hidden bombs, either. You could be opening your refrigerator in your kitchen and detonate a bomb. You could walk into your home, turn on a rigged light switch, and be blown up. You won't be able to stand on the street corner or sit near a window in public without a high-powered rifle zeroing in on you. You'll have to be careful what you light up and smoke, and what you snort up your nose, because it could be poison.

"All this isn't even counting the chaos that could be started inside your organization. One or more of your boys could be greedy and ambitious, or made to be greedy and ambitious by your enemy. All it takes is one guy with one bullet, and you're history, man. I could go on and on about dirty wars and their dirty little tricks. Seventy-five grand isn't a lot of money to Alfano, but he'll never let you live if you don't pay up. What you'd be doing, in effect, is committing suicide, and one of your boys would take over your operation."

I didn't mean to run off at the mouth, but Robinson had gotten me pissed off. I wanted to unnerve the overconfident bastard by telling him about the real world. The burning anger in his eyes told me I might have overdone it a bit. Reaching under the couch, he pulled out a worn attache case. No way in hell was I going to have another case dropped on my damn toes. I couldn't move backward because of Cyclops, but I was prepared to step sideways in either direction to protect my toes.

Instead of flinging the case to the floor, he flung it down broadside on top of the coffee table. There were two porcelain ashtrays full of cigarette butts, a couple of glasses, several joints, and the whiskey bottles on the table. Cigarette butts went flying everywhere, both ashtrays broke, the empty whiskey bottle broke, and the glass table-top shattered into pieces. As for the half bottle of whiskey, somehow it didn't break. What it did do was wobble off the table and bounce off the toes of my left foot, spilling booze on my right shoe and sock. I took this second assault on my toes as a celestial warning that money collecting wasn't my cup of tea.

"You're the fool, you wise-ass house nigger!" roared Robinson. "That old dago's got young college punks like you doing his work on the east side now, huh? You a college boy, ain't you, Uncle Tom? You sound like one. I bet you never even lived in the ghetto, college boy, and the only thing you really know about wars is what you've read in those college books, ain't it? There's your money, punk; you tell that fucking dago we're through doing business. Now get your greasy ass out of my face before I blow you away."

I bent over to pick up the case, thinking that everything was settled. It wasn't. Robinson suddenly backhanded me across the face. I flung my body backward instinctively, forgetting that Cyclops was behind me. Slamming into him was like backing into a brick wall. My knees almost buckled as pain shot through my lower back from the impact. I still had the case in my arms, and I hugged it tightly to my chest. There was no way I was letting go of that case. Cyclops wrapped his beefy arms around me, jerking me off the floor. The case collapsed against my chest, and the two metal fasteners popped open. His powerful arms felt like a steel vise around my chest. I couldn't breathe. He was going to kill me.

"Don't kill him, Cyclops," Robinson said, laughing. "He might be the old dago's favorite pet nigger. I don't want to send him a dead man. I just want to piss the old weasel off a little, that's all."

Cyclops let my feet touch the floor again, easing the enormous pressure on my chest. I was weak and dizzy, hoarsely gulping air into my painful lungs. Walking around the coffee table, Robinson punched me in the stomach twice. I grunted loudly with each blow, and both times, my insides quivered. I became nauseated and dizzy, and things around me got blurry.

My eyes were half closed. I heard the woman suddenly yell out, "Let me hit him too, baby, let me beat him up! I want to see his blood. I want to see him bleed good, baby." She was crazy! The drugs and booze had to be warping her brain or something! She punched me in the face and made my nose bleed. Then the bitch punched me in the left eye and gave me a left uppercut to the jaw. She spit in my face, not just once, but twice. Then she kneed me in the groin, eliciting a short screech from me. I was hurting badly as the woman slapped my face several times, screaming, "Leave my man alone, asshole! Leave him alone, you hear me?"

Her stinging slaps cut the inside of my mouth in a few places, including my upper lip. Blood from my nose and mouth was splattered all over my face and clothes. The right side of my head hurt, my left eye was swollen, my back hurt, and my whole ribcage ached terribly. I was a mess, but I'd taken beatings before, and I was determined to get through this one. No matter what happened, I wasn't letting go of that case unless I was dead or unconscious.

I could still hear Robinson laughing as he told Cyclops to throw me out. Cyclops let me go, and I dropped helplessly to the floor. Roughly grabbing a handful of my suit coat, he dragged me across the rug. The door was held open, and I was kicked a few times as Cyclops dragged me out. I was hauled down the hallway to the last door on the left. Cyclops let me go to unlock the door with a key. He went down a small hallway with a steel door at the other end. After he unlocked that door, he came back and dragged me through both doors, right into an alley. The alley was full of garbage, beer cans, weeds, paper litter, and broken liquor bottles. The stench of urine, cheap booze, and dog waste smothered the air. After dumping me in the alley, Cyclops disappeared back inside.

I lay there drifting in and out of consciousness for a while. Several yards up the alley was the sidewalk and street, where I saw blurry people and cars passing by. I dropped my head back down to the ground; I was in too much pain to move. Then it started. Increased pain ripped through my head. Blinding explosions went off as a hail of imaginary bullets zipped by me. Breathing harder, my heart thumping wildly, I looked around desperately for my weapon. I couldn't find it. I was unarmed. No rifle, no grenades, no knife, nothing. Physically, I was awake in a cold alley, but mentally, I was back in Nam in the A-Shau Valley. I was surrounded by the enemy, and they kept dropping mortars and machine gun fire on me. My body was trembling and jerking from the concussion of each explosion. I heard buzzing bullets ricocheting and inching closer to my position. Frantically, I looked down the other end of the alley, seeking escape.

"Oh, no, no, no!" They were back! Oh, my God! Dozens of dead NVA and VC soldiers. They were back! Crowded into the alley, they were coming for me in slow motion. A grayish, glowing mist encircled them all as they slowly edged closer and closer. All of them were armed with rifles and bayonets, and some of them limped, crawled, and moved like zombies. Blood flowed endlessly from their eyeless sockets and mouths. I wanted my dark side to appear like never before. For once, I honestly wanted to become Nighthawk-One. Only my altered self could look death fearlessly in the eyes with recognition and acceptance.

These dead, vengeful soldiers didn't just want my life; they wanted my very soul, too. In possessing my soul, they'd make me an everlasting member of their eternal death march. The closer they inched, the more terrified I became.

It was uncontrollable panic and fear that prompted my body to move. I was too horrified to stay still and be captured by the very soldiers I'd killed. Now oblivious to my pain and dizziness, I started crawling toward the street. Somehow, still holding the attache case in one arm, I kept moving forward through the filthy debris. Sheer panic and horrifying fear attacked my mind savagely, driving my emotions to their limits.

Still flat on my stomach, I finally made it out of the alleyway and onto the sidewalk. About a dozen or so yards away to my left, there were still people in front of the bar. To my right, several yards down, stood a few teenagers drinking beer. Seeing me crawl out of the alley like a wild man had startled them.

My clothes were soaking wet and ripped. The horrid smell of the alley was in my clothes and on my skin. I tried to get to my feet, but my knees collapsed and I fell back down. I stubbornly struggled to stand up again, and finally, I did it. This area was dangerous. I had to move before I was robbed, killed, or both.

Leaning against a brick building with my head swirling, I started vomiting. The teenagers stared while only a few of the older people looked on from the other group. Cars sped up and down East Ferry while I weakly clutched the attache case to my chest. I wasn't in any shape to drive my car, but I still had to get out of the area fast. Pulling a hundred-dollar bill out of my pocket, I waved it at the teenagers. "Yo, young brothers! Stop me a cab and this is yours!" I groaned.

They ran out into the street, yelling and screaming, and waited anxiously for an empty cab to come by. A few minutes later, they stopped a cab rather abruptly. The cab driver was cursing them as I staggered up to his window. I gave the hundred-dollar bill to the teenagers and a fifty-dollar bill to the cab driver. I told him I'd been mugged and wanted to get home fast. I gave him my address on the west side and slid into the back seat.

About twenty minutes later, the cabby pulled up in front of the apartment. I'd already told him to keep the whole fifty if he helped me to the door. After unlocking the door, I stumbled into the kitchen and tossed the case on the table. The light was on in the living room, along with the TV. My body was sore and aching, and all I wanted to do was take a hot bath in Epsom salt. I slowly took off my shirt and pants as I stumbled into the living room. Toni was sitting on the couch with a glass of vodka in her hand. On the coffee table sat a half bottle of vodka. I'd been noticing recently that Toni had been drinking more and more. Wearing a long white bathrobe, she sat with her legs crossed and her hair in curlers. Her face was red, her eyes watery and bloodshot. She was staring at the TV, practically hypnotized, and I wondered if she even knew what the movie was about. The glass she held in her hand fell to the floor when she saw me. She screamed, "Oh, my God! Robert!"

My nose and mouth had stopped bleeding, but my lip and left eye were still swollen. And I'd scraped some skin off my knees and elbows. Most of the muscles and bones in my body ached. I raised my hand, almost whispering, "Toni, please! Stop screaming before the neighbors think I'm killing you in here."

"Fuck the neighbors!" she yelled, rushing over to me. "My dear God, are you shot or stabbed? Where does it hurt, honey? What happened, Robert?"

"Take it easy," I moaned. "I'm hurting, but it's not as bad as it looks. I got beat up, that's all, baby. Help me upstairs to the bathtub."

On the way upstairs, she blurted, "Let me take you to the hospital. You could have broken bones or internal bleeding, honey!"

"No," I grumbled, "no hospital. I'll be all right in a few days. I just need to rest."

Still upset, she said, "I'm calling Dr. Rubenstein. He's helped people for my father and Alfano before. It's all off the record, honey, he won't say anything."

"No!" I moaned. "No doctor! I'll be okay. I just need a bath and rest, that's all."

In the bathroom, Toni ran hot water in the tub. She sprinkled in some Epsom salt, then helped me undress. She gave me a couple of strong pain pills, and brought me a towel with ice cubes in it. I moved the towel between my eye, my lip, and the side of my head. The water felt soothing as Toni tenderly washed my body. She was weeping and chattering in Italian. After my bath, she threw all the clothes I'd been wearing in the garbage. Then she got into bed with me, pressing her body against mine. She was still weeping and talking rapidly in Italian until she fell asleep. She hadn't said anything outright to me, but I knew she was angry as hell. What could I say? I had no real defense. All I knew in my heart was that I loved and needed her.

For the next couple of days, Toni stayed home from work to nurse me. She brought my car home. Luckily, it hadn't been stolen or broken into. Between the hot baths, pain pills, ointment and food, I started to feel better. My ribs weren't broken, but they still hurt. I kept noticing, too, that the better I got, the more moody Toni got. I'd already called Alfano and told him what happened. It was agreed that I could wait to give him the money until I got better. I'd decided that Boots Robinson was a dead man. I wouldn't kill him quickly, either; I'd torture him slowly with a pair of pliers and a razor blade. He should have killed me when he had the chance.

A few more days went by. I'd been in the house all this time, recuperating. Toni was getting more and more unbearable to deal with. She was argumentative over minor things, constantly drinking, and had sudden, cursing tantrums at times. She knew I was still dealing with Alfano, but she hadn't confronted me about it yet.

After a week, Toni came home from work and all hell broke loose. She was slightly drunk when she walked through the door. I had already cooked supper, and I was stretched out on the couch, half asleep. Stomping into the living room, she threw her purse on the chair and took off her coat. "Robert, wake up! Wake up, now! We're going to talk!"

I mumbled, "What? What happened?"

Sitting down, hands on her lap with her fingers entwined, Toni said nervously, "I'm leaving you, Robert!"

Surprised, I sat up, not knowing if she was serious or not. Her tearful red eyes and flushed face looked ominous. Did she mean it, or was she just using a scare tactic on me? "You're leaving me?" I asked, stunned.

"You heard me," Toni snapped. "I'm leaving you, my father, and brother. I'm going to Italy to live with my mother. I've talked to her on the phone, and she wants me to come, Robert."

I said nothing. I just sat there, bewildered. How could she leave me? I knew she was angry because I was dealing with

Alfano, but leave me? I looked at her, feeling a grieving desperation, and then sadly lowered my eyes. Toni stood up and rubbed her trembling hands together, pacing back and forth across the room. "I don't want to fight, Robert," she said sternly. "This is hard enough as it is, so just listen, please. I love you, but I can't live like this anymore. First my father, then my brother, now you. You're all involved up to your ears in criminal stuff. I hate Maggadino and Alfano. I hate them all. They tore my family apart, and now they're tearing us apart, Robert! I love you, but I can't marry a man involved with people like that. I just can't. And I won't." Toni continued, saying she grew up worrying herself sick about her father being shot or his car blowing up one day. She said she worried herself right into a nervous breakdown when she was seventeen. For six months, her father had her seeing a psychiatrist once a week. She said it was all a waste of time. Her father made her promise that she wouldn't mention anything about him to the psychiatrist, let alone talk about his friends. She said she told lies to the psychiatrist because her father told her that if she told him the truth, the psychiatrist would have to be hurt.

"I was so scared, Robert!" she cried. "The funny part was that it wasn't any big secret about my father being in the mob. My friends in high school told me about it before I even knew myself! Guys I liked in school were nervous around me because of my father's reputation. I was treated like I had a contagious disease or something!"

Getting up, she went into the kitchen and brought back a bottle of bourbon, a can of soda, and two glasses. With tears running down her face, she fixed us both a drink. I'd never seen her drink bourbon before; she usually drank vodka or scotch.

I stared at her, and suddenly it started to sink in. I loved Toni. I needed her. For a few seconds, My Ling flashed in my mind. I'd lost her forever, and now I was losing Toni forever. This couldn't be happening to me. I didn't deserve this. I knew she was hurt and angry inside, and if she wanted to leave for a few days or weeks, I could understand it. But leave for good?

Taking a sip of her drink, she continued pacing. She wiped the tears from her face, only to have them quickly replaced by more tears.

"Toni, sit down here next to me. Let's talk this out, okay?" I asked.

She stopped walking and glared at me. "No, I can't do that, Robert, and you know it. I can't think straight when I'm close to you. It took me a week of fighting with myself to build up the nerve to do this."

Her first drink was gone, and she was already gulping down another. "You've been drinking too much," I said. "Slow down on that stuff or it's going to hurt the baby."

"Don't talk to me about my baby!" she snarled. "You gave up your rights to this baby, and it's because of you that I drink so much! You've already hurt me and the baby, Robert, don't you understand that? My baby's not going to be raised around you and my family here! My child will not be a thug, breaking the law and hurting people, all in the name of the great holy Mafia! Not my child! And if I have a daughter, in God's name, I won't put her through the same things I went through! I won't stand for it, Robert!

"When you came home hurt and bleeding, I was a breath away from another breakdown. My father came home beat up a few times, and once he'd been shot. If you were murdered on the streets out there, I planned on killing myself. That's when I started to realize I had to get away. For my baby's sake, for my sanity, and my life, I have to go. My God, you're going to be killed one day, Robert, and I don't want to be here when it happens. If Alfano's enemies don't kill you, then he'll turn on you for some reason. I won't stay here while you're on the streets, finding ways to get yourself killed. And I won't raise our baby here, either. I can't even function at work anymore. My nerves are shot!"

Crying louder now, she flopped down on a chair, slamming her glass down on the coffee table. "Don't leave me, Toni," I pleaded. "I need you."

"You don't need me." She sounded tired. "I believe you love me, Robert, but you don't really need me. Your first love and real need is living on the edge. That's why you'll always be attracted to the Alfanos of the world. I know that being raised in the ghetto had to be dangerous, and being a Green Beret was dangerous, too. You're used to that way of life, honey, but I'm not used to it and

165

never will be. Damn you, Robert, you had an obligation to me and our baby to stop this craziness!" She buried her face in her hands and sobbed.

Toni was right. The day I moved in, I should have stopped the recklessness. My dealings with Alfano were supposed to make things better for us, not worse. Choosing between Toni and Alfano wasn't a choice at all. I wanted Toni. Alfano would just have to understand and accept that. I wasn't going to lose Toni and our baby for him.

"I'm through with Alfano," I said. "No games this time, no lies. It's over. I'll look harder this time for a decent job, too. I'll wash dishes — anything — to bring legitimate money into the house. I'll prove it to you this time, I swear it, I'll show you."

"No!" Toni cried. She stood up and began pacing again. "I don't believe you. You're lying to me again. My mind's made up. I'm going to Italy to get away from all of you."

I sat there watching her, wondering why this was happening to me. Toni was leaving me; she wasn't coming back. Why was she hurting me like this? Sure, I lied about Alfano, and I heard everything she said about him, her family and herself. But to leave? That was drastic. I screwed up, but leaving me wasn't the answer. Deserting me was what she was really doing, deserting me for her mother! This was unfair. I put my life on the line for us to have sufficient money. How could she condemn me for that? Some men wouldn't have done anything except sit on their asses. At least I tried to do something. She wouldn't even give me that little bit of credit.

I'd worked myself up into an angry frenzy. Fixing myself a straight double-shot of bourbon, I quickly swallowed it down. Then, jumping to my feet, I shouted, "Now hold it a damn minute, woman! Sit down! Now!" Toni stopped dead in her tracks when I started shouting. Then she moved to the nearest chair and sat down. "You had your say. Now I'm going to have mine," I continued. "Don't use me as an excuse to leave! You probably had this planned long before I came along! I said I'd change, but you don't believe me! And that's not *your* baby growing inside you. It's *our* baby. If you want to leave, then leave! But if you really love me, you won't go!"

"It's because I love you that I'm going, Robert!" Toni cried.

"Bullshit!" I yelled back. "I'm packing my clothes and leaving for a few days. If you're here when I get back, we'll start fresh and I'll do the right thing, I swear it! If you're gone, then I'll know you never did give a damn about me."

Stomping upstairs, I packed some clothes into a suitcase. I put Alfano's seventy-five grand in a shopping bag and stuffed it into the suitcase, too. I planned on calling Alfano within the next few days to give him his money. I also planned on telling him that we were through dealing, and the reason why. After stuffing three grand of my own money into my pockets, I came downstairs. Toni was bent over in her chair, crying. I was too angry and drunk to say anything. I just stormed past her and out the door. I stopped at the nearest liquor store to get a couple bottles of bourbon. Then I drove downtown and checked into the Delaware Hotel.

The place wasn't exactly the Statler-Hilton, but it was fairly clean. I was given a room on the third floor. Using water as a chaser for my booze, and sometimes drinking straight, I got myself good and drunk. I was deeply hurt by what Toni had said about leaving. Frustration brought tears to my eyes, and rage made me pound my fists savagely into the wall. In my drunken, enraged state, I cursed loudly, punching away at the wall until my knuckles were skinned and bleeding.

I was making such a loud racket that a hotel security man appeared at my door. He told me to stop the noise or leave. Apologizing, I explained that I had come to the hotel after an argument with my girlfriend. He asked to check my room; he wanted to see if I was alone, and if there were any illegal drugs around. He said that if I had drugs, I'd have to leave; he wanted no more problems with the police. I let him look around the room and the bathroom. He noticed the damaged wall where I'd been punching. Chips of cheap paint and pieces of plaster littered the rug. The guy told me I'd have to pay for the damages. Then he reminded me about keeping the noise down, and that maybe I should get some sleep. I gave him a few hundred dollars for the wall. I also gave him fifty dollars for himself, telling him that everything was okay. I was relieved he didn't kick me out. I wasn't in any shape to go looking for another hotel.

Less than a half hour later, I was stretched out on top of my bed, sound asleep. I ended up staying at the hotel for three days. I spent most of that time in my room, drunk. I'd completely forgotten about calling Alfano. By staying drunk, I conveniently avoided having to deal with my broken heart.

The Delaware Hotel was right off Chippewa Street, which was considered a small red-light district. The Chippewa section stayed crowded every night with drunks, muggers, prostitutes, pimps, and drug pushers. The bars were rowdy and dangerous, and the patrolling cops were as devious as the people they watched. During my stay at the hotel, I bought myself a snub-nosed .38 pistol from a street hustler. Since I was alone in a sleazy area, I wanted adequate personal protection.

After those few days at the hotel, I felt an urge to get back to the apartment. With my typical late afternoon hangover, I packed my clothes and left. I didn't see Toni's car in front of the apartment when I parked. Maybe she was out visiting late after work, or had loaned the car to her girlfriend again. I was nervous and sweaty when I got out of the car. My head throbbed and my stomach ached. The only thing on my mind was Toni. Would she really leave me? *Please be home, Toni! Whatever God or Supreme Creator there is, please let her be home!*

Rushing through the door, I dropped my suitcase on the kitchen floor. In the living room, I paused, yelling Toni's name repeatedly. I panicked as I dashed upstairs to the bedroom. Her dresser drawers were open and empty. The top of her dresser was bare and the closet door was open; all of her clothes and shoes were missing. Toni was gone. She left me. My whole body went numb, and I leaned against the wall. I was shattered.

I wanted to get angry. I wanted to slam my head against the wall until I couldn't take it anymore. I wanted to yell from the utter frustration of it all. I wanted the whole world to pay attention to the agony in my heart. My Toni was gone. With my shoulders drooping, my chin on my chest, I silently cried. *I do love you, Toni. What's wrong with me? Am I crazy or what? I'm always sabotaging myself.*

Ten minutes later, I slowly walked downstairs. Deep inside, I was terrified at the thought of being alone again. I valued My Ling and Toni, and I loved them both. But I lost them, one due to my stupidity and now the other due to my stubbornness. *What a fool I am. Such a hopeless, worthless fool.*

I didn't notice the two men in the living room until I got to the bottom of the stairs. They must have come in while I was still upstairs. They were sitting on the couch, but they quickly stood up when I entered the room. I stared at them, and they stepped to the middle of the floor, staring back at me. One man was heavyset with brown hair. He was in his mid-to-late thirties, about six feet tall, and had a thick neck. He had a beer belly and dangerously brutal eyes. Under his black trench coat, he was wearing a two-piece blue suit. The other man was younger, in his mid-twenties. He was muscular, about 5'10" tall, and had curly blond hair and intense blue eyes. He was wearing a pair of cream-colored pants, a cream-colored shirt, and a burgundy sport coat.

I didn't know them. I had never seen them before. I somehow sensed that they knew me, which meant they knew Toni. Did they help her leave? Were they hiding her somewhere? My immense grief turned into immense anger. I could never adequately deal with sorrow or grief, but I could deal with rage. Rage was something I always seemed to understand. When I was angry, I avoided having to deal with my deep inner feelings. Being an abused child, I had tremendous rage built up inside me. The army taught me how to utilize that rage by turning me into a human killing machine, programmed to destroy other things and eventually self-destruct. My God! What kind of man was I? Death merchant or knight, robot or human being? What?

The human body wasn't physically built to maintain the surge of raging energy I could so easily generate. The side effects were headaches, dizziness, numbness in my fingertips, high blood pressure, and muscles so taut they ached. My body felt like a scorching fireball, with my veins smoldering and blood sizzling.

My mind and eyes locked on these two men with a turbulent intensity. They knew something about Toni, and I wanted to know what it was. If I had to, I'd stomp the hell out of these two men and keep searching for Toni until I found her, or I was killed.

"Where's Toni?" I asked coldly, stepping toward them.

The older one sneered, "Don't worry about Miss Tartaro, boy. You got seventy-five big ones belonging to Mr. Alfano. He wants his money, nigger."

I wasn't trying to steal Alfano's money, and I would have given it to them without a second thought. But after being called a boy and a nigger, I wasn't about to voluntarily give them anything but trouble. Their aggressive body language and the raw assurance in their eyes told me they were an experienced fighting team. I wondered how many men and women these bastards had beaten up and killed for Alfano. They were armed, deadly assassins, and I needed an edge. I'd been trained for high-intensity, life-threatening situations of this nature. In seconds, a series of options and scenarios, both logical and illogical, streaked through my mind until I came up with a viable plan. Being a good actor was just as important to intelligence agents as it was to con men and undercover cops on the streets. Using the pretense of fear to create a diversion, if only for seconds, would be the crucial edge I needed.

Replacing my tough expression with one of fake fear, I stuttered, "Oh, shit, the money. Hey, guys, no problem, take it easy! It's here! I don't want to get hurt, the money's here! I forgot all about it, I swear! I wasn't trying to steal it! You guys take the money, give it to Mr. Alfano, okay?" My body language was totally submissive, adding to the realism. They relaxed slightly and I sensed their overconfidence as they smiled at each other.

They were standing side by side, the older man to my left, the younger one to my right. Turning sharply to my right, I took a quick step. Instead of stepping away from the young man, I pivoted my body around clockwise, hitting him between the eyes with my right elbow. I didn't see him crumple, unconscious, over the coffee table because I was already attacking his partner. Spinning on the ball of my left foot, I did another clockwise rotation, my right leg whipping out into the air, the heel of my shoe smashing into the big man's face. The savage kick hit right under his nose, making him stagger backward. Hitting the corner of the coffee table, he continued backward into the end table and lamp, breaking them both before slamming into the wall.

The brutal force of a roundhouse power kick like that would have dropped an average man, finishing the fight. Blood flowed freely from the man's mouth as he sagged against the wall. He was hurt and stunned, but he was still a threat. Pulling my pistol out, I aimed it with both hands right between his eyes. "You'll live," I yelled. "Do as you're told, and you'll live!"

Breathing hoarsely, he was groaning and sniveling, spitting out globs of blood and a few teeth. His eyes burned into mine with a crazy hatred. Trying in vain to wipe blood from his mouth and nose, he grimaced in pain and stopped. Glancing at the younger man on the floor, I saw a swollen, bloody lump between his eyes. I had the big man turn around and lean against the wall with his feet back and spread apart, police-style. With my pistol pressed firmly against the base of his head, I checked him for weapons. I found a .45 automatic and brass knuckles. Checking the other man, I found a 9mm automatic and a nine-inch blackjack. With my pistol still aimed at the big man, I had him take off his shoelaces and his partner's shoelaces. Then, with one shoelace, I had him tie his partner's little fingers together behind his back. With another shoelace, I had him tie his partner's thumbs together.

The younger man was still unconscious, but he was secured now. I had the big man get on his knees and put his hands behind his back. I tied his little fingers and thumbs together with the other shoelaces. I went into the kitchen and came back with a pitcher of ice-cold water from the refrigerator. I rolled the younger man over on his back, and I slowly poured the water on his face. He regained consciousness and coughed, and I told the man what had happened to him. I turned the radio on loudly to a rock station before I began my interrogation.

Putting my pistol on the coffee table, I grabbed a handful of the young man's hair, holding the blackjack in my other hand. "Where's Toni?" I yelled. "Where's she at, scumbag? Tell me or I'll tattoo your fucking skull with this blackjack!"

"I don't know where she's at. I don't know!" he yelled fearfully. "It's the truth. Only Alfano knows, he'll tell you, he knows!"

I didn't believe him. I was about to hit him behind the ear when I heard a voice behind me snap, "You strike my man and you're dead!" Jerking my head around, I saw Alfano standing in the doorway of the living room. He was wearing light pants and a white shirt with a black cashmere overcoat and a dark fedora. Both of his hands were in his coat pockets, and he was puffing on a cigar. Flanking him were two men holding pistols with silencers attached. Wild-eyed, I glanced back and forth from Alfano to my pistol on the coffee table. The probability of surviving if I went for my pistol was highly unlikely, but I was still going to try. My death had to count for something, which meant taking at least one of them with me. He must have sensed what I was contemplating, because in a softer tone he said, "Don't try it, son. You'll never make it. I know you're angry, but you've hurt my men enough. Try to understand my situation and just calm down. I came to talk about my money and Antoinette."

The man I was holding by the hair yelled, "He was going to kill us, boss! I swear on the sacred Virgin Mary, he was going to kill us!"

"Shut up, meathead!" Alfano shouted sternly. "I heard what you said when he asked about Antoinette. You don't know where she's at. But you still didn't have to rat me out, stupid."

"I'm sorry, boss," the man moaned, "I'm sorry. He went through me and Fat Louie like we was nothing."

"Shut up, will you? Just shut up," Alfano raved. "I'm mad enough already."

Slowly taking his hands out of his pockets and showing me his empty palms, Alfano walked over to the radio and turned it off. "I'm unarmed, Parker," he said. "You want to know about Antoinette, right? So let's talk. I'm not sure what happened here, but my men need a doctor first. How about it?"

I didn't care about Alfano's money, and I cared less about his two hurt executioners needing a doctor. I didn't care about his other two men with their pistols aimed at me, either. I did care about Toni. I wanted to know where she was. I had to see her and beg her to come back. I lowered my arm, tossing the blackjack to the floor. Alfano picked up my pistol and put it in his pocket. With his other hand, he motioned to the men by the door, and they put their weapons away.

"Carmine," Alfano sighed, "get these men to one of our doctors. Johnny, you stay here." After Carmine cut the shoelaces off both men, all three left. Johnny remained by the doorway with his arms folded, his right hand inside his suit jacket.

Alfano and I sat down on the couch. He asked me about his money, and I explained why I kept it for so long. He had Johnny get the money from my suitcase. While Johnny counted the money, Alfano said grimly, "Antoinette is in Italy, and she's not coming back. Now, don't get upset without letting me finish, because you'll be making a big mistake. Everything I'm going to say is basically in your interest. All hell's broken loose, and you're on the chopping block again. And from what I've seen of Louie and Vinnie, you're going to have two more people wanting to murder you now."

Suddenly, Alfano started laughing and patting me on the back. He was laughing so hard he turned red and started coughing. In between coughs, he asked me for a drink. I got him one while Johnny watched me like a hawk. After tasting some of the bourbon, he looked carefully around the room at all the blood. "I can't believe it," he laughed. "I can't believe you whipped two of my best men!"

"I want to talk about Toni," I said bluntly. "Her mother has to have a phone. I can call her, Mr. Alfano."

"Sorry, that's out of the question," responded Alfano. "Joe and Dave still want to kill you. The way they see it, if Antoinette hadn't met you, she never would have left. They're demanding your death again. In their words, you're 'a home-wrecking nigger bastard.'"

"Damn it!" I yelled. "Who the fuck are they kidding? Their home was wrecked before I even met Toni."

"Take it easy," Alfano said. "I have to agree with you on that part, but it doesn't settle anything."

Alfano then told me that just before Toni left, she called Joe and Dave to say goodbye. They tried to talk her out of leaving, but they couldn't. So they went to Alfano and explained what had happened. All three came over here with some of the boys to check things out — and also to search for the money. They didn't find it, so Alfano had the place staked out in case I came back. When I was spotted going into the apartment, Alfano was called. He said he'd told Louie and Vinnie to make sure I stayed at the apartment until he got there so he could talk to me about Antoinette and the money.

"And I've made my decision about both," Alfano stated. "I'm settling this thing once and for all, and no one's going to be killed. I respect all my boys, but I don't like them making demands on me. I've already told Joe and Dave that I'm not having you killed and to stay clear, but at the same time, I can't allow you to keep aggravating them or let you continue to bust up my boys."

Alfano then gave me a hard, level stare. "I don't know who started the fight here, but I want all of you to stay the hell away from each other. I've had a few talks with Joe already about jeopardizing my authority, and I'm telling you now. I like you, son. You're intelligent and you got balls, but after today, you'll no longer exist to me. If I see you on the streets, I'll show no recognition. If anyone asks if I know you, I'll deny it. But you go near Joe or Dave or look for Antoinette, and I'll have you shot dead."

Alfano paused to light his cigar again, giving me time to digest his ultimatum. A minute ticked by silently, and then he continued, in a softer tone.

"If you and the Tartaros really thought about it, you'd all see that the reason you hate each other's guts is because you all love Antoinette. In my opinion, all three of you are responsible for her leaving. But I can't be caught in the middle of this. As of right now, none of us — and I mean *none* of us — ever had any dealings with each other. And I don't think I have to warn you that things could become, well, hard on Antoinette if you don't keep a tight lip."

I flinched with anger at this, but I was so overwhelmed with feelings of loss that I couldn't respond. I just sat there, praying that this was a dream but knowing it wasn't.

"This is the best option for all concerned," he went on. "I'm giving you fifteen grand out of this money, but you can't stay here after today. It's too bad that things turned out like this, but I want your word on respecting my decisions, Parker. Let things lie, understand?"

I felt terrible, physically exhausted and miserably heartbroken. Why was this happening to me? I loved Toni so much, and I'd chased her right out of my life. The realization of that weighed on me tremendously. I was on my fourth drink, but I still sat there, traumatized. I thought about suicide again, but that took the kind of guts that I just didn't have anymore. Alfano didn't want me around, but I didn't care about that. He was unimportant and irrelevant in comparison to Toni. My God! She was gone! I'd never see her again! Would our baby be a boy or a girl? What would our baby look like? I'll never get to hold our baby!

Alfano patted me on the back, then poured more booze into my glass. With my head low, I sighed, "I'll do as you say, Mr. Alfano; you have my word. You spared my life again, but I'm not sure you should have this time. I seem to be my own worst enemy, and it tears me apart inside. When I was in Nam, a Vietnamese woman I loved was killed due to my stupidity. I love Toni, too. She chose to have my baby, and my stubborn pride chased her away. I'm useless, and I don't seem to fit in anywhere. Maybe you should reconsider your offer and just kill me right now."

Alfano gave me an odd look, then swallowed more booze. "You're really serious," he said. "That would make the Tartaros two of the happiest people in Buffalo, among others. Would it make Antoinette happy? Do you really know without a doubt that you'll never see her again? Or see your child? At my home, I saw the way she looked at you. There was nothing but pure love in her eyes for you. She's gone, but I strongly believe she'll always love you. Right now, you're upset and blaming yourself because she left. Hopefully, I won't pick up the newspaper in a few days and read about you shooting yourself or jumping off a building. Wait a few months. See how you feel about things. Then, if you still want to do yourself in, maybe I could understand it a little better."

I sat there rubbing the side of my head. "Maybe you're right," I mumbled. "I'm depressed and tired right now. It's going to take time to accept everything that's happened. I don't want the fifteen grand you're giving me. I want Toni to have it."

"Okay. If that's what you want, I'll take care of it," stated Alfano, standing up. "I have to be going. Don't forget what we've discussed here."

Alfano and his bodyguard started to walk out of the living room. Then Alfano turned around and walked back to me. Taking my pistol out of his pocket, he set it down on the coffee table. He said, "Off the record, if there's anything I can do for you, just let me know discreetly. For the record, I've spared your life twice, and hopefully made you reconsider killing yourself. But if you harass the Tartaro Family, or talk about our dealings together to anyone, you'll die."

He extended his hand and we shook hands. "No problem, Mr. Alfano," I said. "I know what's expected of me."

"Take it easy, son," he remarked solemnly. They both left the apartment, leaving me by myself. For a couple of hours, I stayed on the couch, drinking and wallowing in my dilemma. No longer did I want revenge on Boots Robinson or anyone else. My motivation was gone, and I cared about nothing but Toni and our baby.

Finally getting up, I packed all my personal belongings and put them in my car. I drove back downtown to the Delaware Hotel and got a room for a couple of days. I continued my drinking and vomiting. Then, somehow, I managed to call my mother. I told her I had no place to go and wanted to come home for a while. After almost an hour of listening to her angrily lecture me about my behavior and what she went through raising me, she finally said yes. Before leaving Buffalo, I took my car back to the leasing company. I had no more use for it, and I just didn't want it around anymore. Then I took a cab along with my belongings to the small Steel City of Lackawanna.

Chapter Ten

I continued my drinking spree in Lackawanna, walking around from bar to bar. Between loaning money to so-called friends who never paid me back and buying booze all the time, I was almost broke. With a fanatical determination, I kept my mind in a sort of mental vacuum, avoiding thoughts of Nam, My Ling, and especially Toni and the baby. I stayed sloppy drunk, slept in my clothes, rarely bathed, and ate very little.

After being home for several days, my mother kicked me out of the house. She called me a low-life bum and wished me dead again. My stepfather said I was lazy and no good. My sister said I was an embarrassment to her and the rest of the family. I couldn't even afford a motel room, so I ended up going to my grandmother's house, asking for help. Without hesitation, she let me stay, which was a relief to me. Though I was having problems, it hurt deeply that my own immediate family had turned me away.

For the next couple of weeks, I continued hanging out on the street corners and in bars. I kept getting into fights. I couldn't afford bourbon anymore, so I started drinking cheap whiskey and wine. Winos, bag ladies, and bums taught me how to steal bottles of booze out of liquor stores. And I collected deposit bottles from garbage cans and street curbs to get money, too. I went up to strangers and acquaintances on the street, begging for change to buy booze. At the After-Hours joints in Lackawanna, the owners sometimes paid me to stop fights and keep troublemakers out of their establishments. The owners liked me because I was good at my job, but they only paid me slave wages, which consisted of a few dollars and a couple bottles of cheap whiskey. Behind my back, people in the neighborhood started referring to me as Crazy Bobby. The rumor circulating around was that I was a nice Christian boy growing up, until I went to Vietnam and got shot in the head.

I started to have mental blackouts from my excessive drinking. At times, I'd wake up in the morning and couldn't remember what I had done the night before. People on the streets had to tell me if I had been fighting or arguing. The blackouts lasted for a couple of hours sometimes. I still carried my pistol wherever I went. There were times when I thought about selling it, but I didn't. Without it, I didn't know if I'd be able to protect myself adequately.

Late one night, inebriated as usual, I sat in Fat Jack's Bar on Steelawanna Avenue. It was on this particular night that I met Rosilee Fergurson. Rosy would inadvertently make all the problems and challenges I'd experienced seem almost meaningless. Our meeting would escalate into a series of situations that would truly test my sanity. Fate would seem kind compared to Rosy, because with a startling impact, she would tragically have her most treasured possession stripped away: her life.

The night I first ran into her, she sat next to me at the bar and smiled. "Hi, Bobby. You still remember me after so long?"

At first glance, Rosy had registered clearly in my mind. She and my mother had been friends when I was a kid. Rosy's brother, Leroy, was a couple of years older than I was, and we played together as children. She used to baby-sit my sister and me, which is why I remembered her. I recalled her as always being happy and friendly. The Rosy I stared at now still seemed friendly, but I sensed she was different from the Rosy I knew back then.

She was in her mid-thirties, slightly overweight, with short, dark-brown hair. She was about 5'8" tall and was wearing a green, two-piece pantsuit with knee-high leather boots and a brown, waist-high jacket. She wore no jewelry or watch and carried no purse.

At one time, Rosy was an attractive woman. Her face was worn and tired, now, making her look years older. She seemed jittery, and she had a runny nose that left her sniffling. There was an ugly knife scar across her face. It ran from the right side of her face to the inside corner of her right eye, across the bridge of her nose, and stopped at the left corner of her mouth. I stared at the scar because she didn't have it when I knew her before. I didn't know that the scar had been put there by an angry, jealous woman who had accused Rosy of having an affair with her husband.

I was so deep in thought that she had to ask me a few times if I remembered her. I told her I did, and she asked about my family. She hadn't seen them in a long time. After I said they were okay, she told me her mother lived right across the street from Fat Jack's. After buying her a few drinks and talking for a while, she confessed to being a heroin addict. It really shocked me that she was shooting dope. Then, out of the blue, she asked me, "Would you do me a favor, Bobby? Just a small favor, please?"

"If I can, sure," I answered. "If it's money you want, though, I only have a few dollars to my name."

"It's not about money," she said. "I just need you to stick close to me for a few days, that's all. You know, be my body-guard."

I listened while she talked about some of the drug-shooting dens in the neighborhood. She complained that she'd been beaten, her money and dope had been stolen several times, and she'd been gang raped at the dope dens. She felt that if other drug addicts saw her with me, they'd remember my reputation and leave her alone. With no second thoughts, I told her I'd help for old time's sake.

She wanted to go buy some dope and shoot up, so we left the bar and headed for a nearby shooting den. We walked up Steelawanna Avenue, turned left, went down Ridge Road, and stopped in front of an old, vacant house. The dilapidated wooden dwelling was right across the street from Maxim's Bar. Looking up and down the street for a moment, she took my hand and led me along the side of the house into the pitch-black darkness. At the rear of the house, she gave a code knock on the back door, and we were let in.

The room we were in held little furniture. It was filthy and smelled of cheap wine and urine. It was a pigsty, with living and dead roaches, empty orange juice cartons, beer cans, liquor bottles, and half-eaten moldy food. There was a shadeless lamp in one corner with a bright light bulb in it. The two windows were boarded up tight, and no light could be detected from the outside.

I watched Rosy, along with a dozen other men and women, buy dope, cook it up, and shoot it into various places of their bodies. About twenty minutes later, we left, and I noticed that she no longer had the shakes. She was high as a kite from her fix. I had to put my arm around her waist to keep her from falling on her face.

Going up Ridge Road, we turned right, walking all the way down Steelawanna Avenue and past the red, brick, two-story Baker Homes projects. Across from the projects on the Holbrook

Street side were the greenish-gray, two-story Albright Court projects. Since I was raised in the Baker Homes Projects, I briefly remembered the gang wars and the football and basketball games between the projects as well as the romantic and sometimes violent house and street parties. After crossing Holbrook, there was a large field full of high grass, weeds, bushes, and trees. Through the field was a crooked dirt pathway that was used as a shortcut between the two projects. Rosy lived in Albright Court, and we used the path to get to her apartment.

The two-bedroom apartment was extremely unkempt with dirty, cheap furniture. Some of it was broken and ripped. The place was a haven for roaches and flies. The kitchen sink was stacked with dirty dishes, and the trash bags were overflowing with garbage. In one of the upstairs bedrooms, Rosy's three sons slept, all in the same bed. The oldest looked to be about fourteen years old. In her bedroom, in a small crib, slept her daughter, who was only several months old. Sitting down on the bed, Rosy started to take off her clothes, but she never finished. With her blouse off and her pants still half on, she suddenly fell back on the bed, sound asleep. Between the booze and the dope, she was out cold for the night.

Looking at her, I wondered why she turned to dope. Who the hell was I to wonder about anything, though? I was in the same general predicament. I could very well be just a short step away from shooting dope myself. I'd given up on tomorrow. I despised dope, but I knew I could use it as a way to cope. I took Rosy's pants off and stretched her out on the bed. Then I picked up her bedspread from the floor and covered her up. I kissed her softly on the forehead, and memories of how nice she'd been to me and my sister as kids flashed through my head. I left her apartment and walked to my grandmother's house, where I fell asleep fully clothed on the couch. Life was so mysteriously strange, so dangerously violent, and so pathetically unfair. But deep inside, somewhere, I knew there were moments when life was magnificently beautiful, too.

During the next few days, I stayed close to Rosy. Sometimes, I'd reluctantly give her money for dope because she'd get seriously ill without it. Seeing her in pain, with the shakes, crying, and vomiting was something I just couldn't deal with. Rosy was unmarried and on welfare, so with some of the money I acquired, I bought food for her and her kids. To get the extra money needed for Rosy and at the same time still get my booze, I expanded my ingenuity.

Two of the Bethlehem Steel Plant parking lots were in my immediate neighborhood. The parking lots were heavily guarded by armed security guards on foot patrol and in cars. Late at night, I'd sneak into the parking lots in the neighborhood. Breaking into some of the cars, I'd steal whatever items of value I could find. I sold most of the items to a fence, and I sold the rest on the streets. Sometimes, the fence would pay me in heroin instead of money, and I'd give the dope to Rosy. I even ambushed and mugged a few white and black well-dressed drunks by choking them from behind until they were unconscious. I only took cash and jewelry from my victims, not their ID or credit cards. I did this so I could feel like I wasn't like the other muggers in the city.

I dealt with Rosy like she was an older sister because that's how I felt about her. She was drinking heavily, prostituting, and shooting dope into both arms and inside her thighs. As for me, I had no desire to fall in love again. Love had proven to be emotionally damaging to me.

Rosy and I seemed to get along well together. Maybe it was because we felt falsely secure in each other's company, even though, realistically, we were both desperate and weak individuals. People on the streets who saw us together assumed we were boyfriend and girlfriend, which wasn't true. When asked, we always replied that we were just friends and nothing more. I learned quickly, though, that speculation and false rumors were more exciting to street people than the truth.

People started to warn me about Rosy, too. They told me things that shocked the hell out of me. And these things always centered around the same subject. Rosy was a drug informant for the Feds, they said. They called her a snitch, rat, or narc, depending on the person I was talking to. I heard this from drug pushers, drug addicts, pimps, and hustlers, but I didn't want to believe it. They kept insisting it was true, and they warned me about hanging around with her. They told me that two drug informants had disappeared already, and a third informant was shot dead in the middle of the street in Buffalo. Eventually, I believed what they said because I remembered something that happened while I was sticking close to her.

Late one night, while I was walking down a quiet side street with her, a car came and stopped about fifteen yards ahead of us. Rosy told me to wait where I was while she walked to the car and got in the back seat. There were two white men in the front seat, and she talked to them for ten to fifteen minutes. One of them gave her money and a few bags of dope. It didn't dawn on me then, but Rosy must have told those men something about me for them to feel relaxed enough to talk to her around me. Between the booze and wanting to forget so much, I'd forgotten all about it until now. I started to wonder if the men in the car were Lackawanna or Buffalo police, or if they were with the FBI. I didn't want to get involved, but I had to confront Rosy about it. I was starting to hear street rumors about death threats against her.

Late at night in her apartment, I asked about the two white men in the car. Sounding angry, she answered, "I'm not proud of it, but I'm a snitch, Bobby. I've been a dope fiend for four years, now, and for the past two years, I've been snitching. I had to do it, Bobby, or else I'd be in prison right now. I can't handle prison or being away from my kids. The first time I tried selling some dope, I ended up selling it to a federal undercover agent. I've been snitching on drug dealers in Lackawanna and Buffalo. I've been snitching on robbers and burglars to help the local cops, too. For the past several months, the Feds have really been pushing me for more and more information about drugs in the area."

"What about the two white men in the car, Rosy?" I asked.

"They're Feds," she responded nervously. "When they started seeing us together, they asked a lot of questions about you. I told them you were an ex-Army Green Beret and that you'd been to Vietnam. And I said I used to baby-sit you and your sister a lot when you were kids. I told them you were protecting me on the streets for a while."

When I told her the rumors I'd been hearing on the street about death threats against her, she became terrified. Throwing her arms around my neck, she started crying hysterically, screaming, "I don't want to die, Bobby! I don't want to die! My kids! I don't want my kids hurt! I don't want to be dead!" It took an hour and some booze for her to calm down. Finally, I told her that the rumors could be idle gossip, like so many other street rumors. I didn't believe this myself, but it helped to settle her down. She continued talking, saying the Feds did some checking up on me to make sure she was telling the truth. She said they told her that she was smart to stay close to me because of my street reputation.

Getting frustrated again, Rosy said she had nowhere to run. We sat on the couch and watched TV until she fell asleep. With my pistol on the coffee table, I methodically went over what Rosy had told me. The main thing that stuck out in my boozed-up mind was that neither the local cops nor the Feds had told Rosy about the death threats against her. With other drug informants and undercover narc officers on the streets, it was impossible for the local cops and Feds not to directly or indirectly know about the threats. What were these law enforcement bastards up to? What was their angle? It was possible, though highly improbable, that they thought the threats were groundless and were ignoring them.

I strongly felt that Rosy was playing down the number of people she'd snitched on. The more I thought about it, the more logical it became that certain law enforcement officers had to know that the death threats were real, but saving Rosy's life wasn't their highest priority. It seemed to me that she was intentionally being left on the streets until she was killed. Rosy's role as a snitch had somehow been compromised, so she was no longer important to the local cops or the Feds. It seemed that everyone on the streets knew she was a snitch. She was being offered no police protection, and she hadn't even known about the death threats until I'd told her. She was being set up as a sacrificial lamb. Why? Where was the gain? Who's to profit?

It dawned on me that if Rosy were murdered on the streets, it could prove beneficial to local and federal drug agencies. Her murder would ease drug dealers' minds about leaks, and that would give undiscovered snitches and undercover narc officers in the area a safer and better position for intelligence-gathering. It was highly probable that certain officers purposely leaked information about her being a snitch. They would do it for money, favors, and to keep their own street dealings a secret. The only other logical reason why drug agents might compromise Rosy was that they thought, as I did, that she was emotionally and mentally burning herself out with booze and dope. Because she was a useless snitch, they felt it would be easiest for the streets she lived in to claim her life.

How Rosy got compromised was really irrelevant at this point. There were probably a few other angles to all this, too, but the end result spelled death for Rosy. With the drug agents and the streets against her, she was between a rock and a hard place, and I wondered if she fully understood this. Maybe she understood it better than I did and just didn't care anymore.

I started thinking about my position in this whole mess. Was I being used? Knowing I had a good military background, did the Feds direct her to me, figuring I'd help her? It was probable that Rosy may have been told I was in that bar before she came in. I was the perfect sentimental patsy for her, and she was a bigger patsy for the Feds. When the Feds checked up on me, they must have found out I was AWOL from the army. They did nothing about it because I was being useful to them by making Rosy feel more secure on the streets. They'd been pressuring her for more information on the drug scene, knowing full well she couldn't possibly tell them anything relevant anymore. This was their way of conning her into staying on the streets, exposed. They realized that if she ever found out about the death threats against her, she might take off and disappear. With me in the picture, they were gambling that she'd feel more secure on the streets and remain a target until she was killed.

In the end, the Feds knew that everything depended on the drug dealers and how quickly they wanted her dead. I'd been put in a dangerous position, and the more I thought about it, the angrier I got. With one or two local cops or federal agents on the take, the drug dealers had to know my background. Since the dealers thought that Rosy was my girlfriend, they probably felt I was crazy enough to retaliate if Rosy were murdered. This meant that my life was in just as much danger as Rosy's. I got even angrier as I thought about all this. I didn't need this shit! Damn it, why me? Why the hell me?

After putting Rosy to bed, I checked the kids' bedroom and shut off the lights. Turning the TV off, I stretched out on the couch and slept in combat mode. For the next week, I stayed so close to Rosy that she was screaming and cursing at me to leave her alone. In angry fits, she complained that she needed breathing room so she could hustle some money on the streets. She said she couldn't even go to the bathroom without me standing outside the door. I felt that between the booze, dope, and emotional stress, she didn't mean what she was saying. On June 1st, I gave her a break and I went to a bar by myself. While in the bar, drunk, I overheard a guy making dirty remarks about Rosy. She wasn't there to defend herself, so I told the guy to shut his mouth. We argued and I punched him, and then I challenged anyone else in the bar to a fight. Someone had called the cops, and they came before I could leave. I was arrested for assault and disorderly conduct. I was released the next morning.

On June 5th, someone tried to murder me. It was in the early morning hours after two o'clock, after I'd left Maxim's Bar on Ridge Road. Rosy had become elusive and harder to find during the past few days. She was purposely ducking me, and there was little I could do about it. After leaving the bar, I walked down Steelawanna Avenue, then cut through the middle of the Baker Homes projects. In my jacket pocket, I had a full bottle of whiskey that I'd bought off the bartender in Maxim's. In my other jacket pocket I had my .38 pistol. I was headed for one of the spots I usually went to when I wanted to be alone and drink.

Across the street on one side of the Baker Homes projects was the Roosevelt Elementary School. Right next to the school was a large stone pool. The pool was only a couple feet deep, and it hadn't been filled with water since I was a kid. Alongside the pool was a small stone bathhouse. This is where I was headed. Very rarely would I find someone there this late at night. The school and pool were surrounded by a fence, and there were several entrances. I walked through the nearest entrance and went down a paved slope to the bathhouse. Just before entering the dark bathhouse, I opened my bottle of whiskey and took a long swig. As I entered, I brought the bottle up to my mouth for another swig. The bottle never made it to my lips. Someone hit me squarely in the stomach. The swift, solid punch knocked the air completely out of me. My bottle soared up into the air and then shattered on the concrete floor. My knees shook, then buckled, and my body dropped.

Abruptly, powerful hands gripped my jacket, holding my body up for a split second before tossing me against the far wall. My upper body slammed against the wall, and the back of my head hit the stone wall hard. I slumped to the floor, landing on my butt. My stomach hurt like hell, and my back and head were aching. I was dazed, and I'd urinated on myself. I was lying against the wall, my arms stretched out, my legs wide apart on the floor. There was scant light from a nearby street lamp that filtered through the portholes of the bathhouse. I tried to focus on the son of a bitch standing over me. He was white, tall, muscular, and dark-haired, wearing dark clothes and gloves. The bastard was smiling at me!

"So you're Parker, huh?" he grumbled in a deep voice. "They said you were tough. You don't look tough to me. I'm being paid good money to waste a fucking wino!"

The egotistical bastard started laughing at me. Reaching behind his back, he pulled out a long hunting knife. He was standing there between my legs, and as he started to bend over me, I kicked him in the right kneecap. He shrieked, and the short kick stopped him momentarily. The knife lingered several inches from the left side of my face. My hand was already inside my jacket pocket, feeling for the pistol, but I didn't have time to pull it out. Frantically, I fired the pistol from inside my jacket. The shot echoed loud inside the bathhouse, and the guy was knocked backward several feet. He groaned, and blood splashed on my face and clothing. The knife he'd been holding clattered to the ground. Swaying, with his right hand clutching his left shoulder, he staggered out. I fired again, but he was already gone. Scrambling to my feet, I stumbled painfully out of the bathhouse, wanting to kill the bastard.

The guy was already at the top of the paved slope and on the sidewalk. A car was there with its lights off, motor running, and the back door open. There was another white guy behind the wheel, and the wounded guy dove into the back seat. With the wheels screeching and rubber burning, the car sped off into the night.

I had to get out of the immediate area before someone called the cops or a nearby cop car arrived. Being too sore to run fast, I jogged slowly across the dry pool and out a gate. Crossing the street, I went through another gate and into a large playground. This was the playground I played in as a kid when I was growing up. After exiting the other side of the dark playground, I went up and down side streets until I got to my grandmother's house. Once inside, I took all my clothes off and threw them on the closet floor of my bedroom. It was too dark out for anyone to have seen me clearly. A witness could only give the cops a basic description of my clothes. After washing my body with soap and water from the bathroom sink, I took a few aspirins for my aching head. I was physically exhausted and light-headed as I crawled into bed.

The next day, as a precaution, I wiped my fingerprints off the pistol. Then I buried the pistol near some railroad tracks around Lehigh Avenue and Ridge Road. I didn't want the pistol being found on me or in the house. A quick-thinking criminal could easily manipulate what happened and use it against me. I didn't want to be set up and arrested, charged with weapons possession and attempted murder.

I kept wondering who the hit man was and who had sent him. Had drug dealers paid him because of my closeness to Rosy? Were they planning to kill me first, then her? Maybe this attempted hit had nothing to do with drug dealers. Toni's father and brother could have been responsible for the hit man. Fat Louie and Vinnie the Snake could have sent the guy to get me for payback. That lawyer, Thorton, had threatened me. Or it could have been Carol's pimp, the Ice-man, who sent the guy after me. My analytical mind went back even further, suspecting Major Small, too. Was he still in Nam, or was he stateside now? Was the bastard crazy enough to let that last mission I was on worry him to the point of trying to have me killed? He could be planning to get out of the army and into politics, corporate work, or civilian government intelligence work, and if that were the case, he wouldn't want that mission brought up. It would only take a short conversation with the right people to damage his reputation, even if he stayed in the army. Was Captain Miller, my old section leader, dead? I wouldn't put anything past Major Small; he was a devious cutthroat. That mission still haunted me, but I had no intention of talking about it to anyone. It happened in another lifetime, another place.

I put all these suspects in the same category. It was highly probable that any one of them might try to kill me, and they were all financially capable of hiring a hit man. For a few hours, I racked my brain, trying to pick one person from the group who wanted me dead more than the others. I couldn't do it. All those bastards wanted me dead with a vengeance, it seemed. After giving myself a worse headache from thinking so hard, I decided I didn't care if ten hit men shot me dead. I was too physically and mentally exhausted to care, and I was just too damn sore to worry about it.

I went to Rosy's apartment, but she wasn't home. She was still avoiding me, and I began to realize why. When I wasn't around, it was easier for her to block out her dangerous situation and her problems. When I was with her, my very presence reminded her of them. The death threats and her other problems were things she didn't really want to deal with. I finally caught up to her late that night. She was standing on a street corner with some of her so-called friends. Pulling her aside, I told her what had happened to me in the bathhouse. She was disinterested. I couldn't believe the way she was acting. She was swaying and slurring her words, and I knew she'd had a fix recently. She yelled angrily at me to leave her alone. She told me to go to hell. She didn't want to be around me anymore. The more I tried to make her understand, the louder and angrier she got. Being angry myself, I just walked away, disgusted with her and her dope fiend friends. I didn't need the aggravation of it all. I didn't even care about myself, but like a fool, I was trying to get a dope fiend to care about herself.

Stopping by a liquor store, I bought two bottles of cheap wine. Then I went over to my grandmother's house and stayed in my bedroom. I sat on my bed, drinking and listening to the radio, still angry about my altercation with Rosy. There was still no doubt in my mind that she had drawn me into this. She was going crazy, drinking and shooting dope. She couldn't take the stress anymore, and she was becoming more and more emotionally burned out. For a brief moment, I considered the possibility that she was trying to protect me in her own way. After getting me involved in all this, she might be feeling guilty about using me. The only way she knew how to correct it was to keep away from me. No matter what her motives were, though, I stayed close to my grandmother's house.

The night of June 10th and the morning of June 11th are dates I'll never forget. It was the night of June 10th that I ventured out to Fat Jack's Bar. I'd gotten restless from being cooped up in my bedroom. It was only eleven-thirty when I entered the half-filled bar. A few minutes after two o'clock, Rosy entered the bar with a guy in his late twenties. I couldn't recall his name, but I'd seen him around and knew he sold drugs. From the shadows of my table, I watched them standing at the crowded bar, laughing and talking loudly. Ever since she'd cursed me out on the street corner, I vowed to stay away from her. Seeing her so doped up and drunk she could hardly stand showed me just how pitiful she really was. I really couldn't afford to feel sorry for anyone except myself. But like a fool, sitting there in my drunken state, I felt sorry for her, anyway.

It wasn't jealousy that catapulted me out of my chair. Rosy and I weren't lovers in any way, form, or fashion. What drove me out of my chair was a combination of other things: she had serious death threats against her, she had good kids, the dope was killing her, she was a good person at heart, and she helped care for my sister and me when we were young.

Walking up to them, I tapped her on the shoulder and said, "I'm taking you home, Rosy."

She turned abruptly, and her glazed red eyes met mine. Her shocked expression was one of guilt, and she lowered her eyes, ashamed. The dark brown guy with her said menacingly, "Hey, what's up, Rosy? I thought you said you and Parker weren't tight, baby. You messing with my head or what?"

She regained her doped-up nerve, and her expression changed from shame to angry defiance. "We ain't tight!" she yelled. "Leave me alone, Bobby. I don't need you watching me like a goddamn buzzard!"

Whispering in her ear, I reminded her of the bathhouse incident, the death threats, and that her kids needed her home, not on the streets. She slapped me. It was unexpected and hard, numbing the whole side of my face. "Don't tell me what my kids need!" she screamed. "And what happens to me is none of your goddamn business anymore, Bobby! Leave me the fuck alone!"

The body language of the guy she was with became threatening as he boomed, "Leave her be, man!"

Standing face to face with the guy, I welcomed a physical confrontation to vent the old and new frustrations trapped inside me. I glared at him savagely, mentally challenging his very existence. "This isn't your business, man," I growled. "I'm ready to die if I have to. Are you?"

It must have been the crazy glint in my eyes or the tone in my voice that made him slowly back off. He glanced at Rosy in disgust, mumbling, "You lots of fun, baby, but you ain't worth fighting over." Then, swallowing down the rest of his whiskey, he walked out of the bar. Trembling, Rosy watched the guy leave with panic in her eyes. I knew she was seeing bags of dope disappearing into thin air. Without saying a word, she pushed past me and ran out the door. I was right behind her. The guy had his car parked in front of the bar. By the time she got out the door and down the few steps to the sidewalk, though, he was already driving off. Rosy ran into the middle of the street, yelling, crying, and waving for him to come back. Standing on the sidewalk with my hands in my pockets, I just watched her.

With tears of rage, she turned to me, screaming, "You bastard! You chased him away! I hate your goddamn guts! What am I going to do now, huh? I got no money and need another fix, you son of a bitch! I hope you die!"

Personally, I was glad I chased the guy away. She didn't need to shoot any more of that crap into her body. It was killing her and driving her crazy. Saying nothing, I started to walk down the street to my grandmother's house, which was one street down. Rosy had suddenly stopped screaming and cursing, so I casually glanced over my shoulder at her. She was coming at me with a straight razor in her hand! Within a heartbeat, she was on me, lashing out wildly with the straight razor, screaming, "I'll kill you, Bobby! I needed that dope! I'll kill you for that!" I kept backing up and changing directions to keep out of range. She was out of control! I didn't want to hurt her, so the only thing I could do was keep out of her reach until she got tired.

After a few minutes, she fell to the ground on all fours, exhausted. She was gasping heavily, crying, and spitting on the ground. I was breathing heavily myself, a few yards away from her. Awkwardly, she threw the straight razor at me and missed. Getting even more enraged and frustrated, she dropped flat to the ground, bawling like a baby. I went over and helped her to her feet. She wrapped her arms around my neck and cried convulsively. It took about ten minutes to calm her down. I apologized to her over and over, making promises I knew would be impossible to keep.

"I'm sorry too, Bobby!" she sobbed. "I don't want to hurt you. I'm losing my mind! I'm going crazy! Oh, Bobby, I'm so scared! I don't want to die! Lord knows, I don't want to die!"

She started getting upset again, and it took a few more minutes to calm her down. "I'm starting to get sick," she moaned. "I hurt all over. Do you have any money, Bobby? I need another fix. Just a small one. Help me, please, Bobby." All I had left on me was a five-dollar bill and some change. It wasn't much with the heavy habit she had, but I gave it all to her anyway. "What am I going to do?" she mumbled, more to herself than to me. "Maybe I can borrow some money from my mother again. I'll have to wake her up to open the door; though. She hates that."

"Well, let's go ask her," I blurted out, not wanting her to get any sicker.

"No," she snapped. "I have to go alone. She gets mad when I show up with a guy. I'll be all right, Bobby, don't worry. Go home and get some sleep. I'm sorry for everything, I really am, Bobby. Go home. I'll be all right."

After convincing me she'd be okay, I walked away. I looked back a few times, and she stood on the sidewalk, smiling tearfully and waving· goodbye, until I turned the corner. I couldn't understand why she was smiling. As I continued on, I began to realize that Rosy had tricked me. She wasn't going over to her mother's house; she just wanted to get rid of me! She was probably on her way to the After-Hours joints, looking for that guy she'd been with. Even if she didn't find him, I was sure she'd still get her dope tonight.

I'd warned her about the death threats, and I got cursed at for my troubles. I told her a hit man had almost killed me, and she wished me dead. I tried to stop her from using more dope, and she tried to kill me. I was stupid to get involved with her in the bar. I was in a Catch-22 situation. I didn't want her shooting dope, but I couldn't bear to see how sick she got without it.

In my room, I got undressed and lay on the bed. *I've had it! No more!* I was too tired to care about Rosy or myself. Whatever she wanted to do was fine with me. I had my own problems to deal with.

Waking up at about eleven in the morning, I had the usual headache, stomachache, and shakes. My grandmother, by habit, was always up at dawn, cooking and listening to the radio. I got dressed and sat down at the kitchen table. After a few minutes of conversation, my grandmother mentioned a radio news report she'd heard. It was about a black woman being found dead in a field between the Baker Homes and Albright Courts projects. For an instant, Rosy flashed through my mind, but then I discarded the thought. Violence wasn't unusual in Lackawanna. Just because a black woman's body was found didn't mean it was Rosy. Still, I questioned my grandmother about the news report, wanting to know the details. She told me the police didn't know the woman's name yet because there was no ID on the body. I knew for a fact that Rosy never carried ID. I stayed glued to my chair, waiting for the next news report to come on. When it did, what I heard stunned me. The police had identified the body as being Rosilee Fergurson of Albright Court projects. They said she'd been beaten, and the side of her skull had been crushed by a blunt instrument.

Wide-eyed, my grandmother watched the trauma I was going through. Tears spilled down my face, I trembled, and I could barely breathe from the pain in my chest. My head ached, my nose started running, and muscle spasms rippled uncontrollably through my body. I could barely hear my grandmother when she asked if I was responsible for the woman's death. Through choking, sobbing breaths, I told her no, but that I'd been with her the night before.

After a few minutes, I jumped up, saying I had to go see Rosy's mother and children. I had to talk to them because Rosy was like family to me. Rushing to my bedroom, I grabbed my jacket, then headed for the door. My grandmother was standing in front of the door, begging me not to go see Rosy's family. She explained that because of my violent reputation, people would be thinking I did it. And to go see Rosy's family, she said, would only start emotional accusations and trouble.

Logically, I knew my grandmother was right. Throwing my jacket on the couch, I sat down, trying to relax. *They killed Rosy! They killed her! I warned her, damn it! I told her about the death threats! She wouldn't listen. Now she's dead. I'll get them! They'll pay, I swear it, Rosy!*

I thought about what my grandmother had said. We were seen together on the streets, and I was with her last night. The street gossip had to be in full swing by now, blaming me for her death. Whoever killed Rosy made sure the body was conveniently found. I believed this was done for two reasons. First, it was a message to snitches and potential snitches. Second, the people involved knew I'd be the prime suspect because of my association with her and because of my reputation. Just knowing that sent waves of rage through my veins. They tried to kill me first, but they failed, so they killed Rosy. This way, they'd be getting two birds with one stone, with the help of crooked local cops or Feds. A neat package

I had to wonder if Rosy's enemies were behind her death or if my enemies had done it. My enemies would know that I'd be hurt by her death — and that I'd be the prime suspect. I didn't know what to think. *Who do I take revenge on?* Some of the street people who knew the source of the death threats had been too terrified to even tell me. My mind raced as I tried to figure out angles, options, strategies, and conclusions. I was in a frenzy, feeling emotionally and physically trapped.

Stretching out on the couch, I closed my eyes, trying to relax and concentrate. I'd stay away from Rosy's family. I wasn't running away, though. I refused to run. I wouldn't become a fugitive for something I didn't do. I didn't care if I was killed by my enemies or by Rosy's enemies; I wasn't running. If the cops wanted to arrest me, I didn't care about that, either. I was fed up. I'd had it. Whatever was meant to happen would happen. If I ran, I'd be admitting guilt. If I stayed, I could very well be killed.

For the next week, I stayed in the house, drinking and drowning in self-pity. The neighborhood had collected enough money to pay for Rosy's funeral and burial. The street gossip had spread like wildfire, blaming me, Crazy Bobby, for Rosy's death. The second week after Rosy's death, I started going out again. I couldn't stand the confinement any longer. Most people on the streets shunned me. I could have been ambushed and killed very easily because I wasn't armed. I didn't want a weapon. My death wish was sneaking back, just like it had in Nam. This time, I was unarmed in an asphalt jungle, with enemy forces watching and waiting. What were they waiting for? *Here I am! Do it! Kill me! Get it over with, bastards!*

The local cops picked me up for questioning during the second week. They talked to me for a couple of hours about Rosy. I mentioned nothing about the death threats or any of her meetings with the Feds. I didn't trust the cops or the Feds, and I wasn't saying any more than I had to. Telling everything I knew would have only been manipulated to involve me more. The cops tried to pressure me into confessing to Rosy's murder. Finally, they let me go because there was no evidence against me.

Two more weeks went by, and it was now July. I was still drinking heavily. Almost a month had gone by since Rosy's death. I was starting to think the cops knew I didn't do it and were looking into the case as a drug contract hit.

On July 8th, I stole a car from Lackawanna and drove to Buffalo. I did it because I wanted to talk to some people I knew there who might be able to tell me more about Rosy's death. I never did talk to them, though; I was drunk and got arrested by Buffalo police for crashing the stolen car into two parked cars. My uncle, the paralegal, who happened to be in town visiting, got me out in his custody the next day.

On July 11th, I was arrested for criminal mischief by the Lackawanna police. I'd chased a drug addict I knew and his girlfriend to their apartment, where I proceeded to break several of their windows. I'd heard that this guy knew something about Rosy's death. Maybe I was starting to get some people nervous, because on July 15th, I was arrested again. It was around seven o'clock in the morning, and I was still sound asleep in bed after a night of cheap whiskey and wine. I didn't hear a thing when four Lackawanna police detectives smashed in my grandmother's door. When they charged into my bedroom, I instinctively jumped up. I was still drunk, and I saw blurry figures surrounding my bed. I tried to focus on what was happening, and then a voice boomed, "You're under arrest, Parker, for the murder of Rosilee Fergurson! On your feet, get dressed!"

The detectives had their weapons aimed point blank at me. Being disoriented, it took a few minutes for me to get dressed. While I was being handcuffed, my Miranda rights were read to me. Two detectives searched my room, inch by inch. Finding the set of bloody clothes on the closet floor, one of the detectives asked, "Are these the clothes you wore when you killed Rosilee Fergurson?" I didn't answer. My head was pounding with pain, my stomach ached, and I felt nauseated. I was too tired and drunk to even curse at them. It wasn't Rosy's blood on the clothes, which they eventually found out through forensic tests.

I got a hurried glimpse of my grandmother as they shuffled me out the front door. She was crying. I'd never seen my grandmother cry before, and it was emotionally devastating to me. I was responsible for those tears. *I never should have come here to stay!*

Outside, the day was already warm and humid, and the sun was shining. I was taken to the Lackawanna Police Station. They took my mug shot and fingerprinted me. In a small basement room, I was roughly pushed down in a chair. There were only two detectives in the room. One of them sat down behind a desk with a typewriter on it. Putting a sheet of paper in the typewriter, he typed for a couple of minutes, then stopped. The other detective had his .38 pistol out. He twirled the cylinder, then pointed the pistol at me. He did this repeatedly while I sat there, handcuffed and shackled. I was still drunk, exhausted, and in pain. I barely heard the detective on the typewriter when he started bombarding me with questions. For a few hours, I stayed in that room, trying to answer questions while I listened to the clickety-clack of that damn typewriter.

The questions ranged from my childhood history, to Vietnam, to my martial arts training, to how I knew Rosy, and to her death. They asked again if she was a friend, if she was a girlfriend, if I loved her, and if I knew she was a police informant. They asked me if I killed her out of jealousy, anger, a Vietnam flashback, or if I was paid to kill her. They said Rosy had been beaten by an expert before her head was crushed. I was a martial arts expert, so they assumed I did it. They even showed me black and white pictures of Rosy lying dead in the field. They kept dwelling on Vietnam because they saw that it upset me to talk about Nam. They made me go into great detail about the times I had to enter hand-to-hand combat in Vietnam. The one detective finally stopped typing and set several sheets of typed paper in front of me. He told me to stand up. I obeyed. He took the handcuffs off, then shoved me back down in the chair. The other detective stood out of my range, his pistol ready in case of trouble.

A pen was placed on top of the papers, and I was told to sign them. I refused. They talked to me for fifteen minutes, trying to convince me to sign. Finally, they told me I could go home once I signed the papers. They said that the papers only stated what I'd been saying, that I had nothing to do with Rosy's murder. Being mentally and physically exhausted, as well as in pain and still drunk, I finally signed the papers, thinking I'd be released. I'd told the detectives over and over again that I knew nothing about her death or that she was an informant. Of course, I *did* know that Rosy was going to be killed and that she was an informant, but I wasn't telling that to the police.

I was not released like they had promised. After signing, I was handcuffed and taken to the Erie County Jail on Delaware Avenue in Buffalo. I was being charged with second-degree murder. After mug shots and fingerprints were taken there, I saw a doctor for my headache, stomachache, and dizziness. After that, I was issued bed sheets, a blanket, a pillow, and assigned to a cell. Too tired to make my bed, I stretched out on the bare mattress with my pillow and fell asleep. I wouldn't know for some time that what I had signed at the police station was a statement confessing to Rosy's murder due to a Vietnam flashback. The detectives had deviously manipulated what I'd said to them.

Rosy's death and my signed, fabricated confession would only be part of the strange events that were entering my life. I would feel used and sacrificed, as if I were a pawn in a game of chess. I have yet to discover the full story behind these events. Like the solitary pawn, I was important enough to be involved, but I was the least important when it came to the overall scheme of things.

Chapter Eleven

I had only been in the county jail for a few days when I got into a fight with two other inmates. The inmates had stolen my breakfast and then attacked me. I beat them so severely that they were taken to a medical hospital for treatment.

Still enraged after the fight, I refused to go back to my cell when ordered to by the guards. After locking the other inmates in their cells, several guards who were part of the jailhouse goon squad rushed to physically restrain me. I was sadistically beaten, maced, kicked, stripped naked, handcuffed, shackled, and dragged to the Hole.

The Hole was a solitary confinement cell in total darkness. With a solid steel door, the cell was hot, filthy, and the air was stale, smelling of dried urine and feces. Dead roaches were lying everywhere, live ones scurried about, and the cell was caked with dry blood. On the floor lay a dirty, smelly, ripped mattress.

I'd been in a quiet, depressed rage for a couple of days since I'd been locked up for something I didn't do. So when the two inmates had taken my breakfast and attacked me, they were startled by the extremely violent response they got.

After being in the Hole for two days, I was finally allowed to see a medical doctor for my cuts and bruises. After ten days in the Hole, I was taken out and put on another tier. I found out that the inmates who'd stolen my food were pressing assault charges against me. This surprised the hell out of me, considering they physically attacked me first.

On July 30th, I was handcuffed, shackled, and taken to Lackawanna for my preliminary hearing. The city court judge presiding at this hearing would determine if my case should be thrown out of court, dealt with at the city court level, or handed over to a county grand jury for a possible murder indictment.

What kind of evidence could they possibly have aside from a coerced confession from me? This case has to be thrown out of court, damn it! I didn't kill Rosy! Why am I being put through this?

I sat down near the front and was told to remain seated by the detectives. The courtroom was small with only a few people in it. I watched a man standing near a table on the other side of the courtroom as he talked briskly to the court stenographer. A few times, he stopped for a moment to stare at me before continuing his conversation. I sensed that he was the assistant district attorney assigned to my case. I looked over my shoulder toward the center of the courtroom for a clearer view of the few people I'd passed while coming in. I recognized Rosy's mother as she sat weeping, a handkerchief pressed to her face. She was in her late fifties to early sixties. She looked so weary and drained sitting there. Right next to her sat a middle-aged woman I didn't recognize. The unknown woman was probably a relative or a friend giving moral support. They were both avoiding eye contact with me, so I looked a few seats behind them to see who was sitting there. The dark-skinned, middle-aged, obese woman in the back I recognized as Anna Bishop. What was she doing in the courtroom? If Anna were here to give support to Rosy's mother, why wasn't she sitting with her? Anna owned one of the after-hours places in Lackawanna, and I'd worked for her a few times. Besides the illegal gambling at her place, she also sold drugs on the side. Anna and Rosy's mother lived in the same apartment building, which was right across the street from Fat Jack's Bar on Steelawanna Avenue. Anna was a gossiper, so she was probably here to get an earful. She wouldn't make direct eye contact with me, either, so I turned back around.

I was feeling nervous, angry, and worried as I sat there. I wasn't sure of anything. I felt trapped and depressed, knowing I shouldn't be there, let alone handcuffed and shackled. About fifteen minutes elapsed before the judge entered from a side room. The hearing was called to order, and the murder charge against me was read. After this, the Lackawanna DA called Rosy's mother to the stand.

The DA questioned her carefully about the events that occurred in the dark, early morning hours of June 11th. Rosy's mother tearfully testified that she was asleep in her upstairs apartment when she was suddenly awakened by her daughter's frantic yelling and loud pounding on the downstairs door. Getting out of bed, she went to the window, opened it, and looked out. She said that she saw no one but her daughter at the door. She asked Rosy what was wrong, but Rosy only pleaded desperately for her to come downstairs and open the door. After closing the window, Rosy's mother said that she rushed downstairs and opened the door, but Rosy was no longer there. Rosy's mother was crying, her face soaked in tears. The DA dismissed her from the stand, saying he had no further questions for her.

She left the stand slowly, still sobbing and wiping the tears from her face. My God, I wanted to rush over to her, to touch her, to somehow ease the agonizing pain deep inside her. How could all this be happening? How could it be real? I missed Rosy, too. I cared about her. I loved her as a precious friend. I tried to save her life! I really tried! Rosy's mother never looked at me, but I sensed no hate in her eyes, only tremendous grief. I was self-conscious about the hurt she felt because I was sure she thought I was guilty.

I was shaking uncontrollably as I watched her walk back to her seat. Why wasn't she angry? Why didn't she curse, scream, and condemn me to hell's darkest corner? I could have handled her rage far better than I could handle her enormous grief. What could I possibly say? What could I do to prove to her it wasn't me? Other people wanted Rosy dead; I didn't. I tried to warn her, but she wouldn't listen. Why was it my fault? Why me?

As I sat, pondering these thoughts, I became even more bewildered when the DA called Anna Bishop to the stand. What the hell did she have to do with this hearing? After she took the stand, the DA asked her to identify herself to the court and give her home address. Anna was extremely tense while she spoke, her small brown eyes darting back and forth. Suddenly, her eyes became wide and panic-stricken, and they locked on mine. With a pained expression on her face, she nervously yelled, "They're making me do this! I don't want to do this, I'm sorry! Two detectives came to my home, threatening to close down my after-hours place if I didn't do this."

I could see the stunned expressions on the DA's face and the judge's face as they briefly looked at one another. They were surprised to hear this outburst from her, but they weren't so surprised that they cared to question her further about the legality of the two detectives' actions. It took a couple of minutes for the DA and the judge to calm her down; she kept repeating loudly how the detectives had threatened her.

After Anna calmed down, she testified that she had an upstairs apartment in the same apartment building as Rosy's mother. She said she had windows that faced the street. In the early morning hours of June 11th, she said she was wakened by Rosy's yelling and pounding on the downstairs door. Being curious, she got up and went to the window, opened it, and peeked out. Anna said that Rosy's mother was already on her way downstairs to open the door. During that time, Anna said, a tall black man suddenly appeared out of nowhere and grabbed Rosy from behind. The man had his left arm around Rosy's neck in a choke hold, and with his right hand had Rosy's right arm twisted tightly behind her back. Rosy was trying to resist. Anna said the strong man quickly pushed Rosy down the street and around the corner. The DA asked Anna to describe the clothing the man wore, and she recalled that he was wearing dark clothing and a light applejack-style hat. The applejack hat was one of the newest "in" styles for many street people in Lackawanna and Buffalo. The hat was basically an oversized pullover cap. My heart started racing when I heard Anna mention the hat, because sometimes I wore a blue applejack hat.

After hearing this, I instantly realized what was coming next. The DA asked her if she recognized the man, and Anna reluctantly nodded and said, "Yes." The DA asked if that man was sitting in the courtroom, and again she responded, "Yes." The DA asked her to point to the man she saw grabbing Rosy, and Anna pointed hesitantly at me. Anger surged through me, and I jumped out of my seat, glaring at her. The detectives quickly sat me back down. She was lying! She was deliberately destroying my life to save her after-hours place and avoid arrest for illegal gambling and drug dealing!

The utter frustration of knowing she was lying and the helplessness I felt inside filled me with a tearful fury. Anna avoided my eyes when she left the stand, her head low and her face ashamed. The judge ruled that my case should be turned over to a county grand jury for a possible murder indictment. About a month later, I would be indicted by a grand jury for second-degree murder.

Many years later, I finally found out what Anna had truly seen that night. Several people from Lackawanna told me what Anna had told them just days after Rosy's death. Anna had seen a man grabbing Rosy and forcing her down the street and around the corner. What she failed to mention in court was that there was a car, with its lights off, that slowly followed the man and Rosy around the corner. Anna had also said that she couldn't recognize the man with Rosy because it was too dark outside.

After first hearing this story, I began to realize how Anna got herself into this. She was a gossiper, so she told everyone in the neighborhood about what she saw. Her story on the streets obviously got back to the police. They probably picked her up for questioning, but they weren't too thrilled that she couldn't identify the man. Because I had a tough reputation on the streets and was the prime suspect, I'm sure the police wanted to build a strong, airtight case against me.

They put pressure on Anna, threatening to close her after-hours place and arrest her if she didn't have second thoughts about what she saw. So Anna changed her story and signed a sworn affidavit to her new story.

Anna wasn't stupid, and like many of the street people, she had to know that Rosy was an informant with a murder contract on her head. When she saw an unidentified man grab Rosy and a car follow them, she must have known something was going down. Since she was a hopeless gossiper and an attention seeker, she couldn't resist running her mouth on the streets. By the time she realized that she didn't want any part of a drug-related murder, though, it was already too late.

After the hearing, I was brought back to the county jail. Lying quietly on my bunk, I stared blankly at the ceiling. My God, murder? In prison for the rest of my life? For something I didn't do? Why me? Where the hell did I go wrong? What could I have possibly done in my life to deserve this?

In deep concentration, my eyes closed tightly, my thoughts drifted further and further back through my existence. My mind was ruthlessly searching for a reason, a clue, anything that would help justify my tormented life.

It seems my family and relatives had a strange fascination about well-known names. I say this because my father's full name was Jesse James Parker. One of my uncles was named Douglas MacArthur Smith. I have a cousin named Bonnie Parker. I was named Robert Parker, which was Butch Cassidy's real name. And

I have other relatives named after famous and infamous people. Strange, but true.

My mother was fifteen years old when she became pregnant by my father, who was twenty. They got married during the pregnancy, and a year after I was born, my sister, Deborah, was born. When I was five years old, my parents got divorced. My mother was bitter over the divorce and despised my father. As a result, she started to physically abuse me because I looked so much like him. She'd curse at me while punching me, kicking me, and beating me with an electrical extension cord. There were times when she'd strip me naked, tie up my hands and feet with rope, and beat me. And there were times when she'd put me in the basement in total darkness for hours at a time, telling me that the boogey-man was going to come and eat me. I would actually pass out for short periods of time in the basement because I was so terrified of the boogey-man. Sometimes, she'd come home angry and force me to pack some of my clothes into a paper shopping bag, and then put me in the car and drive me miles from home, and leave me stranded alone on some strange street corner, telling me she didn't want me anymore, and that my father was coming to pick me up. For hours, I'd stand there, scared to death. I always expected to see my father, not realizing that my mother had lied to me again. And I never dared to leave that street corner until she came back, because my mother always threatened to kill me if I did, and there was no doubt in my terrified child-mind that she was capable of killing me whenever she chose to.

When I was in elementary school, a letter was sent to my mother, letting her know how intelligent I was. As a result, she started visualizing me as a medical doctor or some type of specialist or surgeon when I grew up, and then I'd have enough money to take care of her when she got old. To do that, she felt I had to become a perfectionist in school and at home, and so the cursing and beatings increased because I was not living up to her perfectionist standards. She taught me how to cook, sew, knit, wash clothes, iron, and even had me scrubbing the floors on my hands and knees. And if my work in school or at home didn't pass her inspection, she'd get angry, curse me, then beat me.

As a child, I wasn't assertive, outgoing, or physically aggressive at all. Because of this, I kept getting my butt kicked by neighborhood bullies and street gangs. It became the neighborhood pastime to kick my butt. And when I'd come running home, crying, with a swollen lip, eye, or bloody nose, my mother would beat me then, too. She told me I should fight back on the streets when I was attacked instead of running home all the time. I didn't quite understand her reasoning then, but I do now. There's an unwritten law in the ghetto. Not standing up for oneself is considered a serious and embarrassing weakness. In the asphalt jungle of the ghetto, only the strong survived.

My sister was a wild tomboy who would verbally and physically fight back on the streets. My mother felt embarrassed because I was the only boy in the family, but I wouldn't fight. To alleviate this problem, she enrolled me in karate classes three times a week. For two and a half years, I faithfully attended my karate classes. One slight problem prevailed, though: I still wouldn't fight back on the streets. I was highly aggressive in karate classes, but always passive on the streets.

As a kid, I was never afraid of fighting. It was just that I hated violence. I saw absolutely nothing constructive in wanting to hurt another human being. I've seen beatings, stabbings, shootings, and dead people on the streets, and I wanted no part of violence.

My favorite subject in school was history, and I would read all I could in the city library about it. What shocked me so much as a kid was that mankind's history was filled with violence. From violence between two people to entire countries fighting, there was blood being spilled and people being maimed and killed all through history. Why the violence? Why did civilized people do this? No matter how far back in history I went, I found violence. There had to be a better way to resolve problems.

As a poor, naive kid, I despised violence and wanted to wipe it off the face of the earth. I didn't realize it then, but the constant beatings I got from my mother were influential in my hatred of violence. It's hard to imagine a teenage kid believing that violence could be eradicated from the earth. I looked at things as either black or white as a kid, with no gray area whatsoever. To me, there was only good and evil in the world. Violence was evil. Take away or destroy the evil, and only good would be left. It was that simple to me. I was foolish and pathetically naive.

By the end of the tenth grade, I was willing to do anything to get away from my mother. She was a tyrant and brutal to me. I had to get away from her or I was going to go crazy. I was desperate, and I became interested in joining the army. In the army, I felt I'd be able to fight this evil that plagued mankind's very existence. It was also the only way for me to get out of the ghetto, to travel and see the world. And more importantly, joining the army was the only way to get away from my mother at seventeen. It was the summer of 1966. To join military service during this time, a person had to be seventeen with a signed consent form from a parent or guardian. I had serious doubts about my mother signing this form.

I finally got the nerve to show my mother the army consent form. To my surprise, she signed the form. I expected a lecture, cursing, or a beating, but she wasn't hostile at all. I understood why when she told me to send money home every month. I agreed for a chance to get out the house.

My experience in the army was a crash course in the harsh reality of the world. I quickly learned that very few things were black and white or absolute. I learned that the only thing power respects is equal or superior power. And I went from being obsessed with nonviolence to being obsessed with my personal survival, regardless of the violence involved. I became exactly what I'd always hated: an evil entity.

As I lay on the bunk in my jail cell, I tried to make some sense out of my life and put it in perspective. I felt mentally trapped and emotionally unwanted. My loneliness was beyond description.

After a few months in the county jail, I found out that a lawyer named Thomas Polk was assigned to my case. Polk had a suppression hearing on my coerced confession. He was trying to get my confession thrown out, but the judge ruled against it. After he lost the suppression hearing, he talked to me about taking an insanity plea. With my confession and Anna's testimony, he said I'd be found guilty and sent to prison for a very long time.

Polk's breath and clothes reeked heavily of booze. He was an alcoholic. His suits were dingy, his face flushed, and he had bloodshot eyes. But I trusted Polk, simply because I had no one else to turn to. He told me that taking an insanity plea and spending a year or two in a state mental institution was better than prison. From the very beginning, I let him know that I didn't kill Rosy. I told him everything, from the time I met Rosy in the bar to the time I was arrested. He listened, but he seemed disinterested. He explained that the evidence against me would find me guilty in a court of law, and that I should go with the insanity plea.

I was devastated. When I thought of all the things I did do, to be locked up now for something I didn't do seemed incomprehensible. I had panic attacks, flashbacks, nightmares, and I'd quietly cry myself to sleep sometimes. I was feeling hopeless, desperate, and I found myself wishing more and more for a normal, average life. There I was, twenty-one years old, a mental and physical wreck. If destinies are to be believed, was this my impending fate, my imminent purpose?

I started to believe that I was born with a dark cloud over my head, a dark cloud that somehow grew bigger and more sinister as I grew older. It seemed to me that tragedy has stalked me, haunted me, and overwhelmed me in almost every important aspect of my life.

After seeing two psychiatrists, I was put on a psychotropic drug called Thorazine. I took this powerful drug four times a day, seven days a week. The clear, thick liquid was given to me straight. It took my breath away as it went down my throat, leaving me gagging and gasping. Only after taking the Thorazine straight would I be allowed Kool-aid or water.

The Thorazine kept me extremely tired and lethargic. It made my eyes blurry, and it made me sleep a lot and eat twice as much. It kept my mind in a groggy haze, making it hard to concentrate on reading or watching TV. Though I was given a white pill for side-effects, I still suffered severe complications. My jaw muscles became taut and ached and I couldn't close my mouth. My lower back muscles became tight and painful, and would stiffen at an odd angle. The drug seemed to make me more depressed. No matter how hard I tried, I couldn't fight off its eerie effects. Physically, I was held prisoner by steel bars, and mentally, I was held prisoner by a drug. Sometimes, I daydreamed about being married to a good woman, having children, a good job, and being happy with life. I daydreamed about My Ling and Toni, always imagining happy endings. And sometimes, I dreamed about being a kid again who never wanted to grow up because adults were too complicated and dangerous.

I had fantasies about bending the steel bars with my bare hands and floating through the air, a free man. Or I'd see all the jail doors suddenly open, and I'd walk through each one to my freedom. I also had traumatic nightmares about the physical abuse my mother put me through, about being tortured and killed by VC and NVA soldiers, and about being put in the electric chair in prison and killed.

As each day, week, and month went by, I found myself desperately trying to escape reality more and more. This was my mental survival mechanism. Reality only spelled doom and heartache for me. Fatalism had become my reality. At times, I wondered if I really had gone insane, and I tried to pinpoint the moment it had happened. Could I truly be a madman? Was it possible for a madman to recognize his own madness? Was it possible that I could have killed Rosy because I was insane, or had an alcoholic blackout, or a flashback from the war? I remembered everything that happened the night she died. I didn't kill Rosy. But why was I feeling so ashamed and guilty? I didn't realize it at the time, but the shame and guilt I felt was not for killing Rosy, but because I wasn't there to save her. If I had stayed with her that night, she'd still be alive. I believed that with all my heart.

I'd lost my mother, in a way, because we weren't exactly close while I was growing up. I lost My Ling to death in Nam. I came home to find that Carol was a heroin addict who had gone from bad to worse. Toni appeared in my life, and just as fast, she disappeared. Rosy came back into my life as a heroin addict and a friend, and death swept her away. I had warm feelings for all these people in my heart; I loved each one of them in a very special way.

The time I spent in the county jail did not help me emotionally. I didn't believe I was crazy, but I knew something was dreadfully wrong with me. I had two worlds revolving inside me, two entities — the civilized man and the savage man. The civilized man would never have placed himself in such a predicament. So where did my savage part come from? Did it lie dormant inside me from birth until it was harnessed and refined by the military? Was the savage man inside me a part of every man's

206

being? Did a mysterious force come out of the infinite halls of darkness to ignite mankind's dark side? Man still remains a mystery unto himself, a complex puzzle not yet resolved. I am certain, now, that the civilized man and the savage man exist in each and every one of us. Two worlds, two entities fused together as a whole; brutal enemies, but bonded brothers forever.

During the latter part of March in 1972, I went to trial for the murder of Rosy. I had a non-jury trial; the judge made the final ruling in my case. The psychiatrists testified that I was dangerously mentally ill. They told the judge I was hearing imaginary voices, that I was a trained time bomb, and that I talked about violence and killing like other people might talk about a baseball or football game.

On March 30th, 1972, the judge dropped all the minor charges against me and found me not guilty by reason of insanity on the murder charge. This meant that the court had found me guilty of murder, but at the time of the crime, I was mentally ill. Testimony from the two psychiatrists told the judge that I was still dangerously mentally ill. The judge ruled that I be put in the custody of the New York State Department of Mental Hygiene for treatment.

What the NYS Criminal Judicial System did not know or understand was that I was not mentally ill, but suffered from what's called PTSD (Post Traumatic Stress Disorder) from the war. This type of disorder was not known to the criminal courts in the early 1970s, and it would not be officially recognized by the American Psychiatric Association until about 1980. PTSD was widely known in the military as Delayed Stress Reaction or the Wyatt Earp Syndrome. As explained by the American Psychiatric Association, PTSD was not a mental illness but a reaction to the catastrophic stresses experienced in war. The definition of PTSD concerning combat veterans in Southeast Asia was that it had a prolonged effect on a person's personality development, patterns of adjustment, coping styles, and interpersonal functioning. Some of the emotional symptoms of PTSD were psychic or emotional numbness, feeling like a walking time bomb, anxiety and specific fears associated with combat experiences, emotional constriction and unresponsiveness, a tendency to react under stress with survival tactics, sleep disturbances and recurring nightmares of combat, hyper-alertness, suicidal feelings, flashbacks to traumatic events experienced in war, and a fear of losing a loved one through death or rejection.

After almost two years in the county jail, I was transferred by deputy sheriffs to the Buffalo State Psychiatric Hospital in April of 1972. This psychiatric center was on the west side of Buffalo on Forest Avenue. Never in my wildest dreams would I have imagined that my incarceration would last well over thirty years. Had I known in Vietnam that I'd be locked up for over thirty years, I'd have come home in a body bag. To the day I die, I will mean this with the utmost sincerity.

Chapter Twelve

At the Buffalo State Psychiatric Center, I was put in a ward with geriatric patients. After a month of ward restriction, I was given privileges. Employees said I had to stay on the grounds and be back in the ward for all three meals. And I had to be back in the ward in the evenings before it was dark. The Buffalo Psych Center was an open-grounds, minimum security, civil psychiatric institution.

Employees reminded me that if I got into the slightest trouble or ran away, it would result in the police taking me back to the county jail. Just mentioning the county jail sent shivers through my body. I despised that place. Spending almost two years there was enough for any man.

I spent about six months at the psych center. I tried to stay out of trouble, but it seemed that my flimsy willpower just got weaker and weaker. I started drinking again. The booze was supplied to me by patients from the Alcoholic Rehab Unit. I went back to drinking cheap whiskey and wine, wallowing in my own self-pity.

During my stay there, I met a patient by the name of Joan Stevens. Joan inadvertently led me down the disastrous path of violence again. She was white, pretty, and shapely, about 5'7" tall, and had shoulder-length brown hair. Her deep blue eyes were highly noticeable and sensuous. Joan was in her early thirties and had been locked up in state psych centers for most of her life. She'd never married, but she had a baby in her early twenties. The baby was put up for adoption because the state found her unfit to raise the child. Whenever she got angry at a male patient on the grounds, she'd threaten him by saying I would kick his butt. I told her to stop saying that several times, but she kept on doing it anyway. Sometimes, I'd get these really hostile looks from male patients because of her.

Joan had a habit of stealing, and she enjoyed walking off the grounds to nearby stores or shops to do it. She always wanted me to go with her, but I refused. I wasn't about to get arrested because she was a kleptomaniac. I just couldn't go back to the miserable confinement of that county jail again.

She enjoyed smoking reefer whenever she could, too. Her mother lived near the psych center, and on weekends, she walked over there to visit. Many times, she told me how boring it was in psychiatric institutions and that she wanted to run away. She tried to manipulate me into robbing a nearby bank so we could run away together. No way was I robbing a bank with her, or with anyone else, for that matter. We argued about this constantly, and she always ended up calling me a coward. I didn't care what she called me; I wasn't robbing any bank.

On October 20th, Joan and I took an unauthorized walk to the nearby Delaware Park. It was late afternoon. I was already on my second pint of cheap whiskey, and Joan had already smoked a few joints when she started arguing with me again. Angrily pointing a finger at me, she shouted, "You're a coward, Robert! You're not a man! We could steal a car, rob a bank, and be out of here in no time."

I started to get angry and yelled back, "I don't care what you call me, I'm not robbing no bank!" I took another swig of the whiskey and stood there, glaring at her. It was starting to get dark.

"You're a coward, Robert!" she screamed bitterly, her eyes glazed and red from the reefer. "The staff says you're tough and dangerous, but you're just a coward. We could rob a bank easily. I'm fed up with institutions and everyone telling me what to do."

I shouted, "You are one stupid bitch, you know that? What's your problem? Are you dumb? Deaf? What? How many times do I have to tell you? I'm not robbing no bank!"

She ignored what I was saying. She pulled a folding knife out of her purse, saying, "We don't even need a gun. We can use this knife to rob the bank. I bought it the other day while I was visiting home, and it's sharp, too!"

Unfolding the knife, she waved it in my face. I was stunned. I'd never really thought of her as being crazy, but she *had* to be crazy. The knife, stealing a car, robbing a bank, running away — it was *all* crazy. "Give me the knife, Joan," I said, "before you hurt yourself. I'm tossing it in the lake."

She took a swift step back, still holding the knife in front of her, shouting, "No! We don't have to rob a bank! We can rob people with the knife and use the money to run away!"

I stepped closer to her, reaching out for the knife. Trying to dissuade her, I said, "It's getting dark. Let me throw the knife in the lake so we can get back, okay?"

Joan tried to step back again, jerking the knife away from me. I grabbed her wrist this time, pulling the knife toward me. With sudden determination, she grabbed the knife with her other hand and used both hands to pull on the knife. This tug of war went on for a few seconds, and then she suddenly kicked me in the groin. I jumped back in pain, letting go of her wrist. Because I let go so fast and she was still pulling the knife toward her, the knife struck her in the chest, above her blouse. The slight cut was superficial, but still, there was blood. We were both shocked as we stared at the cut and the blood.

Joan began to smile. Then that smile broke into loud laughter as she hollered, "You're in trouble now, Robert! If we go back to the hospital, you'll go back to jail!"

My heart raced. I panicked, saying nervously, "It was an accident! It was an accident!"

"They ain't going to care about that," she said, smiling. "We go back, and you'll go to jail! They'll lock you away forever! *We have to run away now!*" My heart beat even faster and I began to hyperventilate. I kept staring at Joan's cut while the blood oozed out and smeared her white blouse.

Oh my God, I can't go back to jail. I won't be locked up again, I can't! Piercing pain pounded in my head as I stared at the blood. The distinct sound of chopper engines churned loudly in my mind. The harsh sound of light and heavy machine gun fire echoed all around me. With both hands on my head, I crumbled to the ground, screaming. My body twisted and jerked in the grass like a fish out of water. I continued screaming as I saw myself drowning in a sea of blood. All around me, dead bodies were floating, bodies of VC, NVA, and Vietnamese civilians, all bobbing around in the blood. An emotional and mental war raged fiercely in my mind. The pain was unbearable. And from the depths of my soul, the pain brought forth a part of me I wanted to forget. The savage man within me was taking control. With every beat of my heart, it became stronger and more lethal. And savage man was Nighthawk-One.

Nighthawk-One had been created within me to be a survivor and a merchant of death. I stopped thrashing around in the grass as Nighthawk-One took control. Survival was everything, now. To wage a relentless war, Nighthawk-One knew he had to survive. And to survive, he had to escape, which meant he needed money, supplies, and transportation.

About a minute must have passed since I'd fallen to the ground. It was dark outside, and the park's lights were on. I got up, staring oddly at Joan. She was still standing there with the knife in her hand, a bewildered expression on her face. Then her eyes grew wide with fright. She sensed that I had changed. Spinning around, she bolted away, screaming for help. I caught her and took the knife. She kept screaming as I threw her to the ground and sat on her. "Stop screaming!" I yelled. "You do as you're told and you won't be hurt."

"Robert, please," she cried. "What happened? What's wrong with you?"

"Shut up and do as you're told," I warned her. "Now get on your feet."

After she stood up, I put my right arm tightly around her waist. I had her button her sweater all the way up so the cut and bloody blouse couldn't be seen. I told her to put her arm around my waist and to keep it there. We started walking, and to any observers, we were just another couple. After walking for a few minutes, I still had no idea where I was going. All I knew for sure was that I was in enemy territory. I had to escape and evade the enemy or they would destroy me. It didn't matter how I got it, but I needed money, supplies, and transportation.

A plan suddenly dawned on me, and I knew what I had to do. I told Joan to take me to her mother's house. Her mother lived nearby, and I'd get the things I needed from her. It took about fifteen minutes to get there. Joan had told me before that her father was dead and her mother lived alone. She lived on the first floor of a two-story apartment building. I had Joan stand in front of the door so her mother could see her clearly. I stood to the side of the door, out of sight. Joan knocked a few times, and her mother answered the door. She was surprised to see Joan and asked why she wasn't at the hospital.

It was then that I pushed Joan into the apartment and closed the door behind me. We were all in the kitchen. Her mother was short, white haired, and in her early sixties. She was frightened by my sudden appearance. I told them not to scream or try to escape. I told Mrs. Stevens I wanted all the money in the house. She gave me a few dollars and some change, but I needed more. I knew she was on Social Security and had little money, so I checked around the house, looking for anything small and valuable I could sell on the streets. The only items I found were several pieces of jewelry from her bedroom. I was so frustrated I even took Joan's small stash of reefer to sell.

I found a shopping bag and filled it with food from the cupboards and the refrigerator. I found some rope and tied up Mrs. Stevens. Then, picking her up, I took her to the bedroom, where I lay her on the bed. She didn't have a car, and I needed transportation. I asked Joan who lived in the upstairs apartment, and she said a man named Mr. Trevino lived there. She said that Trevino, who was in his early fifties, sometimes drove her back to the hospital and would take her mother to run errands.

I had Joan look out the window to see if his car was parked out front. It was. I then had Joan call him on the phone and tell him that her mother wanted to borrow some money. I was hoping to lure him downstairs, and it worked. She opened the door, and as he stepped in, I grabbed him by his shirt and brought the knife to his throat. I told him to do as he was told and not to struggle. I let him go and demanded his money and car keys. He only had a few dollars on him. I took him into the bedroom, tied and gagged him, and put him on the bed next to Mrs. Stevens.

Whenever I moved around the house, Joan stayed close to my side. She said she wouldn't try anything, and she still wanted to run away with me. Back in the bedroom, I just stood there, staring. She was still frightened, but now there was a gleam of exhilaration in her glazed eyes. She seemed weirdly excited by what was going on. I continued to stare at her mother and Mr. Trevino. A minute went by without me uttering a word.

"What are you thinking about, Robert? What are we going to do now?" Joan asked, her arm around my waist.

I felt a sudden rush of compassion as I stared at Joan's mother and Trevino. Compassion was an extremely poisonous and

213

threatening emotion to Nighthawk-One. As such, Nighthawk-One retreated, fleeing deeper and deeper into the confines of my soul. I became terribly worried as I realized what I had done. What should I do? I didn't want to go back to jail! Should I run, call the police, what?

My first impulse was to untie and comfort Joan's mother and Trevino, but I didn't. I was becoming more anxious as each second ticked by. "Let's go," I said to Joan in a weak voice. I wanted to get out of there fast. My chest hurt and the apartment was smothering me. I just wanted to erase the whole scene from my head and pretend it never happened. I wanted to get out of the apartment and out of the city of Buffalo. No more confinement, no more jail.

Joan grabbed the bag of food, and we went to Trevino's car. A few minutes later, I found the Thruway, and we were on our way out of Buffalo. Joan and I hadn't spoken a word since we got in the car. About an hour later, she suddenly burst into tears, sobbing loudly. She was hysterical, rocking back and forth. Surprised by her sudden outburst, I pulled the car over to the side of the road and stopped.

"I'm scared, Robert!" she sobbed. "I want to go back to the hospital! I want to see my mother! I can't do this, Robert! I can't believe all this is happening! I can't believe you really did all this! My mother could be hurt tied up like that, Robert! Please take me back! I'm begging you, please!"

Putting my arms around Joan, I told her I'd take her back. I was worried about returning to Buffalo, but I got off the Thruway. I began to realize that Joan never really wanted to run away. It was just a fantasy of hers that had abruptly become all too real through me. The reality of it was something she couldn't cope with. The mental institutions she'd been in for most of her life had protected her from the harsher realities of the world. It was this understanding that motivated me to turn back to Buffalo.

Once I was back in the city, I parked the car on a downtown street corner near Lafayette Square. I gave Joan all the change I had in my pocket. I told her to find a phone booth, call the police, and tell them what happened. I reassured her that the police would go to her home immediately. She kept telling me how sorry she was, and she thanked me for bringing her back. Opening the car door, she stepped out, then quickly leaped back in. She kissed me on the lips, then jumped back out again.

After she closed the door, I drove off. I got on Main Street, then turned down a side street, heading for the Thruway. I stopped for a red light at an intersection, and that was as far as I got. A police car screeched to a halt in the center of the intersection. I quickly shifted into reverse, preparing to hit the gas pedal, make a 180-degree turn in the street, and speed off in the opposite direction. Glancing into the rearview mirror, though, I saw another police car come to a halt about twenty yards behind me.

Using their car as cover, the two policemen in front aimed their pistols at me. The policemen behind me were using their open doors as a shield, and their pistols were aimed at me also. One of them yelled for me to put my hands out of the window and told me not to move.

I started to laugh. I sure didn't feel like laughing, but there I was, laughing at the dangerous situation I was in. Again, one of the policemen yelled for me to put my hands out of the window and not to move. I'd heard the command both times, but I just didn't care. I was going to jail, so I didn't care if they shot me dead right there. Still laughing, I opened the car door and got out, putting both hands on top of my head. They rushed forward, threw me against the car, handcuffed me, and took me to jail.

My criminal charges consisted of assault, kidnapping, unlawful imprisonment, robbery, forcible theft, burglary, auto theft, possession of marijuana, and possession of a dangerous weapon. I stayed at the Erie County Jail for nine months. My attitude was very bitter. I was constantly enraged and explosive. Some of the rage was directed inwardly, but the rest of my rage was directed at the world around me. I have no words to describe the intense emotional hurt I felt inside. I hated myself and the world.

I wanted to rip the savage part right out of me. I wanted to destroy it, to pound it into total oblivion. It seems I've been doomed in this world since the moment I was born. When my mother beat me as a child, she would tell me I was no good and evil. I wondered, deep in my soul, if I truly was an evil entity. Was the demonic savage man within me my true self, my truer being? Was I born in spiritual darkness and therefore doomed to live and die on the dark side? Was my soul destined to be evil as a punishment for wrongs perpetrated in another life, another time?

As a child, I didn't deserve the cursing and severe beatings I got. In Vietnam, while better American and Vietnamese people died, I didn't deserve to live.

Why didn't the police just kill me at the intersection when I disobeyed their orders? Why did I survive? Why didn't they shoot me so I could be free of this evil within me? I wanted to die.

I've often wondered about evil. To me, evil should be dealt with intelligently, and not just in religious discourse about God and Satan. The evil inside me was terrifying. It had an intimidating force, a temptation, a mystification, and a grisly charm. This evil was cunning, predatory, and bizarre. It seemed easier to be evil than it was to be good. Evil is used in war to dehumanize the enemy and to dehumanize other groups and races. The art of dehumanization is reprehensible, but its warped logic is incredibly efficient. Evil is brutal, relentless, and even alluring. And evil can be a savage liberation, like a sexual orgasm and a dynamite explosion blended together.

Evil somehow seems more entertaining, fascinating, and attractive than good. It's like a potent drug that is intoxicating and seductive to the human mind because it has to do with control, domination, and power. Is evil necessary to civilization? I don't know the answer to that, but what I do know is that my life has no meaning, no true purpose. I simply exist.

At my trial, I was found not guilty by reason of insanity on all charges. I was not sent back to the Buffalo Psych Center. The Department of Mental Hygiene had recently opened a maximum security forensic mental institution for the criminally insane. It was there that I was sent in July, 1973. The name of this mental institution was the Mid-Hudson Forensic Psychiatric Center. Mid-Hudson would become well known for housing the most dangerous people in the state. At any given time, Mid-Hudson housed about three hundred fifty people from all over New York State.

The employees working in the wards were called TAs (Treatment Aides). Each floor held thirty-five to forty patients. The building I was in was called Oak Hall. Most of the TAs at

Mid-Hudson were barbaric, sadistic, and inhumane to patients. The many violent incidents and brutal acts I witnessed or heard about will be part of me until the day I die. Having to physically restrain a violent, out-of-control patient and put him into a straitjacket, canvas sheet, or solitary confinement is one thing. But brutally beating a patient, before and after he was restrained, to the point where the patient suffers life-altering injuries, is an entirely different matter. The TAs punched, kicked, kneed, choked, cursed, and spat on their patients. It was like seeing a pack of wild, starving jackals descend upon a lone sheep that had been cornered. Many times, the victims had to be taken to an outside medical hospital due to the severe beatings, and sometimes, patients died. The vindictive TAs would laugh, joke, and brag about such incidents.

This type of behavior was easy for them because they simply dehumanized us. We were referred to as scumbags, lowlifes, brain-dead, coconuts, animals, and the scum of the state that nobody wanted. I've seen them throw urine on patients, tie and gag them, and make them eat their own feces. In their boredom, I've seen them antagonize calm patients into becoming violent, and I've seen them manipulate patients into beating other patients. Mid-Hudson made me recognize how easy it is for a group of human beings to completely dehumanize another group, just because they're different. This recognition shocked my senses, making me feel miserable and guilty about what I'd done and seen done to the Vietnamese people. To be on the receiving end of such a horrifying thing can bring serious enlightenment to a person.

There was a small number of TAs whom I will always re-member as being fair and just with their authority. Those TAs did their job properly, not wavering from the rules and regulations of the ward or psych center and being humane and understanding. I wish them all peace and happiness. They are truly an asset and a role model for the Department of Mental Health and for all of humanity.

I stayed at Mid-Hudson for about a year and nine months. The hurt and rage I felt inside did not make me one of Mid-Hudson's better patients. There were several occasions when I had to be restrained and put into a straitjacket, or tied to a bed in a canvas sheet, or stripped of my clothes and put into an isolation room. The average time a patient spent in a straitjacket was one day to several days. The average time spent in the sheet was one to three days. The time spent in the isolation room was one day to several days. These restraints were necessary due to the fights and personal vendettas I had. I never provoked a verbal or physical confrontation with another patient or with a TA, but I never backed off when a patient or a TA verbally harassed or physically attacked me, either. Not only would I fight, I'd ambush and attack patients and TAs who bothered me. I'd attack them in the hallways, in their sleep, at their desks, in the showers, while they were watching TV, in the main yard, and in the bathroom. It became well known throughout Mid-Hudson among patients and staff that I believed in retribution, regardless of the physical or psychological consequences.

During my stay at Mid-Hudson, I became personally and sexually involved with a TA in my ward. Her name was Ann Carlson. She lived in Walden, New York. Ann was white, in her mid-thirties, about 5'6", and had short blonde hair and green eyes. She was very pretty with a lovely figure. She first worked as a security guard at Mid-Hudson before she became a TA assigned to my ward. She talked to me in the ward and in the yard all the time. The conversations became more and more personal. One day, while we were talking in the yard, she told me she was falling in love with me. She said she thought about me constantly at work, at home, and in bed.

I'd been voted in by the other patients as the ward chairman. As ward chairman, I had several duties. One of the duties was to do the ward laundry. Whenever Ann worked the weekends, she always volunteered to escort me to the basement, where she and I had sex together. She gave me a few pictures of herself, and she also gave me a ring off her finger to keep. I hid those things in my dormitory locker. She wrote sexy notes and handed them to me secretly. I read the notes and then destroyed them. Some of the patients started complaining to the staff about Ann spending so much time with me and not enough time talking and interacting with them. They speculated that Ann and I were having a personal relationship. So the staff watched Ann and me more closely. There was no proof that we were personally involved, but her superiors finally talked to her about it anyway. She denied having any personal interest in me. Her superiors talked to me. I denied any personal interest. On one of Ann's pass days, and while I was off the ward, the staff searched my dormitory locker. They found the pictures and ring Ann had given me. We were questioned separately again, and we both denied any personal involvement. I told her superiors I'd stolen the pictures and ring from her purse. They wanted to fire Ann, but they couldn't because they had no proof we were involved. What they did do, though, was take her off the ward and reassign her to work the midnight shift in the female ward in another building.

About a month later, we had a brief talk in the main yard. She had come to pick up her check during the day shift. Ann said she loved me, but she had been warned not to have any contact with me. With tears in her eyes, she smiled and told me she was raised in an all-white community, and she had considered herself a racist until she met me. We were both heartbroken, but I understood the reality of what she was saying. After our short talk, she walked away, and I never saw her again. About ten years later, I heard what happened to Ann. She'd always loved motorcycles, and she had one of her own. While riding down a highway in New Jersey, a car struck her motorcycle. She survived, but tragically, the accident left her crippled for life.

During my stay at Mid-Hudson, the ward social worker questioned me about my military status. I had not given my military status much thought since I came home from Nam. There wasn't anything the army could do for me, so I'd put the matter out of my mind. Besides being AWOL, when a soldier has been in as much trouble with civilian authorities as I have, it was standard procedure to separate the soldier from the army with a dishonorable discharge. This had been done with soldiers who had done a lot less than what I'd been charged with, and they weren't even AWOL at the time. Being found not guilty by reason of insanity on serious criminal charges was considered a legal conviction by civilian and military law. So the US Army wouldn't touch me with a ten-foot pole, because I was AWOL and criminally insane. Or so I thought.

The social worker contacted the US Army, and all hell broke loose. Army officials at Fort Dix and Fort Monmouth, New Jersey, began calling Mid-Hudson, demanding my release to military authorities. The army officials wanted to send a chopper to Mid-Hudson to pick me up. They said that through a computer error, they had lost me in their systems. Unknown to New York State and to me at the time, my special operations background was the reason the US Army was overriding their standard procedure and demanding my custody. There were secret meetings going on in Washington pertaining to a major threat, a threat not only to national security, but to American citizens worldwide. There would be secret meetings like this going on for several years until the late 1970s, when Washington officially announced what it had done as a preventative measure for this type of national security threat. The meetings ultimately involved hundreds of American men with the skills and expertise of special operations. The secret meetings came about due to the massacre of Israeli athletes at the Munich Olympic Games in 1972 by terrorists.

The US Army's argument with Mid-Hudson was that I had never been discharged from the military, and therefore, I was the property of the federal government. Mid-Hudson stated that I was found not guilty by reason of insanity twice in a civilian court. I was getting psychiatric treatment, and as such, I was the property of New York State. To avoid media publicity, the US Army backed off. This was a tactical move by the army, though. I would hear from them again in the coming months.

In April 1975, I was transferred to the Buffalo Psychiatric Center. The Buffalo Psych Center didn't receive me with open arms. I was immediately put in a locked ward. The doctor and treatment team leader told me that the only privilege I might have would be a heavily escorted walk outside once or twice a month. I was given my own room and ate my meals in the ward. I was there with no future, no hope, nothing.

After being in the ward for about four months, one of the employees and I became personally involved. This led to a sexual relationship between us. Her name was Diane Mosley. She was black, in her late twenties, attractive, shapely, and six feet tall. She worked the three-thirty to eleven-thirty shift. She would sneak me off the ward sometimes by using the service elevator. We'd take it to the basement and go into an old employees' lounge to have sex.

Late one afternoon, while I was sitting in my room, Diane came and asked if I wanted to get off the ward for a little while. She wanted to take me to a hotel downtown for a few hours and be back before the next shift came on. Her coworkers agreed it was okay as long as we were back before the shift changed.

I left with Diane, taking the chance that we wouldn't be caught. We left the Psych Center, stopped at a liquor store, and went to a downtown hotel. Diane enjoyed snorting coke, and she had some with her. I was just drinking the booze while she snorted coke and drank. We had sex, and I had more booze, and she had more coke. We had more sex after this, and then she fell asleep in bed. It was getting late, so I tried to wake her up so we could get back. She wouldn't wake up so I kept shaking her. She finally woke up, but she was in an enraged drunken and drugged stupor. She cursed me for waking her, then slapped me hard across the face. Then, lifting a lamp near the bed, she hit me in the head, drawing blood. All this happened fast. Then she leaped out of bed, screaming, and took off naked out of the room. I got dressed in a hurry and nervously left the room, too. By the time I got downstairs to the lobby, though, hotel security was there to stop me. I didn't see or hear Diane; I had no idea where she was. And I would never see her again after that encounter.

The Buffalo Police took me back to the psych center. Everyone wanted to know the details about what happened. I told them all to fuck off. Diane was fired, and I was kept locked up in my room. I was fed meals in my room and escorted to the bathroom and shower. For about a month, my world consisted of talking to very few people and living in that small room. I had a typewriter, and I worked on my autobiography to occupy my time. I had almost two hundred typewritten sheets done. My nightmares and flashbacks increased. My nerves were terrible, and I was filled with anxiety, depression, hate, and rage.

After being at the Psych Center for six months, employees awakened me early in the morning on October 8th. They told me to pack up all my personal belongings. Even though I kept asking what was going on, they told me nothing. My belongings packed, two male employees escorted me out of the building into a state car. I still had no idea what was going on or where we were headed. We went to the Buffalo International Airport. I was turned over to an Air Force Medical Team. The team, in turn, escorted me aboard their Air Force Medical Plane. I was flown to Fort Dix, New Jersey, and I was met by three burly CIA agents from their Office of Security. They put me in a military car and drove me to the Walson Army Medical Hospital on the base. I was admitted to the secure psychiatric ward on the fourth floor of the hospital. One agent stayed with me while the other two left. They were going to work eight-hour shifts, so there would always be an agent with me. I was forbidden to talk to other patients in the ward.

The next day, I met Major Goodman, who was the chief psychiatrist. He told me he'd be my psychiatrist and personally take charge of my stay at Walson. He apologized for the inconvenience of having an agent with me at all times and said it wasn't his idea. Major Goodman was pleasant, and I felt comfortable in his presence. He acted more like a civilian than a military officer. Over the next few days, I had an enormous number of psychiatric and medical tests done. I felt mentally and physically violated by having to endure so many tests in such a short period of time.

Chapter Thirteen

I was truly relieved to be out of the Buffalo Psych Center and New York State. I was told I'd be getting back pay for most of the months I'd spent in civilian jails and mental institutions. I started to feel good about myself. I looked in the mirror sometimes, staring at the strange smile on my face. I seemed so different when I was smiling, so relaxed and content. It had been a long time since I had really smiled.

On October 13th, right after breakfast, I was told that Major Goodman wanted to see me. With an agent beside me, I went to Goodman's office, knocked, and entered. I saw the major sitting behind his desk. The person sitting in front of the desk, grinning, made me stop in my tracks. I panicked. My smile vanished as a haunting, shuddering chill swept through my body. Mixed feelings raced through my mind: emotional pain, mental anguish, suspicion, hostility, hate, rage, and vengeance. My breath became shallow and my heart pounded as I stared at this person. It was Major Small, except now he was Colonel Small. The sight of him flooded my mind with memories I'd tried to forget for years. I still hated Small. I could sense by the icy gleam in his eyes that he was still the same. Men like Small never change. They're too lost in their eccentric, egotistical patriotism for their country and their duty.

Colonel Small got out of his chair to greet me and vigorously shook my hand. He was acting like we were long-lost buddies as he patted me on the back. I had the sudden urge to puke in his face. He was as phony as a three-dollar bill. What was he up to? What was going on here? Whatever it was, I wanted no part of it. My nerves were jumping as Small invited me to sit in his chair. I was too surprised and upset to say anything as I sat down. What did he want? I tried to act calm, but my trembling hands showed my apprehension of being in his presence again.

Major Goodman and the agent left the office. Small sat down behind the desk, hands clasped together on the desktop, and grinned. He knew my mind was racing, analyzing, deducing, trying to figure out what was going on. I didn't fear Small, and yet, he was intimidating to me and knew it. What was it about him that made me feel so uncomfortable? Deep inside, I knew the answer. Small was a viciously ruthless man who was capable of anything. I hated him, and I wanted to scream it at the top of my lungs. But I didn't

"How's things been going, Sergeant?" he asked calmly.

Small wanted to play head games with me. He had to know everything that had happened to me since I left Nam. He wanted me to squirm while I told him how terrible my life has been. I refused to satisfy his sick ego by giving any details. "I've had some problems," I answered simply, shifting in my seat.

"That's the understatement of the decade," he laughed, opening a folder on the desk. "You've been a busy beaver since you came home. You've been charged with damn near every crime in the book: murder, assault, kidnapping, robbery, burglary, etc. And you've been associated with black and white organized crime figures. What have you got to say for yourself, Sergeant?"

What the hell did he expect me to say? I fucked up! We couldn't all be righteous, holy, and perfect like the great Colonel Small. I gave no immediate response.

"Are you aware that New York State wants you back?" he said, grinning.

I bolted upright in my seat after hearing this. Was he serious, or was he playing head games again? He saw the sudden worry in my eyes and the tension in my body. It was the type of reaction he expected and got. Bastard! Without thinking, I stupidly mumbled, "What?"

"That's right, Sergeant," he smirked. "They're saying the doctor on duty at the time made a mistake by discharging you. The State of New York is demanding that you be returned to their jurisdiction."

I was stunned, speechless. This couldn't be happening! I didn't want to go back! My chest was heaving, my lungs fighting for more air. He was sending me back to hell. My mind seemed to stop functioning. I couldn't think. I felt disoriented. I couldn't accept being sent back.

Small was enjoying this, and it showed on his face. There was nothing I could do or say. I was going back. "We have an obligation to New York to send you back," he said calmly. Then he sat back in his chair, just watching me for a minute. Leaning forward again, he asked sarcastically, "How did it feel being in that state asylum? Did it bother you, being surrounded by all those crazies? You must have felt like an unknown disease being peered at and studied by those civilian shrinks."

I was shattered inside as he kept taunting me. I felt like a caged animal again. My life was a joke. Leaning back and folding his arms, he grinned confidently and said, "I can prevent New York from ever getting its hands on you."

My heart almost stopped when I heard this. I was gasping heavily; every breath was painful. I felt so traumatized. Was he playing with me again, building my hopes up just to rip them away? Could it be possible? I'd do anything to keep from going back.

"I'm not kidding, Sergeant," he said, suddenly growing serious. "Whether you like it or not, I'm the only one who can help you now. I want something in return. I'm making this very clear, Sergeant. If I help, I will own you, body and soul. Do you understand me?"

I was making a pact with Satan. What did he want? Did I dare? But anything was better than being confined in a mental institution. I trusted Small about as far as I could throw a building, but I wasn't in any position to bargain. If I refused whatever he wanted, he'd have me back in New York in a heartbeat. He wanted me to surrender to him unconditionally. I had no choice.

"What do you want from me?" I asked solemnly.

"I want you to join one of the newer anti-terrorist teams being formed. Later today, you'll be flown to a CIA training site called Camp Peary in Virginia. You'll be training there for a few months."

Small told me that since the mid-1960s, our country has had anti-terrorist teams created by the Intelligence Community. Of the newer anti-terrorist teams being formed, the most publicized one was called Delta Team. Some of the other teams were named

Seaspray, Task Force-160, the Quick-Reaction team, Yellow Fruit, and the Horsemen.

Each team's mission was to secretly seek out and neutralize anti-American terrorists around the world. The teams were also used for more than just dealing with terrorism. They'd been used in domestic situations, political assassinations, and resolving political unrest in favor of the United States. The team members were mostly ex-Green Berets with assistance from the Air Force, Navy Seals, and Marine Recon. All military personnel on the teams were authorized to wear civilian clothing and carry fake ID during covert ops.

Some of these men had seen a lot of action that would never be reported or found out about by the media. They'd been in firefights in the Mideast, and they were responsible for the assassinations of over a dozen anti-American terrorists around the world. They'd been from Saudi Arabia to South America, to Lebanon, Iran, and other places.

Small said I'd be second in command of a primary team with a support team as backup. The support team's main function was to ensure that the primary team was kept supplied and equipped. The support team also acted as a reactionary force in case the primary team needed help. Small said they were phasing out some of the old teams and improving on the new ones. There would be a few dozen new primary teams created.

"You came highly recommended, and you placed high on the computer system's selection of men profiled for these teams," he explained. "A few other officers and I are in charge of selecting the army personnel for these new teams. You're a natural for this kind of business, Sergeant, and I knew that back in Nam. Like it or not, men like you, myself, and selected others are a necessity in this world. Free societies would become nonexistent if it weren't for men like us. Due to human error, we lost you for a while in the computer systems. When I found out you were locked up in that max-security state hospital, I tried to get you out quietly. They wouldn't release you, so I backed off and attended to other business. I've been busy; I came back from one war just to get involved in another type of war.

"I waited for several months while you were in the Buffalo State Hospital, and then I tried again. I planned to demand your release on a Saturday morning. On weekends, there's usually only a skeleton crew on duty in institutions. I calculated that the doctor on duty would probably just be a random doctor with no insight on your case. I gambled, and it worked. You're here. Had the plan failed, I would have used more drastic means of getting you out. You would have simply escaped with our quiet assistance.

"If New York State goes to court in order to get you back, we'll keep them bogged down for years in the courtroom until we get bored. Then we'll simply fake your death. We'll have witnesses and an official death certificate stating you were accidentally blown to pieces during a training exercise with live ammo and explosives.

"There's one thing I want to make clear, Sergeant. If I help you, I will own you. Your life will belong to me. You will be duly dedicated to the Intelligence Community and to your team, but your loyalties and sympathies will be to me.

"Understand that now, Sergeant Parker. I'm telling you this because you will be given assignments and missions on a solo and team level by the Intelligence Community. After each assignment and mission you complete, you will verbally report to me in detail about that specific assignment or mission. I know you're aware that this is illegal, and that there are severe penalties for compromising security like this within the Intelligence Community. I'm violating security by telling you to do this. But you will do this, because I will own you.

"You will become one of my personal operatives. In between your assigned duties, I may have need of your expertise for my own personal and business reasons. Whatever it is I command you to do, you will treat it as a mission and complete it, Sergeant. I strongly caution you to keep a tight lip about the verbal reports and about being one of my operatives. If you compromise me in any way, confinement in the loony-bin will be the least of your worries. I'll literally have you skinned alive before I kill you. No one would believe you, anyway. My word would certainly override the word of a criminal and ex-mental patient. Leave well enough alone, and you'll be nicely rewarded financially. Rock the boat, and I'll send you straight to hell. Have you got the picture now? I've held nothing back. I want a commitment before I leave this office. Refuse me, and you'll be back in Buffalo by this afternoon."

I'd been perspiring heavily while I listened to him. My head was bent slightly down; I couldn't even look him in the eyes. I stared at the floor, wondering how my life could be so complicated and screwed up. I felt defeated and controlled by Small. I hadn't felt this empty since childhood. He had me by the balls, and he knew it.

Small was obviously part of a bigger picture, an invisible government of politicians, high-level military personnel, and elite shadow warriors like myself. To me, Small was a right-wing extremist of the worst kind. This secret Invisible Government he was part of was a direct threat to average citizens, honest politicians, and decent military leaders, as well as to present and forthcoming Presidents of our nation. This Invisible Government was most likely created to covertly go against our country's final decisions in domestic and foreign policy matters that they disagreed with. I wondered how many people they had manipulated, blackmailed, befriended, and killed in order to create such a devastating force.

With sincere grief, I told Small I needed his help. I just couldn't bear the thought of going back to New York. He was very pleased with my decision. After my training at Camp Peary, he said he'd give me a secure phone number that would reach him at any time.

Small and I had been in the office for about half an hour. After the meeting, the agent and I were sent to the Identification Department on base. I was issued a brand new army ID card. I noticed on the card that my rank of sergeant had been reinstated. Arriving back at the hospital, I packed my personal belongings and waited. A few hours later, the three agents and I were on an army military transport plane, headed for Camp Peary, Virginia. I fell asleep on the plane, not wanting to contemplate my fate. We landed on a runway inside the fenced-in grounds. The place was crowded with people from all over the world, people of different races and nationalities. They were all there for specialized training. Then they'd be returned to their countries to fight, spy, and train others. The instructors were CIA, military personnel, and mercenaries contracted by the Agency.

I was taken to a third-floor office in a red brick building. There were other new brick buildings like this, mixed in with older wooden military structures. The well kept office belonged to a middle-aged CIA officer by the name of Tim Sterling. Sterling would become my agency connection. He was ruggedly slim, about 6'2" tall, with intense blue eyes and shabby blond hair that had streaks of gray in it. I still remember the brown slacks and short-sleeved tan shirt he wore. He wore his glasses slightly down on his nose, and he walked with a slight limp. I never forgot his habit of squinting when he talked.

Sterling shook my hand warmly, welcoming me aboard. He then dismissed the agents with me. In my briefing, he never even mentioned Small once. Sterling told me basically what Small had said about the new anti-terrorist teams being formed. Besides being a counter-terrorist specialist, Sterling said my other duties would be widespread. He said there would be times when I'd be doing security bodyguard work for senior officials of the agency and their dependents. I'd be giving covert security assistance and intelligence-gathering training to selected countries, and I'd train foreign military units in commando-style tactics, bodyguard work, and anti-terrorist tactics. He also mentioned I'd be teaching specific intelligence-gathering through the use of human sources and electronic eavesdropping.

He talked about places like Mexico, with its insurgency in the countryside and extreme poverty; about Central America, its extreme instability being a breeding ground for leftists; and about the Middle East and how it was getting increasingly worse. He said there would be times when the team I was on would be working with the Israeli Mossad (Military Intelligence), or with their Branch 40, which was their coordinator of terrorism intelligence. He mentioned I'd be spending time in places like Colombia, Peru, Burma, Turkey, Spain, the Iran-Pakistan border, the Philippines, and Lebanon, going against terrorists and communist factions, separatists, rebels, Muslim insurgents, and right-wing extremist groups.

Sterling went on to explain about terrorism, drugs, and politics becoming more and more united around the world. Drugs were becoming an annual multibillion-dollar business, and terrorist groups around the world recognized the potential opportunity of the drug trade. Drug deals were increasingly providing the financial backing for urban terrorists, rural insurgents, liberation movements, subversives, arms-traffickers, left and right political groups, and high-level officials. Terrorism and drugs together were extremely dangerous; they were a threat to the social and political stability of nations around the world. He also repeated that a function of the counter-terrorist teams would be tracking down and assassinating selected drug dealers, terrorists, and their relatives. He carefully stressed that I was restricted from discussing my duties with anyone. At the end of the briefing, he said he'd be talking to me periodically during my training. I spent the rest of the day and evening being issued bedding, fatigues, equipment, a sleeping area, and being oriented to the grounds.

My training was mentally and physically intense, lasting from sunrise to sunset in classes and in the field. Some of the training I'd had before and went through again. For a few weeks, some of the things I was taught were the Aims and Methods of America's Political Intelligence System, which was basically domestic spying by our government. The whole idea was to spy on certain American citizens, groups, and organizations, and restrict or suppress all forms of political dissent and movements for social change. Aggressive Intelligence meant we could harass and use disinformation campaigns, frame a person to be arrested, or kill a person, making it look like an accident or suicide.

I was taught more about electronic eavesdropping and counter-electronic eavesdropping. I was taught undercover operations regarding espionage and how to recruit undercover people to help me. I learned about briefing and debriefing undercover agents, how to acquire informers to work for me, and about the best weapons to carry with me on an undercover assignment. I was shown physical surveillance, how to follow a person on foot or in a car by using radios, decoys, disguises, and deception, and how to disappear from people following me. I was also taught how to plan and execute the overthrow of a government, mainly third world governments. I was taught how to break into nuclear power plants by forcibly penetrating over thirty different barriers commonly found at industrial and commercial nuclear facilities, and how to do it by only using hand-carried portable tools.

I was shown more about jungle guerrilla warfare, urban guerrilla warfare, and demolition. I learned how to make all types of homemade bombs, which were as powerful as the regular plastic explosives and RDX explosives. I was taught bodyguard work, shown more on how assassinations are set up, how kidnappers and terrorists choose their targets, and was taught about escape and evasive driving, weapon concealment, body armor, and how to use special purpose weapons.

I was taught how to find missing persons by using common techniques, and I was shown more about picking common door locks. I was shown more about computer hacking and disappearing easily by using false identification. I was shown how FBI agents do their intelligence gathering when they spy on organized crime groups and drug traffickers.

I was taught deadly karate moves that could kill a man instantly, and about the body's weakness and psychological reactions to pain, shock, paralysis, and unconsciousness. I was taught disruptive terrorism, and I learned about deadly substances and how to get them from natural sources, substances like saxitoxin, which is more deadly than curare or tetrodozin; deadly nerve poison that can be extracted from a common fish; and ricin, a deadly poison that can be extracted from beans and has no known antidote.

Toward the end of those few weeks, it was becoming obvious to people around me that I was starting to suffer from extreme mental exhaustion. My stress attacks had started again. I was suffering severe flashbacks, and my nightmares became increasingly worse. In some of the nightmares, terrorists viciously tortured me while they laughed loudly. I'd wake up several times each night in a breathless, cold, trembling sweat, screaming. Two to three times each day, I'd suddenly burst into severe shakes. I felt worthless. I started drinking again, and I could only sleep for a couple of hours at night. My senses were acutely attuned to everything around me. Loud noises irritated me, and sudden movements near me would leave me nervous and jumpy.

I was sent to see an agency psychiatrist, whom I neither trusted nor liked. While I talked to him, I frequently broke down uncontrollably and cursed the world. I told him I was fed up with this dog-eat-dog world where no one seemed to give a damn about anyone else. As far as I was concerned, they could stop the world right now and I'd gladly get off. I raged on, telling him that sometimes I felt like getting blocks of C-4 explosives and blowing up some of those push-button, office-desk warriors in Washington who called themselves generals and politicians. I told him I was tired of killing and learning how to spy on people, tired of having flashbacks, and fed up with nightmares where my brain was splattered all over the place.

The agency psychiatrist had never been in Vietnam, never been a field agent, and was fresh out of college. How could he even begin to understand my feelings? It frustrated me even more that he seemed to be at a complete loss as to why I was so bitter toward our government. He started asking me if I was leaning toward communism or having militant or terrorist thoughts or ideas. He asked repeatedly if I'd defect or sell classified secrets to other countries if I were approached by foreign agents. I kept telling him I wouldn't, but he kept asking me the same questions in different ways. I was so enraged by the psychiatrist that I refused to talk further with him and left the room. That same day, I was suspended from further training and restricted to my sleeping quarters. The next day, under escort, I was flown from Camp Peary back to the psych ward at Walson Army Medical Hospital, Fort Dix, New Jersey.

The CIA had deemed me unfit for any further training, stating that I was emotionally burnt out, antisocial, hostile, and extremely distrustful of the US Government. The CIA also stated that because of my covert and intelligence background, my recent opinions and criticisms of the government made me a potential national security threat. The agency felt that my current views would make me not only sympathetic but possibly personally involved with domestic or foreign groups and organizations that were enemies of the United States.

With me targeted as a possible national security threat, the agency would conduct periodic visual and electronic surveillance indefinitely, whether I stayed in the army or not. The agency would advise Army Intelligence to do the same, too, due to the possibility of me turning into a hardcore militant or terrorist. If that were to happen, the agency would normally suggest my "coordinated termination" before I became a formidable enemy.

I'd been put on medication when I went back to Walson, and I felt slightly better after a few days. My panic and anxiety attacks put the army and the CIA in a delicate position. Their only choice was to distance themselves from me as quickly as possible. Major Goodman, who had a few top-secret security clearances, told me he had attended two classified meetings concerning me and that certain decisions had finally been reached. He said that after all my military paperwork was done, I'd be sent back to Buffalo State Hospital. He also said I was being demoted from sergeant to private again, my medals were being revoked, and I wouldn't be receiving back pay for most of my time spent in civilian jails and mental institutions. He informed me that I'd be receiving a medical discharge under honorable conditions. I'd receive semi-retirement pay monthly for about a year, and then I'd get switched over to non-service disability. Major Goodman strongly advised me to forget my stay at Camp Peary and Walson once I was gone.

I strongly sensed Major Small's expertise in all this along with the CIA. I would never see Colonel Small again, but I would never forget him. I hated him in Vietnam, despised him at Walson, and I'd hate and despise him until I dropped dead. And if there's a hell, I'm sure to see Colonel Small there, and I'd be delighted to hate and despise him for eternity. Demoting me, denying me back pay, giving me a medical discharge and non-service disability instead of service-connected disability was the army's and the CIA's way of plausible deniability in the long run. They were doing this in case I did something really crazy one day, like assassinate the President or some other high government official, or join some militant or terrorist group. This way, they could claim I was deemed unstable by military authorities, reprimanded for whatever improprieties they dreamed up, given a psycho discharge, and returned to Buffalo State Hospital for further treatment. I guessed they could have done worse; they could have not given me any disability at all. I was smart enough not to challenge their decisions because I knew I'd lose. I hadn't won at anything important in my life; I wasn't about to beat my head against the wall over this.

Major Goodman told me it would take a few weeks until all my paperwork was done. I was powerless. I had no control whatsoever over my fate. To my so-called civilized society, I was a certified psycho, a nonentity, with no past or future. I was too emotionally devastated to be angry. I became even more depressed, and I was lost in my own empty void of hellish reality.

On November 15th, I was surprised when Major Goodman told me I could start having liberty passes until my paperwork was finalized. On that same day, I was issued an overnight pass. Why was I suddenly being granted liberty passes? The army and CIA had deemed me a potential national security threat, right? They felt I was emotionally burnt out and hostile, which meant I was unpredictable and dangerous, right? They granted me passes because they were compassionate, sensitive, and caring, right? I didn't think so, but I eagerly welcomed the passes because they meant temporary freedom.

Because I was depressed and medicated, I was not suspicious of these generous passes. Under normal conditions, my analytical mind would have foreseen some type of devious situation developing. My depression and medication had put my mind in a type of idle void.

In Wrightstown, New Jersey, on my very first pass, there was an attempt on my life. Had I been killed, my death would have been seen as a typical mugging that got out of control. The incident happened while I was in the parking lot of a bar. I was lured there by the most potent and effective weapon known to man: a beautiful woman. Because of the publicity generated by the incident, the US Army emphatically denied to the media and the police that I was issued a pass. The army stated I had simply escaped and gone AWOL, which was a lie. Had I escaped, I certainly would not have remained in the immediate area! The murder attempt was a black bag covert action special!

That day, after signing out on pass in the late afternoon, I went straight to one of the clubs on base. I stayed in the club until early evening and had several drinks. I was miserably sad and lonely. It felt good, though, to be free for a while. I was determined to enjoy my freedom by drinking myself into a stupor. (Being emotionally and physically helpless, I was drinking to forget my dreaded fate.) After leaving the club, I caught a base cab to Wrightstown, which was right next to Fort Dix. The town was always packed with service people from Fort Dix and McGuire Air Force Base, which was close by. I walked around town for about an hour, just enjoying my freedom of movement. There were bars, discos, restaurants, and motels in and around Wrightstown for me to choose from after my walk.

As I was walking down a side street, a big brown Caddy pulled up near me and stopped. The car horn blared to get my attention. Looking into passenger side of the car, I saw a beautiful woman smiling at me. She looked to be in her early thirties. She was light-skinned, stunning, and sensual. Like a little kid, I stared wide-eyed and open-mouthed at her. She wore a long, white fur coat with a long, deep-red evening gown under it. She had the gown pulled back, exposing her thighs. The black nylon stockings she wore hugged her shapely legs perfectly. Around her waist she wore a wide black belt with a big gold buckle. She was wearing shiny, black high-heeled shoes. I imagined running my fingers through her short, curly brown hair and touching every inch of her deep, creamy, smooth thighs. Her erotic green eyes seemed to caress me, consuming me emotionally and mentally. Her lips were so full and inviting that I trembled at the thought of them pressing against my lips. I would learn that she was of mixed blood, with a white mother and black father.

"Hi," she said in a soft, alluring voice. "Would you like to go riding with me? I hate riding alone."

I was surprised. I couldn't believe my luck. She was probably a high-priced prostitute looking for some action, but I didn't care what she was — I wasn't about to let her get away. I would have ridden to hell and back with her if she wanted.

I tried to look calm and casual as I got into the car. As she drove off, she turned the radio on to some music. After lighting a cigarette, she said, "My name's Pamela Cooper. What's yours?" I told her my name as I stared at her sensuous legs. "You probably think I'm some kind of whore, Robert, but I'm not," she said sweetly. "I'm just bored. I passed you twice while driving around town. You're a handsome guy and I like the way you walk."

"Flattery will get you everywhere with me," I teased.

She laughed, saying, "Good, I was hoping it would. I was a little nervous at first, stopping like I did. I've never done that before. Usually, I'm the one guys are trying to pick up."

Pamela drove out of town. I had no idea where she was going. I didn't care. Her perfume held a magnetism that was overwhelming and delightful. She drove to an isolated wooded area a few miles out of town. She brought out a bottle of vodka, two cups, and a can of soda for a chaser. For a while, we just sat there, drinking and talking. She told me she'd been on a date earlier with an air force sergeant from McGuire Air Base. The guy became obnoxious and loud with her in a restaurant, so she left. She'd been married, divorced, and had a daughter. She worked as a barmaid in a Wrightstown bar. I told her I was single, recently stationed at Fort Dix, and that I was from Buffalo, New York.

After our conversation and drinks, we made love in the front seat. Twice we made love, and I passionately wanted her. I wanted to try every sexual coupling position I knew with her. I wanted to keep kissing, tasting, and feeling myself in her soft, drenching loins.

It was already dark outside, and Pamela had to be at work in a little while. She wanted me to come with her to the bar and hang around until she finished work. Then she said we could get a motel room and spend the night together. I agreed. She put on a pair of jeans, sweatshirt, and sneakers, which were on the back seat floor in a plastic bag. She had me drive back to Wrightstown.

The bar she worked in had an 'Off Limits to Military Person-nel' sign in front of it, but I didn't care. The parking lot was in the rear of the bar. It was dark; the only light was a bright bulb over the rear entrance to the bar. After locking the car, Pamela told me to hold on to the keys. The bar was crowded, smoky, and noisy, and the music was blasting. After she gave me a moist kiss, she relieved one of the barmaids behind the bar. For the next few hours I stayed in the bar, playing pool and socializing. Pamela kept bringing me bourbon and Cokes, saying they were on the house. I watched her as she laughed and chatted while fixing drinks; she seemed to know almost everyone in the place. Later, I got hungry and left the bar for about forty-five minutes. I went across the street to a pizza parlor and had something to eat. After returning to the bar, Pamela started bringing drinks to me again.

It was about two o'clock in the morning when she got off work. We went out the rear door into the dark parking lot. I was drunk and horny, and she kept talking and laughing as we walked to the car. As I was unlocking the car door, I noticed that Pamela had abruptly become silent. Then she quickly backed up a few steps. I turned my head to the right to see what she was doing, and as it turns out, my head movement at that instant saved me from being brutally knocked unconscious. I hadn't heard the two black men sneak up behind me. They each had some type of blunt instrument. One of them struck me on the right side of the head, but it only grazed me. Still standing, I fell hard against the car. I had a small bump on my head that was bleeding.

Pamela blurted, "Kill him, Leon! They said kill him or we ain't getting paid!" The other man had his right arm in the air, preparing to strike me. My combat survival instincts took over. Pamela had set me up for a mugging. That pissed me off.

They think I'm too drunk to fight, but I'm not! As the man swung downward with his blunt instrument, I blocked his arm with my left forearm. I followed through with a swift right kick that struck him in the ribcage. He grunted like a pig and tumbled backward to the ground. The other man raised his arm, ready to strike again. With my left hand, I grabbed a handful of his shirt, and I put my right arm between his legs. I lifted him completely off the ground and slammed him upside down against the car. I then rushed over to the other man, who was still on the ground, and kicked him in the side of the head.

Pamela came up behind me and started beating me in the head with her purse, shouting, "Leave them alone! Leave them alone!" I grabbed her around the throat with my left hand, choking her. I could have crushed her throat easily, leaving her gurgling to death. In fact, I could have killed all three of them had I wanted to. Instead, I just pushed Pamela to the ground. She bounced right back up and ran toward the bar. "Help me! Help me!" she screamed at the top of her lungs.

I was drunk, but I damn sure wasn't stupid. I knew she was smart; she was going to go running into the bar with phony tears, pretending to be hysterical. She'd convince the rowdy patrons that she was a damsel in distress and I was the bad guy. They all knew her, and they probably knew the two punks on the ground, too. They didn't know me. This was the type of bar where most people carried a knife, gun, or both. Since most of them were liquored or drugged up, or both, they wouldn't be interested in what I had to say. I could be severely hurt or killed trying to reason with a mob in this parking lot, especially with Pamela along, psyching them up. I had to get out of town fast.

I noticed that the key was still in the car door. Jumping into the car, I started it up and sped out of the parking lot. I had no idea where I was going. After turning down a few streets, I saw a sign that said 'Newark.' I took the turn off to the Thruway and headed for Newark. I did ninety and over all the way. Newark was about sixty-five miles from Wrightstown. It was sheer luck that I wasn't spotted by New Jersey's infamous state troopers. After getting to Newark, I drove around for a while. I suddenly became tired and sleepy, and I didn't know what to do. I spotted a big parking lot filled with cars. Driving into the middle of the lot, I found an empty space. The car would be concealed. I was too exhausted to think anymore, so I curled up in the back seat and fell asleep.

The next morning, I woke up with my head aching and throbbing. I had a wicked hangover, and the bump on my head was sore. I sat up, moaning as I remembered what had happened. Pamela probably had the cops looking for me because I took her car, but I knew I'd rather be alive and wanted for car theft than be dead in the county morgue. I thought about running away, maybe even leaving the country. Being locked up in jail again wasn't appealing to me at all, but being a fugitive for the rest of my life didn't sit too well with me, either. I had to decide on a course of action and do it quickly.

After a few minutes, I decided to call Major Goodman and see what the situation was. I had forgotten all about Pamela's blurted remark in the parking lot. It would be years before I remembered what she'd said to the guy named Leon. Had I remembered that she'd told them to kill me or they wouldn't be paid, I never would have called Major Goodman. I would have left the country in disguise with a fake passport. There were third world governments that would pay dearly for my skills. I got out of the car and found a nearby phone booth. Through the information operator, I got the Fort Dix number and Walson. Major Goodman sounded agitated on the phone. His voice was high, jittery, and alarmed. I was the one in trouble, but he sounded close to a nervous breakdown. "My God! Thank God you called! All hell's broken loose around here. Where are you, Parker? Are you okay?" the major shouted.

"I'm in Newark and I'm okay," I replied. "What's the situation?"

"There's a lot of people looking for you," he remarked nervously. "Officially, the MPs, the CID (Criminal Investigation Division), the local police, sheriffs, troopers, and the FBI are after you. Unofficially, Army Intelligence, the CIA, and a few anti-terrorist teams are looking for you, Parker. What the hell happened?"

"A woman and two men tried to mug me in a parking lot," I said. "I fought back and took her car to keep from being killed. I didn't stop driving until I got to Newark."

"Mugging? Two men?" The major sounded surprised. "I heard nothing about a mugging, only that you tried to kill a prostitute and had stolen her car. I've had a weird feeling about this whole thing ever since I was ordered to give you liberty passes."

"What are you talking about?" I asked.

"Nothing," the major snapped back. "Forget I said that. Listen, Parker, you've got to give yourself up. The faster you do, the safer it will be for you. We seem to have gotten along well together, so I'm asking you to turn yourself in."

I thought about what he had said, and I realized that with my past criminal and mental record, the cops would believe anything Pamela told them. The two men who'd been with her were probably long gone by the time the cops got to the bar. With a lawyer representing me, though, maybe Pamela could be forced to tell the truth. It was a long shot, but I didn't want to be a fugitive with an attempted murder rap hanging over my head.

"Okay," I said, "I'm coming in. I'll be at Dix in a couple of hours."

"No, no!" shouted the major. "Don't come here. I want you in custody of the civilian authorities, not the army. This is in your best interest. Find the federal building and stand in front of it. I'm going to call the Newark Police and tell them you're turning yourself in. I won't be talking to you anymore after this. My involvement ends here, Sergeant Parker. Good luck, and may God be with you." Without saying another word, the major hung up the phone.

On my way back to the car, I asked a few people where the federal building was located. After finding it, I parked the car right in front of the building. For the first few minutes, I just stood on the sidewalk, watching the people come and go. Emotional agony and mental grief filled my very being. Tears filled my eyes as I thought about my good-for-nothing life. Why me? Why the hell me? Why couldn't I be like most of the people walking by, with normal problems and responsibilities?

I spotted a liquor store across the street and walked over to it. I bought a pint of bourbon and went back over to the federal building. Since I was getting arrested, I might as well be boozed up along with being miserable. For about twenty minutes, I stood there, drinking from my brown bag. I was drinking to forget my past, my hopeless future, and why I was standing there.

An old shabby van suddenly stopped on the street in front of me. The hippie van looked like it was right out of the sixties, with bright psychedelic colors and designs painted all over it. Two young, long-haired white men dressed like hippies jumped out of the van. Between us was a parked car. "Hey, are you Sergeant Robert Parker?" one of them asked.

I had no idea who the two hippies were, so I growled, "Who's asking?"

Right then, both guys leaned across the roof of the parked car, arms extended, pistols pointed at my head. "Police, don't move!" the one hippie said. A big dark police truck came out of nowhere, screeching to a halt behind the van. Several fully armed special weapons policemen rushed out of the truck toward me. I was handcuffed and jailed.

The next morning, at about five a.m., I was again handcuffed, shackled, and put into a police van. Wrightstown was in Burlington County, so I was being transported to a town called Mount Holly, where the Burlington County Jail was. I was given an unmotivated army lawyer and an overworked public defender to represent me.

Chapter Fourteen

After being in the Burlington County Jail for a few weeks, two army MPs brought my personal belongings from Fort Dix. My belongings were intact: my clothes, typewriter, jewelry, cash, etc. Everything was there — except for one thing. My autobiography manuscript was missing. I was stunned, and I kept searching through my belongings for the manuscript. I furiously questioned the MPs about my manuscript, but they denied knowing anything about it. I was beyond upset when I realized that my manuscript was gone. Someone had deliberately taken it. Was the person who took it working for Army Intelligence, the CIA, or Colonel Small? Did they all have a hand in this? I didn't know. For days, I would angrily brood over this. They probably took it because I wrote a lot about the top secret special operations group I was in. Most of our covert activities would be considered illegal and inhumane as far as the Geneva Convention and the world community were concerned.

While in the county jail, I started to write my manuscript over again. I was determined to defy the army and the CIA by writing my autobiography, including Vietnam and other aspects of my life in it.

My army and civilian lawyers kept trying to talk me out of going to trial. If I went to trial and lost, I'd be sentenced to fifteen to twenty years for attempted murder. With my violent criminal history, they said I'd lose. They weren't interested in hearing about or pursuing the two men who were with Pamela that night. They did tell me that the State of New York wanted me back in their custody. Technically, New York State had no jurisdiction over me after the Buffalo Psych Center, but New York State kept creeping back into my life with a vengeance.

The lawyers told me that New York now had a detainer on me at the jail. They said that while I was locked up, the New York State Department of Mental Hygiene had gone to court about me. A Buffalo judge had put me on a five-year mental hygiene conditional release in my absence, and then said I violated the conditional release, making it legal to put a detainer on me in New

Jersey. The judge said I had violated the conditional release by getting into trouble and getting locked up again.

I couldn't believe this. They did all this while I was in the county jail. To this day, I still question the legality of what New York State did. I wasn't on any conditional release when I got into trouble. How could they do all that after the fact? With the detainer on me, even if I'd gone to trial and won, New Jersey could not set me free. They had to turn me over to New York. Had I lost the trial and been sent to prison, I would not have been released to the streets after serving my prison time. With the detainer on me, prison authorities would have turned me over to New York.

For months, the lawyers kept trying to talk me into signing extradition papers to expedite my return to New York. They finally told me that if I signed the papers, the State of New Jersey would be willing to drop the attempted murder charge down to 'threatening to take a life.' I'd then be granted time served on this charge along with the auto theft charge. To me, it seemed extremely odd to have a serious charge like attempted murder dropped down to a simple verbal threat — unless there were people who knew the attempted murder charge against me was a farce. And since they knew the charge was untrue, it was easy to lower it to a charge of 'verbally threatening' as an enticement for me to sign the extradition papers. If I wanted to fight the extradition, it would have taken New Jersey a long time to force me back to New York legally. It was evident that New Jersey and the army wanted me out of their hair. For several months, I refused to sign the papers, wanting to go to trial instead. The lawyers kept telling me I wouldn't be going to trial and I would stay in jail until I changed my mind.

One thing about being locked up is that you have plenty of time to think about things you normally wouldn't think about on the streets. One of the things I thought deeply about was how I seemed to get into so much trouble when it came to women. As a teenager, I had girlfriends, but I seemed more attracted to girls I had no business fooling around with. For instance, there was Patty Basil, whose father was a preacher with his own church. Rev. Basil was totally against any boy fooling around with his pretty, luscious daughter. He watched over her like she was a family heirloom. When Patty let me know she had feelings for me, I became a tactical genius in finding ways for us to be alone together. Rev. Basil began to suspect that something was going on between his daughter and me. When he saw me on the streets, he'd point his finger angrily at me, saying, "Boy, you stay away from my daughter, you hear me? I'll rip your sinful heart out if you go near my daughter again." He even went to my mother to complain about me. My mother would beat me, then tell me to stay away from Patty. But Rev. Basil and my mother only made me want to see Patty more. Their intense disapproval made the thought of Patty and me being together even more romantic, daring, and exciting.

Then there was the time as a teenager when I had two girl-friends at the same time. That turned into a disaster; it almost cost me my life. I was going with a girl named Joy first. I wanted to be cool, like some of my buddies who had two girlfriends, so I got another girlfriend. Her name was Vicki. Joy and Vicki didn't know about each other at first, but eventually, they did. I got busted at a Fourth of July picnic at a state park called Chestnut Ridge. I was with Joy at the picnic, and it never dawned on me that Vicki would show up at the same picnic to surprise me. And surprise me she did! Standing with my arm around Joy, I never saw Vicki behind me. She was slowly walking toward me with a butcher knife in her hand. Only when some nearby people yelled for me to watch my back did I turn around. When I did, she was only a few yards away from me. She had this crazy, distorted glare in her eyes. Tears were pouring down her face from the anger and hurt she must have felt. She dropped the knife, turned around, and slowly walked away with her head down. I lost both Vicki and Joy as girlfriends that day.

As a teenager, I must have had a fascination about living on that dangerous edge. I say this because my next escapade was to get involved with a girl named Tanya. What made Tanya forbid-den territory was her boyfriend, who was the undisputed terror of the projects and the neighborhood. Joe was short, but he was wide and thick with huge muscles everywhere. He was also a one-man crime wave who crushed bones and rearranged faces for recrea-tion. No one in his right mind messed around with Joe or his girlfriend. Everyone feared Joe. Gangs feared Joe. Grown men feared Joe. The police feared Joe. Hell, I feared Joe! So why did I fool around with his girlfriend? I don't know. I just did.

Tanya was someone who should be admired at a safe distance, like radioactive material; if you got too close, she proved to be hazardous to your health. I used to admire her at a distance like all the other guys did, but one day, she told me how much she liked and adored me, and that did it. From that day on, common sense and logic evaded me. I got into Tanya's panties every chance I got. Joe, who was part grizzly bear and part pit-bull, got wind of what was going on. Every time he saw me, he sent me home bleeding, limping, and in pain. I'd hurt for days after one of his beatings. Joe didn't realize it, but the more he beat me, the more I enjoyed screwing Tanya just to get even.

Carol Wilson, my girlfriend while I was in the army, definitely wasn't good for me. She manipulated me and took advantage of me. While stationed in Germany, I went out with plenty of women. I was still attracted to women I had no business fooling around with. In Munich, I met a Turkish woman named Kead. She had two big brothers and worked as a barmaid in a Turkish bar. I started going to the bar to see Kead. Most of the Turkish patrons in the bar disliked Americans and strangers. I was both.

Kead's two brothers didn't want me to see her, and they would pick fights with me in the bar to discourage me. First one brother would fight me, and then the other would step in. Kead always got involved, helping me fight them off. Sometimes they kicked my butt, and sometimes Kead and I kicked their butts. I'd still hang around the bar until Kead got off work. We'd go out on the town and spend the night together. I could have easily avoided the bar and her brothers by meeting her somewhere else, but I had to prove to her brothers that I wouldn't be intimidated. My stubbornness paid off. I was finally accepted by her brothers and the others as a friend and patron of the bar.

I had another affair with a pretty French woman named Monique. My affair with her got me into deep trouble because she was married to a full bird colonel. I met her while I was stationed in Heidelberg. Word got back to her husband, and my immediate superiors were all over me. It is a cardinal sin and against military law for an enlisted man to have relations with an officer's wife. To be caught with a full bird colonel's wife was outright disastrous. I was given an abrupt ultimatum: either I volunteer for Vietnam immediately or be sent to the prison stockade. *Vietnam, here I come!*

To help occupy my time in the county jail, I started teaching several of the other inmates martial arts. I taught them about strength, explosiveness, endurance, timing, and discipline. I taught them choke holds, strangles, breakaways, releases, locks, throws, sweeps, and countermoves. I taught them punching, rear attacks, defending against a knife or club, and fighting from the ground on their backs. I taught them knife-fighting, carrying methods, guard and grip positions, slashing and thrusting, human target areas, quick-kill strikes, footwork, and deceptive movements. I also trained them on lock-picking tools and had them take notes. I taught them how to open pin tumbler locks, mushroom and spool pin tumbler locks, wafer tumbler locks, disk tumbler locks, tubular cylinder locks, magnetic locks, padlocks, and automobile locks.

I taught them how to acquire new identities by giving them the addresses of a few barely legal companies that specialized in ID paperwork. From these companies, they could get photo ID cards, passports, social security cards, drivers licenses, birth certificates, divorce papers, union cards, marriage licenses, reporter press cards, clergy ID, police ID, and even some badges.

I taught them about different methods of disguise, how to give themselves a complete or partial makeover, and how to permanently or temporarily disappear. I gave them mail order sources for wigs, makeup, and latex material to change their facial and body profiles, and I taught them how to use mail drops and use the untraceable signature. I taught them escape-and-evasive driving, about cornering right and left turns, hairpin turns, boot-legger turns, moonshiner turns, ramming procedures, and double-vehicle blockades. Teaching these men all this and more was my personal payback to the State of New Jersey for the royal screwing they were giving me.

After ten months in the county jail, I finally signed the extradition papers. My lawyers weren't doing anything except letting me rot in jail until I signed. I wanted to forget this whole mess, and that meant getting out of New Jersey. After signing the papers, I was convicted of threatening to take a life and auto theft. I was given time served on both convictions while I waited for New York to come and get me. On July 29th, 1976, two Erie County deputy sheriffs came and drove me to the county jail in Buffalo, New York. For two months, I stayed in the county jail.

On September 29th, two deputy sheriffs took me back to the maximum security Mid-Hudson Forensic Psychiatric Center. I spent almost two years at Mid-Hudson this time. During the first part of 1978, while I was still there, my grandmother died. I was very close to my grandmother and loved her dearly. It truly broke my heart when I was told she had died in her sleep. I was so upset that I cried for days. It seemed like whenever I chose to love someone or become close friends with someone, I ended up losing that person. The marine buddy I met on the plane going to Vietnam was shot and killed in Nam while he sat next to me. I truly loved My Ling, but I lost her, too. Even though Carol wasn't good for me, I still lost her through her addiction to drugs. Rosilee, who used to baby-sit my sister and me, was killed on the streets. I loved Toni, and I lost her through my stubbornness and greed. Now I had lost my grandmother. Why me? Why me, all the time? I was ravaged with guilt; if I wasn't constantly getting into trouble, I could have been out there when she died.

I recalled the speeches she gave me about my negative behavior when I came home from Nam. For weeks, her words echoed over and over again in my mind while I was at Mid-Hudson. I swore an oath to myself and my deceased grandmother that I'd never use my martial arts to severely hurt anyone again.

My grandmother's death changed me in another way, too. I found out that I was no longer capable of becoming Nighthawk-One. That raging entity within me had somehow been destroyed and no longer existed. I felt an indescribable, overwhelming sense of relief deep within my mind and soul. I felt like I'd had major surgery, and a deadly, cancerous growth had been extracted. It's hard to explain, but I learned the human art of being fearful and afraid again. I could be afraid of being physically hurt by someone, fearful of living on the edge, and afraid of the unknown. It may sound crazy, but I relished those feelings. I embraced them openly and eagerly. They made me feel like a normal human being, like maybe I did fit in somewhere in this world. I wanted to get my life together again, to be a positive and constructive part of society. My grandmother had wanted that so much for me. Her death had become my motivation; I truly wanted to change. But what I failed to realize was that my life was no longer mine to control. Parts of my personality, soul, and physical being belonged to numerous agencies, organizations, and places. I was merely a pawn surrounded by kings, bishops, and knights. My malicious mistreatment had already left an irrevocable mark on my morality, and I would encounter others in the system who would include irresponsibility, negligence, misconduct, harassment, and outright racism in their treatment of me.

At the end of August, 1978, I was sent from Mid-Hudson to the Buffalo Psych Center again. I was sent to four different wards, and each ward psychiatrist refused to accept me as a patient. The assistant director of the psych center had to intervene and designate a ward to accept me. I spent almost two years at the Buffalo Psych Center. I met a Polish woman named Marjorie Kowlowski who was in her mid-thirties. She worked in the ward I was put in. She was about 5'9" and overweight. She had a pretty face with long brown hair and dark brown eyes

Marjorie was a senior employee who had gone all the way through nursing school, but she never graduated due to marital problems. Her husband worked at the psych center, but they were separated and in the process of getting divorced. Marjorie's father also worked at the psych center. Marjorie was assigned as my therapist. She and I would become personally and sexually involved. She would also become my common-law wife because we would be together for the next eight years. When she and her husband had lived together, she cheated on him a lot. At the same time, he cheated on her. Marjorie would also cheat on me, but I wouldn't end the relationship. I was too terrified of being alone again. Though she cheated, she showed concern and cared for me when no one else bothered to. I eventually learned to love Marjorie in my own way.

I was relieved that Marjorie was Polish and not Italian, Jewish, or Irish. Toni had shocked me by having relatives in the mob. That couldn't happen with Marjorie, right? I'd heard of Italian, Jewish, and Irish mob organizations, but I'd never heard of any Polish mob organizations. Marjorie being Polish was quite comforting to me. It was nearly impossible to have another girlfriend with a mob relative, right? Well, guess what? The nearly impossible happened.

Marjorie had a relative who would give me glimpses of a seductive and horrifying world. All that I had been through in my life would not prepare me for this. I was allowed to peer into a sinister reality that was beyond anything I could have ever imagined. Truth is indeed stranger than fiction. To the day I die, I will never discuss in detail everything I've seen or been told by Marjorie's relative. If I did, you would think I was a babbling lunatic who had lost all his senses and reasoning. Some things, though, I will discuss, to give a general idea about her relative and his activities.

The ward I'd been put in had a white, middle-aged unit team leader by the name of Bill Morgan. The unit team leader worked right under the ward psychiatrist and had two to three wards under his control. Bill hated me at first sight, and he set out to make my life a living nightmare. He started one-to-one therapy sessions with me every week in his office. In each session, he constantly threatened to have me sent back to jail if I lied to him about anything. He also threatened to write bad reports in my chart, which he did anyway, if I lied to him. Sometimes, we talked about the women I'd known, and he always asked if the women were black or white. Personally, I didn't think it made any difference what color the woman was. When I questioned him about this, he got angry. He yelled that it made a hell of a difference in this society. He said I should only be involved with women of my race because race mixing was forbidden. At the end of each session, he reminded me not to repeat what we discussed or I'd be severely punished and never be released.

Bill was a bastard who reminded me more and more of Colonel Small. When I was quiet and content, Bill said that I was depressed. When I talked more and socialized, he said I was hiding my true feelings. He was turning me into a nervous wreck. He got me so upset that I became physically sick with stomach pains, vomiting, and headaches. When I tried to have a decent friendship with another patient or employee, Bill intervened by telling the person lies about me and advising him or her to stay away from me.

After being restricted to the ward for several months, I was allowed to go to programs, group therapy meetings, and work in the Rehabilitation Building. I was allowed free time in the evenings, from six to eight o'clock, to walk the grounds. Whenever I left the ward, I had a special sign-out sheet where I would put down my destination, the time I left, and when I returned.

After I was at the psych center for almost a year, I was allowed weekend home visits.

I attended group therapy sessions twice a week, and a psychologist ran the group. Several other patients and I met with him in a room in the Rehab Building. One day, the psychologist asked me if I wanted to be on the Board of Visitors Committee as a representative and spokesman for the other patients at the psych center. He explained that the committee was made up of five people: two psychiatrists, two respected representatives from the community, and myself. The function of the committee would be to meet four times a year to make sure that the Rehab Building was doing all it could to help the patients by checking out programs, staff members, etc. The psychologist said that a majority of the employees in the Rehab Building felt I would make a good patient committee member. Even if I were discharged, the psychologist said he still wanted me to be on the committee. I accepted, but it had to go through the unit team for approval, which meant it had to go through Bill. A few days later, the psychologist told me that Bill refused to let me on the committee; Bill said I didn't deserve it.

In the ward, we had a public telephone for the patients' use. Bill harassed me about the phone. There were times when I actually caught him hiding around the corner, listening to my phone conversations. He questioned me a lot about the people I talked to on the phone and what I talked about. I felt it was none of his business.

In one of my rehab programs, I worked in the machine shop during the day along with several other patients. We had twenty-minute breaks in the mornings and afternoons. Bill started harassing my shop boss about me. All the patients in the shop had their twenty-minute breaks in the restaurant area of the Rehab Building. Bill wanted me to start taking my breaks right in the machine shop. The shop boss refused to do this; he thought I should be able to take my breaks in the restaurant area like the other patients. Bill went over his head and spoke to the Rehab Building director. A few days later, my shop boss was ordered to have me spend my breaks in the shop.

I was allowed to go off the grounds to school, where I started taking a college prep course. Bill accused me of skipping classes and stopped me from going to school. A team meeting was called, and every team member except Bill felt I should be allowed to go back to school. They felt this way because there was indisputable evidence that I was not skipping classes. Bill didn't like this and got angry with everyone at the meeting. He overruled them all by reminding them that he was the unit team leader. I know this because I was there during the whole meeting.

I got into a weight-lifting program at the gym in the Rehab Building. I enjoyed lifting weights, but Bill had me thrown out of the program.

I had suffered a couple of head wounds while I was in Vietnam. Sometimes, when I had flashbacks and nightmares, I'd get excruciating pain on the right side of my head. My right eye would pour with tears like a faucet, and the pain would be piercing and sharp. These were called cluster headaches, and I'd get these head pains when I was under extreme stress. Only prescription pain pills were strong enough to stop the pain. Mid-Hudson and the county jail gave me prescription pain pills for the head pains, but Bill wouldn't allow anything but aspirin to be given to me, and aspirin was useless.

Once, I had to have a rectal operation. What I had was called a fissure, meaning that right inside my anal passage, the skin was ripped, leaving an open wound. I got the fissure from a combination of things at the psych center. I had to stand up all day to work the machine I was assigned to in the machine shop. Right after work, I used to go and lift weights. During most of my evening free time, I'd sit on a concrete slab on the grounds. That bastard, Bill, who kept me under tremendous stress, may have also contributed to the fissure.

When I first started having severe pain from the fissure, I complained to the staff. I was given a laxative, which did nothing but agitate and worsen the pain. The fissure was extremely uncomfortable and painful. It hurt when I walked, stood still, sat down, and lay in bed. Bill still made me go to work and attend all my other programs. I kept complaining about the pain, and I was finally sent to see a doctor about it in another building. A month had gone by since I had this fissure. The doctor checked me out and told me not to worry. He said I should soak my rectal area in warm water and use suppositories. I did this for a few weeks, and the pain got worse.

I was suffering mentally as well as physically. My ward doctor gave me some type of clear liquid to cleanse my bowels. This liquid turned out to be more damaging to the fissure. I could barely stand from the pain, let alone walk. I literally cried and pleaded for pain pills. I only got aspirin, thanks to Bill.

The only person who was concerned about my extreme suffering was my therapist, Marjorie. Through her, I finally got an appointment at a medical hospital. The doctors were upset that the psych center had let me suffer for so long. I stayed in the hospital for a week, and I had an operation to stitch the fissure up. The doctors wanted me on bed rest for several days after I got back to the psych center. Bill, the barbarian, had me attending my programs the very next day after I returned.

Whenever we got a new ward psychiatrist, I was never allowed to meet him or her personally like the other patients. Instead, Bill always briefed the doctor about me privately. Bill scared this one new ward psychiatrist so badly that the psychiatrist wrote a letter to the chief building psychiatrist, stating that he refused to be my psychiatrist under any circumstances and another psychiatrist should be appointed to me. To this day, I still wonder what that bastard was telling those people about me.

One of my programs was cooking class. It consisted of several male and female patients, one employee, and the female cooking instructor. On this particular day, one of the male patients started flipping out and screaming hysterically. He threw his chair through the air, hitting another male patient in the face. Then he grabbed one of the steak knives from the table and headed for the door. Marjorie bolted to the doorway to stop him from leaving. The patient angrily swung the knife at her throat. She screamed and backed out of the doorway; the knife had narrowly missed her. I followed the patient into the hallway and disarmed him without harming him.

During another incident, I helped a male employee in the ward. A male patient had gone berserk and had grabbed the TV, trying to smash it to the floor. The employee was by himself in the ward, which was totally against psych center rules and regulations. The male employee couldn't handle the patient alone. I applied a pressure point hold to the patient's neck, and he quickly let go of the TV set. I then kept the patient pinned, unharmed, on the floor while the employee went for help.

Several other times, I helped to control violent or upset patients. During a meeting of some of the psych center employees, the subject of me receiving a psych center commendation for my help was brought up. They said that many of the patients respected and confided in me and that I gave them positive reinforcement. But Bill, the bastard, told the employees that I would receive nothing. He said it would be embarrassing for the psych center to give me, a patient, a commendation because it would imply that the employees weren't doing their jobs.

The most serious incident was when a big, black, muscular patient became violent and jumped a black male employee from behind. The employee fell to the floor, and the patient viciously kicked him in the head and body. The patient broke the employee's ankle, bruised his ribs, and gave him a severe concussion. No other employees were in the ward at the time. I ran into the dayroom and restrained the patient without hurting him. The employee stated that he could have been hurt worse or even killed if I had not intervened; he was out for about a year due to his injuries.

Before Bill stopped me from going to school, I got involved in another situation. While riding the bus back to the psych center one afternoon, four black teenagers got on the overcrowded bus. The teenagers and I were the only black people on the bus. They were cursing loudly, and they started pushing and intimidating some of the people. They also threw firecrackers down the aisle from the rear of the bus. The exploding firecrackers had people jumping, ducking, screaming, and crying for help. One old lady started to cry. The white bus driver stopped the bus and went back to the rear. He angrily told the teenagers to get off the bus or he was calling the police. Two of the teenagers started pushing him around and threatening to beat him up. The frightened bus driver yelled for someone to help him, but no one moved. I finally got out of my seat and confronted the teenagers. I told them to leave the bus driver alone or I was going to start shooting. Then I told them, pretending to be angry, that I had a long day at work, I was tired, and I wanted to get the fuck home. I put my hand in my coat pocket, pretending to have a pistol there. I had no weapon of any kind on me, but I wasn't about to tell them that. I was gambling that the most they might have would be knives and not pistols. The bluff worked; they got off the bus, cursing at me. As the bus driver drove away, they threw a few firecrackers at the bus.

Right after the bus incident, the bus driver asked for my name and address. The men and women on the bus kept shaking my hand and hugging me, thanking me for my help. A few days later, the bus company called the psych center. They said I was an outstanding citizen, and they wanted to put me in for a citizens' commendation from the city. Bill shot the whole idea down, though. He convinced everyone that I wasn't a good citizen or patient.

Had the teenagers chosen to use violence, I would have been in deep trouble. They could have seriously hurt or killed me because I was limited in what I could do to protect myself. This was due to the oath I'd sworn on my grandmother's death about not using martial arts to seriously hurt anyone again. I had embedded that oath deep within my conscience, so deep that I still fear hurting another human being. I will never compromise that oath to my beloved grandmother. I probably could have overpowered one or two of the teenagers without really hurting them, but there was no way I could have taken on all four of them, armed or unarmed, without using extreme or lethal force. In life-threatening situations it is instinctive and natural for human beings to fight back to survive, but I would have let those teenagers kill me before I seriously hurt or killed one of them.

For some reason, I only seemed to function in extremes. I either loved or hated people. I was aggressive or passive, obsessed or bored, argumentative or silent, stubborn or complacent. Living like this was wreaking havoc on my blood pressure.

Chapter Fifteen

When I first got to the ward, Marjorie made up excuses to talk to me. Her husband, a 6'3" burly Polish man, was nicknamed Big John. On weekends, most of the professionals and ward staff employees had time off. Many of the ward patients went home for weekend visits. Most of the patients slept in the dormitory, but there were also private rooms for patients. Marjorie worked the day shift, and on weekends, we'd go into the dormitory, where I'd help her change sheets on the beds. The other ward employees would be busy doing their own things, like gossiping on the phone, watching TV, sleeping, or visiting other wards. Because Marjorie and I were alone in the dormitory several times, we went from talking to having a sexual affair.

When I first started getting privileges, I saw Marjorie's husband on the grounds. Big John gave me the meanest looks he could conjure up. Evidently, word had gotten back to him that I was having an affair with his wife. Even though they were separated, he still confronted me a few times on the grounds and tried to pick a fight. He yelled racial slurs and threatened me for fooling around with Marjorie. But regardless of how much of a sleazebag I thought he was, he was an employee. I was just a criminal mental patient, which was the lowest form of life in New York State. He could easily set me up by attacking me first, then calling the cops to press assault charges on me after telling them that I attacked him. The cops would definitely believe him before they believed me. A couple of times, he pushed me, trying to provoke me into starting a fight. I did nothing. I'd listen to his ravings until he got tired and went away.

I was allowed to start weekend visits, but I could only go if my mother or father signed me out for visits at their homes. I had told them both about Marjorie, and they had met her a few times at the psych center. My mother wasn't really interested in me having weekend visits, so Marjorie made a deal with her. My mother would come to the psych center on Saturday morning and sign me out for the weekend. She'd take me home with her, and a few hours later, Marjorie would come and get me. She and I would then spend the weekend together, and all I had to do was be back at the psych center by nine p.m. on Sunday night.

My mother didn't have to sign me back into the psych center; I just had to be back by Sunday night. This suited my mother just fine because she was too busy on weekends with her girlfriends and boyfriends to have me hanging around. Whenever my father signed me out on weekends, he did the same thing my mother did.

I got my driver's license back while I was with Marjorie, and I drove her car. Sometimes, we went out on the town together, and sometimes, I just took the car and went out by myself. I enjoyed driving while listening to the radio, and I would do this for hours. I'd drive around town and the suburbs all night until dawn. I enjoyed the freedom of movement and the wide open spaces around me.

I began to notice that whenever I was on the streets, I was being followed. I didn't tell Marjorie about this because I didn't want to worry her. Sometimes, it was just one middle-aged white man. Other times, he'd be with a younger white man. They were very professional in their surveillance and never made any attempt to approach or ambush me. I didn't know what to think or do at first. Were they city detectives? The FBI? Army Intelligence? The CIA? Colonel Small's men? I still had enemies in the Buffalo area, too, so I was quite concerned about this. My life experiences had taught me to take nothing for granted. I was being followed, and I wanted to find out why.

One weekend, I went out driving by myself. It was around three o'clock in the morning, and as usual, I was followed. I drove to the east side of town and parked the car on Wyoming Avenue. I got out and started walking down the dark avenue. The man trailing me parked his car and followed me on foot. I went to the end of the avenue, turned the corner, and hid in some tall bushes near the sidewalk. When the middle-aged man turned the corner, I jumped him. Not wanting to hurt him, I put him in a combination half-nelson and choke-hold. I applied only enough pressure to his neck to weaken him so he wouldn't fight back.

I searched him quickly for ID and found a pistol on him. His ID stated he was a licensed private investigator from New York City. Why was a New York City private investigator following me? I questioned the man, wanting to know his interest in me. For every question I asked, the only answer I got back was "Fuck you!" He was an experienced hard-rock, and guys like him only respond to sheer intimidation.

I put the barrel of the pistol between his eyes and cocked the weapon. I told him I'd shoot if I got one more "Fuck you." I wouldn't have actually shot him, but he didn't know that. I asked him again why he was following me. This time, he turned into quite a chatterbox. "Take it easy, Parker. No need to get excited, okay? Me and my partner work full time for only one employer as investigators and bodyguards. We were ordered to do a bio-file (biography file) on you from the day you were born until now. We're thorough. We even have copies of your dental records. We were ordered to be in Buffalo for all your weekend visits from the hospital. We have to follow you everywhere you go. We weren't ordered to harm you; we were ordered to protect you. You have enemies in the Buffalo area, and our employer was concerned for your safety."

"Who's your employer?" I asked roughly.

"You might as well blow my head off now," he said tiredly, "because I can't tell you who he is. If I did, he'd have me killed for sure. I fear him a hell of a lot more than I do you or anyone else. Give me a break, okay? Let me do my job."

I was surprised. I had several people who would like me dead, and now there was someone who wanted me protected? I was confused, but I didn't know what else to ask the man. I felt angry because my life was so complicated and frustrating. After giving the man back his pistol and ID, I just walked away. The thought of being protected on the streets made me feel good, but not knowing the benefactor of that protection left me a bit shaken and curious. I decided I wasn't going to worry myself into a nervous wreck over it, though; it was out of my control, like so many other things in my life.

Two weekends later, I found out who the private investigators worked for. Their employer was Marjorie's grandfather. I also found out that Marjorie was not fully Polish. She was half Polish and half Syrian. Her father was Polish, her mother was Syrian, and her grandfather and grandmother were Syrian. After her grandmother died from cancer in her late forties, her grandfather remarried. He'd been with his second wife for about twenty-five years. Marjorie's grandfather was also a noted multimillionaire. I would later find out that he was actually a billionaire. His name was Thomas Cutter, and he lived in the suburbs of Utica, New York.

It was around three o'clock in the morning when he showed up at Marjorie's apartment with four armed bodyguards. Marjorie and I had been asleep in bed. She was surprised because she hadn't seen him for a long time. He and I talked for the next few hours, well into the early dawn. He asked me a lot of personal questions and seemed very interested in me. He said he knew more about me than any one person or agency would ever know. He said he liked my intelligence, my military background, and the fact that I wasn't afraid to use violence when it was necessary. He also told me he had blacks, Italians, the Spanish, Sicilians, and other races and nationalities working for him.

Marjorie had called him "Poppy" all her life, and he wanted me to call him that, too. Poppy was in his late sixties to early seventies. He had white hair and a bald spot on top of his head. Most of the time, he carried a cane with him; it had a solid gold cobra head on the end. He was a retired engineer who had worked all over the world for an international corporation. Whenever Marjorie mentioned his two sons, he'd get angry. He bitterly disliked his sons, saying they only wanted his money and cared nothing about him. He said he was going to disinherit both sons so they wouldn't get a penny. After talking and eating, he left, saying he'd be back the next weekend.

Poppy started coming frequently on weekends, and he'd talk mostly with me. Marjorie would usually get tired and go back to bed, and sometimes, she never got up at all. She had always believed that Poppy was an upstanding citizen who had gained his money only through legal endeavors. I was sure Poppy had always led her to believe that. At first, I wasn't sure why he had decided to tell me about some of his illegal activities. Marjorie had told me once that he was very secretive and eccentric. As time went on, I began to understand why. Poppy was bitter toward his sons because they had no interest in following in his footsteps. He'd wanted his sons to take over the worldwide criminal organization he had built from the ground up. One of his sons worked for the Kodak Company in Rochester, New York.

Poppy overwhelmed and captivated me during our many talks. He had large bank accounts all over the world and in the United States. He once had Marjorie and me call a bank in Geneva, Switzerland to check on one of his accounts. In that bank account alone, he had over seven hundred million dollars! Poppy had legal and illegal businesses all over the world in places like Lebanon, Iran, Cuba, Syria, Brazil, Peru, Canada, Italy, Spain, Sicily, Egypt, Puerto Rico, Jamaica, France, England, Nigeria, and the United States. As a baby, Marjorie had been kidnapped by some of his enemies and held for ransom, which he paid. When she was a little girl, he took Marjorie on frequent vacations to his heavily guarded villas in Milan and near Venice, Italy. He also had a big place in Mexico. Worldwide, he owned offices, companies, corporations, restaurants, hotels, beer companies, oil assets, stocks and bonds, yachts, horses, ranches, homes, camels, and more. He had interest in gambling casinos and establishments all over the world. He had what he called "asset agents" in places like Cuba, Libya, Beirut, South Africa, Nicaragua, Colombia, Panama, Honduras, El Salvador, Costa Rica, Iran, Iraq, and Syria.

Whenever major trouble started anywhere in the world, he would send agents there for information and to find out ways to make money. He also had connections with international terrorist groups, and he would send millions of dollars to Syria every year. He was also involved in international drug trafficking, the lucrative slave trade, arms-trafficking, and espionage. He owned shopping malls and businesses in New York State. He used those businesses to hide large quantities of drugs as his part in the now busted "Pizza Connection," which involved a Sicilian Mafia organization and an Italian-American Mafia organization.

Poppy was an honorary member of a Sicilian Mafia organization. Because he was Syrian and not Sicilian, that was the only way he could become an active member. He held the rank of a don, or godfather, and was even given Sicilian mob soldiers to command. Some of his bodyguards were Italian, Sicilian, black, and Spanish. All this was amazing to me. I was looking into a world that was part of our reality but rarely seen by most people. It was frightening but yet so alluring. Not only was Poppy a high-ranking Sicilian mob leader, he was the leader of his own worldwide criminal organization. It is still difficult for me to fully comprehend the magnitude of power he held in his hands.

Poppy started bringing his Sicilian chief capo, who worked directly under him, to the apartment. He was in his early to mid-sixties and introduced himself as Giuseppe. Giuseppe was also second in command of Poppy's own organization. Poppy had some of his other mob soldiers working for him at different levels in his organization, too. Third in command was the chief lieutenant, a Sicilian by the name of Francesco who lived in France.

Poppy's organization consisted of twenty-five groups spread out around the world. Each of these groups had a capo and two lieutenants. Each group could contain a hundred to thousands of people, and they consisted of Sicilian mob members, associates, and connections. Each group had its own supply of weapons and special equipment. Each capo was paid half a million dollars a year, and each lieutenant was paid two hundred fifty thousand dollars a year plus expenses. Each capo was given an annual thirty-day vacation, and each lieutenant got two weeks of vacation.

Poppy started taking me on weekend trips with him to Toronto, Montreal, and New York City. Sometimes, we stayed in the Buffalo area, where he introduced me to some business people. He told everyone we met that I was his grandson. He never mentioned my last name to any of these people. I noticed that some people knew him by different names. I realized that Poppy had several fake names that he used in his business dealings. He taught me about laundering illegal money by using false IDs, forming companies, using offshore corporations and tax-havens, using mail drops and remote call-forwarding, and how to invest money without reporting it to the IRS. He taught me how important it is to have good business friends and associates, how to avoid getting caught, and what to do if I did get caught.

He had a silver Mercedes Benz limousine and a black Lincoln limousine. There were bodyguards inside the limo with us and a chase car following with two more bodyguards in it. On our trips to New York City, we always took one of his planes down. In New York City, Poppy introduced me to mob soldiers who secretly worked for him by spying on their own mob families. He also introduced me to numerous businessmen in the area. I met some of these people while I was staying at the Hyatt Hotel in midtown Manhattan. For instance, I met a Puerto Rican businessman who owned hotels and motels in Puerto Rico, I met a Jewish immigration lawyer with an office in Manhattan, and I met the owner of a Manhattan funeral home. I met a Nigerian who was involved in Nigerian organized crime and had contacts in the American militant BLA (Black Liberation Army). I overheard conversations about a mass grave in upstate Orange County and near Peru, New York. I met a Jewish man who was a broker and also under federal indictment. Many of these people seemed a little nervous around Poppy, and they gave him the utmost respect.

Giuseppe sometimes came to the psych center to visit me during the evenings, which is when I had the privilege of walking around the grounds. He talked to me about his family and relatives, and he told me how many of them lived with him on his farm in Sicily. He told me that Poppy considered his own sons to be cowards, wimps, and money hungry. He said Poppy was thinking about retiring, and that's why he was introducing me to people and telling me things, little by little. Poppy was grooming me for an upper-echelon position in his organization, which meant having a position with his Sicilian connection. His theory was that the American, Italian, and Sicilian authorities would never guess that a black American had a major role in his organization and the Sicilian connection.

Giuseppe said that Poppy had absolute power to appoint me to any position he wanted in his organization, even over the Sicilian mob soldiers he controlled, without the approval of the other Sicilian bosses. He said Poppy was discussing me with them out of respect and wanted their input. Giuseppe told me that the majority of Sicilian mob bosses in the Sicilian Commission were against putting me in a major role. They felt I should start at the bottom and earn my way into a major role. Poppy countered, Giuseppe said, by telling them that if they pressured him into appointing someone else to a major role after his retirement, he'd do everything within his power to destabilize and ruin that person. Giuseppe said they'd been discussing this and other issues the last few times Poppy had attended meetings in Italy and Mexico.

Giuseppe also told me that Poppy was a very powerful and ruthless man to deal with. He said the people working for him were terrified of him because he ruled with an iron hand. He also said that Poppy was trying to get younger blood into his organization and among his Sicilian soldiers. Giuseppe said that there were a lot of problems in the organization and among the mob soldiers due to Poppy's iron-clad leadership.

Giuseppe was worried that Poppy might have him killed instead of letting him retire and that he'd appoint a younger person to take his position. He said that if I did get appointed to his position or to Poppy's position, he was asking now to be given a chance to retire and not be killed. For what it was worth, I told him not to worry.

Sometimes, Poppy brought Colombians and Peruvians to the apartment late at night to eat, drink, and discuss business. Sometimes, he brought Italian and Sicilian men to the apartment, too. A few times, Poppy brought two of his lawyers with him so Marjorie and I could sign papers. I had no idea what most of the papers contained because most of them were in Italian. Poppy just told us to trust him and sign the papers. He had Marjorie and me sign power-of-attorney papers, also. They stated that if he was sick, in a coma, or incompetent, only Marjorie, Marjorie's mother, and I, together, could make decisions in his personal and business affairs.

Chapter Sixteen

Bill, the unit team leader, started harassing Marjorie. He did it because Marjorie was the only one in the ward who complained about my treatment. Other ward employees were leery of Bill because he'd been known to have employees fired. He harassed Marjorie so much that she changed shifts, going from the day shift to the midnight shift. She eventually went to the midnight shift in a female ward to get away from Bill. Marjorie had spent over nineteen years as a state employee. In all those years, Bill was the only one to give her a substandard evaluation.

I began to have serious thoughts about killing Bill or having him killed. I knew he had heart trouble, and if I used a certain chemical poison, I could make it look like his death was caused by a natural heart attack. I despised Bill. I put him in the same hate category in which I put Colonel Small. I had friends from my past who would kill the bastard for me. I also knew that if I went to Poppy and Giuseppe about him, he was a dead man. I wanted Bill dead, but I couldn't motivate myself to do it or have it done. I was strongly against the use of extreme or deadly force, directly or indirectly. Instead, I would murder Bill over and over again in my mind. For rest of his life, he will never know how dangerously close he came to being murdered. Knowing that secret was soothing to me whenever I saw the bastard.

A forensic ward was going to be opened up at the Gowanda Psychiatric Center. The small town of Gowanda was about forty miles from Buffalo, and the psych center was a few miles out of town. These new forensic wards would be opened up at selected state psych centers throughout the state. They would have maximum security, housing mostly criminal patients and county jail people sent there for mental evaluations. The forensic ward employees were supposed to be specially trained to deal with any situation that arose concerning criminal patients. The theory behind the creation of these forensic wards was that they would eventually make the max-secured Mid-Hudson Forensic Center obsolete. Instead of dangerous patients being sent to Mid-Hudson from all over the state, they would simply be sent to the nearest forensic ward in their area. Forensic ward TAs at Gowanda would boast that due to their elite training, no patient of theirs would ever have to be sent to Mid-Hudson. That was their theory, right? Well, guess what? I would be the first patient in the Gowanda forensic ward to disprove that theory.

A group of mental health forensic professionals was sent to the Buffalo Psych Center to evaluate all the criminal patients. Their evaluations would decide who would be sent to the Gowanda forensic ward and who would stay at the Buffalo Psych Center. I met with a forensic psychologist, who interviewed me for about an hour. At the end of the interview, he told me I was not dangerous to myself or others and saw no reason for me to be sent to Gowanda.

The next day, Bill called me to his office. He was furious that the psychologist didn't want me sent to Gowanda, and he told me I'd be sent to Gowanda come hell or high water. He wanted me to see another forensic specialist from the group, a psychiatrist. At first, I refused to see someone else because even an idiot could tell it was a setup, but he said I'd be restricted to the ward with no privileges until I agreed to see the psychiatrist. The next day, I saw this psychiatrist for about fifteen minutes. At the end of the interview, he let me know that I would most likely be going to Gowanda.

By having me see the psychiatrist, Bill had put a rope around my neck, and what he did a week later tightened that rope. Bill showed up about ten minutes after I came back to the ward from my evening free time on the grounds. He was not alone, and he had that twisted, sinister smile on his face again. With him were a psych center security guard and several male employees. Standing in front of me, Bill said I was going to the Intensive Treatment Unit, which was in another building of the psych center. Patients were sent to the ITU when they became uncontrollable or violent in the regular ward.

I asked why I was being sent to the ITU. Bill gleamed as he told me I had been seen leaving the psych center grounds by the security guard who was standing with him. I glared angrily at the fat security guard, knowing he was lying. I knew this was all part of Bill's master plan to get me transferred to Gowanda. I stared back at Bill, hating him with all my heart. I wanted to kill him. Just one quick blow to the throat or between the ribcage, and I could rid humanity of this piece of shit once and for all. He brutally abused his authority, and that's what made him so dangerous. He was dangerous to patients and employees, just as a hoodlum was dangerous to people in general. I could kill him before the goon squad with him had a chance to respond.

Bill was wrong. Why was he doing this to me? Why? I was enraged, but I was extremely hurt, too. I thought I understood most people to a reasonable degree, but sometimes I wondered. I will never understand people like Colonel Small and Bill. I'm no angel myself, but Colonel Small and Bill were predatory beasts that hid behind their jobs like gutless wimps. I was escorted by the goon squad to my room, where I tearfully packed my belongings and was taken to the ITU.

Altogether, I spent a few months in the secured ITU. While I was there, I found out from employees that the security guard who claimed he saw me off-grounds was a good friend of Bill. This security guard apparently had a few serious incidents at the psych center that were hushed up. One of these incidents involved stealing state property, and another incident involved him getting a juvenile female patient pregnant.

Bill was a cunning, sleazy, barbaric bastard. He had this off-grounds crap held over my head so I could be sent to Gowanda. Why Bill hated me so much, I will never know. There were other patients of his who were really doing wrong, and he did very little or nothing to stop them. For instance, there was one Italian criminal patient named Joe who had jumped through his mother-in-law's window with an automatic assault rifle. Bill pampered Joe and rarely reprimanded him. Joe used to come back to the ward drunk. He'd have tantrums and scream hysterically at other patients and employees, and Bill would do nothing to him. When Joe beat his patient girlfriend up in front of the Rehab building, with patients and employees looking on, all Bill did was keep him restricted to the ward for one day.

Another criminal patient, whose name was John, was a weapons specialist who had shot and wounded three policemen on a rampage. When John heard that Senator Kennedy was coming to town, he let it be known at the psych center that he was going to kill him. All Bill did was have John put in the ITU during the weekend Kennedy was in Buffalo.

A criminal patient named Russo ran away from the psych center and stayed out all night, getting drunk. Bill restricted him to the ward for one day. There was a female criminal patient named Patricia who had killed her husband on their wedding night. Her relatives brought her back to the psych center late and drunk from a weekend visit. Her relatives tried to bribe the evening supervisor to overlook the incident. Bill had Patricia restricted to the ward for one day. There was a patient named Sam who had killed another patient at the psych center. He came back to his ward one night and broke furniture and assaulted employees. Bill sent him to the ITU for two days. None of the patients I mentioned were sent to Gowanda. Why did I have to stay in the ITU for three months and then be sent to Gowanda?

At the end of July, 1980, I was sent to the forensic ward at the Gowanda Psych Center. I would stay at Gowanda for two years. Marjorie visited me frequently and brought me messages from Poppy and Giuseppe. I was voted in by the other patients as the president of our patient government meetings, which were held once a week. After being asked by the staff, I wrote a set of rules and bylaws for the meetings and the elections. The patient-president would hold office for three months, and then elections would be held again. The other patients liked and respected me so much that they kept voting me in as patient-president. The staff finally stepped in, telling the patients I could no longer be president.

I was appointed by staff to be the patient coordinator in the OT (or occupational therapy) shop. I learned to make ceramic articles like chess pieces, tea sets, fancy figurines, cups, Christmas trees, etc. I had more orders than I could possibly fill by employees who wanted to buy my ceramic pieces. I was appointed by the staff and patients to be the chief editor for a newly created ward newspaper called the *Forensic Journal*. The *Forensic Journal* would be circulated throughout the psych center. Employees could also take them home for family and friends to read. Only forensic ward patients could contribute to the newspaper. I wrote poems for the newspaper, and I also wrote personal newspaper commentaries on local and world events. In the Gowanda town newspaper, high school students paid tribute to me for my inspiring and sensitive poetry. During my time at the psych center, I also sent five-hundred-word articles to the Buffalo

Courier Express newspaper for possible publication in their editorial section. The newspaper would only print a selected person's article once, but they printed every article I sent them. I wrote articles on subjects concerning antiterrorist teams, terrorism, black-on-black crime, depression, and more.

I was appointed by the staff and patients to be the chairman of all the patient coordinators in each ward program. We held patient coordinator meetings once a week to discuss program problems and improvements. I did so well as patient coordinator in the OT shop that I was taken out of OT and put in the newly formed carpentry shop. I was in charge of hundreds of tools and small machinery.

Out of thirty-five patients in the ward, I was the first one to be given off-ward privileges. I started having escorted and then unescorted privileges to the weekly dances and movies at the psych center. I started assisting a male employee in running the ward commissary cart almost every evening. The large, wooden commissary cart was on wheels and was stored on the second floor, which was closed down and used mainly for storing equipment. To get the cart, the employee and I had to go off the ward into the hallway and take the elevator to the second floor. After getting the cart, we brought it on the elevator and into the ward. After patients bought all the goodies they wanted, we took it back upstairs to do inventory and restock it. It took from forty-five minutes to an hour to restock and inventory the supplies.

I started working on-grounds three times a week in the afternoon at a company called AgFab. AgFab was a privately owned company that specialized in repairing farm equipment and putting together new farm equipment. There were several other patients who worked with me at AgFab. The bosses at AgFab told my treatment team that I learned extremely fast and was an excellent worker. They also told the team I had learned everything about the tools, machines, schematics, etc., and there wasn't anything else they could possibly teach me. The team was having trouble finding me a job that was comparable to my intelligence. All the regular patient jobs at the psych center were deemed unsatisfactory for me by the team. I was very good at typing and filing, and I knew two types of shorthand. The team thought about getting me an office job at the psych center doing these things, but the idea was discarded. If I were to work in the office, psych center information would pass through my hands, information that was confidential and forbidden for me to see as a patient.

I was finally taken out of AgFab and given a job at the psych center garage. The garage had never accepted a patient to work there before. Because I came so highly recommended, though, the garage boss decided to take me. I knew the basics about car and truck maintenance, but they taught me many things and I became good worker.

The white garage boss was a nice man who treated me well, but the other four white employees working under him were racist and vindictive toward me. Gowanda was a small town with only a few black families living in it. The Gowanda Psych Center only had a few black patients, and it had only recently hired several black employees from Buffalo. I was the only black person working at the garage. I had to endure racist jokes and comments that really pissed me off. I never said anything back, though, because I didn't want to lose my job or get negative evaluations. Keeping my job was an important part of my therapy, the treatment team said. Three days a week, I worked mornings and afternoons at the garage. I took my lunch breaks in the ward, and then I walked back to work. I was usually the first person back to the garage after the lunch break. Several times, after returning to the garage, I found that the white employees had left insensitive and cruel "gifts" for me. For instance, upon returning to the garage, there was once a rope made into a hangman's noose hung from a wooden ceiling beam. The noose was around the neck of a handmade dummy that had been painted black. Across the chest of the dummy, written in white paint, were the words: "Nigger go home." This was done other times, too, with phrases like "KKK," "Coon go home," and "Die, nigger."

I became so enraged over these racist incidents that I got stomachaches and headaches, and my blood pressure went sky high.

After each of these incidents, I'd take the rope and dummy down before anyone else got back to work. I'd untie the noose and put the rope away, and then I'd rip the dummy to pieces and throw it in the garbage dump outside. I had every right to complain to the garage boss and my treatment team, but I didn't. I wasn't about to give those racist bastards that pleasure. They'd really enjoy it if I complained and felt intimidated by all this. I was determined not to be run off by a bunch of inept hillbillies. They had stereotyped the wrong black man by messing with me. After each of these racist incidents, I went about my job as if nothing had happened.

The therapist assigned to me was a man named Jim Fox. Once a week, I had escorted privileges with Jim off the grounds. These escorted privileges lasted for several hours, and Jim took me to movies, restaurants, and to Marjorie's apartment.

My treatment team wanted me to start making speeches supporting the forensic unit and its goals. I didn't want to do this; I just wanted to stay out of trouble and be treated like the other patients, but it wasn't to be. I was not keen on being their patient public relations man, as they put it. I told them nicely that I wasn't interested. They countered by telling me it would be therapeutic. They also added that if I kept refusing, it wouldn't look good on my record. That was outright blackmail, but it worked. I finally consented to doing the speeches because of their persistence. The treatment team confided in me, saying that the statewide forensic units were an experiment in a different kind of approach to dealing with criminal patients. They said I was the best asset they had to show that forensic wards were worthwhile. They said the forensic wards would get more money from Albany if they could prove they were productive.

I was allowed to write my own speech as long as it was approved by the team. I wrote a several-page speech titled "The Forensic Philosophy: Steps to a Conditional Release." The speech was accepted by the team as excellent. I gave the speech at a few mental health seminars that were held at the Gowanda Psych Center. Professionals with psychiatric backgrounds from the tri-state area attended these seminars. I also gave the speech at a seminar for the New York State Council of Churches at the psych center. I was scheduled to give this speech at other psych centers, too. I did so well at giving the speech and answering questions that the team said they wanted me to continue giving the speech even if I got discharged.

Several different times, groups of people stopped by the ward for a tour. The team had me give the tour and answer their questions. Groups of psychiatrists, psychologists, social workers, lawyers, judges, and college students came for the tour. When we had our yearly open house day, which was when the community and psych center employees could tour the ward, it was I who planned and wrote the foundation for open house presentations. Another reason the team enjoyed all this was because the forensic wards were being ridiculed by some newspapers and psychiatrists, who claimed it was a useless project.

A majority of the nonprofessional forensic employees in the forensic ward at the Gowanda Psych Center were complaining to their union and the newspapers, saying they wanted higher state grades and more money. The employees were actually physically fighting and harassing each other. The complainers felt they should have the same grade and the same amount of money that employees at the Mid-Hudson Forensic Psych Center got. The complainers also constructed a slow-down strike in the ward as part of their grievance. The ward psychiatrist and unit team leader called me into the office one day. They wanted me to spy on the nonprofessional employees to find out who the troublemakers were. I told them both I didn't want to get involved. They gave me a fifteen-minute speech on why I should get involved and told me to think about it.

The whole thing really angered me because I already knew who the leaders of the complaining employees were. I knew because they had talked to me already, wanting me to spy on the professionals. They also wanted me to help keep the other patients calm during their slow-down strike. I told them the same thing, that I didn't want to get involved. What kind of crap was this? I was a patient. They had no right trying to get me involved in their disputes. Why me? But my problems would get worse, not better.

The type of therapy given the patients in the ward was called Eskalapeon-Synannon. This type of therapy was created in state prisons for hardcore and long-term convicts and was not created for mental patients, but it was illegally being used in the ward. I thought it was a good program at first, but I quickly changed my mind. The ward team leader used hardcore confrontation in one-to-one and group therapy sessions. Patients were getting upset, threatening, suicidal, and violent. They punched out windows, broke toilet bowls, punched holes in the walls, cut their wrists and throats, and tried to hang themselves. This type of therapy was totally confusing to most patients in the ward.

Our ward team leader was a middle-aged woman named Tina. Tina was white, obese, and looked masculine. She was also moody, self-centered, overly aggressive, and very cunning at getting her way. She was the one who had started these hardcore therapy programs in the ward. I was the only patient who knew that these hardcore programs were not designed for use on mentally ill patients. The Department of Mental Health in Albany had no idea that these programs were being implemented in the forensic ward at Gowanda.

I felt that Tina was too aggressive in punishing us, and I let her know that. She told me to butt out or I'd start having problems of my own. Punishments consisted of things like forcing a patient to sit in a chair in the corner of a room, facing the wall. The patient was forced to do this from a couple of days to a few weeks for eighteen hours a day. The only time the patient was allowed to move was for meals, medication, and bedtime. Because of this, patients suffered delusions, breakdowns, and suicidal tendencies. Another punishment was Tina telling the patients not to talk or interact with a particular patient. This, too, would go on from a couple of days to a few weeks.

Sometimes, the patient had to wear a sign across his chest that labeled him a wimp, sissy, liar, or less than a man. If a patient was caught cursing in the ward, he got punished by being put on cigarette and commissary restrictions. If a patient was caught with porno magazines or raised his voice in anger about anything, he got punished. If he refused to go to programs or refused medication, he got punished. Patients' records were supposed to be confidential and not openly discussed with other patients, but Tina and the other employees openly discussed all aspects of patients' records in group therapy. Tina would tell us in group therapy that when males are incarcerated, it's normal for two men to have a sexual relationship. The same went for incarcerated women. She also told us that a man looking at a woman with lust and sex on his mind was sick and disgusting.

I was involved in the reassigning of three employees from the forensic ward to regular wards at the psych center. These three employees brutally beat up a patient. I complained about it to the mental health investigators when they investigated the incident. Most of the employees in the ward disliked me after that, but I didn't care.

While at the psych center, I was assigned a black rehab counselor by the name of Joe. Joe was a Muslim, and he was extremely militant. Instead of being concerned about me on a professional level, all he wanted to talk about was my Green Beret training, small arms weapons, urban guerrilla warfare, ambush tactics, sniper training, explosives, etc. He even tried enticing me to become a black militant hit man, but I refused. Then he gave me reasons why I should hate the white race and why they had to be either exterminated or controlled. He said that would only come about through a bloody race war. He was very serious and adamant. At times, he'd get raging angry when he talked about a race war and white people. Personally, I felt Joe was crazier than all hell, and I complained to Jim, my therapist, about him. Jim did nothing about this; he said I was exaggerating and overacting because I didn't like the man. Jim made me angry when he told me that. I knew myself better than that.

Joe was finally taken off the forensic ward and put in a regular ward at the psych center. He was not taken off the ward due to my complaint but because he was constantly arguing with his coworkers. He started calling me on the phone at the garage, saying he needed to talk to me. I told him I was too busy to talk and would get in trouble if he kept calling. He kept calling anyway. I complained to the team about him, and still, no one did anything. He continued harassing me over the phone about joining his black Muslim militant group. While I was walking back to the garage after lunch one day, he confronted me with two other black Muslims. This time, he outright threatened my life if I didn't join his group and teach them what I knew. I was very angry about being threatened like that, but I kept my composure. After work, I went straight to the psych center's security office and complained about him. They listened and said they'd get back to me, but they never did. I wanted no trouble with anyone, and I definitely didn't want to be put in a position where I lost control while physically protecting myself.

Shortly after this, Joe was arrested and then fired from his job. He was not arrested and fired because of the things he did to me, though. While he was arguing with a female coworker in his ward, he seriously assaulted her, which resulted in his arrest. Only after this incident did people take notice that he was a fanatic and dangerous. I'd been telling them this for some time. It should not have taken an employee getting seriously beat up for them to take action.

I was also inadvertently involved in another situation in the ward. The situation this time concerned a black patient named Steward and a pretty, well-formed white female employee named Doris. They were having a personal and sexual affair in the ward. This was obvious to me and several other patients. On several occasions on the weekends, we saw them disappear together for about a half hour. I didn't consider this a problem; it wasn't any of my business.

Doris was a rather strange person. She was indignant, rude, and quick-tempered with most of the patients in the ward. I had a heated dispute with her after being in the ward for only a few months. The dispute happened while all the patients were out in the fenced-in forensic yard. It was starting to get dark outside, so Doris and the other employees yelled that it was time to go back inside. The door to the ward was wide open, so most of the patients went through the door, including me. This was how it was always done when we were outside. This particular time, though, Doris felt we should have waited at the door for her before going inside. Of all the patients who went through the door, she singled me out to start yelling at. She was very angry, pointing a finger at me and cursing loudly. She wasn't yelling and cursing at any of the other patients, only me. I got angry and told her I wasn't the first patient through the door; I was only following the other patients. She paid no attention to what I was saying and told me to shut my mouth or she was putting me on report and restriction. I got even angrier after hearing that, and I started yelling and cursing back at her. Then I walked away into the dayroom, mumbling and cursing under my breath.

It normally takes a lot to get me angry, but her mouth yelping a mile a minute like that touched a nerve. A few employees came over and tried to calm me down, and a few employees were with Doris trying to calm her down. She actually wrote me up for creating a disturbance in the ward. The next day, my therapist, Jim, told me that Doris was having a lot of personal problems with her husband and her life. Those problems were starting to affect her job performance. She was quick-tempered and angry most of the time with everyone, he said.

As the months went on, I noticed that she was coming to work with black eyes and bruised lips and arms. Sometimes, she would be limping painfully. I didn't know it at the time, but Doris was cheating a lot on her husband and evidently getting caught. Several of the male employees in the ward had been to bed with Doris. Her husband worked at the psych center, too, but he was in another building. She was seeing a marriage counselor and a therapist about her problems. I was asked to be flexible and cooperative with Doris until her attitude improved. Being flexible and cooperative with Doris would lead to my downfall at the Gowanda Psych Center.

A few patients came to me, wanting me to go with them while they reported the affair between Doris and Steward to the staff. For about fifteen minutes, I tried to talk them out of it. They wouldn't listen to me. They kept demanding that I go with them because I was the top patient role model and the patient-president. I was tempted to tell my fellow peers to eat shit and die with this role model and patient-president crap, but if I kept refusing to go with them, they'd tell Tina on me for sure.

I went with them to the office, and they chattered on about Doris and Steward. Doris was reprimanded and put on a probational status as an employee. Some of the employees chose to believe that I was the one who spearheaded the campaign against Doris. Even Doris believed this. I could see the hate in her eyes whenever she stared at me. I never opened my mouth once while I was in the office with the other patients, but yet, I was the only patient being given the cold shoulder by most of the employees. My luck really sucks. I will probably end up being the only human being in the world to be struck by lightning twice while in the same city, standing on the same corner.

As part of my therapy, Tina wanted me to work closely with a Spanish patient named Carlos. I didn't mind doing this except for the fact that Carlos was incompetent, psychotic, and assaultive. He was about 6'3" and well over two hundred pounds. I knew Carlos from the Buffalo Psych Center. He would go into sudden vicious rages where he growled like a wild animal and seriously assaulted patients and employees. In one of his assaults, he stabbed two employees continuously with a metal fork in the dining room. It took seven male employees to hold him down. I told Tina I didn't want to work with Carlos because I knew he would eventually assault me. Tina didn't take my refusal lightly, and what she did was a bit on the extreme side. She called all the patients together for a meeting in the dayroom. Then she proceeded to tell them that I was a coward not to work with Carlos. In front of the other patients, she called me gutless, a quitter, and said I had a yellow streak down my back. Tina was deliberately attacking my manhood in front of the patients and employees. This was her crude way of trying to embarrass me into working with Carlos.

I did not fear Carlos. I simply didn't like being put in a position where I might be assaulted. By the end of the meeting, though, I reluctantly agreed to work with him. I was supposed to teach Carlos how to eat properly instead of stuffing food in his mouth. I was to make sure he took a shower, used deodorant, combed his hair, brushed his teeth, and washed his clothes. I felt that working this close with Carlos was a job for the employees, not another patient. They were getting the hazardous-duty pay for working with patients like this. I wasn't.

A few days after I began taking care of Carlos, he flatly refused to take a shower one morning. I told him that if he didn't take a shower, I'd have to report him to the office, which meant he wouldn't be allowed to smoke. This is what I was instructed to tell Carlos if he refused to do anything I asked of him. As soon as I said this, he viciously punched me in the face. Instinctively, I wanted to retaliate with a rigid forward palm thrust to his nose that would have killed or seriously injured him. But instead of hurting him, I simply got behind him and wrapped my arms around his neck. I purposely didn't have my forearm against his throat because that would have killed him or seriously hurt him, too. Instead, I applied brief pressure to both sides of his neck, which caught off the supply of oxygen to his brain. He stopped struggling, started swaying, and went limp. I kept yelling for the employees. That same day, I told Tina that I was through working with Carlos. She yelled cowardly names at me, but I didn't care this time. I told her if she was so tough, she should work with him and see what it was like. I really got her angry by saying that, but enough was enough.

About a week later, Carlos took a large metal ashtray and attacked another patient. He struck the patient several times in the head. There were no employees in the dayroom, and I was the one who subdued Carlos before he could hit the patient more. The injured patient had to have over twenty stitches. A few days later, Carlos assaulted employees on two different occasions with a chair. He was arrested and sent to jail this time.

While I was at Gowanda, Marjorie was assaulted by two female patients in the ward at the Buffalo Psych Center. Her lower back was severely injured and she went on compensation. She would never return to work. Ultimately, she would receive permanent disability from the state and be given early retirement. Marjorie also found out that she had lymphoma. That shattered us both. I was more upset by it than she was. Marjorie was a strong person, and that helped me cope with her cancer. She had major operations to remove the cancer and stop the spreading, but the cancer continued to spread. Her grandmother had died from cancer, and her father had cancer, too.

I tried not to show Marjorie how devastated I was. What if she died? I was horrified at the thought of being alone again. Who would care about me?

Chapter Seventeen

My flexible cooperation with Doris led to a strange and destructive alliance. I disliked Doris. Her negative attitude toward me showed she disliked me. She had written me up, saying I had created a disturbance in the ward, right? I had been with several patients who turned her in for having a personal and sexual affair with a patient, right? Doris blamed me for turning her in, right? I felt that Doris was having too many personal problems to be efficient as a ward employee, but that was my personal opinion, and I never told it to anyone. Many of the ward employees already disliked me because three employees were transferred to another ward for beating a patient.

I was no longer working on the commissary cart because I had other duties. There were other patients who now had the privilege of working on the cart with an employee. The male employee who had worked on the cart with me had been taken off it, too. The employee who was now in charge of running the cart was none other than Doris! One evening, Doris took me into a side office and said she wanted me to help her run the commissary cart. I was stunned. Was she crazy? I didn't even like her, let alone want to work with her. There were other patients who had the privilege to work with her on the cart. I flatly refused her request. Just being alone with her made me feel uncomfortable. She was persistent in wanting me to help her, though. She told me that she had already okayed it with the team. I was really confused. She promised to write only good reports on me if I helped her. If I kept refusing, she said she'd have to write a negative report on me, and it wouldn't look good in court for a judge to read that. She was blackmailing me. Why is it that whenever I refuse to do something, I get blackmailed or have my manhood questioned?

I reluctantly agreed to help her. We had to go upstairs to the deserted second floor to get the cart, bring it back downstairs for the patients, and then take it back upstairs to restock it and pull inventory. Between getting the cart and returning it, Doris and I spent about an hour together every day. She constantly talked to me about her personal problems. She believed her husband was cheating on her, so she felt justified in cheating on him. She complained about her two kids, saying she loved them but felt she got married too early in life. Some nights, she was so upset from fighting with her husband that she'd go into crying spells, wanting me to hold her and comfort her until she stopped. Several times, she showed me black and blue marks on her legs, arms, and torso where her husband had beat her. A few times, she wore sunglasses to work to hide her black eyes.

Holding each other led to kissing, which eventually led to us having sex together upstairs after returning the cart. She really disliked her husband and some of the people she worked with. She said they were always gossiping about her. She told me that if she ever got the nerve, she was going to kill her husband for beating her so much.

She wrote me letters and sneaked them to me in the ward. In her letters, she wrote about wanting to kill her husband, and she felt I was very understanding in listening to her problems. She said I was the only person she could confide in without being judged, and she loved me for that. In one letter, she named all the male employees at the psych center she had gone to bed with. In another letter, she told me that her husband had pistols, shotguns, and ammunition, and that as long as I took her with me, she would help me escape and get some of his weapons for me. She sneaked me several nude pictures of herself to keep. Instead of going to the psych center dances on Tuesday nights or the movies on Friday nights, I secretly began to meet with Doris on the grounds. Numerous times, we sneaked into a room in the basement of a building and had sex.

I definitely should not have been fooling around with Doris. I seem to gravitate toward any woman who shows affection toward me. I want to hold on to that affection desperately, regardless of the consequences. Could that stem from the way my mother never showed me affection? Could it be because she didn't touch me, hug me, and tell me I was loved as a child? Is that the reason I was willing to live on the edge and be self-destructive — because of this compulsive need to be cared for, needed, and loved?

Living on the edge in a variety of ways was exciting, intoxicating, and stimulating to me. As a teenager, I wasn't involved in gang wars or criminal activities to prove my adolescent courage. I lived on the edge by purposely fooling around with girls whose boyfriends or brothers were bullies or psychotic gang members. My adolescent courage was proven by the constant beatings I endured at the hands of those tough guys. No matter how badly I got beaten, I continued to make love to their girlfriends and sisters.

This courage was strange, I agree, but it was my courage. When I joined the army and became an Airborne Ranger, a Green Beret, and part of a covert operations group, that was another way of living dangerously. And I continued to fool around with women I had no business getting involved with. I was told by one of my best friends that I was something of a paradox, an enigma to most people, that God had given me the uncanny gifts of perception and leadership. But in giving me these gifts, God, in his infinite wisdom — or humor — had taken away some of my common sense.

I went from one extreme of disliking Doris to feeling extreme compassion for her. Becoming close to Doris may have also been my odd way of dealing with Marjorie's cancer. If she died, I would be totally alone, and I feared loneliness more than anything in the world. Therefore, I needed Doris to keep the loneliness away in case Marjorie passed away.

One evening, while we were restocking the cart and pulling inventory, Doris started complaining about the bills her husband made her pay. She said he hardly left her any money for herself and asked if I could help her. I told her I would. Within the next few days, I had Doris get several ID pictures of herself made. Giuseppe had given Marjorie his girlfriend's name, address, and phone number, and she had given that information to me so I could write or call him whenever I wanted. The number and address were for a Brooklyn home where he stayed sometimes. Using one of the public phones on the grounds, I called Giuseppe for the first time, explaining what I wanted. I had already sent the pictures to the address, using his girlfriend's name on the letter.

Several days later in the early evening, Doris and I met Giuseppe on the grounds. He had driven up in his girlfriend's car with his Sicilian cousin, Lorenzo. Lorenzo was short and slim with dark features like Giuseppe. He was in his early to mid-fifties, and he was very friendly to Doris and me. We all sat in the car, with Doris and me in the back seat.

Giuseppe gave Doris a set of fake identification, which included a birth certificate, a high school diploma, a social security card, a driver's license, and a voter's registration card. Some of the ID cards had her picture on them, but they all had a fake name. The address on the fake ID was to a real home in Buffalo. Doris was even given two major credit cards in her fake name as well as a bank account book. The bank book was to a savings account that had been opened in a Buffalo bank under her fake name. Five thousand dollars had been deposited in the account; every month, two thousand dollars would be deposited in that account for her, too. Giuseppe gave her five hundred dollars in cash in the car. Any mail that came to the Buffalo address in her fake name would be saved for her to pick up. An old Sicilian couple lived at the address; they were paid to do this for several other people, too.

Giuseppe asked if it was okay to talk openly for a minute in front of Doris. I told him it was okay. He said that Poppy wanted me to meet Lorenzo because he was thinking about retiring soon, and Lorenzo would be put in by him as acting boss until I got out. This had finally been agreed to by Poppy and the other mob bosses as the practical thing to do. Poppy had wanted my input on this, and I told Giuseppe it was fine by me. Poppy wanted me to know that things would be okay until I was discharged.

Poppy had ordered Giuseppe some time ago to do whatever I asked of him. When I got sent to Gowanda, Marjorie told Poppy and Giuseppe about Bill, the team leader, at the Buffalo Psych Center. She told them about all the things Bill had done to me and her while we were at the Buffalo Psych Center. They were really angry, and they wanted to know if I wanted Bill kidnapped and murdered. I did want Bill dead, but I told them I didn't want it done. I felt this way because of the oath I'd made to my beloved grandmother. Having the power of life and death in your hands carries a certain type of responsibility with it. I learned that quickly in Vietnam. I couldn't order people to be murdered just because they got me angry. Besides, I'd have a long list of people to get rid of before I got around to Bill if I did that.

That's what I told Marjorie to tell Poppy, and he was quite pleased by my decision. I wasn't letting myself be led by my emotions, and good leaders aren't led by their emotions, either.

Giuseppe and Lorenzo warned Doris not to tell her husband or anyone else about the ID, about them, or what was discussed in the car. Doris got out of the car first and went to our hiding place in the basement. About ten minutes later, I got out and met her there. Giuseppe and Lorenzo were on their way to Buffalo for a few days, and then they'd go back to New York City. Doris was astonished about the ID, the money, and what had transpired in the car. I told her the two men were mob members who were friends of mine and owed me favors. I told her this so she would remember their warning about keeping her mouth shut. All the money she had been given and would be given was organization and mob money. Doris could now disappear from her husband for days, weeks, or forever if she wanted. I wanted her to get used to taking trips to Buffalo while I was locked up. When I got discharged, I planned on getting her an apartment of her own in Buffalo, too. My dreadful fear of loneliness motivated me into reckless and precarious situations.

A few weeks later, things started falling apart for me. Doris and I had met in the basement and had sex, as usual. On this particular evening, though, I was supposed to be at the psych center's dance in the Rehab building. Instead of going to the dances and movies every week, I had been meeting Doris. Unknown to me, on this particular night, an employee from the forensic ward was escorting a patient to the dance for the first time. I was with Doris and didn't get to the Rehab building until the dance was over. The forensic employee told the team the next day that I had been gone during the dance. The team demanded to know where I'd been. I told them I went for a walk. I didn't expect them to believe that, but I couldn't tell them I had been with Doris. I wanted to protect her and her job. All my privileges were taken away, and I was restricted to the ward until I told them where I'd been. Doris was almost hysterical at first and pleaded with me not to tell them I'd been with her.

For several weeks, I kept my mouth shut, sacrificing my privileges to keep her out of trouble. During those weeks, Doris and I met alone in the nurses' station or in the dormitory a few times and had sex. During those weeks, I also overheard conversations between employees about Doris partying on the streets and having sex. I got angry about this because there I was, locked up and miserable, and it wasn't even fazing her. She was buying clothes and partying with these men with the money I'd supplied to her. My common sense finally kicked in; I realized that if she cheated on her husband, then of course she'd cheat on me.

While I was in the forensic yard one day, I saw her go by on a motorcycle with a male forensic employee. Seeing that really got me angry. The next day, when she came to work, I angrily demanded the fake ID, money, and credit cards back. Doris was arrogant and bold; she said she wasn't giving me one penny back. She also told me that I was just a patient, and if I told on her, I would get the worst of it. I was almost out of control with anger, and I told her that if I didn't get my money back, I just might go to the team and tell them about us.

Later on, when we were all in the yard, she quietly stared at me as I paced up and down. She looked worried and panicky. I had no intention of telling anyone about our affair, but she didn't know that. Doris suddenly walked over to my therapist and started talking to him. A few minutes later, I saw her burst into tears. About fifteen minutes later, they both went inside the building. That would be the last time I ever saw Doris. She had obviously told my therapist something about us.

The next day, I went to my therapist, wanting to talk about Doris. He flatly told me that he didn't want to discuss her. I went to another employee and asked to see my doctor. The employee told me that the doctor was too busy. I didn't know it at the time, but within a few days, every employee in the ward knew about Doris and me. Exactly what they knew, I had no idea, because no one would discuss her with me. I was deliberately being ostracized by the employees. Why wasn't I being confronted by my doctor and the team about Doris?

The following week, on a Wednesday morning at about eleven o'clock, the usual patient government meeting was called together. This particular meeting, however, was nowhere near usual. Most of the employees from the day shift, evening shift, and midnight shift were there. This was very unusual. We were all in the dayroom, and the other patients were excited, wondering what was going on. I was totally unprepared for what was about to transpire.

Tina called the meeting to order. She said there was a serious problem that needed their attention. Then she pointed an accusing finger at me and said that the problem was me. She accused me of continuously raping and beating Doris! Tina screamed that today was my judgment day. I was dumbfounded, bewildered, startled! Rape? Beatings? My mind raced as sudden panic and realization set in. Doris had told them this. She was lying! I never raped anyone in my life! Doris was running scared. She was lying through her teeth to protect her butt.

I leaped out of my chair, yelling that I never raped Doris. Tina shouted at me to sit down and shut up. She proceeded to call me an animal, snake, dog, and other appalling names. She screamed that I was going to jail for this. The patients were shocked at hearing this; they just sat there, staring at me. The other employees started in on me, calling me humiliating names. It was open house on my ass that day.

Many of the employees had been hoping I'd get into some kind of trouble. They were more than happy to oblige Tina with the name-calling. Tina then turned the meeting over to the patients so they could degrade me. The patients were stunned, not really knowing what to say at first. Tina whipped them up into a frenzy by saying more negative things about me, and then about half the patients began calling me names and taunting me. Some of the patients started crying because they liked me a lot and couldn't deal with what was going on. They asked Tina if they could be excused from the meeting, but she refused to let them. This was definitely wrong. I was the only patient with unescorted privileges in the ward. This meant that all the other patients still had serious coping problems. Was it right to commit them to this kangaroo court that was going on?

The meeting went on for about a half hour. I was angry and hurt about Doris telling such vicious lies. Every time I stood up to say something, Tina would tell me to sit down. You could almost taste the hostility in the faces and eyes of the employees. I felt helpless and humiliated by them. Tina did not allow me to defend myself. I wanted them to hear my side of the story, but Tina had them too wound up.

I gave up on them, emotionally and mentally. I went deep inside myself. I numbed my feelings so I couldn't care about what they believed or what they did to me. At the end of the meeting, I was manhandled by several male employees. They pulled and ripped my sweater, shirt, pants, socks, and shoes off me. While calling me degrading names, they pushed me out of the dayroom, down the hall, and into one of the seclusion rooms. Stripped down to my undershorts, I was given a shot by the nurse. The male employees called racial slurs at me, saying I should be castrated and hanged.

Tina was there and told me I'd be in the room until the police took me to jail. She said I'd be allowed no visits and no phone calls. She told me that she hoped I'd rot in jail. Finally, they all left, locking the door behind them.

The next day, a state trooper came to question me about Doris. I told the trooper I never raped or beat Doris. I also told him that she and I did have a personal and sexual relationship together through mutual consent. The trooper told me that they could prove through fiber-testing that I'd been in the basement with her. I responded by telling him that she and I had met there over a dozen times to have sex. I never denied being with her in that room. The trooper said he had already talked to Doris and taken her statement.

After taking my statement, he left. The police investigation concluded that nothing criminal happened between Doris and me. The police also found out about a nurse in the ward who was fired because she became personally and sexually involved with a patient from the county jail; he had been sent to the forensic ward for a mental evaluation.

I stayed locked up in the seclusion room for two weeks. I was put on a strong psychotropic drug four times a day. Doris had obviously mentioned nothing to them about Giuseppe, Lorenzo, and her fake ID and bank account. My doctor and therapist came to see me a few times while I was locked up. They told me that Doris was being fired. They also told me about an incident that happened at her home while I was locked up. The incident drove her into a severe nervous breakdown and shock, leaving her incompetent and incoherent. They said she was now in a mental institution, but they wouldn't tell me which one.

They said that Doris's husband had gone to answer their front door, and when he opened it, there were some men standing there, holding a coffin. Doris was standing behind her husband, and one of the men said they had come for Doris's body. She flipped out right there in the doorway and started screaming hysterically. Then she took off running through the house and out the back door. Someone had played a cruel joke on Doris. The men were from a local funeral parlor. Someone had called the funeral parlor, saying that his sister had died at home and he wanted someone to come and get the body. The person gave them Doris's name and address.

My doctor and therapist couldn't understand why she'd reacted that way. They asked me if I knew anything about the incident with Doris and if I could explain it to them. I told them I knew nothing about the incident; I'd been isolated in a single room. Even if I had known who was behind it, I wouldn't have told them. Hearing this news about Doris didn't exactly fill me with sorrow and compassion for her. Poppy and Giuseppe could have been behind this. They knew me well enough to know I wouldn't want her killed. They might have done it as a way of telling her that what she did to me was wrong. The incident could also be a warning, saying that this time it was a joke, but next time it would be real hit men coming for her. There were also other people I knew from my past who could have heard about my predicament and done this to her.

My doctor and therapist told me that Marjorie kept demanding to see me and talk to me. They questioned me about what was happening in the ward that they should know about. I began to tell them about some of the things that were going on. I told them about Sharon, who was an employee in the ward. Sharon liked me a lot and wanted me to teach her karate so she could protect herself on the streets. I taught her some basic forms of self-defense and dirty street fighting. Several times, she had taken me to the back dormitory when it was empty, where we kissed, hugged, and fondled each other. Twice, we had sex. I told them about Connie, a nurse. She was constantly pinching and fondling my rear end every chance she had, and she'd sneak up behind me, wrap her arms tightly around my waist, and rotate her hips against me sensuously.

I also told them about the middle-aged female employee named Nancy. While I was sitting in the dayroom, she came and sat down next to me. She asked if I'd been watching the news on TV lately. I told her I had. Nancy was married to a deputy sheriff who was thinking about running for county sheriff. She was cheating on her husband. She told me about a trial that was going

284

on concerning two men who were paid by a third party to murder a man. The two hired men, riding in a van, pulled up alongside the victim, who was on a motorcycle, and shot and killed him. Nancy told me that she and the young victim had been lovers. She was in tears as she told me this, and she said she'd been attending the trial of the two men since it started. She was hoping and praying that the two men and the man who hired them went to prison and got killed by other prisoners. If the three men were still out on the streets, she said she would have given me money and sex to kill all three of them for her.

I told them more things, too, about what was happening in the ward. They were both stunned by my revelations, saying that it was no wonder there wasn't any proper therapy being done in the ward.

After two weeks in the seclusion room, I was sent back to the Mid-Hudson Psych Center in early July, 1982. I was transferred because I'd become an embarrassment to Gowanda's forensic ward. Doris eventually retracted her statement about me raping and beating her. I spent about a year and ten months at Mid-Hudson. During my time there, Marjorie moved from Buffalo to Middletown, which was only a few miles from Mid-Hudson. She wanted to be closer to me. Marjorie visited me almost daily and brought me messages from Poppy and Giuseppe.

After I had been at Mid-Hudson for several months, my ward doctor recommended that I see an independent psychiatrist, a doctor who doesn't work directly for the state but is selected and paid by the state to evaluate mental patients in state psych centers.

My doctor felt I should not have been sent back to Mid-Hudson. He wanted me in a less secure civil psych center. He said that the support of an independent psychiatrist's evaluation would be helpful in getting me out. A psychiatrist named Hendricks was picked to see me. He came to Mid-Hudson, and we talked privately for about an hour. He had already read my file before he saw me. He talked to me about Vietnam. Hendricks had been an officer and a psychiatrist in the Marine Corp, and he had served in Vietnam, where he gave psychiatric help to combat troops. I was given a negative evaluation by Hendricks. It angered my doctor that he did this, but there was nothing my doctor could do about it. I had to stay at Mid-Hudson.

While I was at Mid-Hudson, Poppy received a letter from the federal government. The letter stated that he must be at the federal building in Albany on a specific date to discuss the millions of dollars he was sending to Syria every year. Poppy was enraged and refused to show up. He said that the US government wasn't going to boss him around. Poppy was eccentric and stubborn like that. Marjorie's mother and Poppy's wife had called Marjorie to ask me what they should do. They were concerned about what the government would do to Poppy if he didn't show up in Albany. They knew that Poppy liked and respected me. I told Marjorie that I couldn't see Poppy going to Albany. I remembered him telling me that his cousin, Samuel Logan, took care of some of his personal and business affairs. Logan was a lawyer who lived in Geneva, New York. I told Marjorie to call her mother and have her contact Logan to see if he would go to Albany to represent Poppy. A few days later, I found out through Marjorie that Logan had agreed to handle the situation. I never did find out exactly what Logan did; he didn't talk about it with Marjorie or her mother.

A few weeks later, Poppy had a severe heart attack and went to the hospital. He was in a coma and on a life-support machine. His wife, his two sons, his daughter, and several other relatives spent a lot of time with him at the hospital. Poppy's two sons wanted him taken off the life-support machine so he could die in peace. Poppy's daughter, Marjorie's mother, had a copy of the power of attorney papers and showed them to Poppy's doctor. The papers showed that only Marjorie, her mother, and I had the legal right to have him taken off the machine. The two sons weren't pleased about hearing this.

Marjorie's mother and Poppy's wife called Marjorie, telling her to talk to me. The decision to take Poppy off the machine or leave him on it was left entirely up to me because I wasn't a relative. I told Marjorie on our visit that I wanted Poppy kept on the machine for a few more weeks. If there was no change in his condition during that time, it would then be all right to take him off. A week later, he came out of the coma, got stronger, and was taken off the machine. When he heard that his sons had wanted him off the machine early, he was furious. A few weeks later, he was out of the hospital, and he started visiting Marjorie at her Middletown apartment. He told her he was going to talk to his cousin Logan and have his will changed so that Marjorie and I were in it.

While Poppy was having his will changed, he decided to look into several other personal and business matters that Logan was handling for him. To his surprise, he discovered that Logan had been secretly stealing a lot of money from him for years. Poppy was angry and told Logan that he would no longer be handling any of his personal or business affairs and that he was no longer in his will. Logan was angry about being caught and blamed Marjorie and me. He felt his thievery would never have been discovered if it wasn't for Marjorie and me getting into Poppy's business. Logan started calling Marjorie on the phone, threatening to kill me and her. He did this several times, saying there was a murder contract on both of us.

Poppy had two bodyguards staying inside Marjorie's apartment and two bodyguards outside the apartment in a car. They had Marjorie wear a bulletproof vest every time she left the apartment. These bodyguards pulled shifts with other bodyguards so she was never left alone. Poppy had two men put electronic bugs in the apartment and on the phone so that the bodyguards in the car outside could hear everything that was said in the apartment or on the phone. All this went on for several days. Then Poppy told Marjorie that everything was all right and we didn't have to worry about his cousin anymore. He refused to discuss what had happened to Logan and told us not to talk about it. He did tell us that he had made it official law within his organization that whenever I got out, whether that happened in one year or twenty years, I would legally and rightfully inherit his organization and mob soldiers. He said again that Lorenzo would only be acting boss when he retired.

Over a year later, my ward doctor presented me to the Mid-Hudson Forensic Committee. The committee consisted of several psychiatrists and sometimes a social worker. Every criminal patient at Mid-Hudson had to pass this committee in order to be transferred to a less secure psych center. If the patient passed, the committee would recommend to the court that the patient be transferred. Most of the time, the judge would go along with the committee's negative or positive recommendation concerning a patient. Every professional on the committee had to agree with the transfer for it to go through.

After interviewing me for about an hour, they all agreed that I should be transferred to a less secure psych center. The next day, when it came time for everyone on the committee to sign the papers for my recommended transfer, the social worker refused to sign. She had abruptly changed her mind. The psychiatrists on the committee were not pleased with her for doing this. Without her signature, the recommendation could not go through. Weeks later, it was concluded by the whole committee that I wasn't ready for transfer.

Chapter Eighteen

Months later, Poppy gave Marjorie some money to hire a lawyer to get me out of Mid-Hudson. I was seen by the Forensic Committee again, excluding the social worker. This time, the committee passed me. Marjorie hired William Schwartz, who was one of the best lawyers in Middletown and Orange County. Schwartz was an ex-FBI agent, and at one time, he had been the Orange County District Attorney. A court hearing date was set. Since I was a criminal patient, the district attorney's office from the county I was from had the legal right to approve or contest my possible transfer. The Buffalo District Attorney's office said that they would strongly contest my transfer to a less secure psych center. They said that they never wanted me back at the Buffalo Psych Center or living within the city limits of Buffalo. The State Attorney General's office was involved in all the court hearings having to do with criminal patients' transfers, acquired privileges in civil psych centers, and conditional releases.

My doctor felt I was ready to be transferred to a civil psych center. He was prepared to come to my court hearing and testify. An assistant attorney general would be coming to my hearing to help my doctor and the committee get my transfer. An assistant district attorney from the Buffalo Special Investigations Bureau and the social worker who had previously refused to sign my transfer papers would be at my hearing to protest my transfer.

The social worker was talking negatively about me at the psych center. She had a dislike for me that seemed more personal than professional. She was a skinny, unattractive, unkempt woman who seemed very strange to me. She wore the same worn, tattered, dirty clothes for several days before changing, and a few times, she had been reprimanded about her hygiene because of her body odor. Whenever she saw me in the psych center, she stared at me with intense hostility. I had no idea why she was so bitter toward me.

Court hearings for patients were held in the library once a month at Mid-Hudson. The judge would come to the psych center to preside over these hearings. On the day of my hearing, the library was packed with employees who were curious about my case. The Assistant DA from Buffalo protested my transfer venomously, saying I was still dangerous and violent. The social worker testified to the same thing. She also testified about incidents that had happened while I was in Vietnam. Why she brought up my experiences in Nam, I don't know. What I did in the war should not have been relevant to whether I could go to a civil psych center or not.

One of the incidents she mentioned was when my team was going through a village, looking for Viet Cong or "infrastructure personnel." A few members of my team, including myself, had been attacked. The social worker stated that a middle-aged Vietnamese woman had angrily thrown a bucket of water on me and that I retaliated by literally ripping a portion of her throat out with my hand. The social worker's version was only partly true. The woman didn't throw a bucket of water on me at all. What she did do was charge out of her hooch screaming, swinging a machete at me. She was on me so fast, I didn't even have time to shoot. I blocked the downward swing of the machete with my rifle. Then I grabbed her wrist, twisting it, and karate-chopped her in the throat with my other hand. She died right there. In her hooch, buried underground, were several rifles, pistols, and homemade explosives.

Another incident she mentioned was when my team and I were in Laos. Our mission was to kidnap and bring back a live NVA soldier. Headquarters wanted one for intense interrogation. We got a soldier, but he killed two of my men first. I secured the man by tying his hands behind his back. When he realized that he wasn't going to be shot, he took off running, trying to escape. We captured him. I was angry. I tied a frag grenade to a rope and then tied the rope around his neck. I pulled the grenade pin, then kicked him into a bombed-out crater. The explosion killed him.

My lawyer, Schwartz, said that all these incidents involved killing the enemy and not civilians. He told the judge that the attitude of the social worker toward me seemed more personal than professional. The Assistant Attorney General spoke in my favor, and my doctor wasn't even called to testify. The judge had heard enough and granted my transfer.

In the middle of April, 1984, I was transferred from Mid-Hudson to the Middletown Psychiatric Center in Middletown, New York. I spent about three months at the psych center. I hated Mid-Hudson and was glad to be out of that place. I never wanted to go back. I wanted to do whatever was best so I could get out and live my life quietly. Marjorie wanted that. Poppy wanted me out, too, but only for his personal reasons. I'm sure Poppy thought he was helping me in his own way. But I was having serious doubts about wanting to be involved with his organization and mob soldiers. I didn't want the army controlling my life, and I didn't want Poppy and his organization controlling my life, either. To me, the army and the mob were the same. I wanted no part of criminal activities anymore, personal or organized. I just wanted to be left alone to live my own life.

I was having difficulty dealing with Marjorie's cancer. She'd started chemotherapy, and the side effects were terrible. It was frightening to watch her hair fall out, to see her in extreme pain and vomiting a lot. She was still in good spirits, but deep inside, I was horrified. She insisted on visiting me even when she was sick. I felt so helpless. I wanted to rip that cancer right out of her body. I wanted it completely destroyed. No one else will ever know how much I wanted that cancer destroyed so she could be healthy again. But there was absolutely nothing I could do. Knowing that was traumatic for me. I couldn't handle the emotional pain and grief of it. It wasn't fair!

Everyone thinks I'm strong person inside, but in many ways, I'm sensitive and vulnerable. I've always had poor coping skills in dealing with emotional pain, grief, and sorrow. I knew I was dysfunctional in some ways, but I wasn't crazy. Psychiatrists diagnosed me with personality disorders, antisocial traits, alcohol dependency, and post-traumatic stress disorder from the war. These are not considered mental illnesses by definition. I've never been diagnosed as being psychotic by any psychiatrist. I never had any premeditated intentions of getting personally involved with any female employees in the psych centers. But once a female employee showed a personal interest in me, I responded impulsively and emotionally instead of using my reasoning abilities. I had an extremely deep craving to be cared for, needed, and loved. I wanted no personal involvement with any female employees at the Middletown Psych Center. My reasoning and common sense dictated that it only brought trouble and pain. But I let my emotions and impulses override everything else again without thinking about the consequences.

At the Middletown Psych Center, I got involved with a female nurse in the ward. Her name was Jennifer Rossi. She was Italian, in her late thirties, and very pretty and well-formed. She was about 5'7" tall with long, black, curly hair, brown eyes, and a dark complexion. Jennifer was divorced and had two sons. She was with the psychiatrist and the two male employees who interviewed me when I first got to the psych center. Weeks later, she told me she was attracted to me at first sight. Instead of being put in the dormitory, I was given my own private room. There were only a few other patients who had their own rooms. She started talking to me a lot. She worked the day shift, and before she went home, she always searched the ward for me to say goodbye.

The first few times she asked to read my manuscript, I refused. I was self-conscious and ashamed of letting someone I knew read the manuscript. I felt this way because of the violent things I'd done in Nam and on the streets. I didn't want anyone who was spending time around me to read it and think I was some kind of demented, crazy person. I explained this to her, but she became more persistent about reading it. I finally gave her my finished typed sheets to read, and she took them home for a few days. When she returned the manuscript, she was surprised by the many things that had transpired in my life.

Sometimes, she worked the evening shift and midnight shift for extra money. She started bringing me homemade food to eat. She wrote me a letter, saying she couldn't fight her feelings anymore; she was falling in love with me. There was a public telephone for patients in the dayroom, and Jennifer started calling me in the ward. One night, when she was working extra duty on the midnight shift, Jennifer slipped quietly into my room. The other night employees were either asleep, watching TV, or visiting other wards. She woke me up by kissing me on the side of my face. I was quite shocked by this. Then she took all her clothes off and got into bed with me. She told me to put my arms around her and just hold her for a few minutes. She just rubbed and stroked my back and shoulders firmly, moaning sensually until she had a full, erotic orgasm. Then we made love twice that night.

The visiting room was small, with a bathroom attached, and only one patient with visitors was allowed in at a time. The visiting room was only open from nine o'clock in the morning to nine o'clock at night. When Jennifer worked extra duty on the evening shift, I always pretended to go to bed at nine o'clock. The other ward employees watched TV, went to sleep, played cards, or visited other wards. Jennifer would sneak down and unlock the door to the visiting room in the hallway. Then she'd go back into the dayroom or the office. I'd then sneak out of my room and go into the visiting room and wait. Ten to fifteen minutes later, she'd tell the other employees she was going off the ward. She'd go to the front door in the hallway, unlock it, open and shut it again loudly, then lock the door quietly. Doing this made it sound like she had actually left the ward. She'd then sneak quietly into the visiting room and lock the door. From there, we went into the visiting room bathroom and locked the door. I had a bedspread that we'd spread out on the floor. We were usually on the bathroom floor or in my room when we made love. We would have several sexual rendezvous like this. Jennifer kept telling me that she wanted my baby and wanted to be my mistress. It was against ward policy to be in the nurses' station with a patient while the door was closed or locked. But Jennifer would take me into the nurses' station and lock the door many times. We would hug, kiss, and fondle each other there.

One afternoon, she came into my room and gave me three keys. One of the keys was to her car. The second key opened doors in the ward, and the third key was to the ward's back door exit. When I entered the mental health system, I learned that it wasn't unusual for an employee to have one or two extra sets of psych center keys. They weren't supposed to have the extra keys, but they did. She told me to keep the keys and hide them in my room. She said that she didn't want to lose me, and if the psych center treated me unfairly and didn't give me a discharge soon enough, we'd have to take things into our own hands and she'd help me escape. She said she and her kids would go with me, and we could go to California, Florida, or Canada and live under a new name. I hid the keys, hoping I'd never have to use them.

It was starting to become obvious to some of her coworkers that something was going on between us. A few of them even went to the chief psychiatrist to tell him about their suspicions.

Jennifer was called to the unit chief's office about the suspicions. She denied being personally involved with me. She was very worried that our relationship would be discovered. There was no solid proof of our involvement, but she remained quite distraught. She was worried about losing her job and her nursing license. Some of her coworkers began talking to her about our involvement, too.

What probably drove Jennifer to the edge was when she found out in one of the team meetings that the patients' phone in the ward was bugged. She came bursting tearfully into my room to tell me. One of the patients in the ward had been calling the state troopers on the phone and cursing at them. The troopers started tapping the phone to find out which patient was doing it. As soon as Jennifer told me this, I told her to calm down. She kept insisting that the troopers had heard her talking to me on the phone and had reported it to the unit chief. She was convinced the unit chief was going to fire her and have her license revoked.

I told her that the troopers and the unit chief knew nothing about us. With my background in surveillance, I knew about civilian laws relating to electronic eavesdropping. I told her that the patient telephone wasn't bugged; the line was only bugged at the troopers' barracks. Anyone who called the troopers from the patient phone would automatically have his or her voice recorded at the troopers' barracks. If a patient called anyone else, the patient would not be recorded, and if anyone called the patient phone, they wouldn't be overheard by the troopers, either.

The patient phone was a public telephone, and it would take a court order from a judge to have a public phone fully bugged. Judges were careful about signing bugging orders, and they did so only in extreme cases. A mental patient in a psych center calling the troopers and cursing at them wouldn't warrant a full electronic bugging of a public phone. I explained all this to her, but she didn't seem convinced.

The next day, Jennifer didn't come to work. That afternoon, I was called to the office to see the team and unit chief. They said that Jennifer had called earlier and told them I had threatened her. They said she was too afraid to come to work as long as I was in the ward. Ambushed again! It was a lie! I had never threatened Jennifer. I was devastated at hearing this. She was sacrificing me in order to save her job and her license. Once she heard about the patient phone and listened to her coworkers, Jennifer had turned her back on me.

All my ward privileges were taken away until the investigation about Jennifer and me was finished. I was put under close observation. Close observation meant moving my bed into the dayroom, where I would sleep near the office. I was restricted to the dayroom and ate my meals there. There was no doubt in my mind that after the investigation, I'd be sent back to Mid-Hudson. This had happened in Gowanda, and I had been sent back to Mid-Hudson then. I wasn't going to sit quietly and have them do that to me again without a fight. Jennifer was ruthless and by no means stupid. She was ruthless because she'd accused me of threatening her when I hadn't. She wasn't stupid because she didn't tell them about the keys she'd given me. Telling them that would have been incriminating to her, and she knew it. I was going to use that to my advantage.

The next evening, a little after eight o'clock, I told one of the employees that I needed to take a shower. He escorted me to my room to get my robe, towel, and soap. While I was getting these things, two patients started fighting near my room in the hallway. The employee left the doorway of my room to break up the fight. I used that opportunity to get the three keys and put them in my pocket. After showering, I put my clothes back on and went back into the dayroom. A little after nine o'clock, the employees started playing cards in the dayroom. I asked permission to use the bathroom. It was right next to the dayroom, and I was allowed to go by myself. The bathroom had a back door that was always locked and led to the dormitory. Since I was alone in the bathroom, I quickly unlocked the back door. After locking the door behind me, I walked through the dark dormitory into the hallway. Right outside the dormitory, through the hallway, was the ward's back door exit. No one from the dayroom could see me unless they walked out of the dayroom, down a short hallway, and into the main hallway. I unlocked the ward's exit door and silently went through. Then I locked the door, went down a few flights of stairs, and out the door of the building. I locked the exit door so I could gain time to escape. Once the employees realized I was missing, they'd check the ward's front and back doors to be sure they were locked. After that, they'd assume I was still in the ward and begin a thorough search.

I stayed in the shadows and kept my distance from anyone walking on the grounds. I hid in the bushes, behind trees, and under parked cars whenever a car drove by. I did this to avoid any psych center security cars from approaching me and perhaps stopping me.

I made my way to the back of the psych center and walked off the grounds. A few blocks away, I caught a cab to Marjorie's apartment. She lived on Stratford Lane in a complex called the Stratford Apartments. After I knocked a few times on the door, she opened it. She was definitely surprised to see me. Inside the apartment, Marjorie kept hugging and kissing me, asking how I got out. I told her that Jennifer had accused me of threatening her, and I had escaped to avoid being sent back to Mid-Hudson. Marjorie started crying, and I told her not to worry. From her purse on the living room table, I took her car keys. I told her to call the cops as soon as I left and tell them I came and took the car. I didn't want the cops harassing her, which is why I got the keys myself instead of asking her for them.

I was only in the apartment for a few minutes; then, I left. Her car was in front of the apartment. I got in and drove off. I made it to New York City, which was about sixty miles from Middletown. I parked the car on a side street in midtown Manhattan. It was after midnight, warm, and humid. I walked a few blocks to 42nd Street and Eighth Avenue. I was across the street from the Port Authority Bus Station. The sidewalks were filled with people, and the streets were jammed with cars. A variety of music could be heard from passing cars, ghetto-blasters, and establishments. I stood on the corner for a while, enjoying my freedom. Then I started walking down 42nd Street, still thinking about my situation. I didn't want to contact any friends because the police would be doing the same thing. I needed a place to stay until I could change my features and get a new identity.

While I was walking, someone tapped me on the shoulder. I turned quickly, instinctively going into a defensive karate stance. Standing in front of me, smiling from ear to ear, was Giuseppe. He wrapped both his arms around me and patted me on the back several times. I was so surprised that I didn't know what to say.

Finally, I asked him how he found me. With his arm around my shoulders, he said we needed a drink first. Then he'd explain. We went into a nearby bar. Giuseppe said that Poppy's cousin, the lawyer, was no longer a problem, but Poppy still wanted the apartment bugs in place in case another threatening situation popped up from somewhere else. Giuseppe said that a husband and wife bodyguard team had rented an apartment in the complex, near Marjorie's place, to keep an eye on her. They were also electronic eavesdropping specialists, and they had equipment to hear everything that went on in her apartment. Poppy felt it was better that Marjorie and I not be told about the team. When I went to Marjorie's place for the car keys, the whole conversation was overheard by the team. The husband had followed me in his car, reporting my whereabouts to Giuseppe over his car phone. Giuseppe was already in midtown on some business, and the husband directed him right to me.

I was amazed at Poppy's efficiency in security matters. A person didn't get to be his age and acquire what he had, though, if he wasn't extremely careful. Giuseppe seemed thrilled that I was out. The way he talked, it sounded like he'd made up his mind some time ago that I'd be better for the organization and the mob soldiers than Poppy was. He made a phone call while we were in the bar, and about thirty minutes later, we left. In front of the bar, a dark limousine was waiting for us. We got in and headed for the exclusive East Hampton Village on Long Island. The limo stopped in front of a large, white, two-story traditional house. The house was one of many owned by Poppy. Giuseppe said I'd be hiding out there until Poppy got me out of the country.

The house had to be worth a couple million dollars and had a swimming pool, tennis court, library, and several bedrooms. Giuseppe, three bodyguards, a maid, and a cook were staying at the house. The maid and cook were relatives of mob soldiers. The house was near the beach, but I never ventured out into the immediate area. I stayed there for about a month. Various newspapers were brought to the house so I could read the articles written about me. I dyed my black hair so that it was all gray. I was given a gray-and-black fake beard to wear whenever I needed it and a metal brace to wear on my lower left leg so it looked like I was slightly crippled. I was given a cane to use when I walked with the metal brace, and I had foam rubber to wear around my waist, under my clothes, so I looked ten to fifteen pounds heavier. All types of sport coats, pants, suits, and shoes were bought for me to wear.

Poppy was still out of the country and didn't want anything done with me until he got back. I had talked to him several times over the phone while I was at the house. There were several different times when I had the limo take me to New York City. I went to different boroughs of the city and used public phone booths to call Marjorie. I wanted to be sure she was all right, and I wanted her to know how I was. The last time I called was on a phone at the Port Authority bus station. Marjorie was quite upset and angry with me. She had somehow come to the conclusion that she'd never see me again. In her hysterical state, she kept saying I didn't love her anymore because she had cancer. That was not true, but she wouldn't listen to me. I was going to go away for a few months and then come back and start seeing her periodically.

Poppy had told me over the phone that I shouldn't tell her I was on Long Island or had any contact with him. The only thing she knew was that I was staying with a friend in New York City. That would be the only thing the police knew if they were still tapping the phone. Marjorie was making me feel extremely guilty and ashamed over the phone. She kept telling me that I was leaving to be with another woman. She pleaded with me not to go, but I didn't know what else to say. I was at a loss for words, and she made me feel guiltier and guiltier. She was having chemo once a week, now, and there was no way for her to come with me. She felt that, in leaving, I was putting my freedom ahead of her.

In a manner of speaking, I was, and that made me feel miserable. She reminded me over the phone how she stood by my side at the Buffalo Psych Center when no one else would. Was she being unfair by telling me this? Was she within her rights to say that to me? I didn't know what to think anymore. I thought she'd be happy that I had my freedom back. I became so overwhelmed by emotion that tears poured down my face. What did she want from me? What did she want me to do? I didn't know, so I asked her. She wanted me to turn myself in to the police. Her reasoning was that if I were locked up, she'd be able to visit me regularly until she died. How could she ask me this? It was unfair. She said that if I really loved her I would do this.

She was asking me to choose between my freedom and her. Why was she doing this? I cared about her and I loved her, but I needed my freedom. Why did it have to come to a choice? This would be one of the most painful choices of my life. And I would come to regret my choice a thousand times over. I told Marjorie I'd give myself up to the police. She wanted me to come by the apartment first to see her before I turned myself in. I told her I would. I asked her to give me a few days, and then I'd call to let her know I was coming.

While riding back to Long Island, I was terribly upset. I got drunk from the bar in the limo. Back at the house, I told Giuseppe what I was going to do. He stared at me like I was crazy. I didn't want to turn myself in, but I felt compelled to do it. If I didn't do it and she died from the cancer, I'd never be able to live with the guilt. Memories of her and of not doing what she wanted would have haunted me forever. In Marjorie's mind, even though I'd be locked up, I would still be there for her. I didn't want her to feel alone and abandoned; I knew the power of loneliness, and it was horrifying. Perhaps I was wrong in feeling such enormous guilt. I don't know. If she didn't have cancer and wasn't having chemo, I definitely wouldn't be turning myself in.

Giuseppe talked to me for about an hour, trying to change my mind, but I wouldn't. The bodyguards talked to me, too, but it didn't do any good. Giuseppe called Poppy and told him what I was planning to do. Two days later, late in the evening, Poppy arrived at the house with Lorenzo trailing him. Poppy was raging angry, and we drank and argued all night about me turning myself in. He yelled and cursed so much that a private doctor on the payroll had to be called to the house and put on standby. Poppy was so enraged that he pounded his cane furiously on the floor, the walls, and the tables. When two of his bodyguards respectfully suggested he calm down because of his heart, Poppy beat both of them savagely with his cane.

He threatened to change his will if I went back. I told him I didn't care. He kept telling me I was a fool and that the system would just keep me locked up until I was insane or dead. He said that if I stayed with him as his grandson, he'd make me a rich and powerful person. I still refused. He told me he'd killed every person that had ever tried walking out on him. He said he'd have had his sons killed if they had known as much about the organization as I did and tried walking away. He told me angrily that he loved Marjorie, too, but I was a fool to give up my freedom. He threatened to have his doctor give me a shot to knock me out. Then he'd have his bodyguards put me on his private jet and fly me to his home in Mexico and keep me there until I came to my senses.

Poppy told me that Marjorie was being selfish. She knew how much I wanted my freedom. He kept telling me that I was foolish to sacrifice my freedom for Marjorie. He lectured me about how he built his organization from nothing. Poppy said I was his last hope, and he went from being angry to trying to plead and reason with me. I still refused. He said that if I went back, it was over between us, and he'd never forgive me for turning my back on him. He raved on, saying that he had things all planned out for me and that I was betraying him.

By early morning, Poppy was calmer but still frustrated and angry. He said he'd never condone my feelings, but he would respect them even though I was making a terrible mistake. He reminisced for a while about how much he had loved his first wife and how depressed he was after her death. He talked about romantic times, funny times, and sad times with his first wife. He talked about when his daughter was a child, and also about Marjorie when she was a child. By the time he finished talking, he was crying. Poppy was disappointed and hurt by my stubbornness, and I truly felt sorry for him. He called me a traitor and told his bodyguards to get me out of his sight before he had me cut up into little pieces.

A limo took me to Middletown, and I got out a few blocks from Marjorie's apartment. It was early August, in the morning, and it was starting to get light outside. I didn't care about being seen. There was no reason to hide anymore. It didn't matter if the neighbors recognized me from newspaper photos. At the apartment, Marjorie and I hugged, kissed, and talked for about twenty minutes. Someone had seen me going into the apartment. Three state trooper cars quietly pulled up outside. Several heavily armed troopers forced through the front and back doors. I was secured, searched, handcuffed, and taken to their barracks. The troopers were friendly and courteous, and we talked for a while. They told me I'd been described to them as a crazy, violent maniac who had a black belt in karate, was an ex-Army Green

300

Beret, and a Vietnam veteran. They said I wasn't what they had expected. I understood what they meant; some of the newspaper articles had called me a madman and said I was dangerous. Also, some of the articles stated that I was still suffering from flashbacks of Vietnam, where I was maiming, crippling, and killing people.

The district attorney's office in Buffalo stated in the newspaper that since I'd been captured, the judges, assistant district attorneys, police officers, and witnesses who were ever involved in any of my cases no longer had to keep a low profile.

Chapter Nineteen

I was taken by the troopers to the town of Goshen, where the Orange County Jail was. To my surprise, I was being charged with class E felony escape under the New York State Criminal Procedure Law. How could this be? I was a mental patient who ran away from an open grounds, minimum-secured civil psychiatric center. How the hell could I be charged with felony escape? Under the New York State Criminal Procedure Law, and under the New York State Mental Health Law, running away from a civil psychiatric center was not considered criminal felony escape. It was not a crime for a mental patient in a civil psych center to run away. I could only be charged with felony escape if I had run away from a detention-type facility or center. Prisons were considered detention facilities, and the Mid-Hudson Forensic Psych Center was also considered a detention center. If I had gotten away from the civil psych center using violence or a weapon, I would go to jail, but I got away through nonviolent means. Under the mental health law, when a mental patient ran away from a civil psych center, the police were to be notified. If the police caught the patient, they could not put him in jail unless he had broken the law. The police could only return the patient to the civil psych center he or she had come from.

I was at the Orange County Jail in Goshen for several months. Marjorie retained Schwartz as my lawyer again. Schwartz treated me with total indifference this time instead of working diligently for me like he had before. He even suggested I sign myself back into Mid-Hudson. I refused. I wasn't voluntarily signing myself into any psych center for him or anyone else. He told the newspaper I was the most incompetent person he had ever met. That was a lie. Why was he trying to mislead the media and the police? A year later, I discovered his motivation for doing that. Schwartz was running for public office again in the county, and getting me quietly back into Mid-Hudson would have been a feather in his cap. When he took me on as a client again, he knew he was going to be running for public office.

Marjorie visited me at the jail two to three times a week. During her visits, she met a young woman in her early twenties by the name of Josie Fairbanks. Josie was coming to the jail twice a week to visit a girlfriend of hers. Josie was about 5'5". She had long blonde hair, blue eyes, and a pretty shape. She was on welfare and lived in the city of Newburgh. She was on the verge of being kicked out of her apartment because she hadn't paid her rent. Marjorie liked Josie, and she wanted her to move in with her until she found a place to live. Marjorie wanted my approval, and at first, I refused to give it. I didn't like Josie. She seemed sneaky and manipulative, and I didn't trust her. I told Marjorie how I felt, and she told me I was wrong. Marjorie pressured me into changing my mind by saying she needed someone at the apartment because of her cancer and chemotherapy. She said that Josie could help with the cleaning and cooking, and she could help take care of her when she got sick.

So Josie moved in with Marjorie, but I still did not like or trust her. Josie made no attempt to contribute any of her welfare money toward the rent or food. She lived free on Marjorie's money and my money. Marjorie even let her borrow the car whenever she wanted. With Josie living like this, I seriously doubted that she was actually looking for another place to stay. My strong suspicions about Josie proved to be correct.

Josie eventually told Marjorie that she was with a motorcycle gang known as the Pagans. The Pagans were one of the top five motorcycle gangs in the country. They were highly organized, had mob connections, and were involved in drug trafficking, prostitution, murder contracts, and loan sharking. Josie told Marjorie that she was on federal probation for bank robbery. She and a few male members had tried to rob a bank in Manhattan and got caught. All the members involved in the attempted robbery got stiff prison sentences except for Josie. Oddly enough, she got probation. She didn't bother to tell us that she was also a federal informant.

Josie had a boyfriend who was a Pagan member and lived in the area. He and other members had heard and read about me in the newspapers, over the radio, and on local TV. They tried to recruit me into the Pagans. Through Josie, they promised to get one of their lawyers to represent me, and they guaranteed that I would only do county jail time for the escape if I joined them. I had no idea how they could guarantee me this. I refused the offer.

I didn't turn down Poppy just to get involved with an organized motorcycle gang.

Through reading the newspapers and watching the news on TV, I found out more about a Sicilian mob boss named Thomas Buscetta. Poppy had mentioned this man's name to me on several occasions. Buscetta was second-in-command of a Sicilian mob organization. He had also been instrumental in creating the French Connection drug line and later the Sicilian Pizza Connection drug line. He had also been involved in several mob murders. Buscetta had been highly respected at one time in Sicilian mob circles. From the late 1970s to the early 1980s, though, Buscetta was on the losing side of a Sicilian mob war. The war cost the lives of his two sons, his brothers, his nephew, and a dozen other relatives. He was on the run from Sicilian hit men as well as the United States and Italian authorities. He was caught by Brazilian authorities, and the Italian police brought him back to Italy. Buscetta was bitter over the killings of his relatives and agreed to testify against American and Sicilian mob organizations and many of their associates. He was the highest ranking man in Mafia history to testify against the mob. What he told the authorities resulted in hundreds of arrests and touched every mob organization in Sicily. He was then brought to the United States and hidden in the New York City area until he testified about the American Mafia. Buscetta would give the severest blow to the Mafia since its birth. After learning about Buscetta, I knew that Poppy was in deep trouble. Marjorie and I later found out that Poppy was on the run from American and Italian authorities, too.

Without consulting me, my lawyer had made a deal with the district attorney's office. I was called to court, and the judge sentenced me to one to three years for the class E felony escape. I was stunned. *Prison! I'm going to prison! How can this be? I'm a mental patient who ran away from a civil psych center. How could they send me to prison?*

I stared in disbelief at Schwartz as he quickly stepped away from me. I was taken back to my cell block. The maximum prison sentence a person could get for class E felony escape was one to three years. It was very unusual for a person to get the maximum sentence for his first felony conviction, especially when it was nonviolent.

About a week later, the deputy sheriffs took me to the maximum-secured Downstate Fishkill Prison. I was at Downstate Fishkill for about a month while I was indoctrinated into the prison system. I was designated a maximum security prisoner with a CMC. CMC stood for "constant monitoring classification," which meant that no matter which maximum-secured prison I was sent to, I would be carefully watched by corrections officers because I was an escape risk and because of my violent background and my ties to organized crime. From Downstate Fishkill, I was sent to Sing Sing Prison in Ossining, New York to serve my time. I was assigned to A-Block, L-288. There were a couple hundred prisoners or more on A-Block. There were several tiers to the block, and L-tier was the highest. While I was in Sing Sing, I became a literacy volunteer and began teaching illiterate prisoners how to read and write.

Marjorie visited me. Her cancer got worse, and she spent weeks and sometimes months in the hospital. In early March, 1986, Marjorie died at the Horton Medical Hospital in Middletown. I was devastated. I cried for days in my cell. Her death was a severe blow to me. It left me depressed, and I had stomachaches, chest pains, headaches, and diarrhea. I became so lethargic that I had to quit teaching classes. I was bitter and enraged. I wanted to believe in a God. I wanted to fall to my knees and pray to Him to look after Marjorie. I wanted to beg Him to forgive me for all my mortal sins, and I wanted to cry out desperately to Him for mercy and plead to Him for spiritual guidance. That is what I would have done had I believed in a religious God. I wanted to believe; with all my heart, I sincerely wanted to believe in something. But I couldn't believe. Sing Sing denied me the privilege of being taken to the funeral home and viewing her body due to security problems. That hurt me even more.

Josie came to visit me. She wanted me to give her full legal power of attorney so she could do whatever I wanted done. I already had power of attorney over Marjorie's personal and business affairs. Marjorie stipulated that if she died, she wanted to be cremated. I told Josie that I wanted everything in the house sold — the furniture, the appliances, even the car. I told Josie to send me all the personal papers belonging to Marjorie and me. Marjorie and I had a joint bank account, too. I told Josie to close the account and send the money to me. After all this was done, I said I'd pay her generously for helping me.

I wasn't enthused about Josie handling these matters, but I didn't have much choice. I didn't know anyone else in the Middletown area who would do this for me. So I gave her full power of attorney. To the day I die, I will regret doing that. Marjorie's body was cremated, and the remains were sent to her parents at their request. Josie then proceeded to rob Marjorie and me of everything we owned. With the POA I'd given her, she put ownership of the car in her name. She closed the bank account and kept the money. She took all the furniture, jewelry, stereos, and appliances from the apartment, and she threw away our personal papers. I was so upset and enraged about this that I was on the verge of a nervous breakdown.

I found out the name and address of Josie's federal probation officer in Middletown. I wrote him several letters explaining what Josie had done. I pleaded with him to have Josie give back everything she'd stolen from me. The probation officer did nothing. He never even answered any of my letters. I was so bereaved and enraged that I wrote him one more letter, threatening to kill him if I didn't get my money and property back. Because of that letter, I was officially charged with threatening a federal probation officer.

About a month and a half after Marjorie's death, two men from the Drug Enforcement Administration came to visit me. They wanted information about Poppy — where he was, what we talked about, his associates, and his legal transactions. I told them nothing. They said they knew that Poppy and I were close. They tried to make a deal with me, saying they'd put me in their witness protection program if I cooperated with them. I still refused. Then they tried intimidation, saying the DEA could make it difficult for me to be released. I still refused to cooperate.

During the next two months, I received visits from the FBI and from Washington's office on counterterrorism. They offered me my freedom, along with a new name and life. I refused them. They tried to intimidate and threaten me, too, but it didn't work. That was the second time I sacrificed my freedom by putting it second to stronger convictions.

During the early part of June, I received a letter from the Department of Mental Health. It said that two psychiatrists would be coming to Sing Sing to examine me. Their examination would be instrumental in deciding if I should be paroled to the streets or not. If they found me mentally ill and dangerous, I would be paroled to the maximum security Mid-Hudson Forensic Psych Center. This was a setup, and that really aggravated me. The two psychiatrists were not going to let me be paroled to the streets. They were sent to give me a royal screwing, using the legal system to keep me locked up. Even if I were the most well balanced person in the world, the psychiatrists wouldn't approve my parole to the streets. I knew it, they knew it, New York State knew it, and I'm sure certain federal authorities and intelligence agencies knew it, too.

In late June, the two psychiatrists examined me. I had no violent incidents of any kind while I was at Sing Sing. I wasn't even put in the satellite unit of the prison, which was where they put prisoners with mental problems. I was in the regular prison population on A-block in Sing Sing. The two psychiatrists still found me to be mentally ill and dangerous.

At the end of July, I was paroled to the Mid-Hudson Psych Center. I was there for about a year and ten months. Because I was sent there, the charge of threatening a federal probation officer was dropped. I was transferred from Sing Sing to Mid-Hudson so fast that I wasn't even allowed to bring my personal belongings. I was told they'd be sent to me. They weren't. My personal belongings at Sing Sing were either lost or stolen by other prisoners. I didn't care about losing my typewriter, clothes, books, and magazines. But while I was in prison, I'd written and completed a full novel while I was still working on my autobiography. The novel was now lost or stolen, and I had no copies. Losing the novel was really upsetting because I'd put a lot of work into it.

I started having pains in my chest while I was at Mid-Hudson. I was given x-rays and examined at the Horton Medical Hospital. It was discovered that the middle part of my right lung was slightly collapsed and filled with fluid and lumps. Two employees took me back to Horton for a bronchoscopy. While I was still awake, a doctor put a long tube up my nose, and it went into my right lung. They wanted to take samples of the lumps in my right lung to see if they were cancerous. They weren't.

At Mid-Hudson, I saw a renowned psychiatrist from Albany Medical College. This psychiatrist was an independent consultant for the State of New York. He went to different psych centers throughout the state, giving his expert opinion on special cases. He, along with a room full of professionals, interviewed me for a couple of hours. He concluded that I was not psychotic and that Mid-Hudson was not the place for me. He said that an Alcoholic Anonymous group, a Vietnam group, and an Adult Children of Alcoholics group would be appropriate for me. He also recommended close supervision of any female psychotherapist assigned to work with me.

To get me out of Mid-Hudson, the Forensic Committee interviewed me for three days before recommending my transfer to a civil psych center. This was the longest interview the committee had ever done with a patient. The average patient interviews lasted only an hour.

At the end of May, 1989, I was sent to the Willard Psych Center. I had never heard of the place. It was about forty miles from Ithaca, New York, and about sixty-five miles from Rochester, New York. The psych center was right across the street from the town of Willard. Willard seemed to be more of a hamlet than a town, though. The psych center, which was over one hundred years old, was in the scenic Finger Lakes region. It was located on the eastern shore of Seneca Lake.

During the ward patient trips on weekends, I went with employees on van rides in the area. They left me fascinated. I never realized that New York State had such beautiful countryside. I was amazed by the friendliness of the people in this rural area.

For the first several months at Willard Psych Center, I was restricted to the building and the ward. After this, I was given unescorted privileges on the grounds. Many men and women would come there for treatment and be discharged after a few weeks or a couple of months. They came from cities and towns like Rochester, Ithaca, Geneva, Romulus, and Seneca Falls; they came from farms, hamlets, mountain cabins, and small villages.

I was given a job in the geriatric ward. I worked there four days a week and was paid minimum wage. I was the only patient ever accepted by the geriatric staff to work in the ward. My boss was a very pretty woman by the name of Valerie. She was a physical therapist in her mid-thirties, and she had long blonde hair and an excellent figure. Valerie was a nice person, and jogging was her favorite hobby. She taught me a lot about working with geriatric patients.

Basically, I had the same duties as the staff members. I was taught how to take blood pressures, temperatures, give first-aid, and how to exercise patients in various ways. I was shown how to operate the computerized exercise machines, how to lift, carry, and put down a patient, how to use the whirlpools, how to make beds, how to make and use hot compresses, and how to feed patients. I also took them for walks and pushed their wheelchairs. During the dance hour, I danced and sang right along with patients, and I participated in other therapeutic programs with them, too. I truly enjoyed listening to them talk about themselves, their relatives, and their friends. I read newspapers and magazine articles to some of them, and I talked about current events. For a while, they even had me hopelessly hooked on afternoon soap operas. Coming to work in the morning and finding out that one of them had died was something I couldn't fully accept. I adored them all. They appreciated me, but I appreciated them even more. They made me feel like I had a purpose in life. They wanted and needed me, and I wanted, needed, and loved all of them in a very special way. Some of the elderly women in the ward were quite frisky. One of them would sometimes sneak up behind me and pinch my butt. It would hurt, too! She would just burst out laughing and clap her hands loudly.

While I was at Willard, a student nurse and an employee made sexual advances toward me. Usually, I would have responded impulsively by having sex with both women separately. Instead, I discreetly reported both women to my treatment team. I acted appropriately, and that surprised me. I was through fooling around with employees, nurses, and student nurses. I had looked temptation square in the face and stood my ground. This was a big step for me. It was a short-lived big step, but it was still a first for me.

My father died from cancer during this time. Two employees escorted me to the funeral home in Buffalo. I met a dozen of my relatives and cousins. My father requested on his deathbed that I be given a gold watch he owned. The watch was his favorite, and it had his name engraved on it. He made this request in front of his sister, his brother, my mother, my sister, and a few other relatives. My mother agreed to do it since she was the one who now had the watch. At the funeral home, though, my mother refused to give me the watch. She was keeping it for herself. My sister and several relatives were angry at her for not giving me the watch, but that was the way my mother was; she hadn't changed. How could she do that to me? I'm her son, her only biological. I cared nothing about the value of the watch. I wanted it for sentimental reasons and because he wanted me to have it. My mother never had any respect for me as a human being or as her son. I was angry, but I said nothing. I didn't want my relatives thinking I was a crazy maniac, which is what my mother kept telling them. Even the two employees with me were surprised at her conduct and attitude. My mother had disappointed and hurt me deeply again. It was yet another emotional scar to add to the many others she'd given me.

A black woman in her mid-thirties was admitted to Willard Psych Center. Her name was Shirley Cooper. She was about 5'10" tall, and she had a light brown complexion, pretty brown eyes, and was very attractive. Shirley was a heavy drug user, primarily taking crack cocaine. She had various charges against her, consisting of assault, robbery, burglary, disorderly conduct, and destroying private property. She was suicidal when the police brought her to the psych center.

After a few weeks on medication, she was feeling better. She and I were in the same group therapy sessions along with several other patients. Whenever she saw me in the dining room or on the grounds, she spoke to me. We started talking to each other a lot.

I started liking Shirley, and I assumed she liked me, but she didn't. She was a predator of the worst kind. She had no idea what friendship and caring were really about. Shirley manipulated my feelings and eventually brought my world tumbling down on me.

When Shirley told me at the psych center that she liked me, I was dumb enough to believe her. A few weeks later, she was about to be discharged, and she asked me for a few hundred dollars to secure an apartment in Ithaca. She told me she'd lost her old apartment due to being arrested, and she couldn't get on welfare because of problems with the welfare department. I gave her the money in cash. After she was discharged, I only heard from her sporadically over the next few months.

Shirley had never intended to use the money I'd given her to secure an apartment. Instead, she used the money for crack and booze. The last time she called me, she begged me for more money, but I refused.

A few years later, I realized how foolish I was to ever get involved with her. She brought me nothing but trouble and heartache. Maybe part of it had to do with my fear of loneliness and abandonment, and part of it had to do with my need to feel wanted, needed, and loved. I seem to attach myself to anyone who shows me affection, whether that affection is real or false. I convinced myself that I was wanted and needed even when I really wasn't.

Shirley went to North Carolina to live with a relative. She left because the police were going to question her about some of her criminal activities in the Ithaca area.

Through the psych center lawyer from the Mental Hygiene Legal Services, I filed a writ of habeas corpus in court. I did this in June of 1990. I asked the court that I be released from the psych center and Department of Mental Hygiene. The state attorney general's office and the Buffalo district attorney's office strongly opposed my release to society. In October of 1990, a compromise was reached between the court, my psych center lawyer, the attorney general's office, and the district attorney's office. I was going to be allowed to slowly reenter society by going through a set of specific conditions and rules. If I completed the conditions and abided by the rules, the court would release me from the psych center on a five-year conditional release, which was a type of parole. To do this, I first had to withdraw my court request for a writ of habeas corpus.

The attorney general's office and the district attorney's office were being shrewd by offering me this compromise. They didn't want me going to court on my habeas corpus and possibly winning, which meant I'd be released unconditionally. The attorney general's office and the district attorney's office wanted me to be seen by an independent psychiatrist of their choice. I did, and he gave me a passing evaluation. I then saw an independent psychiatrist designated by my psych center lawyer. This psychiatrist gave me a passing evaluation, too. I saw two more independent psychiatrists as well as the assistant director of the

State Mental Health Forensic Department. It was very unusual to see so many psychiatrists, let alone the forensic assistant director, but I had been told many times that I wasn't their usual type of patient. Normally, a patient only saw one independent psychiatrist.

The conditions and rules set up for me consisted of having escorted, then unescorted privileges into the community. My social worker started by taking me into Ithaca every week to eat out or go to a movie in order to familiarize myself with the area. Then he started taking me to Ithaca and letting me go wherever I wanted for a few hours by myself. The hours turned into spending all day in Ithaca. I was then supposed to be given overnight passes in Ithaca so I could stay in a motel or hotel for a few days on my own. After doing that, I was supposed to be allowed a chance to find myself an apartment to live in. This did not come to be because the psych center reneged on this part of the deal at the last moment. Instead, they wanted me to stay in a family care home in Ithaca. I'd be allowed to spend up to fourteen days at the family care home. Then, I would be returned to the psych center for one day. The next day, I'd be taken back to the family care home for fourteen more days. After doing this for several months to a year, the psych center would decide whether I could get an apartment.

I was disappointed and angry about not getting my own apartment for up to a year. A family care home was a house owned by a private resident who was paid by the state to board patients from the state psych centers. Having to be watched and evaluated for up to a year by some family care home resident was not very appealing to me.

Before I went to the family care home, other things happened. The attorney general and the district attorney's office wanted my picture taken and sent to them. I asked my psych center lawyer why they wanted the picture. He was evasive at first, but I really wanted to know. The system had dozens of my mug shots; they could use any one of them. The lawyer told me that there were some people who had moved into the Ithaca area who feared for their lives if I were released. He said that in my past, I had either directly or indirectly threatened or intimated these people, and they were still afraid of me. Each of these people had requested a current picture of me so they could recognize me on the street.

That was what I was told. It was unbelievable; I was either being told a half-truth or a complete lie. I was not eager to have my picture taken and copies circulated to people unknown to me. I refused to have a current picture taken and told them to take one from my files instead. The attorney general's office and the district attorney's office were obviously letting people from my past know that I was going to be living in the Ithaca area. That meant my enemies knew I was in the Ithaca area, too.

The director and assistant director of the Willard Psych Center started getting numerous calls from individual people and agencies protesting my release. In my ward, there was a public phone for the patients' use. I received several threatening, intimidating, and harassing phone calls. Some callers told me I should be locked up forever, while others actually threatened my life. Other times, hard rock music blared into my ear when I was called to the phone. The calls came from several different men, and I was apprehensive at first about mentioning these calls to my team. I didn't want the calls to interfere with me being released. I finally did mention it to my treatment team, but they just told me the calls were probably pranks and I shouldn't take them seriously.

I began my family care home visits. I went from spending one day to spending weekends, a week, and then two weeks there. The family care home selected for me in Ithaca was owned by a black man in his mid-to-late twenties. His name was Jeff Osborne. His mother used to run the home until he took it over for her. She was in her mid-to-late forties and attractive. She was divorced and had her own home in Ithaca, and she had adopted two little girls. There were four other patients staying at Jeff's. On numerous occasions, Ms. Osborne came to visit Jeff and talk to the patients. Sometimes, Jeff took me with him when he went to visit her.

Jeff and his mother were two of the nicest people I've ever met in my life. Their kindness overwhelmed me. I could sense their friendliness was real and not false. I was not accustomed to being around people like this. They were truly sincere, and sometimes, I felt awkward in their presence. I felt a guarded sense of peacefulness and serenity around them. Emotionally, I desperately wanted to reach out to their sincerity. I wanted to embrace them both, to shed tears on their shoulders and tell them all my doubts, suspicions and fears. I wanted their reassurance that things might finally be okay after so many years. I needed their type of caring and guidance, not the guidance of sterile professionals in psych centers, jails, and the military. I wanted to pour my heart out to these two very rare and special people. But I couldn't. My reasoning overruled my emotions by reminding me that they were part of the state system. I wanted to trust them, but I didn't dare. Trusting had brought me a lot of disappointment and grief during my life.

Jeff was mature and independent for a young man his age. He was highly intelligent, organized, and took excellent care of his patients. He was the kind of young person any man would have been proud to call his son. To watch and listen to him made me realize even more how pathetic my life had been.

Ms. Osborne was the kind of woman most men needed, but most men would go through their lives never realizing that. She was honest, opinionated, and strong. I could sense and see the beauty within her. And she had a smile that tingled my heart whenever I saw it.

I had a sign-out and sign-in sheet to complete whenever I left the family care home. I was supposed to leave the phone number of the place I was going so I could be reached at any time. The police had been notified about me being in Ithaca, too. I had to call Jeff at the house every two hours when I was out. I was not allowed to spend the night anywhere except at the family care home. I was not allowed to stay out all night. I was forbidden to drink or hang out in bars. I had to take an Antabuse pill every morning, supervised by Jeff, before I could leave the house. Antabuse pills were given to many alcoholics so they couldn't drink without getting extremely sick.

I was forbidden to leave the city limits of Ithaca. Upon request by the psych center, the state attorney general, or the Buffalo district attorney's office, I had to willingly submit to a psychiatric evaluation by any of the independent psychiatrists who had seen me already. I could not break the law, be involved in any incidents, or exhibit any inappropriate conduct. If I failed to sign out or return to the family care home, Jeff was told to notify the police immediately and then notify the psych center. All these things were part of the conditions and rules set by the court.

Jeff had to report weekly to the psych center by phone about my conduct and social behavior when I stayed at his home. This bothered me and made me feel uncomfortable. I felt like I was being constantly analyzed under a giant microscope. Jeff was only doing what he was told to do, but still, I felt nervous and uneasy about it. I was always afraid of saying something wrong, or doing the wrong thing, or being opinionated about anything. I was afraid that in just being my natural self, I would somehow say or do something that would offend him. Jeff was a nice person, but he was the state's eyes and ears. And I didn't trust the state. In my mind, Jeff was literally my judge and jury. He had the power to take all my privileges away and have me returned to the psych center indefinitely. I tried to stay away from him as much as possible, which meant staying on the streets as long as I could. When he asked me to go with him to college basketball games, movies, and outpatient dances, I politely declined. I liked Jeff a lot, but he was spying on me for the state. I had no intention of doing anything wrong or illegal; I just felt uncomfortable around him and his mother because of this.

I'd sign out from the house early in the morning, listing several places I would be going to. I listed places like restaurants, movies, a health club, shopping malls, the YMCA, Cornell University, window shopping, downtown, etc. I wanted to stay away from the house as much as possible.

I kept thinking that if I had my own apartment, I wouldn't be spending so much time on the streets. They could have let me get my own place with random visits from the team. Why did they promise to let me get an apartment, then change their minds at the last minute? Living in a family care home, being watched, and having maze of conditions and rules to follow wasn't quite my idea of freedom.

One cold winter night, I was walking around downtown Ithaca. If I had my own apartment, I could have been there, sleeping, reading, watching TV, listening to the radio, working on my manuscript, or doing a dozen other things. I was freezing on the streets, but I just didn't want to go back to the house. I heard a female voice behind me call my name. I turned, and standing there was Shirley Cooper. She hugged and kissed me and asked if I was out for good. I told her I was on passes from Willard. Then she started crying, telling me how messed up her life had been. She said she loved me and was glad I was out on passes. She said I was the only one who could help her get her life back together. She took me to her place, which was a studio apartment on West State Street. It was on the second floor of an apartment building. The front part of the building held a hall that being used for karate classes and African dance and music lessons. Shirley was living like a pauper and still using crack and freebasing. She'd lost a lot of weight, and the winter coat she had was two sizes too small. Instead of curtains, she had a white sheet hanging over the window. She had a twelve-inch black-and-white TV set. Her refrigerator was bare except for some milk and several potatoes. Her cupboards were bare except for a few bags of beans and a few cans of vegetables. She was eating off paper plates and using plastic forks and spoons. What little food she had she got from the Salvation Army. She got the small wooden table and chairs when someone had thrown them out on the curb. She only had one sheet and a spread on her bed, and she was wearing men's cotton underwear. She had few clothes, no shoes, and wore an old pair of sneakers on her feet.

She told me she owed the landlord a few months back rent. She said she had been living in North Carolina for a few months, but she got bored and came back. She said the police had been looking for her, but she had straightened things out with them.

I was shocked at the way she was living. I asked her how she got money to pay for the drugs. She said she was stealing, forging stolen checks with friends, and prostituting. After hearing that, I regretted ever asking the question. Sometimes, she got the drugs for free when she brought other customers to her Colombian and black connections in town. The Colombians and blacks were rivals and the major dealers in town. She dealt mostly with the Colombians because they gave her better quality drugs.

Shirley said that since I was out on passes and soon to be discharged, she'd quit using drugs, prostituting, and stealing. She said she wanted to settle down and be a good girlfriend to me. Why I ever believed her, I'll never know. She had her own place, though, and I was quite happy about that. I no longer had to freeze in the cold, or hang out in public places. But Shirley would become my black widow spider, condemning me to a fate worse than death.

Chapter Twenty

Shirley gave me an extra key to her apartment. I bought her sheets, spreads, and quilt blankets for the bed and enough food to keep her refrigerator and cupboards filled. I bought her a new kitchen table and chairs, a remote-controlled color TV set, and a stereo. I even bought curtains, towels, face cloths, wall pictures, clothes, underwear and shoes for her. And I also paid her back rent.

Sometimes, I'd go over to her place and she'd have fresh bruises and belt marks all over her body. I'd ask her what happened, and she'd say she was in a fight. She'd never tell me if it was another woman, a man, or a group of people she got into these fights with. When we had sex, I'd notice numerous healed scars and bruises on her body. When I asked about the scars, she told me they were from fights, too. But Shirley wasn't getting into any fights. I started thinking that maybe she was into kinky sex or something. I even confronted her a few times about this, but she always denied it. There were other things I caught her lying about, too, and I realized she was a chronic liar.

On one occasion, I came over to her place and heard loud music coming from inside. I unlocked the door and went in. She was lying on the bed with another black woman. They were both naked and engaging in a sexual act. I noticed a black leather belt on the bed and fresh belt marks on Shirley's body and on the other woman's body. Shirley looked up, saw me, smiled, and said hello. I apologized, saying I'd be back later. They asked me not to go; they said I could take my clothes off and join them. I didn't think having two women in bed at the same time was kinky. I simply considered it a gift. But I declined the offer because I wasn't into that kinky stuff with the belt and because the belt marks on them turned me off.

A few times, I thought about leaving Shirley. She was becoming a burden to me, financially and emotionally. If I did leave, though, I'd have to give up staying at her place. I'd also be putting myself in the position of being alone again, and that really worried me.

I started having severe chest pains again. I was taken by the psych center employees to a medical hospital in the small town of Clifton Springs. The town was about twenty-five miles from Willard. After being examined for hours, a date was set for me to be admitted for three days. The middle part of my right lung was hurting again and still slightly collapsed. During my three-day stay at the hospital, I was put on an operating table and put to sleep. An incision was made in my throat, and a tube was put through the incision and into my chest. This operation was necessary for the doctors to have a better look inside my chest and right lung. From their initial examination, the doctors thought I had a cancerous disease. Although the middle part of my collapsed lung still had fluids and lumps, they found no evidence of any cancerous disease. After leaving the hospital, I spent a week at the psych center, recuperating. Then I continued my extended passes to the family care home.

Several weeks later, things fell apart. On the night of February 25th, 1991, I told Shirley I couldn't see her anymore. She and I got into an argument. She tried furiously to change my mind. She even tried to seduce me by taking her clothes off, but it didn't work. I told her she could keep all the things I bought her. She wasn't satisfied with that. I was her meal and drug ticket, and she didn't want it to end. With a bitter vengeance, she said she'd call the psych center and tell them I beat her up and tried to kill her. I was stunned and hurt after hearing that. I didn't believe she'd do that to me after all the things I'd done for her. To lie like that! I'd be sent back to Mid-Hudson. She knew that. Shirley also threatened to tell them that I spent most of my time with her instead of the various places I'd been listing on my sign-out sheet. That was true, but she wouldn't do that to me! She wouldn't! I'd given her more than any man had ever before. I'd helped her more than any relative or friend ever had. This is why I couldn't believe she would hurt me like that. I told her I'd be by the next day to pick up my clothes and personal papers. I told her we could talk more if she wanted, but my mind was made up. It was getting close to my midnight deadline, so I left with Shirley still cursing at me.

The next morning, I went back over to Shirley's place, but she wasn't home. It wasn't unusual to find her gone when I came over, though. I showered and shaved like I'd done many times

318

before, then fixed breakfast. I started packing my clothes and papers into two shopping bags. Then I waited for Shirley to come home, to see if she had calmed down or was still angry. I had to call Jeff every two hours when I was out. My first two hours were up, so I went to a public phone booth in front of the building and called.

Jeff told me that my team psychologist needed to talk to me, that it was an emergency. I called the psychologist at Willard, and he was frantic. He told me to give him my location on the street and not to move. He said he was coming to Ithaca with two security guards to pick me up. He told me I was being returned to the psych center until the investigation was over.

"What investigation?" I asked him.

At first, he didn't want to tell me what was going on. Finally, he said that Shirley had called the psych center and the Ithaca police and told them that I beat her up and threatened to kill her. The psychologist said the police were looking for me.

My body went limp, and I almost fainted from the news. *She did it! She actually did it to me!* I started trembling and felt tears forming in my eyes. *Twenty years incarcerated, and I let a crazy, drugged-up thief, prostitute, and pathological liar do me in. What a fool I am!*

The psychologist told me that Shirley had belt marks on her back and butt. I hadn't put those marks on her, but I had a good idea who had. She told him that I had her running all over Ithaca looking for guns to buy, too. This was a lie. Shirley was smart enough to know that mixing my name with violence, death threats, and weapons would get me plenty of attention. She had destroyed me. Actually, I had destroyed myself by getting involved with her. I started to panic, knowing I'd be put away for the rest of my life. With my background, I knew I'd never be given another chance like this. Depression and desperation swept over me like a plague. I wanted to die. I've always believed that there are things far worse than death, and being incarcerated for the rest of my life in Mid-Hudson was definitely one of those things.

The psychologist was still talking as I slowly dropped the phone, letting it hang by the cable. My mind was in a fog as I walked back to Shirley's place. I thought seriously about hanging myself. Strangulation was painful and slow, though. I stared at the gas stove. I thought about filling the room with gas and lighting a match. The explosion would kill me instantly. It would also kill and injure others in the apartment building, and I didn't want that. I went to a drawer under the kitchen sink that was filled with butcher knives, steak knives, and butter knives. I took one of the butter knives out of the drawer and put it in my pocket. My thoughts had switched abruptly to running away. If the police tried to stop me, I'd attack them with the knife, forcing them to shoot me dead. I chose the butter knife over the butcher knife and steak knife because I really didn't want to hurt anyone. I just wanted to die. I walked out of Shirley's apartment, not even bothering to close the door.

The morning seemed drastically different, now. I was looking at everything through the eyes of a condemned man. My change in perception had somehow made things around me seem distant and strange. My heart was beating rapidly, and I tried to keep my mind focused. Adrenaline was surging through my body, making me feel lightheaded.

I only had a few dollars on me, so I started hitchhiking, wanting to get out of Ithaca fast. I'd gotten about twenty miles out of Ithaca when I started having reservations about running away. While I was on the road with my thumb out, I decided to give myself up. Running away would only give credibility to her lies. I started hitchhiking back toward the psych center. A few rides later, I was standing in front of the Willard Psych Center. But I couldn't bring myself to go any further. I felt I was doing the right thing by turning myself in. At the same time, though, I was voluntarily locking myself up for the rest of my life. There was a vicious internal conflict going on in my mind. I didn't know what to do. If I could have become Nighthawk-One, I'd have had no problem deciding what to do. As Nighthawk-One, I would have been a decisive predator, stealing, robbing, maiming, and killing for the money, transportation, and refuge I needed. Nighthawk-One was no longer a part of me, though. It was gone forever, vanquished and irretrievable. As such, I had no desire to steal, rob, or hurt anyone.

It started drizzling as I stood there in front of the psych center. I began to walk slowly away, trying to hitchhike again. I wanted to get as far away from the psych center as I could. I had changed my mind about turning myself in. I couldn't bring myself to give up voluntarily like before. A trucker stopped and picked me up. About fifteen or twenty minutes later, he let me out and turned down a side road. I didn't realize that a psych center security car had been following me. The lone security guard stopped his car right in front of me. He got out and opened the back door, telling me to get in. He was unarmed and only carried a walkie-talkie on his belt. He had evidently spotted me standing in front of the psych center and followed me when I got into the truck. He kept telling me to get in the car, but I wouldn't move. He took his walkie-talkie out, saying he'd have to call the sheriffs and the state troopers if I didn't get in. No way was I voluntarily getting into that car, and I told him that.

I turned and ran off the road into an open field. It was still drizzling, and the field was muddy and sticky. The security guard followed me after I'd put a few hundred yards between us. He kept talking over the walkie-talkie as he watched me. I could have easily attacked him, taken away his walkie-talkie and car keys, and gotten away before the police came. I chose not to do that. I didn't want to harm him. I kept running through large, open fields; I was over a mile from the road. There was no concealment and no cover in the fields. I saw a few uniformed and plainclothes policemen with the security guard. There was another group closing in from a different direction. They were flanking me, probably trying to run me into an unseen group that was waiting close by. I saw a nearby cyclone fence with barbed wire on top. I staggered for the fence. There were signs on the fence, stating, "Restricted area — no trespassing — property of U.S. Army." Unknown to me at the time, this was an army depot that stored nuclear weapons. The depot was well known in New York State; there had been many demonstrations against nuclear weapons there.

The police had already alerted military security at the depot. I saw wooded areas, heavy vegetation, large buildings, and houses on the other side of the fence. I was exhausted as I slowly started climbing over the fence. I was almost over it when two policemen grabbed my legs and pulled me down. I fell to the muddy ground. I thought about the butter knife, but I didn't pull it out. They backed off and pulled their pistols out. Other policemen came, and I was handcuffed and searched.

The police took me to the Willard Psych Center. I was put in the secure ward there and heavily medicated. On February 28th, in the early evening, I was handcuffed, shackled, and put in a van. With two security guards and two male employees, I was taken to the Mid-Hudson Forensic Psych Center. Months later, I realized that attempting to trespass on an army depot housing nuclear weapons was definitely not a good idea. As I said before, I had no idea the depot stored nuclear weapons. But there are some people in our government who don't think anything in life is a mere coincidence.

Chapter Twenty-One

The Mid-Hudson Psych Center was on Route 17M, a few miles from Middletown, New York. Mid-Hudson was close to a hundred years old. It stood a few hundred yards back from the road, and it looked like an old, sinister castle with medieval towers. I remembered gazing upon Mid-Hudson for the first time, back in the early 1970s, when I was first admitted there. I recalled my sudden shiver of apprehension — or could it have been panic? — as we drew closer to the menacing place. I had forgotten that haunting feeling until now.

I suffered from emotional trauma during my first few months back at Mid-Hudson. I felt so helpless and hopeless. Being back was a terrifying nightmare come true. It was as if Satan himself were toying with my soul, making me suffer my final years in complete damnation. *How could Shirley have lied about me like that? How could she hurt me like that? I treated her with respect, and she turned on me like a snake!* I felt miserable because of what she did to me, and I felt angry at myself for allowing it to happen.

I was put on a relaxation medication during my first few months back. It would take that long, and longer, to deal with the impact of what Shirley had done.

I was put in ward 46, on the top floor in the Forest Hall Building. There were only three floors in Forest Hall, with wards 45 and 46 sharing the third floor. The first floor held wards 41 and 42, and the second floor held wards 43 and 44. The other buildings that housed patients were called Oak Hall and Denton Hall.

The Forest Hall Building sat back a distance from the other buildings of Mid-Hudson. To get to Forest Hall, you had to walk through what was called 'The Tunnel.' The tunnel was not underground. It was simply a straight stretch of pavement about a hundred yards long and three yards wide. There was a tall cyclone fence on each side and aluminum roofing. There was also a slight incline; Forest Hall was on higher ground than the rest of the buildings. To the right was the yard for the Forest Hall patients. The yard was modest and sat on a small hill with a wooden pavilion on it. Most of the time, all the patients in the building were out in the yard. Aside from listening to our Walkman radios and cassette players, though, there was nothing recreational to do in this small yard, which is why we named it 'Little Alcatraz.'

The main yard was circular and much larger than the Forest Hall one. Oak Hall, Denton Hall, and the dining room building encircled the main yard, which had two pavilions, two paved basketball courts, a baseball area, and a volleyball area. Forest Hall wards were denied access to the main yard most of the time because the superiors said we had our own yard. The real reason, though, was because Forest Hall patients were rowdier and more prone to violence than the patients of Oak Hall and Denton Hall. The main yard was like the Times Square area of Mid-Hudson. Doctors, nurses, TAs, maintenance and house-cleaning workers, and sexy secretaries walked through the main yard or sat on benches to chat with other employees. Denton Hall had two female wards. They used the yard, too, but they were separated from the male patients. The superiors felt that Forest Hall patients would taint their beautiful main yard. Even when groups of visitors were given a tour of Mid-Hudson, they rarely brought them through the tunnel to Forest Hall. Instead, they were only shown Oak Hall and Denton Hall.

Next to the Forest Hall yard, across a cyclone fence, stood a modern brick building. There was a gym, swimming pool, church service room, and offices in this building. The gym held a running track, several basketball hoops, a barber shop, and a weight-lifting room. The building was on the same little hill our yard was on. Several years later, the building was drastically remodeled and expanded, which made our yard even smaller.

On the other side of this building, at the base of the hill, stood the visiting room. The square visiting room wasn't big; it could only hold thirty to forty people at a time. There was a soda and coffee machine, an ice cream and sandwich machine, and two microwaves. One of the locked doors in the visiting room led right into a short hallway that opened up to the security room. The security room door, which should always be closed, was kept wide open most of the time. When visitors or employees of Mid-Hudson wanted to leave, they pushed a button on the wall that buzzed the security room, and one of the security people in the room would push a button that opened the door. After walking through the short hallway and past the Plexiglas security room, they walked out of the building. After several steps, security pushed another button, which opened the door through the high fence made of barbed wire and razor wire.

Patients were allowed to wear their watches and their own clothes at Mid-Hudson, and they could receive food packages from family and friends. Patients with no money in their accounts were given thirty-five dollars a month to spend on commissary. We were also allowed to carry up to three dollars in change, or nine dollars if we had an honor card and stayed out of trouble. The visiting room closed at three o'clock every day, and once a week, right after supper, each floor was allowed to go to the visiting room for an hour to use the soda, candy, and food machines. This hour was called the weekly canteen.

The top floor of the Forest Hall Building was considered the strictest floor in Mid-Hudson. The TAs on that floor were the ones who were most likely to beat a patient and put him in the hospital. Forest Hall was known as the badass building due to the TAs and patients being so physically aggressive.

Some patients committed suicide, mostly by hanging, after coming to Mid-Hudson. On several occasions, patients were unintentionally killed by TAs due to over-aggressiveness, and the matter was covered up. On many occasions, the TAs would beat a patient so badly he would suffer life-altering injuries.

Of course, the TAs countered this by saying that they were the victims at Mid-Hudson. They'd state the statistics, that there were over several hundred assaults against them by patients every year. I've been eyewitness to TAs purposely provoking a patient to violence against them or against another patient simply because they were bored or wanted a superficial injury to get off work with full pay. I've listened to them brag about their manipulation of patients, which is a cheap shot at TAs who legitimately get hurt while doing their jobs.

There were some cases in which the TAs just snapped, emotionally and mentally, due to having such high stress jobs. Once, a TA locked himself in a closet and refused to come out. There was another TA who was involved in drug-dealing on the streets and a drive-by shooting.

In another incident, one of the senior TAs was involved. A senior TA was the immediate superior of the TAs working in the wards. This particular male senior TA, along with a few other TAs, kicked a patient so brutally that the patient's groin area had swollen profusely and the patient had to be hospitalized. A TA who was not involved in the beating but witnessed it testified against the other TAs. All the TAs lost their jobs except for the senior TA. The TA who had testified was harassed by having his car tires slashed, sugar poured into his gas tank, and getting death-threat phone calls.

In one incident, a patient already in a straitjacket had scalding water poured on him by the TAs. The TAs had criminal charges put on them, but they were found not guilty by a jury because the patient was too incompetent and delusional to point out the TAs.

There is a pipe, several inches in diameter, on each floor that extends from the ceiling to the floor. Patients have been tied to this pipe while sitting in a chair, gagged, and had drawers filled with feces thrown over their faces or urine poured on them simply because they questioned the TAs authority.

The TAs would brag to me about the parties they had. Sometimes, they got out of hand, and they physically fought each other. They also bragged that some of the female TAs would show their bare breasts at these parties. Some stripped naked and danced on the tables, and a few gave blowjobs in the parking lot. Very few things are kept secret at Mid-Hudson because there's so much gossiping, in-house cheating, and backstabbing going on.

At the minimum, there are four TAs on each floor, with the norm being six to eight. On each floor, there was an average of thirty-five patients. Sometimes, there were as many as forty patients on a floor. On average, each floor should only hold twenty-five patients. Everyone working there, from the professionals to the TAs, knew that they were violating the building fire codes, but none of them ever made it an issue.

The Psychiatric Center Inspection Teams from Albany usually alerted Mid-Hudson that they were coming weeks in advance, which always gave Mid-Hudson plenty of time to drop its patient census to about twenty-five a floor and have the extra beds taken off the ward. To drop the census, Mid-Hudson would refuse to take any more people from statewide county jails, including

Riker's Island in New York City. Then, Mid-Hudson would start sending people back to county jails and to Riker's Island. When the Inspection Teams left, the beds were brought back and the patient census increased again.

Before the New York State Department of Mental Health took over in the early 1970s, Mid-Hudson was home to juvenile boys from all over the state. The boys spent much of their time planting, growing, and eating their own crops on the state land. After the Department of Mental Health turned Mid-Hudson into a psychiatric center for the criminally insane, two high-security fences were put up along with barbed wire and razor wire. Electronic cameras and a microwave movement detector were also installed. Blue-uniformed state safety officers maintained perimeter security, and TAs trained in maximum security procedures were instituted. Even with all these precautions, though, there were still some escapes from Mid-Hudson throughout the years. When a patient escaped, Mid-Hudson turned on a loud, blaring siren to alert the community.

There were shakedown searches at least once a month at Mid-Hudson. There have been confiscations of contraband from guns, real knives, homemade knives, razors, pieces of steel pipes, metal files, bricks, wire garrotes, socks with fist-size rocks in them, and homemade booze and drugs. There were also random on-the-spot searches of patients at the discretion of the TAs.

Toward the end of those first few months, I saw my treatment team. Treatment teams consisted of a psychiatrist, a psychologist, a social worker, a ward nurse, a recreation person, and sometimes a TA from the ward the patient was assigned to. The conference room was through one of the locked dayroom doors, and this was where they held ward treatment team meetings. There was a long, rectangular wooden table in the conference room with several metal chairs surrounding it. The psychiatrist would sit at the head of the table, and the patient would sit at the opposite end of the table.

My ward psychiatrist, Dr. Budo, was an arrogant, middle-aged, dark-brown man from Pakistan. He spoke English with a heavy accent. He was about 5'9" tall, a hundred fifty pounds, and had pimples all over his face. I'd seen him plenty of times before in the building and on the grounds during my other admissions.

Dr. Budo had a reputation for being tough and not compassionate toward the patients. It had been rumored during a few of my other stays here that Dr. Budo had nothing but utter contempt for me.

As I entered the conference room, I sensed disaster. There was nothing but doom in their eyes as I sat down at the end of the table. I felt cornered, like a cat that's suddenly been surrounded by several dogs. *I don't need this crap on top of what's already happened to me.*

"Good morning, Mr. Parker," Dr. Budo said, with that fake crooked smile on his face. "Do you know everyone here?" I glanced at the social worker, Mrs. Carlson, first, who was sitting to the left of the doctor. She was white, in her early sixties, with short gray hair and blue eyes. Her facial expression was professionally blank, but her eyes were bitter as she stared at me. I'd never spoken with her personally, but I'd seen her plenty of times on the grounds.

To her immediate left sat the recreation man, Mr. Smith. He was white, short, solidly built, and in his mid-forties. Mr. Smith and I used to argue a lot in the gym while playing basketball because he always cheated. In fact, he cheated at almost everything that was competitive — cards, volleyball, basketball, and baseball. This led to endless arguments with TAs and patients. He glared at me with a cocky sneer on his face. Mr. Smith didn't like himself, so I could never imagine him liking anyone else.

To the doctor's immediate right sat Ms. Davis, the psychologist. She was white, about 5'7" tall, and stout, with a solid square chin and rough, masculine features. Her eyes were brown, and her hair was black, cut extremely short in a Marine Corps crew cut fashion. She was about thirty-five years old, and she always wore dingy jeans, worn-out sneakers, and tacky short-sleeve shirts. Ms. Davis was also a lesbian extremist who was well known around Mid-Hudson as being a man-hater and a ball-buster. Freud said that the reason women hate men is because they envy men for having penises. If Freud was right about this, Ms. Davis was the epitome of what he was talking about. Her hostile look was a form of mental castration to any man who dared to look her in the eyes.

To her immediate right sat the ward nurse, Miss Murphy. She was white, short, and pretty, with deep blue eyes and shoulder-length blonde hair. Miss Murphy had only worked here for a few years, and I recalled seeing her a few times on my last admission. There was no hostility in her eyes as she looked at me. Her expression seemed to be one of neutrality. Miss Murphy went along with everything the rest of the treatment team agreed upon. She didn't drink, and she was a shy, reserved introvert. Perhaps that is why she was engaged to an alcoholic, physically aggressive TA from the second floor.

"I've seen or met everyone before," I replied in a low voice.

"Well, that's good," stated Dr. Budo as he wiped that fake smile off his face. "We can proceed, then." There was a thick chart open on the table in front of him. He fingered through several pages before looking back at me, saying grimly, "You have a reputation here, Mr. Parker, that seems to grow stronger and more infamous with each admission. Within the last few months, I've had TAs, social workers, doctors, and psychologists from all over the compound approach me to give me their opinion about you. And it seems I can't go anywhere around here without overhearing gossip about you and your past exploits. You're well known in Albany, too, because I've gotten calls and had to return calls pertaining to you. All eyes are on me, now, because you were assigned to my ward. I don't like all this attention."

After saying this, he glanced at the rest of his team before settling back in his seat, his icy eyes locked on mine. For several seconds, he just frowned at me. *He's preparing to come down on me like a brick wall. These people have never talked to me before, and yet their minds are already made up.* It amazed me that the people who had the strongest opinions about me were the very ones who never attempted to have a decent conversation with me.

Straightening back up in the chair, he glanced at the chart in front of him again. Then, with a stern look, he said, "I'm not going to tolerate you fighting with my TAs and patients, Mr. Parker. You hurt anyone in my ward, and I'll have you spending most of your time four-pointed in the box. And I'll have you medicated so much that you won't remember your name. You're going to be with us for the rest of your life, so I want things clear right now. I'm not going to ask you how you got back here. Obviously, you're aware of what happened. We're also aware of what happened. It's all in this report in front of me."

"We didn't want to waste time by going over why you're back," stated Mrs. Carlson. "It's the same old story anyway, isn't it? You get out of here, you get into trouble, and you get sent back here."

If only my life were that simple. I shook my head slowly from side to side. *I'm here for the rest of my life, and there's absolutely nothing I can do about it.*

"Is there anything you'd like to say?" asked Ms. Davis.

I knew the routine. They wanted me to become argumentative and defensive, denying what was written in my chart. That would give them a starting point when they wrote that I was still an angry, raging, impulsive, violent person who's dangerous to himself and others. I wasn't going to give them that satisfaction. They would gloat for days, knowing they had manipulated me into an angry, verbal altercation.

"I don't have anything to say," I replied, defeated.

"I have all your admission dates right here in front of me," Dr. Budo said flatly, thumping his right index finger on the chart. "I also have every violent incident you have ever been involved in at Mid-Hudson."

Dr. Budo then proceeded to name each of my admission dates and the incidents I'd been involved in during each admission. I had completely forgotten about some of them until he reminded me.

Until then, I had never fully realized just how much trouble I'd gotten into at Mid-Hudson. Then it dawned on me. My God! No wonder people are so opinionated about, interested in, and fascinated with my life. After all the gossip and rumors about me year after year, and after all those newspaper articles about me, too, my reputation had taken on a life of its own. It became so immense that no human being could possibly live up to such an exaggeration. I was more doomed by the ever-growing flow of gossip and rumors than by my actual deeds at Mid-Hudson.

It took Dr. Budo almost a half hour to go through my admissions and incidents. Every few minutes of that half hour, he paused to ask me if I had anything to say. Each time, I answered no. At the end of the meeting, Dr. Budo warned me again about getting into trouble and told me that I would be watched very closely.

Sitting in my chair in the dayroom, I tiredly went over what the doctor had read about my admissions and incidents.

My very first incident during my first admission was when I broke another patient's jaw in two places. He was a mean-looking, dark-haired, brown-eyed Irish guy in his mid-twenties. He stood about 5'10" tall, and he was muscular. He was a freelance hit man who was arrested for a homicide in New York City and suspected of three more in the tri-state area.

One evening, he got angry at me over which station to listen to on the ward radio. He was right in my face, yelling and cursing. I could have handled the yelling and cursing as long as he didn't put his hands on me, but when he called me a nigger, I lost control. I hit him in the jaw with a swift, solid, left uppercut that lifted him a few inches off the floor. He was taken to an outside hospital and had to have his jaw wired shut. Then he was brought back to Mid-Hudson and put in the infirmary for a few weeks. I had to spend a few days in the straitjacket for that incident, but I had no further problems with him when he returned to the ward.

My second incident involved a metal card table. I was having a painful stress headache, and I went to the ward TAs at the desk and asked them to call the nurse for the pain pill that had been prescribed for me. They were reading a couple of *Playboy* magazines, but they told me they'd give the nurse a call in a minute. A half hour went by, and they still hadn't called the nurse. So I approached the desk and requested the pain pill again, and again, they said they'd call in a minute. Another half hour went by. They were still laughing and joking over the *Playboy* magazines, and they still hadn't called the nurse.

I finally lost my temper and decided to do something to get their attention. There were a few metal card tables in the ward, and I grabbed one, flipped it over, and pulled one of the metal table legs off. After doing this, I rushed over and started pounding their desk hard with the table leg, cursing at them in a rage about my pill. I'll never forget the looks of astonishment on their faces. They were so shocked that they didn't move an inch or say a word until I had exhausted myself from beating the hell out of that desk. I definitely got my pain pill then, along with two shots in the ass and a visit to the box for a few days.

My third incident involved me and the goon squad. The Mid-Hudson goon squad consisted of several hand-picked male TAs who would rush anywhere on the grounds if there was a violent situation involving a patient. When they got there, they normally beat the patient to a pulp, put him in the straitjacket, and beat him on the way to the box. Most of the goon squad consisted of men who could be defensive linemen for a pro-football team.

During the dayshift in the dormitory area, I got into an argument with a ward TA. The goon squad was called to the dormitory, and I argued with the five TAs who showed up. The argument resulted in them trying to put me into the straitjacket, which turned into a big rumble. There were five of them against one of me, and they couldn't take me to the floor. I had them ramming into each other, slamming into the wall, tripping over beds, and flipping in the air in their futile attempt to subdue me. It was almost comical to see them sprawled out all over the dormitory. I hadn't punched, karate-chopped, elbowed, kneed, or used a power kick on any of them, either. I was entertaining myself by using their own forceful, awkward momentum to throw them around the dormitory.

While my back was to the dormitory door, the sixth goon squad member snuck in and hit me from behind. It was a well executed football tackle, and it dropped me to the floor like a sack of bricks. They all jumped me then, handcuffed me from behind, put shackles on me, and took me to the box. I was four-pointed on a bare mattress in a canvas sheet that stretched all the way down to my ankles. I lay like that for three days, and I was only let out to use the bathroom every eight hours. This incident with the goon squad was gossiped about over and over in Mid-Hudson by old and new staff as well as patients. I was known as the first patient to take the goon squad down before they took me down.

My fourth incident was a complete accident. I was in the yard, teaching several other patients martial arts. One guy was behind me with his right arm around my neck and throat. I was teaching the guys how to flip someone in the air when they're grabbed from behind. The guy with his arm around my neck was named Jack. He was white, twenty years old, and slim, with blonde hair and blue eyes. Jack liked to pull pranks on me, and instead of keeping his

332

arm loose around my neck, he tightened his arm around my neck and throat, choking me and pulling me backward. Instinctively, I had Jack's body doing a swift spiral in the air before I consciously realized what I'd done. Instead of landing fully in the grass, part of his body landed on the concrete sidewalk, where his right elbow slammed into the concrete. He had to be taken to an outside medical hospital, and a steel pin had to be put into his elbow permanently. Needless to say, I was strictly forbidden to teach martial arts to my peers after that.

On my second admission to Mid-Hudson, my first incident involved a fight in the dining room. A guy had been sent to Mid-Hudson from prison for a psychiatric evaluation before he was paroled to the streets. The guy was white, about 6' tall, and weighed over two hundred pounds. He had brown hair and blue eyes. The guy was stocky and had solid muscles from lifting weights in prison for several years. We got into an argument in the yard about whether his ward or my ward owned the football. I ultimately gave him the football, not wanting to argue about it any longer. I assumed the argument was over, but at lunch, the guy sat across from me and started cursing at me again about the football. As I mentioned before, I don't mind if someone curses and yells at me as long as he doesn't put his hands on me. But the guy chose to call me a nigger, and that changed the rules. Lifting myself slightly up from my chair, I punched the guy between the eyes so hard that he slid off his chair and fell to the floor, unconscious. The guy was out for several minutes with a concussion before he regained consciousness in the infirmary, where he stayed for a week. I was ceremoniously put in the straitjacket for two days. This guy sent messages to me through other patients, saying that he was going to kick my ass when he got back to the building. I only sent him back one message through a patient. It stated that if he even looked at me wrong, I would kill him. I'm not sure if it was just my message or if the patients and TAs told him that I don't make idle threats, but his messages abruptly changed; he started talking about peaceful coexistence, instead.

My second incident was with a TA. This Puerto Rican TA was about 5'7" tall and weighed about a hundred thirty pounds. I was not well liked by most of the TAs because I spoke up for myself. I wasn't afraid to fight patients or TAs, regardless of the box, straitjacket, and four-point. Still, it would take years for me to fully understand why this particular TA disliked me so much. He was constantly trying to argue with me, trying to get me into fights. He would do this in the dining room, the yard, the gym, and the basement recreation area. He wasn't even assigned to my ward, but he would leave his ward without permission from his superiors and come to my ward for the sole purpose of trying to pick fights with me. I'd never done or said anything to this guy before, so I was at a complete lost as to why he was always in my face. I heard that he was taking karate lessons in Middletown, and he bragged to patients and TAs that he could kick my butt.

He would get really emotional and raging angry. The veins bulged in his neck when he cursed, yelled, and challenged me to a fight. As irritating as this guy was, I couldn't see him as a serious threat to my physical wellbeing.

One afternoon, I was sitting in my chair, watching TV with the other patients in the ward. This TA walked into the ward. Without saying a word to the TAs at the desk, he walked over and stood behind me, saying angrily, "I'll kick your ass, Parker! You don't scare me, man!" I ignored him and kept watching TV. He seemed to really get pissed off about that because what he did next surprised me. He kicked the back of my chair and backed up a few feet, going into a karate stance. "Come on, Parker!" he raged. "Me and you, a fight to the death!" After feeling him kick my chair, I had jumped out of my seat, staring angrily at him, saying, "You little piece of shit, I'll fuck you up!" He screamed and raged even louder. His voice went really high as he shrieked, "Come on, man! A death match, me and you!"

"Ah, man!" I said to myself, calming down. "This guy has seen too many Chinese Kung-Fu movies!

Two of my ward TAs came over, one on each side of him, and told him that he couldn't just walk into their ward and start trouble with one of their patients. They asked him to leave, but he started screaming about having that damn death match with me again. By this time, there were several other TAs in the ward, too, after hearing all the noise. The two ward TAs asked him to leave again, and still, that stubborn bastard wouldn't budge. He was still in that damn karate stance, too, screaming at the top of his lungs. Finally, the ward TAs, who were over two hundred pounds each, put an arm under each of his arms, lifted him easily off the floor, and carried him off the ward.

As they carried him away, he was still yelling for that death match. His feet were about a foot off the ground, and his legs were moving rapidly, as if he were pedaling an invisible bicycle. The scene was straight out of a cartoon; it was so funny seeing his legs pumping through the air like that while he was carried off the ward. It was so funny that some of the TAs burst out laughing, and the ones who weren't laughing had to turn their heads away from the scene to keep from laughing out loud. The patients were laughing so hard that some of them actually fell to the floor because they couldn't stand and laugh at the same time any longer.

My third predicament involved a patient and a TA. I was playing basketball with other patients on the basketball court in the main yard, in front of Denton Hall. One of the other patients and I got into an argument over a basketball call. I started a fight with him that was quickly resolved, ending with him on his back, semiconscious. Several TAs calmly came over and said I'd have to go in the straitjacket. Ordinarily, the TAs would have rushed over and beat the crap out of whoever was still standing while they put him in the straitjacket, and then they'd kick his ass all the way to the box.

As I stood there, waiting for a straitjacket to be found, I noticed fast movement to my far left in my peripheral vision. A TA who had been working at Mid-Hudson for only a few weeks was charging straight toward me at a full run. I'd seen this big white TA involved in several other patient altercations. His favorite technique to subdue a patient was to charge the patient and wrap an arm around the patient's neck in a choke hold. This aggressive move would choke the patient while snatching him off his feet and slamming him to the ground. Then the TA would tighten his choke hold until the patient was docile from lack of oxygen to the brain.

Well, he was charging me, now, intending to do to me what he'd done to other patients. There was no reason for him to be charging me like this; the incident was over and I was calm, and the other TAs were calm, too. The charging TA was trying to build himself a quick reputation among the patients and staff, and there was no better way to do that than for him to be seen taking me down and choking me single-handedly.

This idiot obviously made the mistake of thinking I was like the other patients. No way was I going to let him hurt me. As he neared, running at full speed, he extended his left arm to yank me by the neck. He had no idea that I was anticipating his sneak attack. Just before he could grab me, I quickly turned to my left, facing him momentarily before swiftly stepping to my right, out of his path. With my left hand, I grabbed his left wrist, twisting his arm. At the same time, I stuck my left foot out, tripping his left leg. The combination of doing both these things at that precise time turned his charging momentum against him. His body arced head first into a spiral that sent him flipping through the air. He landed roughly on his back, bouncing in the grass and skidding for a few yards. He got up slowly, stumbling, with his face in pain as he rubbed his lower back with both hands. Then anger replaced the pained look on his face, and he cursed loudly at me as he stupidly charged me again. This time, I didn't move out his path. I grabbed his shirt with both hands. Using his own power and weight against him again, I fell backward on my back, with both my feet on his stomach, and cartwheeled him over my head through the air. He went flying upside-down again. This time, he landed on the basketball court's black pavement. He seriously hurt his neck and lower back, and he lay there, screaming in pain. He would be out from work for several months. I spent a week in the box, four-pointed to a bed in a canvas sheet for that.

My fourth situation involved another patient and myself. There was a white patient in our ward who stood about 5'6" tall and weighed about a hundred ten pounds. There was also a black patient in our ward from Albany, New York named Dwight. He was six feet tall and weighed two hundred fifty pounds. Dwight intimidated, strong-armed, and bullied the little white guy for most of his commissary money and dining room food. One day, while we ate lunch in the dining room, Dwight told the guy how he was going screw him up the butt, and he told the guy to bring some hair grease to the shower that evening. The little guy started crying because he was terrified of Dwight. The little guy had complained numerous times to the TAs about Dwight, but each time, the TAs would curse at him, telling him to stop being a wimp and stand up for himself.

I've seen these kinds of rapes before in prison and at Mid-Hudson, and no one dares to intervene because it's safer to mind your own business. I've seen guys get seriously hurt and killed when they tried to stop a rape.

I should have kept my damn mouth shut, but after seeing that little guy crying like a baby right next to me, I got angry. The guy was giving Dwight everything he owned, and now Dwight wanted to take what manhood he had left by screwing him up the butt!

I got into an argument with Dwight in the dining room. I told him to leave the guy alone from now on. He started cursing me and making derogatory statements about my mother. We agreed to fight once we got outside, and fight we did. It was a short fight, though; soon, I had his whole body in the air and slammed him to the concrete on his back. Before I slammed him down, Dwight had accidentally scratched me in my right eye, leaving a small red mark on my eyeball. I didn't know this at the time. Dwight was stunned and couldn't get up. The nurses and doctor wanted to send him to the infirmary for a few days, but he refused to go.

Only after looking in the mirror back in the ward did I notice the small red mark. The mark was superficial and would disappear in a few days, but I still got angry. I told Dwight in front of the TAs and the other patients that I was going to mark him just as he had marked me.

A few days later, after our ward was walking back to the building from lunch, I made my move. I sneaked up behind Dwight, grabbed a handful of his hair, pulled his head back, and quickly cut him across both eyes several times. I used a sharp, broken piece of porcelain I'd stolen from the ceramic shop to cut him. He had to go to the outside medical hospital emergency room for stitches. He had to wear large gauze pads on each eye in the infirmary, and he was blind for several weeks before he regained his eyesight. Dwight was lucky. I was trying to blind him permanently. He never bothered me or the little guy after that. I spent two weeks in the box and a few more days in the straitjacket.

During my third admission, my first predicament involved a fight. While I was in the gym, I got into an argument with a patient named Leroy, who was also from Buffalo. Leroy had a history of extreme raging violence and had been to prison a few times. While he was in the Forensic ward at the Gowanda Psychiatric Center, Leroy had attacked a female OT worker in the OT shop while they were there alone, working. He used a sharp, knifelike instrument that was normally used for ceramics, and he stabbed the OT worker many times, mostly in the head, almost killing her. Her injuries were so severe that she couldn't remember the attack or who had attacked her. Leroy tried to flush his blood-soaked clothes down the toilet, but he was caught by TAs. He was arrested and sent to the county jail, where he was found not guilty by reason of insanity and sent to Mid-Hudson.

I didn't want to fight Leroy. I'd known him for a long time and we were friends. But Leroy punched me in the face. The punch didn't hurt and didn't even draw blood, but it did get me angry. I only punched Leroy once between the eyes, and he dropped limply to the gym floor, unconscious. He was bleeding profusely from the cut I'd made between his eyes with the punch. The TAs tried to wake him up, but he remained unconscious for about five minutes. In the emergency room at the outside medical hospital, they said he had suffered a severe concussion. He stayed at the outside hospital for three days and then spent a week in the infirmary. Because I wasn't the aggressor and didn't throw the first blow, I wasn't sent to the box or put in the straitjacket.

My second situation involved a riot in the ward. One evening, a black TA who was working in our ward got into an argument with a seventeen-year-old patient. The enraged TA started choking the young boy with both hands, shaking him vigorously. The young boy's body went limp, but the raging TA kept choking him. I jumped out of my seat, picked up my chair, and threatened to hit the TA in the head if he didn't let the young boy go. What happened next really blew my mind. Twenty to twenty-five patients in the ward suddenly started throwing chairs at the walls, the TV, the windows, and at the TAs, chasing them off the ward. The patients had sharp pencils, chairs, and homemade knives and other weapons in their hands. They were chanting my last name at first, and then they started yelling "Attica." They trashed the whole dayroom, turning over desks, tables and lockers.

I was shocked! I didn't expect this just because I wanted to help that young kid. Over a dozen TAs gathered in the hallway, but not one of them would enter the dayroom. Only when the supervisor came and talked to me did things calm down. The black TA was strongly reprimanded and almost fired for choking the boy and for inadvertently starting a riot.

No patients were put in the straitjacket or the box because there were just too many of us involved. I got a severe write-up in my chart and was sternly told by the director, several doctors, and the supervisors to come to them from now on if I had a complaint about anything. They said that a lot of patients in the building and the psych center looked up to me and respected me as a leader. Because of this, they said I had to be careful about what I said and did around the other patients; if I wasn't careful, there could be major disturbances and riots, with people getting hurt or killed. This had never dawned on me before. For the rest of that stay at Mid-Hudson, I was careful not to incite other patients against the TAs.

My fourth and fifth admissions to Mid-Hudson were fairly uneventful. I was getting older and a little wiser. I wasn't as physically aggressive and argumentative as I used to be.

Chapter Twenty-Two

I'd been at Mid-Hudson for several months on my sixth and current admission. Whenever I saw Dr. Budo in the ward or in the yard, I would smile and say hello. I only did this because I knew it pissed him off. He still didn't want me as his patient, but quite frankly, I didn't want him as my doctor, either.

I'd been voted in by the patients of wards 45 and 46 to be their patient ward chairman. I'd also been appointed by the ward TAs as the laundry-man for both wards, too. And I was appointed boss of the patients' clean-up crew in the evenings, which is when the whole dayroom was cleaned.

There was a female TA in her early thirties who worked in my ward. Her name was Mrs. Collins. She'd been trying to get closer and closer to me since I got there. She was about 5'8" tall, and she had a nice shape, shoulder-length blonde hair, hazel eyes, and nice breasts. She was not beautiful or pretty, but she was oddly attractive in her own way. I wasn't even interested in talking to Mrs. Collins, let alone having an affair with her, because I hadn't fully recovered from my last relationship.

Every time Mrs. Collins needed a patient to do a chore, she called me. Numerous times, she would come and sit next to me in the ward and talk to me. Sometimes, when I was in the yard, she would walk over to me and start talking. She worked the dayshift, and a few times a week, she would have me sweep and mop the floor and help her tidy the beds in the dormitory. We would be in the dormitory by ourselves for about an hour.

She told me that some of the TAs, supervisors, and doctors had warned her about me before I even got to the ward. They told her to stay away from me and to read my chart to see the trouble I'd been in with women before. If they had already warned her about me, why was she in my face all the time? I asked her. She said that after reading my history and listening to all the gossip about me, finally seeing me in the flesh had aroused her. She told me she had masturbated at home several times already, thinking about us having sex.

I was put in an awkward position because I didn't want a personal or sexual relationship with Mrs. Collins. I looked okay on the outside, but inside, I was still hurting from my last relationship. At the same time, I didn't want her angry at me. I didn't need any problems from her or from any of the other TAs in the ward. I was going to be at Mid-Hudson for a very long time, and I wanted to keep the peace between the TAs and me.

I didn't do anything to entice Mrs. Collins, but she was all over me like a cheap suit. She started giving me part of her lunch each day and bringing in sub sandwiches for me to eat.

She started grabbing, patting, and squeezing my ass sometimes when we were alone. Then she got bolder and put her hand between my legs, massaging me there. She started kissing me wetly on the lips, too, but I never kissed her back or held her in my arms. She told me she didn't care if I kissed her back or held her; just touching me was erotic enough. I think she was having little orgasms while she touched me sometimes.

A few times, I told her that I felt uncomfortable with her touching me and that we could get into serious trouble. She would always smile and tell me that she was too careful for us to get caught. Then she would immediately tell me that if I ever said anything about us to anyone, she'd tell the doctors I was the one making the sexual advances. I believed her with every fiber in my being, too. She would play the innocent lamb, and I would be the big, bad wolf. Talk about déjà vu, right?

On weekends, after breakfast and lunch, patients were given the option of going back to the dormitory for a couple hours of sleep. Things were more relaxed and laid back on the weekends. The TAs would watch TV, play cards, or run between floors. On weekends, it wasn't unusual for a TA to take a patient off the ward to the basement. Each building had a recreation floor in the basement with pool tables, table tennis, card tables, and soda and candy machines.

One weekend, in the afternoon, Mrs. Collins told the other TAs that she was going to the basement to use the machines. She told them she was taking me along to get some candy. She rushed me down the few flights of stairs, where she unlocked a door to our left and locked it again behind us. From there, we went through a hallway to another locked door. Through this door, we entered the large recreation room. There was a patient bathroom in the recreation room that was always locked when the room wasn't being used. She went to the bathroom door and unlocked it. We went in, and she quickly locked it again. There were no windows in the bathroom, and she had to turn the light on because it was totally dark inside.

She was breathing heavily. Her breasts heaved up and down, and her rigid nipples pressed tautly against her blouse. Mrs. Collins licked her lips sensuously and briskly took off my shirt. She started kissing and licking my bare chest. Then she did something to me that was totally unexpected. She started licking, nibbling, and sucking on my nipples. I had never thought about a woman licking and sucking on a man's nipples before. It felt good! It was stimulating. Then she put one hand between my legs and started massaging me there until it became rigid. She got down on her knees in front of me, unzipped my pants, and pulled out my manhood. In an instant, her hot, wet mouth was all over me. My body betrayed me, as did my emotional and mental state of being. I felt a tremendous flaming fireball deep in my loins, and it exploded into this huge wave of jubilant warmth that rippled up and down my body. It shot down my legs to my feet and curled my toes. The rippling warmth of passionate elation glazed my eyes, blinding me. Emotionally, I felt as if I had embraced pure ecstasy. Mentally, the intensity was so sensational that I briefly lost track of time and space. This blissful warmth compelled me to release burst upon burst of my moist essence into her, and she graciously consumed all I had to give.

Right afterward, I felt guilty and angry inside. My body's unfaithfulness had led me down the path of immediate sexual gratification again. From the time we left the ward and got back, no more than fifteen to twenty minutes had elapsed. I took a shower; I wanted to wash her perfume and her smell off my body. I felt bitter because I didn't want her touching me, but what could I do about it? No one would believe my side of the story. I knew that from past experience.

For well over three years, Mrs. Collins continued to slap, rub, grab, and pinch my ass, along with giving me endless kisses and a dozen blowjobs in the basement and the dormitory.

Along with horny Mrs. Collins keeping me stressed and uncomfortable, the other TAs on the floor made me feel stressed and uncomfortable, too. They had never given me a hard time, and they had no idea I was feeling that way. The problem was that I'd seen the TAs, on dozens and dozens of occasions, beat and kick a patient bloody, sometimes until he was unconscious. Most of these patients ended up in the emergency room of an outside medical hospital or in the infirmary on the grounds. Restraining patients was part of their job, but punching and kicking patients was not. The more I saw these beatings, the harder it was for me to keep my mouth shut. The other patients in the ward didn't get involved. If they said anything, they knew the TAs would beat them, too. So it was in the best interest of a patient to ignore what he saw and to keep his mouth shut.

There was one particular incident, though, that made me break my code of silence and brought the wrath of the TAs down on me. It was about one o'clock in the afternoon. A black patient named Tony had been complaining all morning about having side-effects from his medication. The ward TAs started getting angry at him because he kept asking to see the nurse.

The patient bathroom was down the hall from the dayroom, and patients had to get permission from the TAs at the desk to use the bathroom. Tony asked to use the bathroom, and the TAs, already angry at him, said no. Tony explained that he had to take a crap real bad and needed to use the bathroom. The TAs told him to sit down and shut up or he'd be put in the straitjacket. Tony sat quiet for about ten minutes. Then he started crying and begging to use the bathroom, saying he couldn't hold it much longer. Still, the TAs refused to let him go to the bathroom.

A few more minutes went by, and Tony suddenly jumped out of his seat, pulled his pants and undershorts down to his ankles, squatted down, and took a crap on the dayroom floor. The TAs beat him so severely that he had to go to an outside medical hospital. Blood was splattered all over a portion of the floor, the wall, and some of the chairs.

I was raging angry, and right after the beating, I started yelling at the TAs, saying that all the guy wanted was to use the fucking bathroom. The TAs told me to mind my own business, but I kept telling them how fucked up it was to beat the guy up for shitting on the floor after they refused to let him go to the bathroom. The TAs ignored me. I raved on for a few more minutes in front of them and the other patients before finally settling down and shutting up. Normally, the TAs would have beat up any patient who interfered in their business, but they knew my reputation at Mid-Hudson and that I wasn't afraid to fight them. They also knew that in trying to hurt me, it was very likely that they would be hurt, as well.

What the TAs didn't know was that I wasn't as physically aggressive as I used to be. I didn't like fighting anymore. But the TAs didn't know that, and I damn sure wasn't telling them.

State investigators from Mental Health came a few days later to question each patient in the ward about the incident. All the patients had witnessed the incident, but they were too afraid to say anything. I was the only patient who made a statement about what had happened and which TAs were involved. All the TAs on the floor thought I had lost my mind or something. They couldn't understand my sudden involvement after almost four years on the floor. I didn't care what the other patients thought or what the TAs thought, either. I was just tired of seeing patients get beat up like that.

Of course, during the next few months, the ward TAs got me back for this. They took away my laundry-man position and took me off the cleaning crew, too. Those two positions were the top patient positions in the ward; they included special privileges and favors from the TAs.

Then they started harassing me using the commissary. Every week, the patients filled out a commissary order sheet for items like coffee, food, soap, etc. The following week, patients received the items they had ordered. Every week, I filled out a commissary order sheet, but my order sheet never made it off the ward. The TAs were taking my order sheet and throwing it away.

They also harassed me by inspecting my dormitory locker and area a few times a week. They would take my clothes, books, letters, and other things and throw them all over the floor.

In the evening, when it was time to go to sleep, I'd sometimes go to my dormitory sleeping area to find that some of my clothes had been ripped or thrown out the window. I knew that the TAs were either doing this directly or had a patient doing it for them. A few times, I found that someone had dumped urine on my bed, or that a large amount of salt or sugar had been poured between my bed sheets.

The patient laundry-man position and the captain of the patient cleaning crew position had been given to a racist Romanian patient by the name of Sergo. Sergo had been charged with kidnapping and attempted murder while in the United States on a visa. He was 6'2" tall, in his early thirties, weighed two hundred thirty muscular pounds, and had short brown hair and black eyes. He was always bragging about being a Romanian Secret Service agent. He did a lot of martial arts exercises and katas, and he bragged about being trained by the Russian KGB and Army Spetsnaz. Russian Army Spetsnaz soldiers was equivalent to our Army Green Berets. Although he had an accent, Sergo spoke good English. But when he spoke to his treatment team, or if he didn't like something a staff member said, he would start speaking broken English, saying he didn't understand.

The TAs knew that Sergo was a racist, and they let him know I was an ex-Green Beret. I had it made in the ward for years and gave it all up to stand firm on the issue of patient abuse.

With the TAs harassing me so much, I figured I had nothing to lose by harassing them back. On several occasions during those few months, if I witnessed or heard about the TAs physically abusing a patient, I called the mental health hotline to Albany and turned them in. Other patients in the ward started calling the hotline number, too, to complain about patient abuse. The patients were also more vocal in their treatment team meetings about the TAs physically abusing them or harassing them. I had most of the patients in the ward speaking up for their rights as patients under the mental health laws and rules.

Sergo made several attempts to provoke me into a fight. He would yell, curse, and call me names in his Romanian dialect. I didn't understand his native language, but I did understand his body language and intent.

He even pushed me one day, almost knocking me off my feet, and still, I walked away. I didn't like fighting anymore, and I didn't want to physically hurt anyone ever again. I had no intention of fighting Sergo, but sometimes, even good intentions can backfire. One afternoon, while I was in the dayroom, I asked the TAs at the desk if I could get a book from my dormitory locker. They said it was okay, so I went through the hallway and past the patient bathroom to another TA desk next to the dormitory door. There was always a TA at this desk, and I informed the TA on duty that I had permission to get a book from the dorm.

Opening the door, I entered the empty dorm and went into another hallway. It had three doors to the left and right. Through each door were five to six beds and clothes lockers that were assigned to patients. My room was the first one on the right. I got my book, but as I walked out of my room into the hallway, someone punched the left side of my jaw. The swift, massive blow staggered me, and blood gushed from my mouth. The inside of my jaw had been cut. I went into a defensive karate stance, which was a conditioned response.

Sergo was the perpetrator. He had hidden right outside the door and blindsided me. I was angry because Sergo had made me bleed. I was also angry because I knew the TAs had sent him back here to harass me or physically hurt me. There was no way he could have gotten from the dayroom to the dormitory without the consent of the TAs. But as angry as I was at the situation, I still didn't want to fight.

No longer in the karate stance, I wiped blood from my bleeding mouth with my shirt sleeve and stated firmly, "Sergo, I don't want to fight you! Just leave me alone, okay?"

Sergo was standing several feet from me in a fighting stance. I recognized the fighting style right away and realized just how dangerous he was. He had been trained in the famous Russian fighting style called "SAMBO." Russia's KGB, GRU-Military Intelligence, and elite Spetsnaz soldiers were taught SAMBO. It was an explosive blend of striking, throwing, and grappling methods that were specifically designed to fight multiple armed and unarmed attackers.

After telling Sergo I didn't want to fight, I quickly started to walk around him toward the dormitory door. I didn't quite make it. With a quick, stiff, arcing right arm, he clotheslined me in the throat. The momentum of me moving forward and being clotheslined at the same time swept my feet completely off the floor. I landed roughly on my back, and my head hit the floor hard.

"Fuck you, nigger boy!" he spat, his face twisted in rage. My back ached, my head hurt, and I was still bleeding. Being called a nigger was usually enough to make me fight, but I didn't. Deep inside, I felt good about that. I lay on the floor, dazed and in pain, with angry, frustrated tears in my eyes.

"Sergo," I moaned, "I don't want to fight, man! Don't listen to the TAs! Leave me alone!"

Slowly, I tried to get up, still talking. "I've never done anything to you." Dizzy and breathless, I raised myself up on my hands and knees. My body was drenched in sweat, and my chest heaved as Sergo towered over me. *My God! All I want is to live in peace! Why is that so hard?*

My head was hanging low between my arms, but I still saw Sergo raise his right foot off the floor. He was going to stomp me in the head! Even though I was already on the floor, bleeding and in pain, he wanted to inflict more damage on me!

For one second, I became enraged. It wasn't the type of rage I used to feel as Nighthawk-One, but it was enough for me to want to hurt Sergo because he had no compassion for me when I was already down. Before he could bring his foot down on my head, I struck him with the open palm of my right hand, still on my knees. The blow struck him in the chest between his ribcage.

The open-palm technique was one of several techniques that were taught to me by one of my combat instructors. Techniques like this were based on striking acupuncture meridians and vital neurological points of the body with the intent of stunning, crippling, or killing in a matter of seconds.

Sergo's knees buckled, his eyes fluttered, and he started gasping. Gurgling sounds came from his mouth. Then his face turned beet red, and he dropped straight to the floor on his back. His eyes were wide open and unblinking, and his breathing became raspy and more impaired. Then he stopped breathing. I started to panic. *Oh my God! He's going to die!* In my state of panic, I swung both his arms out to the side, away from his body. Then, using both my hands, I massaged his heart, pushing down between his ribcage every few seconds. After doing this several times, I pushed his head all the way back, pinched his nose, opened his mouth, and breathed air into his lungs. After doing this several times, I went back to massaging his heart. After three sets of massaging his heart and three sets of breathing air into his lungs, Sergo started breathing again. Still on the floor, I lay with my back against the wall. My body was shaking and my heart was pounding wildly as I gave a big sigh of relief. Sergo's body had gone into shock, and the shock had stopped his heart. If I hadn't massaged his heart and breathed air into his lungs, Sergo would have died. For the rest of his life, he would never realize this, but for the rest of my life, I would never forget it.

After lying against the wall for a few minutes, the dormitory door opened, and three TAs saw Sergo and me on the floor. I could tell by the arrogant smirks on their faces that they had been part of it. Sergo was taken to the nurse's station, and he was okay. I was bleeding and had a swollen bump on the back of my head.

Sergo, still being the macho man, admitted to the doctors that he had attacked me first, so I didn't go to the box or in the straitjacket. He also told the TAs and the doctors that he had kicked my butt good, too. I let them believe what they wanted. What they thought wasn't important to me. What was important and comforting to me was that Sergo didn't die or suffer any serious injuries.

A week after the incident, I was called into the ward conference room. The room was packed with people, including my treatment team, the clinical director, the unit chief, the supervisor, the senior TA, and several other TAs from the building. My treatment team told me that the ward TAs had been complaining about my disruptive behavior. Their biggest complaint was that they said they no longer had control over the patients because the patients listened to me instead of them. This was crap. The TAs were taking my presence in the ward and blowing it way out of proportion. They were up to something, and they obviously needed the support of everyone in the room to do it.

I quickly found out what it was. Dr. Budo told me that I was being transferred downstairs to the first floor. In fact, while I was in the conference room, other TAs were packing my personal belongings into plastic bags and taking them to the first floor. The ward TAs had convinced my doctor that moving me was necessary. He, in turn, convinced the unit chief, who informed the supervisor, who informed the senior TA of my imminent transfer.

Without realizing it, the TAs had done me an immense favor by having me transferred downstairs. The patients and the TAs were less violent on the first floor, and that relaxed me a lot.

After being on the first floor for about two years, I had an experience that has stayed with me to this day. I can only describe it as a mysterious, spiritual type of experience. I have no idea if it was of a religious nature, a natural phenomenon, UFO connected, or a supernatural event. All I know is that the encounter hit me with raw abruptness. I still remember the day. It was a Friday night, just before bedtime. I had been thinking about my life and how wasted it's been.

As I sat in the dayroom, tears filled my eyes as I fully realized that I was going to be at Mid-Hudson for the rest of my life. *My God! Life has been so cruel to me! I have been so lonely for most of my life.* I'm talking about that endless, horrible, cold, lifeless abyss of loneliness. I feared loneliness more than anything, even more than death itself. I'm terrified of being alone in this world. All I ever wanted was love because it relieved loneliness.

I went to bed that night and cried uncontrollably into my pillow. I couldn't stop crying. It was as if all my frustrations, worries, and hurts had reached the breaking point at the same time. I tried to muffle my sobs and cries of anguish with my pillow, but the tears kept flowing. I cried myself into a deep sleep.

At about three o'clock in the morning, I suddenly woke up and found myself getting out of bed. I felt drawn to the big window, and I looked up at the serene night sky. It was filled with beautiful, glittering stars that resembled hundreds of tiny, sparkling diamonds. The moon was full and unusually bright, and I felt its warmth and saw its radiance shining through the window, bathing my whole body. I felt a strong sense of joy as I stood there. For the first time in my life, I actually felt emotionally and spiritually free.

This spiritual experience hit me like a bolt of lightning. I still do the same things I normally do, but at the same time, I know that nothing will ever be the way it was before. What happened to me was real and sweetly wonderful, even though none of it conformed to the logical, scientific way I was brought up to believe the world worked. The experience didn't relieve me from pain or shield me from life, but after it happened, I found that I related differently, more positively, to the world around me.

The experience brought me inner peace. There's a quiet happiness inside me, even when things don't seem to be going well, because I'm filled with inner joy, acceptance, and the desire to remain in that sweet space inside myself.

I went back to bed with my mind reorganizing itself. I felt overwhelmed with sudden wisdom. I began to understand that everyone, not just me, would experience a time of supreme challenges. A time when every emotional and mental resource would be tested. A time when life would seem unfair. A time when our beliefs, personal ethics, patience, humanity, and ability to persevere would be pushed to the limit and beyond. I began to understand that these ultimate challenges were opportunities to become a better person.

It had been difficult for me to feel because most of my feelings were connected to past traumas. I realize now, though, that if I can't endure the bad, it's impossible for me to survive long enough to see the good. There is no joy in life without sorrow, too.

When a person is just learning to trust his or her feelings, it can be an agonizing experience. It means trusting the reality of your needs and desires and your right to express them. To look deep inside myself took self-acceptance and self-love.

The next morning, a Saturday, I got up and told some of the TAs about how extremely bright the stars and moon had been on Friday night. They looked at me strangely, saying that the stars and moon hadn't been out because of heavy clouds. I was shocked. I became panicky. I asked a few nurses and a few people from the maintenance department, and they all said it had been a starless, moonless night. Even the day-old newspaper had predicted dark clouds and fog.

I was almost traumatized. What happened to me was real, not my imagination! I'm not a delusional or psychotic person! After careful consideration, I finally decided that some type of strange phenomenon had happened to me. After fully accepting this, I felt a sudden warmth and peacefulness throughout my body.

That same Saturday morning was the beginning of a whole new life for me. Ever since I came back to Mid-Hudson, I'd been smoking two packs of cigarettes a day. I was spending two hundred dollars a month on cigarettes alone. That Saturday morning, after lighting my cigarette in the yard, I inhaled the smoke as usual — and gagged! I stared in disbelief at my cigarette. The taste and smell of it were disgusting to me. But I worshiped cigarettes! How could this be? I threw the cigarette on the ground, crushed it with my shoe, and I haven't smoked since. It shocked me that I had actually stopped smoking, just like that.

That same Saturday night, I had the urge to start praying again, too, and I've been praying ever since. I hadn't prayed since I was in Nam because I felt that God had forsaken me. After the amazing experience I had, though, I realized that it was I who had done the forsaking.

For most of my life, I had believed in nothing but myself, and that left me hollow, angry, and bitter inside. Believing in something else was like waking up from a long sleep with warm, caring arms around me.

In this material and chaotic world we live in, it's easy to forget that life is lived from within. I'm always striving, now, to live in the spirit and always be conscious of the internal universe within myself. I try to encourage and express that internal divinity so that I can stay faithfully connected and happy. I try to take an inner journey deep inside myself every day because that's the most important thing I can do for myself emotionally, mentally, and spiritually.

Chapter Twenty-Three

Almost two years had gone by at Mid-Hudson since my strange, spiritual experience. During those two years, I was physically attacked several times and hurt by violent, psychotic peers. I could have easily protected myself each time by hurting the person who was intent on hurting me. Instead, I chose to be hurt; I didn't want to hurt anyone ever again. I didn't get angry when I was assaulted, either, because I didn't take it personally. I have gotten angry about some things because I'm only human, but I will never again be angry enough to physically lash out at another human being.

There had been a rumor circulating that I might be sent to the Rochester Psychiatric Center's Forensic Unit because it was closer to my home of Buffalo. The city of Rochester was only sixty miles from Buffalo. Staying at Mid-Hudson meant a life sentence for me. The doctors there would never have me transferred to a less secure civil psychiatric center. If I were sent to another forensic place, I would have another chance to be a free man, so the chance of being transferred, even to another forensic unit, was slim to none. Still, I swore an oath to myself that if I were ever sent to Rochester Psych Center, I would never again do anything to jeopardize my freedom. I continued to pray every night, asking for one more chance.

In December of 2000, I pulled a lower disc in my back while exercising. The back pain was excruciating, and I was in the infirmary for weeks because I couldn't walk. During this time, the ward psychologist came to the infirmary to bring me some bad news. My sister, Deborah, had died. She was a year younger than I was. Being a longtime nurse, she had access to a lot of legal drugs. Those drugs, combined with her heavy drinking, caused her liver to stop functioning. I cried for days. I was so grief-stricken. I was in a sort of void as I mourned my sister. We looked so much alike that people thought we were twins. I still look at her pictures sometimes, not wanting to believe she's gone. *My dear God! Why am I suffering such tragedies? Such trials and tribulations?* To this very day, I still sometimes find myself expecting a letter or a visit from her.

On January 10th, 2001, my prayers were answered. On the afternoon of that day, I was told to pack my personal belongings because I was being transferred to the Forensic Unit at the Rochester Psychiatric Center. I was overwhelmed with joy. A miracle had happened! Without that transfer, I would still be in Mid-Hudson today. Had my home city been in the New York City area, I wouldn't have been transferred. But because all my relatives were in Buffalo, and because there was a Forensic Unit closer to Buffalo, the Mental Health Department in Albany ordered Mid-Hudson to transfer me. The Mental Health Department in Albany was doing this with a lot of patients throughout the state, and in doing this, they had inadvertently given me another chance at life. It was a miracle in every sense of the word. At another forensic unit, I would be dealt with as the person I am, and after a few years there, I'd hopefully be sent to a less secure civil psychiatric center. From the civil psych center, I'd be allowed to gradually work my way into the community. At Mid-Hudson, I was always judged on my past reputation, not on my past several years of good behavior and insight.

Two New York State Mental Health Safety Security Officers and a Forensic TA from the Rochester Psychiatric Center picked me up. They put me in handcuffs, shackles, and sat me in the backseat of a state security van that resembled a police van.

As the van went through the security gates, I turned my head around to get one last look at the place. Being there was like being emotionally and mentally dead. I vowed that I would never come back to Mid-Hudson. I had spent nine years there that time. I was fifty-one years old, and I was simply tired of being tired.

I had been to Mid-Hudson several times, and altogether, that time added up to almost twenty years. I spent twenty years in a god-forsaken wasteland. Being there was like being in a time warp; I'd look through the security fences to see the real world rushing by. I gave a deep sigh of humble relief as the van took me farther away. The Rochester Psychiatric Center was about three hundred sixty miles away. It was wintertime, and it snowing lightly, with lots of snow on the ground already, as we started our journey.

After driving for several hours and making a few coffee stops, we reached our destination. I had never been to the city of

Rochester before. It was near Lake Ontario, on the southern side, with a population of about three hundred thousand people.

The two-story Forensic Unit sat apart from most of the other buildings on the grounds. It was surrounded by two cyclone security fences with constantine wire on top of both of them. There were also a lot of closed-circuit cameras around the building. After entering through the security gates, the van stopped near the side of the building, and I was escorted into an office. I then saw the admissions doctor, who welcomed me to the Forensic Unit and took some basic information from me. After that, I took a shower in the same area. Most of my clothes were put in the basement because patients were only allowed to have a certain number of articles of clothing in the ward.

I was then taken to the second floor, which was called the acute ward. There were two wards that made up the unit. Every patient who comes to the Forensic Unit starts off on the second floor under close observation. Criminal patients who have been found not guilty by reason of insanity or mental defect are put into the custody of the New York State Department of Mental Health, and the Department of Mental Health puts those patients in maximum-security forensic units throughout the state. Male and female inmates from the Monroe county jail are put on the second floor, too. They often stay for months at a time; they're given a psychiatric evaluation and then sent back to jail. Patients are stabilized on this floor because they're usually loud, uncooperative, and sometimes assaultive when they come in. Psychiatric medication was a big help in stabilizing patients. There were about twenty-five patients on each floor at any given time, which suited me just fine. At Mid-Hudson, there were usually thirty-five to forty patients per floor.

Criminal patients who show good behavior on the second floor for several months are then sent to the first floor. The first floor is much quieter, and the patients have more privileges.

There was a level system in place in both wards to deal with privileges. Privileges depended on the amount of credits a patient acquired. The level system generally went from level one to level five. A patient at level one had to remain within a TA's line of sight at all times and couldn't leave the dayroom without a TA. To gain higher levels and maintain those levels, patients had to attend therapeutic programs. All patients were given a card to carry. After a patient attended a program, the program instructor would write "one credit" on the patient's card and initial it. The more credits a patient attained each week, the higher his or her level went until they reached level five. To maintain level five, a patient had to attend at least fifteen programs every week.

If a patient broke any of the rules, he or she was given a written violation slip. The violation slips came in two forms — small violations and major violations. A small violation usually meant that the patient maintained his or her level but still had an infraction. A major violation usually resulted in a patient's level being lowered, sometimes all the way down to one.

Criminal patients on the first floor who show good behavior, insight, and maintain a status of level five without violations are given "furloughs." Furloughs are when patients are allowed off the unit with two to three staff members escorting them. The patients are taken, without handcuffs or shackles, to activities on the psych center grounds, like swimming, bowling, roller-blading, picnics, musical events, and so on.

Criminal patients spend various amounts of time in state forensic units. The amount of time they spend primarily depends on their treatment team's evaluation. I've known some patients who only spent two years in a forensic unit before they were sent to a less secure psych center. I also know patients who had been incarcerated in forensic units for over thirty years.

My doctor had recently become a psychiatrist. He was a young, Swedish-American man named Jan Hansson (the *J* was pronounced like an *H*). That man was the second miracle in my life. He was the most hardworking, intelligent state psychiatrist I will ever meet. He stood about 6'5" tall, and he had short brown hair and a lean, muscled body. His grip was so powerful that every time he shook my hand, I thought he'd rip it right off my arm. To keep pace with him, I almost had to double my stride.

Dr. Hansson was a refined man who made some men feel self-conscious by his mere presence. To see him when he's wearing his glasses is like envisioning Clark Kent in a telephone booth before he rips his shirt apart to expose the "S" on his Superman uniform. Dr. Hansson will always be a superhero to me. He dared to question thirty-one years of myths, hearsay, half-truths, lies, and discrimination that has haunted most of my life. Only a man of steel would have the moral courage and fidelity to do that.

Dr. Hansson told me that he had read a brief history on me, but he wanted more information. He said he wanted school records, military records, and criminal records as well as records from all the psych centers and prisons I'd been in. I had been incarcerated for thirty-one years, and none of my other assigned psychiatrists had requested all my records before.

With the help of my assigned social worker, they tediously worked at gathering all the information they could about me. He said that the best, most honest way to help a patient is to first gather all the information possible about the person. From this information and from interviews with the patient, the treatment team could effectively evaluate and treat the patient.

After a few months, I did something I thought I'd never, ever do. I started trusting a state psychiatrist. Dr. Hansson didn't treat his patients like nonentities or livestock. He brought something refreshing and unusual to the mental health system — he cared! To me, finding a New York State psychiatrist who cared about patients was equivalent to going to the mountains and spotting Bigfoot!

The more information Dr. Hansson received, the more he became convinced that I was never actually insane. Most of the psychiatrists I had seen since being in the system had deemed me a lunatic. For months, I was given all sorts of psychiatric tests. I had more tests at the Rochester Psych Center than I'd had at any other state psych center.

He spoke about having a friend who was one of the best forensic psychiatrists in the country. They agreed that at one time, I had suffered from a severe case of PTSD due to extreme combat in Vietnam. They also agreed that I had an antisocial personality and was alcohol-dependent. I was comfortable with having an antisocial personality because many people, such as judges, policemen, politicians, actors, writers, etc., have antisocial personalities.

Dr. Hansson explained to me that my only actual documented violence on the streets was when I was with the female patient in the park in the early 1970s. Aside from that incident, everything violent I'd ever been accused of was always on hearsay.

When he asked me about the homicide, I decided to tell him the truth. He'd been honest, truthful, and helpful to me ever since I met him. To lie to him about anything would leave me feeling uncomfortable and guilty. I felt good karma from him, and I wasn't about to turn it into bad karma by lying. For thirty-one years, psych center psychiatrists and treatment teams forced me to admit to a homicide I didn't commit. If I didn't admit to it, they thought I was in denial with no insight and no remorse. They told me I wouldn't be given any privileges unless I admitted to the homicide. So I would always admit to the homicide, saying it happened during a Vietnam flashback. That was what they wanted to hear because that was what I'd told the police in a confession. But I'd never confessed to killing Rosy. The police confession was a fake, but who was going to take my word over the word of two detectives? I had carried that lie with me for over thirty-one years, and I felt tremendous relief when I told the truth.

For the first time in all my incarcerated years, I actually had some professionals doubting my guilt in the homicide. They told me that there really wasn't anything they could do about the conviction after so long, but I didn't need anything done about the conviction. Just knowing that there were a few people in the system who doubted my guilt was enough of a blessing.

The question asked most about the homicide was this: why had the police waited a whole month before arresting me? Especially when the police stated that they had an eyewitness? Their eyewitness, Anna, was a shady woman who ran an illegal after-hours joint and was also a drug trafficker in the neighborhood. Also, at my preliminary hearing, Anna had yelled to me from the witness chair that she didn't want to be there, that the detectives were making her do it. It was also well known that Rosy was a heroin addict and a police informant.

The Buffalo District Attorney's Office was the only place that still had copies of my preliminary hearing and trial in the early 1970s. Dr. Hansson had spoken to people at the DA's office several times over the phone, requesting a copy of my hearing and trial. The DA's office gave him the run-around about my records, which meant they weren't giving them to him. My doctor then sent letters to the DA's office with the same negative results

I finally sent the DA's Office a Freedom Of Information/Privacy Act request, asking for a copy of my hearing and trial. They wrote back, telling me that because the homicide was so long ago, it would take time to search for my records. That was an outrageous lie; when my doctor was talking to one of the secretaries there, she stated to him that my file was sitting on her desk. Why was the DA's office giving us such a hard time? Were they hiding something that would prove beneficial to me, or outright exonerate me from the homicide?

The Buffalo DA's office had also stated to newspapers that in their opinion, I was still suffering from Vietnam flashbacks where I was maiming, crippling, and killing people.

While I was at the Mid-Hudson Psych Center, they obtained a copy of my military records from the army's Personnel Department in St. Louis, Missouri. Those records followed me to Rochester, and Dr. Hansson read every word. After thirty-one years in the system, he was the only one to patiently go over my military records, word by word, and question their contents. He concluded, in amazement, that my military records didn't make any sense. He said my records were extremely contradictory. Some of the records were missing, and sometimes the dates showed me in two places at the same time. It became obvious to my doctor that the US Army was intent on misleading anyone who read my records, making them believe that I was never in Special Forces, which meant I was never in the top-secret MACV-SOG, which meant I was never at the CIA's secret training site in Virginia.

Dr. Hansson and my social worker, with time-consuming effort, researched more of my civilian and military past, and the deeper they went, the more intrigued they became. They were shocked at how much I'd been through emotionally, mentally and physically. Most of my military training certificates had conveniently disappeared from my records. The army and the CIA had gone to great lengths to distance themselves from me. They were good at it, but they weren't perfect because they left a trail. Unbeknownst to the army and the CIA, I had copies of some of my training, including my special forces training. Also, Dr.

358

Hansson had researched the army Special Forces archives and found proof of me being in Special Forces and Nha Trang, which is where the 5th Special Forces' headquarters were in Vietnam. My records from St. Louis had no mention of this at all.

I knew that the Special Operations Group I was in was top-secret. What I didn't know until Dr. Hansson told me was that SOG was the most top-secret covert operation in Vietnam. It was so secret that the US Government had actually denied its very existence on several occasions.

Dr. Hansson questioned me extensively about the US Army trying to get me out of Mid-Hudson and ultimately getting me out of the Buffalo Psych Center. He said it was astonishing, almost unbelievable, that the army would do such a thing, especially with them knowing my past criminal and psychiatric background. He was in awe that the army, after getting me back in their control at the Walson Army Hospital, immediately reinstated me with my full rank. He had seen a copy of the reinstatement orders in my records. Obviously, the army had made the mistake of overlooking that; they wouldn't want the public to know that they had taken a man out of a psychiatric institution, fully knowing his criminal and psychiatric history, and had his full rank reinstated like nothing had happened.

Dr. Hansson told me he had copies of my state and national criminal record and that there was no mention of me ever being arrested in New Jersey. He also thought it quite odd that I would be arrested for a serious charge like attempted murder only to have it dropped down to a simple charge of being verbally threatening.

He wrote several letters to the Walson Army Hospital requesting my records, but he never got an answer back. I wrote Walson as well, requesting the same records, and I did get an answer. They told me that my records had been sent to the Army Personnel Department in St. Louis.

Dr. Hansson, therefore, requested another copy of my military records from St. Louis, hoping that more of my records would be sent. He wrote and called the Army Personnel Department in St. Louis, requesting the copies. The Personnel Department sent him nothing. Someone, or some organization or agency, had stopped the department from sending anyone my records.

My doctor also thought it was interesting that when I was taken by the TAs from the Buffalo Psychiatric Center to the Buffalo International Airport, I was turned over to an Air Force Detachment and flown in an Air Force Transport to Fort Dix, New Jersey — an army base. Clearly, there was joint military cooperation involved. I truly believe, as did Dr. Hansson, that if the Buffalo Psych Center hadn't had the papers to prove I was turned over to the military, the U.S. Army would completely deny ever having me back under their control

My doctor found out, too, that on my military discharge paper, DD-214, it stated in army code that I was discharged due to a predisposed condition. This meant that I was discharged due to a psychiatric condition I had before I joined the army. That was an outright lie! I had no psychiatric condition of any kind prior to joining the army. I had never been to any psychiatric institutions or seen a psychiatrist before then. There was also nothing in any of my school records that indicated psychiatric problems as I was growing up. That coded notation was deceitfully put on my discharge papers to stop me from ever seeking service-connected disability. It also helped to distance the US Army and the CIA from me in case I got into serious domestic or international trouble.

I've had more than my share of tragedies in my life. I know what emotional pain is, and it's the worst kind of pain and suffering a human being can possibly endure.

Each and every day, I try to draw positive strength from those tragedies because I never want to lose faith in myself again. I believe, now, that everything that happens to us in life happens for a reason or a purpose. The idea is to find that reason or purpose and try to have it serve you productively in some way.

All I want out of life is the essence of love and the essence of happiness. I know it exists because I experienced it for a moment. It's there. It's always been there for people. All it takes is the emotional and spiritual merging of two people. It has to be embraced fully with no inhibitions or doubts and accepted gracefully, honestly, and openly.

I've been in the Forensic Unit at the Rochester Psych Center for two years, now. I pray every night, and three times a week, I practice a Chinese health art called Qigong ("*chee gong*"). Tai Chi and Kung Fu, as well as other martial arts styles, were taken from Qigong. It's really amazing what simple movements, visualization, and correct breathing can do for your overall health, emotionally, mentally, physically, and spiritually.

I've gained a lot of knowledge throughout my life, but I've realized that wisdom was something I could only give myself. I'm not incompetent or psychotic. In fact, I'm quite intelligent. But intelligence means nothing to a person with poor emotional self-control. I was too impulsive, and I reacted more through my emotions than through my common sense. I'm much more open to discussing difficulties in my life, and I'm better at finding ways of coping with painful and stressful situations without resorting to antisocial behavior. I see things more clearly than ever before, and I'm grateful for the answers that had eluded me for most of my life.

From Dr. Hansson, I learned about the rage inside me that had been there since my abusive childhood, and how the army nurtured that unique rage by bringing it to the surface.

I learned that I had a self-sabotaging attitude that kept me in trouble and prone to panic. This was mainly brought about by my mother's verbal and physical abuse of me. She made me feel worthless, and I had no self esteem. She made me feel like no one would ever want me, care for me, or love me. I went through many years believing this, always trying to meet her expectations and gain her approval, not realizing that her expectations were far too high.

I gradually learned how to deal with my mother at arm's length so that she will never be able to crucially hurt me again. I'm more assertive with her, now, and more opinionated as an individual. I've stopped unconsciously fearing her as an entity higher than God Himself. She can no longer make me feel helpless and worthless. And I no longer have a deep love/hate complex toward her. She's my mother, but I realize, now, that she's also a person and a human being. When I was born, she was just a teenager. I was a child being raised by a child. I understand, now, that she had problems of her own before and after I was born. I was just the object of her frustrations, a symbol of how helpless she felt about her life. Her alcohol abuse compounded those frustrations. My adopted brother was raised with the care and love

I never got. I sometimes feel that adopting him was her way of redeeming herself from the mistakes she made with me.

My self-sabotaging ways affected me socially and intimately, too. My low self esteem made me need endless expressions of love, attention, and signs of affection. I've learned to set limits, mentally and emotionally, on certain domestic patterns of risk behavior. I've learned that life doesn't come with a guarantee that I will be loved, and that the degree to which I will be loved can only be measured by my own lovability. I was simply looking for love too hard in the wrong places.

With Dr. Hansson's guidance, I've dealt with the many losses I've suffered in my life — not only the loss of people I've loved through death, but loss through people leaving me, the loss of my younger self, and the loss of impossible expectations and romantic dreams. I now know that time stops for no one, and I must adjust to change by not living in the past. I have to go on with my life. I have to understand and deal with every loss I have ever experienced. I learned that our loss experiences greatly influence who we are and how we live. My past will always dwell in my present, and only through understanding and learning from my losses and mistakes can the present be made easier and my future enhanced.

To fight against loss, some people have a compulsive need to take care of other people. That was something I was quite familiar with. I did that to forget my feelings of worthlessness and helplessness. Instead of identifying and dealing with my own feelings of hurt, I sympathized and identified with other people's hurts and problems.

I will never again be ashamed of my tears. They reflect my courage and my humbleness, and they make me human, like everyone else. I may be incarcerated, but my inner peace has given me victories beyond my wildest dreams.

It's very important to know your true worth in life. Every day, I try to look into my conscience and remedy my mistakes. I am no longer ashamed of who I am. I have accepted the truth of my being, and I will never again try to deceive myself about anything.

I finally have the wisdom to realize that I cannot change my mother or the other people who have hurt me in my life. I can't change the way our government and our military functions. What I can change, though, is my attitude toward them. I've learned to forgive the harm that has been done to me, beg forgiveness for the harm I've done to others, and to let go of the past. I did it one day at a time until it became a permanent part of myself. I had to let go of my anger and resentment toward other people and toward our government and military. I had to focus on taking care of myself, and then I could forgive them. Without forgiveness, our lives would be governed by an endless cycle of anger, resentment and retribution.

THE END